Titles available from boyd & fraser

BASIC Programming
Applesoft BASIC Fundamentals and Style
BASIC Fundamentals and Style
Complete BASIC for the Short Course
QuickBASIC Fundamentals and Style
Structured BASIC Fundamentals and Style for the IBM® PC and Compatibles
Structured Microsoft BASIC: Essentials for Business

COBOL Programming
Advanced Structured COBOL: Batch and Interactive
COBOL: Structured Programming Techniques for Solving Problems
Comprehensive Structured COBOL
Fundamentals of Structured COBOL

Database
A Guide to SQL, Second Edition
Database Systems: Management and Design, Second Edition

Computer Information Systems
Applications Software Programming with Fourth-Generation Languages
Data Communications for Business, Second Edition
Ethical Issues in Information Systems
Expert Systems for Business: Concepts and Applications
Investment Management: Decision Support and Expert Systems
Management of Information Technology
Pascal Programming for Information Systems
Structured Systems Development: Analysis, Design, Implementation

Microcomputer Applications
A Guide to Networking
An Introduction to Desktop Publishing
Business Graphics
Contemporary Microcomputer Tools: WordPerfect® 5.0, Lotus 1-2-3®, and dBASE III PLUS®
dBASE III PLUS® Programming, Second Edition
DOS: Complete and Simplified
DOS Essentials
Local Area Networking with Novell® Software
Lotus 1-2-3® Quick, Second Edition
Macintosh Productivity Tools
Mastering and Using Lotus 1-2-3®, Release 3
Mastering and Using Lotus 1-2-3®, Version 2.2
Mastering and Using WordPerfect® 5.1
Mastering Lotus 1-2-3®
Microcomputer Applications: A Practical Approach
Microcomputer Applications: Using Small Systems Software, Second Edition
Microcomputer Database Management Using dBASE III PLUS®, Second Edition
Microcomputer Database Management Using dBASE IV®
Microcomputer Database Management Using R:BASE System V®
Microcomputer Productivity Tools
Microcomputer Systems Management and Applications
Microsoft Works: Tutorial and Applications
PC-DOS®/MS-DOS® Simplified, Second Edition
Using Application Software
Using Computers Lab Manual, Second Edition
Using dBASE III PLUS®
Using Enable®: An Introduction to Integrated Software
Using Enable/OA®
Using Harvard Graphics for Business Presentations
VAX BASIC Programming

Shelly Cashman Series Titles
BASIC Programming for the IBM Personal Computer
Computer Concepts
Computer Concepts with Microcomputer Applications (Lotus 1-2-3® and VP-Planner Plus® versions)
Computer Concepts with Microcomputer Applications: WordPerfect® 5.0/5.1, Lotus 1-2-3®, and dBASE III PLUS®
Computer Fundamentals with Application Software
Essential Computer Concepts
Learning to Use dBASE III PLUS®
Learning to use dBASE IV®
Learning to Use Lotus 1-2-3®
Learning to Use Lotus 1-2-3® Release 2.2
Learning to Use Microsoft Word® 5.0
Learning to Use SuperCalc®3, dBASE III®, and WordStar® 3.3: An Introduction
Learning to Use WordPerfect®
Learning to Use WordPerfect® 5.0/5.1
Learning to Use WordPerfect®, Lotus 1-2-3®, and dBASE III PLUS®
Learning to Use WordPerfect®, VP-Planner Plus®, and dBASE III PLUS®
Learning to Use WordPerfect® 5.0/5.1, Lotus 1-2-3®, and dBASE III PLUS®
Learning to Use WordPerfect® 5.0/5.1, Lotus 1-2-3® Release 2.2, and dBASE III PLUS®
Learning to Use WordPerfect® 5.0/5.1, Lotus 1-2-3®, and dBASE III PLUS®, Alternate Edition
Learning to Use WordPerfect® 5.0/5.1, Lotus 1-2-3® Release 2.2, and dBASE III PLUS®, Alternate Edition
Learning to Use WordStar® 6.0
Learning to Use VP-Planner Plus®
RPG II, RPG III, & RPG/400
Structured COBOL: Flowchart and Pseudocode Editions
Systems Analysis and Design

Software Training and Reference (STAR) Series
dBASE III PLUS®
Lotus 1-2-3®
WordPerfect®

EXPERT SYSTEMS FOR BUSINESS
Concepts And Applications

Featuring VP-Expert®

D. V. Pigford
Western Kentucky University

Greg Baur
Western Kentucky University

bf

boyd & fraser publishing company

Credits:

Publisher: Tom Walker
Acquisitions Editor: James H. Edwards
Editor: Donna Villanucci
Director of Production: Becky Herrington
Cover Design: Ken Russo
Cover Photo: H. Armstrong Roberts
Manufacturing Director: Dean Sherman
Typesetting: CopyRight

A Division of South-Western Publishing Company
Boston, MA 02116

Manufactured in the United States of America

Library of Congress Cataloging-in-Publication Data

Baur, Gregory R.
Expert systems for business : concepts and applications / Greg Baur, Darleen Pigford.
p. cm.
Includes bibliographical references.
ISBN 0-87835-439-5
1. Expert systems (Computer science) 2. Business--Data processing. I. Pigford, Darleen, 1943- . II. Title.
QA76.9.E95B38 1990
006.3'3--dc19 89-17480
CIP

2 3 4 5 6 7 8 9 10 D 4 3 2 1 0

To

Dr. Gene Henry
— a true expert

ORDER INFORMATION AND FACULTY SUPPORT INFORMATION

For the quickest service, refer to the map below for the South-Western Regional Office serving your area.

1 **ORDER INFORMATION**
5101 Madison Road
Cincinnati, OH 45227-1490
General Telephone–513-527-6945
Telephone: 1-800-543-8440
FAX: 513-527-6979
Telex: 214371

FACULTY SUPPORT INFORMATION
5101 Madison Road
Cincinnati, OH 45227-1490
General Telephone–513-527-6950
Telephone: 1-800-543-8444

Alabama	Massachusetts	Ohio
Connecticut	Michigan	Pennsylvania
Delaware	Minnesota	Rhode Island
Florida	Mississippi	South Carolina
Georgia	Missouri	South Dakota
Illinois	Nebraska	Tennessee
Indiana	New Hampshire	Vermont
Iowa	New Jersey	Virginia
Kentucky	New York	West Virginia
Maine	North Carolina	Wisconsin
Maryland	North Dakota	District of Columbia

2 **ORDER INFORMATION**
13800 Senlac Drive
Suite 100
Dallas, TX 75234
General Telephone–214-241-8541
Telephone: 1-800-543-7972

FACULTY SUPPORT INFORMATION
5101 Madison Road
Cincinnati, OH 45227-1490
General Telephone–513-527-6950
Telephone: 1-800-543-8444

Arkansas	Louisiana	Texas
Colorado	New Mexico	Wyoming
Kansas	Oklahoma	

3 **ORDER INFORMATION and FACULTY SUPPORT INFORMATION**
6185 Industrial Way
Livermore, CA 94550
General Telephone–415-449-2280
Telephone: 1-800-543-7972

Alaska	Idaho	Oregon
Arizona	Montana	Utah
California	Nevada	Washington
Hawaii		

CONTENTS

Module 5 Using Databases and Spreadsheets with the Knowledge Base 293

Module 6 Using Confidence Factors 337

Module 7 Implementing the User Interface 353

PREFACE

Overview of the Text

The primary goal of this book is to give its user a basic understanding of expert systems and how they are developed. To aid the user's achievement of this goal, a specific expert system development tool, VP-Expert (educational version from Paperback Software), is included.

The book is a blend of theory and practice. The first part of the book features theory and gives the user a broad background in expert systems, a branch of applied artificial intelligence. The second part of the book presents a practical hands-on approach as the user learns to use VP-Expert as an expert system development tool.

We believe that the theory/practice approach is a viable one. With a combined total of over forty-five years of teaching experience in a variety of disciplines, we have found that a person who is actively involved in the learning situation has a more successful learning experience than one who is not.

Why use VP-Expert for the practice segment? There are certainly a number of good expert system development tools available. We chose VP-Expert because of its user friendliness, power, ease of use, cost, and interface with spreadsheets/databases.

The use of the two-part approach also allows for a wider range of users. Users who have little or no background in expert systems will find that the first part of the book will prepare them to deal with the process of expert system development. On the other hand, users with a background in expert systems can proceed directly to the second part of the book to begin work immediately with VP-Expert, using the theory as a reference, if necessary.

The book is intended for a variety of users. We assume that the users have some background experience with IBM or IBM-compatible microcomputers, but we do not assume any prior knowledge or experience with expert systems or expert system development tools. However, users with a background in the aforementioned areas will be able to pursue topics presented in the book in greater depth.

Potential users include students enrolled in an introductory course on expert systems or artificial intelligence at the undergraduate and/or two-year college level. Students enrolled in other disciplines, such as business, management information, sciences, or data processing, would also be able to use the book, but the examples are geared toward the business user.

Practicing professionals are also a viable user population. The book is ideal for a user who wants to learn something about expert systems and how to use a development tool for his or her own application.

Coverage of the Text

The coverage of the book will give the user a basic understanding of expert systems and is designed to be introductory in nature. Since expert systems are a part of artificial intelligence (AI), some AI concepts are included, but only as we feel necessary. There are also some concepts related to expert systems which have not been included; it is our opinion that the excluded topics are advanced in nature and beyond the scope of this book. With the coverage presented, the user will feel comfortable with the notion of expert systems and be able to deal quite satisfactorily with VP-Expert.

In Chapter 1, we give a description of artificial intelligence (AI) and how it compares with human intelligence. We also describe what is meant by the term intelligent computer. Finally, we briefly explain the nature of applied AI and its advantages and limitations.

Chapter 2 presents an overview of expert systems technology. It includes a definition of expert systems and knowledge and a brief historical perspective. Also discussed are the components and features of expert systems and a brief description of expert systems development tools. Finally, a discussion of expert system applications and their advantages and limitations completes the coverage of this chapter. Many of these topics are described in greater depth in subsequent chapters.

Chapter 3 deals with the problem of knowledge representation and the characteristics of knowledge. Several knowledge representation models, including production rules, frames, semantic nets, and predicate calculus, are introduced.

Chapter 4 begins with various methods of reasoning. The concept of heuristics, an integral part of expert systems, and the problems of search are discussed. Inference strategies such as deduction, induction, and abduction are explained. The chapter describes uncertainty and how it is dealt with by expert systems. Finally, we define forward and backward chaining, which are the primary reasoning control structures used in expert systems.

In Chapter 5, the activities involved in creating and updating the knowledge base are presented. The choices of an appropriate problem for expert systems development and the right development tool are the first topics of discussion. The processes of acquiring and organizing the knowledge are then examined. The final discussion in the chapter centers on the update and maintenance of the knowledge base.

Chapter 6 describes activities performed by the inference engine. The capability of the inference engine to deal with uncertainty and its associated problems, such as resolving rule conflicts, is explained.

In Chapter 7, the third major component of the expert system, the user interface, is examined. The value of the user interface is discussed. Human factors are compared to the relative aspects of the user interface.

Chapter 8 focuses on the relationship of software engineering to expert systems development, the final system development, and its integration into the organization. Topics of discussion include the software life cycle, the expert systems life cycle, and the software engineering life cycle. The development stages of prototyping and full system development are examined. A number of difficulties occurring in expert systems development are resolved. Finally, the chapter examines how the expert system should be integrated into the organization.

Chapter 9 looks at the future of expert systems and their development. Future trends in knowledge representation, knowledge acquisition, system development tools, and user interfaces are interpreted. Future availability and cost of expert systems technology are examined. Finally, the chapter presents the notion of intelligent systems.

Module 1 contains a brief introduction and discusses some examples of expert systems. It then moves to its primary purpose: getting started with VP-Expert. System requirements and initial software installation procedures are introduced.

Module 2 presents an overview of the main components of VP-Expert. The structure of the Main Menu, the use of the consultation with an expert system, and obtaining help from VP-Expert are the focus of this module.

In Module 3, details of forming rules with VP-Expert are defined. The creation of an expert system from a table is developed, including the complete cycle involved.

Details of how VP-Expert deals with reasoning and uncertainty are discussed in Module 4. The use of several utilities such as TRACE and SET are furnished along with the use of forward and backward chaining.

The emphasis in Module 5 is how VP-Expert links to peripheral software packages. Details of the linkage to both database and spreadsheet software are discussed.

Module 6 describes how VP-Expert deals with uncertainty through the use of confidence factors. Procedures for calculating confidence factors in their use with various rule forms are examined.

Module 7 discusses the VP-Expert user interface. The topics of formatting the screen, controlling the printer, improving the run-time environment, and using a mouse are the main thrust of this module.

Finally, Module 8 contains a summary of VP-Expert commands and their use. It also includes a discussion of some of the advanced programming features of VP-Expert.

Use of the Text

The text may be used in a variety of ways dependent on the desires of the user. These include Chapters 1–9 alone, Modules 1–8 alone, Chapters 1–9 followed by Modules 1–8 or the integration of chapters and modules (e.g., Chapter 1 followed by Module 1, Chapter 2 followed by Module 2, and so on).

For classroom use, we suggest the latter use of integrating chapters and modules. We have attempted to write the chapters and modules in parallel. In this way, students can study theory and then follow immediately with a study of the implementation of the theory. Certain users can choose one of the other methods of coverage, dependent on their needs and desires, also using the text effectively.

Contained within the text are the answers to the odd-numbered exercises for the chapters and modules. Answers to the even-numbered exercises are contained in an accompanying instructor's manual. Because of their open-ended nature, selected solutions to the module assignments are provided in the instructor's manual.

In addition to the answers to the even-numbered exercises, the Instructor's Manual contains the following:

- A brief summary of each chapter and module.
- A detailed teaching outline for each chapter and module.
- Transparency masters.

Finally, all software required to use the text is packaged with the book, with the exception of the DOS operating system. An educational version of VP-Expert is provided on one disk and a set of the needed sample files is provided on a second disk. There is also a hierarchy chart of the VP-Expert command structure which can be easily removed from the back for easier use.

We sincerely hope that you find the use of the text enjoyable and beneficial. We have enjoyed its preparation.

D.V. Pigford
Greg Baur

ACKNOWLEDGMENTS

We wish to thank a number of people who assisted us in the writing of this book. The following people assisted us in the preparation of the manuscript: Lana Appling, Todd Bacon, Earlene Cantrell, Sheri Daniel, Ann Hardy, Bev Harrison, Noel Hauser, Anthony Honocker, and Ruth Schoeber.

We are also grateful to our reviewers: Professor R. Waldo Roth, Taylor University; Professor Margaret A. Marx, Tunix Community College; Professor Gary T. Hughes, University of North Texas; Professor John Hammond, San Diego City College; Dr. Randolph H. Forsstrom, Bergen Community College; Professor Judith H. Morrel, Butler University; and Professor Mike Michaelson, Palomar College for their helpful comments and suggestions.

We are indebted to Virginia Harvey, our copyeditor, for her excellent suggestions and comments.

We wish to acknowledge Paperback Software for the use of VP-Expert and for their technical assistance. Their cooperation has been very valuable to our efforts.

We are especially grateful to two people: Dr. Ken Modesitt, our department chair, for his cooperation and encouragement of our project, and Donna Villanucci, our editor, for her patience, cooperation, guidance, and support.

Part I

THE CONCEPTS

1

THE INTELLIGENT COMPUTER

***Artificial intelligence (AI)** is a segment of computer science devoted to the development of computer hardware and software that is designed to imitate the human mind. As such, AI has as its main goal the task of solving the problem of making computers smarter; that is, the capability to do more and more things that are considered by people to require some level of intelligence.*

Computers have already demonstrated that they can perform a number of tasks faster and more accurately than human beings. They can, among other things, perform mathematical calculations, manipulate data in the forms of letters and numbers (including storage and retrieval), and make simple decisions. AI researchers are working to improve these current capabilities and to find new ways to use computers requiring even more intelligence.

In this chapter, we will discuss what is meant by intelligence, both human and artificial, and how intelligent computing compares with conventional computing. We will also examine what is meant by applied artificial intelligence and how expert systems fit into the picture. We will discuss advantages and limitations of artificial intelligence. Finally, we will examine the role of AI in the business world.

The Nature of Intelligence

A good place to begin our discussion is to answer the question: "What is intelligence?" According to *Webster's Second Edition New World Dictionary,* intelligence is "the ability to learn or understand from experience; the ability to acquire and retain knowledge; the ability to respond quickly and successfully to new situations; or the use of the faculty of reason in solving problems, directing conduct, etc., effectively."

If we pause and look at this definition for a moment, there is nothing really startling about it: it contains terms that most of us would associate with intelligence and behaviors exhibited by human beings.

We can summarize this definition by saying that intelligence is the ability to acquire knowledge and use it. In this process, we use thinking and reasoning. This description characterizes what we commonly call human intelligence.

On the other hand, artificial intelligence attempts to imitate human characteristics with a computer. This is accomplished through the use of computer hardware and software, and the end result produces what we can call an intelligent computer. At this point in time, the imitation capability is limited but continues to progress.

AI systems today are good at taking knowledge given by humans and storing it for later retrieval. The body of knowledge possessed by the system is called its **knowledge base** and consists of facts, concepts, procedures, and relationships. This knowledge has been organized by a human being so that it is understandable and can be readily used in problem-solving or decision-making systems. One limiting characteristic of this knowledge is that its scope represents a particular subject or domain; it does not have the same breadth that would be expected from a human being. For example, consider an AI system designed to diagnose lung cancer. The knowledge base could consist of facts (patient vital signs), concepts (human will to live), procedures (treatments and surgery), and relationships (incidence of smoking and lung problems). Professionals would have to identify and gather all relevant data for the knowledge base, and the system development team would organize and implement a usable computer system to assist doctors in diagnosing lung cancer. Obviously, this system's scope is relevant for lung cancer but not for other forms of cancer.

A second component of artificial intelligence is concerned with techniques that are used to allow the computer to think and reason. With these capabilities, the computer can draw inferences and make conclusions based on the knowledge it possesses. In the lung cancer example, the system implementation could make inferences and judgments to assist the doctor.

Thus, the intelligent computer is one that can do more than solve problems; whose solutions require calculation, data storage and retrieval, or simple control. It is sometimes referred to as a *knowledge-based system.* In later chapters, we will discuss details of how knowledge is represented in the computer and how the computer can think and reason.

Intelligent Computing versus Conventional Computing

We have already alluded to the fact that there are differences between intelligent computing and conventional computing. It can be basically summarized in this way (at the risk of oversimplification): in conventional computing, the human gives a problem to the computer and tells it how to solve the problem; in intelligent computing, the human gives the problem to the computer but does not tell it how to solve the problem.

When creating a conventional computer program, a programmer creates a step-by-step procedure for solving the problem and converts it into a certain computer language. The computer then takes that procedure and applies it to a given set of data to produce a result. The conventional program guarantees a solution which will change only if a different set of data is used. However, for any given set of data, the program will produce consistent and reliable results. The conventional computer program is capable of solving exactly one problem at a time with the given step-by-step procedure or *algorithm*; a different problem requires the use of another algorithm. Examples of conventional computer programs include payroll, tax computation, inventory, exception reporting, and so on. Conventional programs are very efficient at doing what they are intended to do but are not capable of deviating from the problem at hand.

By contrast, a programmer creating an intelligent computer program gives the problem to the computer but makes no attempt to tell the computer how to solve it. The computer does not guarantee a solution nor does it guarantee totally consistent results. In this vein, it behaves much like a human expert who is attempting to solve a given problem.

The intelligent computer depends on its preprogrammed knowledge base and inferencing strategies to solve the problem. It is also capable of solving other related problems without any changes to its knowledge base or set of inferencing strategies. The intelligent computer may make use of algorithms, especially for search and pattern-matching activities with its knowledge base, but these algorithms are not the driving force behind the problem-solution process, as would be the case with conventional computing. Our preceding discussion is summarized in Figure 1.1.

Intelligent Computing	Conventional Computing
1. Does not guarantee a solution to a given problem.	1. Guarantees a solution to a given problem.
2. Results may not be reliable and consistent.	2. Results are inconsistent and reliable.
3. Programmer does not tell the system how to solve the given problem.	3. Programmer tells the system exactly how to solve the given problem.
4. Can solve a range of problems in a given domain.	4. Can solve only one problem at a time in a given domain.

FIGURE 1.1 INTELLIGENT COMPUTING VERSUS CONVENTIONAL COMPUTING

In a very real sense, it is not a matter of saying that intelligent computing is better than conventional computing or vice versa. That would be like comparing apples and oranges. While there may be some common elements to the techniques used, they are not designed to solve the same kinds of problems. Conventional computing represents a mature technology that will only be improved with increases in computing speed and faster main memory access. Intelligent computing is currently a less mature technology but is progressing as researchers develop ways for computers to modify their knowledge bases internally; they will become much more powerful, with a greater range of possible applications.

Applied Artificial Intelligence

Interest in artificial intelligence has grown in recent years because several commercially feasible applications have been developed. More and more industrial companies are using AI technologies and have begun to hire professionals to work specifically in these areas. In this section, we wish to briefly discuss these technologies, where they are now relative to development, and where they may be headed.

To begin our discussion, consider the diagram in Figure 1.2. The diagram gives an overall perspective of AI today. We recognize that there are many other areas of possible applications, but the areas shown in the figure have the greatest impact on the industrial world today. We will discuss each of these applied areas of AI: general problem solving, expert systems, natural language, computer vision, and robotics.

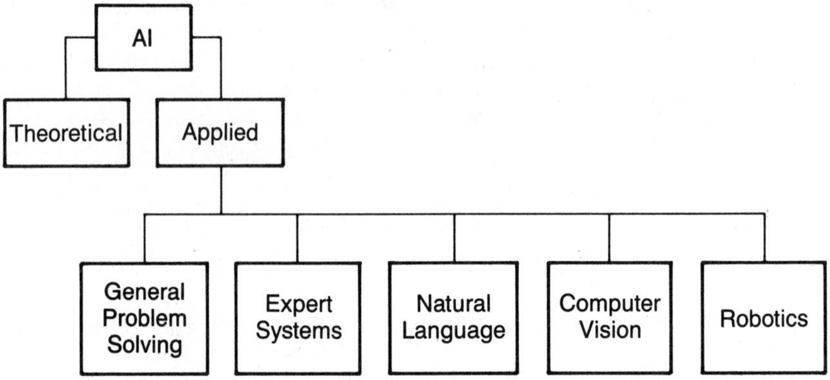

FIGURE 1.2 AN OVERVIEW OF AI TODAY

General Problem Solving

One of the goals of AI research over the years has been to develop techniques to help people such as scientists, engineers, and mathematicians solve problems. Efforts in the 1950s and 1960s were focused on the development of a model which would solve a wide range of complex problems. The results were quite frustrating to AI researchers because as the range of problem-solving capability grew, the power of the model diminished. In the early 1970s, AI researchers finally recognized that, in order to develop a model powerful enough to be useful, the range of problems to be solved had to be narrowed to specific subject domains. This recognition was the catalyst for a number of advancements in problem-solving capabilities.

Planning and scheduling are two problems that are of special interest to business and manufacturing professionals. A plan is a step-by-step sequence of actions designed to achieve some goal. The task is to come up with an optimal plan, one that maximizes efficiency and minimizes cost.

Existing AI programs have been developed to attain an optimal plan. The steps and situation constraints are given to the program, which will examine and sequence the steps, combining some if necessary, to produce the final result.

Scheduling is another major problem for many companies. It may involve personnel, production, inventory, or any number of other areas. Again, the goal is to maximize efficiency and minimize cost. AI programs are available that can deal with the complex nature of scheduling problems.

A third type of problem is one that is often found in basic research and system design development. AI techniques of *theorem proving* and *formula reduction* are sometimes used to verify the results of work done in the laboratory or the system development area.

As AI techniques become more sophisticated, the number of applications in which they will be used will increase dramatically. Previously unsolvable problems will meet their match.

Expert Systems

A second area of applied artificial intelligence is **expert systems (ES).** These are systems that are designed to simulate the behavior of a human expert as he or she attempts to solve some complex problem in a particular domain.

The key to the success of an expert system is the validity and completeness of the knowledge possessed by the system. When this knowledge is combined with various AI inferencing techniques, the outcome is a system that can solve problems, and obtain results that sometimes exceed the performance of a human expert.

Any area in which human experts solve problems is a potential area for the use of expert systems. There are a number of issues regarding problem selection and system development, and we will discuss these in detail throughout this book.

Natural Language

Since the beginning of computer production, communication between computers and people has been unnatural in a human sense. With the ever-increasing number of people now using computers, increased attention is being given to improvement of human/computer communication.

Many people believe that the ideal way to communicate with a computer is via the English language in an everyday form through the use of keyboard, voice, or bar code formats, to name a few. Notable research is taking place to improve the use of *natural language,* but only with moderate success.

The problem is a complex one. The English language is not an easy language to understand—just ask a person who has English as a second language! The English language contains a number of words that have multiple meanings; meanings also depend on the context in which words or phrases are used. Systems developed utilizing natural language thus far have had limited success in realizing a general understanding of English.

Natural-language understanding systems basically use one of two techniques: key word or syntactic/semantic analysis. A system using the **key words technique** attempts to infer a meaning from the communication through the meaning of key words. Such a system is not capable of readily dealing with words that have multiple meanings.

The **syntactic/semantic analysis technique** holds the most promise for the development of a commercially feasible understanding system. This technique breaks down a given sentence into its parts of speech (subject, verbs, and so on for diagramming sentences), and attempts to infer a meaning from this analysis. Systems developed so far have had limited vocabulary capability because of the almost infinite possible combinations of sentence structure. These systems also require a great deal of computer memory for storage of the *lexicon* (dictionary) for the words that the system can deal with.

It is also difficult for the understanding system to generate appropriate responses to the communication. Current systems, such as Eliza, usually have preprogrammed phrases or sentences for response purposes, but these are not always appropriate. Systems do not yet really possess the capability of constructing sentences on a word-by-word basis.

Speech-recognition systems are natural-language understanding systems that accept voice instead of keyboard input. The voice signal must be translated into a digital format so the computer can process the input. Most of these systems are voice dependent; that is, they can recognize only one human voice. Because each person speaks differently, the system must match the spoken word to a unique voice print (like a fingerprint) of that word against some word form stored in memory in order to recognize it. This recognition process must be completed before the understanding process can begin.

Speech synthesis (computer-generated speech) is in its rudimentary stages. Techniques are not yet well developed that can adjust pitch, frequency, and inflection, which are characteristics expected by humans listening to oral communication.

Natural-language understanding systems have improved since their inception; however, it will be some time before we can truly engage in natural language (English) communication with the computer.

Computer Vision

A fourth area of applied AI is computer vision. **Vision systems** are used when the computer requires vision capabilities to perform certain tasks.

Through the use of *computer vision,* a computer can identify features of real objects or images of objects (as in a photograph), and use this information to solve some problem. The problem-solving system uses techniques of search and pattern matching to process the visual information. Since the techniques are exhaustive in nature, it is possible that a vision system may find details that are missed by the human eye. Applications exist in several fields, including the military (examination of photographs for intelligence information) and robots (determination of a robot's location in a problem-solving situation).

A vision system uses a camera (two cameras for stereoptic applications) to obtain a picture or image. This image is in the form of an *analog signal* much like the picture on a television screen. It must then be converted to a *digital signal* so that the image can be processed by the computer. The image then goes through a series of steps (processing, analysis, and understanding) to obtain the desired information.

Vision systems are very complex and require a great deal of computer resources. At this point, they have limited use in real-time situations; improved processing speed and memory-management techniques will make vision systems more useful.

Robotics

Science fiction has been instrumental in making people aware of *robots.* In reality, robots are pictured unrealistically and are not capable of what is seen in the movies.

However, robots do have a number of capabilities and can perform a number of useful tasks, especially in manufacturing applications. Robots have the advantage that they can perform many tedious and repetitive tasks. They can be put into situations that would be dangerous or unhealthy for human beings (mining, explosives, and so on).

Most robots have an arm with several joints that is moved by actuators, with a master system controller which is preprogrammed to perform one or a series of tasks in sequence. Robots are either fixed or mobile, depending on the need.

A goal of robotics researchers is to embed AI software into the robot. This will allow the robot to perform tasks that require some degree of intelligence. The ultimate intelligent robot might be one that utilizes expert systems, speech recognition/syntheses, and vision technologies.

Thus, all of these areas—general problem solving, expert systems, natural language, computer vision, and robotics—constitute the area commonly called applied artificial intelligence.

Advantages and Limitations of Artificial Intelligence

Thus far in this chapter, we have tried to present a perspective of what artificial intelligence is and what it is not. A number of interesting possibilities exist for the use of artificial intelligence to solve problems, but AI, as such, is not a panacea.

On the positive side, we have seen that AI techniques can be used to solve a number of complex problems. Computers will become much more useful as AI techniques are incorporated into both hardware and software to accomplish certain tasks much more efficiently and at lower cost. Problems that were unsolvable before may become solvable through the use of AI techniques. Possible benefits include increased productivity, continuation of acquired expertise, and safer work environments for humans.

On the negative side, the development of AI software has been difficult at best. Development work is expensive and time consuming, particularly if a computer language such as LISP or PROLOG has to be learned. There are not many commercial AI systems, although this situation is changing. Many research breakthroughs are a long way from happening. Added to this is a lack of trained personnel to work together in teams to develop and implement AI systems.

Even though progress will be slow, it is clear that AI has already had a major impact on computer technology. This impact will increase in some application areas faster than others. The intelligent computer is here to stay and will grow steadily as systems with high paybacks in productivity are implemented.

The Role of AI in Business

Historically, computers have played a major role in the business world and will continue to expand that role as advances in hardware and software are realized. The evolution of the computer's role began with data processing systems (DPS) and has progressed through the stages of management information systems (MIS), decision support systems (DSS), and expert systems (ES). The role of artificial intelligence really had its beginnings with the development of expert systems, but it is useful to briefly describe the characteristics of the other systems.

Data processing systems (DPS) use predetermined procedures to manipulate huge volumes of data. Examples of such systems include payroll and inventory and, in general, involve transaction processing. Those systems are used as tools to help solve problems such as "Should the out-of-stock item be backordered?" or "Should the customer be given credit for the purchase of a large quantity of item Y?" The available data is manipulated by the DPS so the result can be interpreted by the decision maker to solve the problem (answer the question). However, because of the huge volume of data generated in the business world, more sophistication was needed.

Management information systems (MIS) were the next step. The purpose of an MIS system is to summarize and select data from the massive DP files so as to give meaning to the computer output. It is common to characterize MIS systems by the terms *exception reporting* or *management by exception.*

In an MIS, managers embed data-selection criteria, based on content relevance, into the computer program, which will operate on a DP file. A typical MIS system might deal with inventory control or purchasing for replacement of stock. One method that might be used could be to assign minimum levels of stock inventory. An MIS program could determine if the level was below the established minimum, and if so, this exception would be reported to the manager and the process of reordering could begin.

MIS systems are very good at dealing with situations that have a known problem structure. These problems have a predictable set of solutions that are usually based on past experience.

Unfortunately, as problems become larger and more complex, it is often the case that an MIS is inadequate, especially when it is used by an individual in making a decision where he/she does not have any relevant past experience in solving the problem. Decision support systems can be used in these situations.

Decision support systems (DSS) are designed to help managers make more effective and efficient decisions. The manager ultimately makes the decision, but the DSS allows for the use of judgment as it supports the manager's decision process. The DSS is not designed to generate solutions or recommendations, but is designed to help managers deal with problems where their level of ability to solve the problem is below a certain threshold. For example, from the inventory control problem we discussed, a DSS would be used by a manager who has had little experience with such problems.

A number of AI areas are of interest to DSS builders as they attempt to build intelligent features into the DSS. Natural language processing and expert systems are of special interest because of the desire to make DSS more powerful and a concern for the ease of use of the human/machine interface.

It may seem from the very brief descriptions of both DSS and expert systems (ES) in this chapter that there is a great deal of similarity between them. It is, in fact, true that there are a number of similarities, but there are also some major differences. Let us first examine some similarities.

Both DSS and ES evolved from similar disciplines. DSS evolved from organizational behavior and information systems, while ES evolved from cognitive psychology and information systems. Both involve the use of the computer to make better decisions.

There are, however, some distinct differences. In general, the goal of an expert system is to replace the human expert by capturing his or her knowledge and expertise. On the other hand, the general goal of a decision support system is to assist rather than replace an expert.

This distinction, however, is not as clear cut as it might appear. Even though the expert system is used to replace a human expert, the user of the expert system is still using the system to help make a decision. While the expert system suggests a solution or makes recommendations, there is no obligation on the part of the user to implement what the expert system has proposed. In that sense, there is little difference between the expert system and the decision support system. We will discuss more about the features of both DSS and ES in Chapter 9.

So far in this section, we have discussed how AI is used in the business world to help people make more efficient and effective decisions and solve problems. There are a number of other business areas in which AI is already playing, and will increasingly play a major role.

The area of manufacturing is especially fertile. Robotics is already well established in a number of applications such as the automated factory and assembly-line tasks that are boring and/or dangerous for humans. Vision techniques are being used in some applications involving robots. Natural-language processing is being used more and more as an integral part of the human/machine interface. We are only now at the tip of the iceberg!

Key Points

- Artificial intelligence (AI) is a branch of computer science that is devoted to the study of computer hardware and software designed to imitate the thinking and reasoning powers of the human mind.
- Human intelligence is the ability of humans to understand from experience, to acquire new knowledge, and to integrate experience and knowledge to successfully solve problem situations.
- An AI system consists of two parts:
  - Knowledge base (facts, concepts, procedures, and relationships)
  - Software/hardware to manipulate the knowledge base to produce thinking and reason as output
- An AI system can determine many ways to solve a given problem, whereas a conventional computer program solves a problem by step-by-step code. If the given problem is altered, the AI system may be able to handle the situation, but the conventional computer program will not.
- Another name for an AI system is an intelligent computer.
- AI is divided into theory and applications.
- Applied AI systems include:
  - General problem solving
  - Expert systems
  - Natural language
  - Computer vision
  - Robotics
- General problem solving is an applied AI system that includes planning, scheduling, and system design and development.

- An expert system is an applied AI system which simulates the behavior of a human expert in a narrowly defined or restricted domain.
- Natural language is an applied AI area that allows a user to orally communicate with the system in ordinary English sentences (as opposed to specific commands or predetermined menus).
- Computer vision is an applied AI system that allows visual input and interpretation from 2-D objects (pictures) or 3-D objects (real world).
- Robotics is an applied AI system consisting of fixed or moving mechanical arm(s) to perform given tasks (paint or assemble a car, plant explosives, explore a damaged nuclear plant, and so on).
- Advantages of AI systems include:
  - Solution of complex problems
  - Increase in productivity
  - Prevention of the loss of human expertise
  - Removal of people from working in selected dangerous environments
- Disadvantages of AI systems include:
  - Large overhead in time, money, and resources
  - Time required to learn new computer languages
  - Lack of inexpensive, usable, and reliable AI development tools to implement needed systems
  - Lack of qualified professionals to work on teams to implement AI systems
- Artificial intelligence techniques will play an increasingly greater role in the business world, especially in decision-making and problem-solving situations.
- Decision-making and problem-solving aids have evolved over the years through:
  - Data processing systems (DPS)
  - Management information systems (MIS)
  - Decision support systems (DSS)
  - Expert systems (ES)
- Robotics, vision, and natural-language processing already have a major impact on many manufacturing applications.

Exercises

1. Consult your dictionary for a definition of intelligence.
2. Define artificial intelligence. How does it differ from human intelligence?
3. Name five conventional computer systems that exist in your educational or business organization. Define the purpose of each.

Name of System	Purpose of System
____________________	____________________
____________________	____________________
____________________	____________________
____________________	____________________
____________________	____________________

4. Name the five applied areas of artificial intelligence (AI).
5. What are the advantages and limitations of AI systems?
6. What is the role of AI in the business world?
7. Contrast among data processing systems, management systems, decision support systems, and expert systems.

Assignments

1. Many computer magazines feature articles on a given topic for that particular issue. *Byte, PC World, PC Magazine,* and *Datamation* are a few magazines where the topic is printed on the binding of the publication. For example, the August 1, 1987, edition of *Datamation* focuses on artificial intelligence with a feature article on "Smart Buys in Artificial Intelligence." Find special issues, if possible, on each of the applied AI areas. (AI is also featured in *Datamation,* August 1, 1986, and November 1, 1984.)
2. Many magazines and journals print an index by topics in the December or January issue of their yearly publications. Search the December or January issues of selected magazines in your library for articles on each of the applied AI areas. (For example, *PC World* publishes the yearly index in January.) A listing of articles may also be found in the *Reader's Guide to Periodical Literature* or in a database which can be accessed in the library. Ask your librarian for assistance in using these sources.
3. There are five new magazines/journals that deal with AI and/or expert systems. Check your library to see if the following publications are available.

Publications	Available	Dates
IEEE Expert	__________	__________
AI Expert	__________	__________
PC AI	__________	__________
AI Magazine	__________	__________
AI Journal	__________	__________

   Issues of *AI Expert* and *PC AI* can be purchased at a local newsstand for under five dollars an issue.
4. Robotics have been highly publicized in recent movies. If you have seen one or more of these movies, use what you have learned in this chapter and critique the movie(s) for technical accuracy about the capability of robots. In your own business, what routine activity could a robot do for you? In your household, what tasks could a robot do?
5. Whether your major activity is educational, business, or engineering, what expert system would be useful to you in your work?

2

EXPERT SYSTEMS TECHNOLOGY

Over the past decade or so, artificial intelligence (AI) has come to be recognized as a viable area for research and commercial activities. The use of the computer to perform certain tasks which had previously been done by human beings has resulted in the development of new and varied applications and has sparked a great deal of interest among professionals both in and out of computer science.

One of the newest applications for the computer has been the creation of expert systems. In this chapter, we will discuss some basic concepts of expert systems including descriptions of expert systems and knowledge, a historical perspective, component parts, development tools, desirable system features, general applications, specific examples, and advantages/limitations. This discussion will give you a good foundation for the further in-depth treatment of topics in later chapters. The case study, WPHELP, will be introduced. This expert system has been designed to assist in selecting word processing software and will be used throughout the chapters.

What is an Expert System?

Simply put, an **expert system** is a computer program that emulates the behavior of human experts who are solving real-world problems associated with a particular domain of knowledge. For example, an expert system might be built to diagnose a person's ailment when the symptoms of the ailment are input. Another example of an expert system might be one to help choose a word processing package for an office.

While the concept of an expert system seems simple and straightforward, the creation of the expert system is far more complex. Creating an expert system involves: (1) extracting from the expert(s) the knowledge and methods used to solve the problem, and (2) the reforming of the knowledge/methods into an organized form for later use. The processes of extraction and reformation are known as *knowledge acquisition* and *representation*, respectively, and are complex and time-consuming processes. The sum of the two processes is known as *knowledge engineering*.

Expert systems differ from conventional computer programs in several ways. Perhaps the most basic difference is that expert systems manipulate knowledge while conventional computer programs manipulate only data. We will say more about the difference between knowledge and data in the next section.

Conventional computer programs are algorithmic in nature and are characterized by the use of repetitive processes. Thus, conventional programs guarantee a solution to the problem to be solved such as payroll, accounts receivable, or inventory. Even a database program (which generates reports and makes requested queries) falls into this category.

On the other hand, expert systems are characterized by the use of *heuristics* (rules of thumb) and make use of *inferential processes.*

Heuristics are often used by human beings to solve a problem or make a decision. Heuristics often are based on past experience or knowledge. For example, suppose that a complex piece of equipment in a manufacturing process breaks down. A repair person (an expert) is brought in to fix the equipment. From past experience, the repair person knows that the breakdown was likely caused by a burned-out bearing. Hence, the success of diagnosing the cause of the breakdown is found by checking the bearings. Heuristics have been used to start the process of determining the cause of breakdown. Of course, the cause of the breakdown may be other than a burned-out bearing, but heuristics gave the repair person a place to start.

Inferential processes involve the use of reasoning. Commonly used reasoning strategies in solving problems include deduction, induction, and abduction; expert systems make use of such strategies. We will discuss these strategies in more detail in Chapter 4.

An expert system does not guarantee a solution to a problem and is designed to work on problems that require non-algorithmic solutions; in other words, the kinds of problems that require human expertise.

Waterman [1986] states that expert systems must have four basic characteristics:

1. Expertise
2. Depth
3. Symbolic reasoning
4. Self-knowledge

Expert systems must have **expertise**, that is, the ability to perform at least at the level of a human expert. This includes not only the capability to solve the given problem but to do so in as short a time frame as possible. Expertise also means that the knowledge about the problem domain possessed by an expert system must have breadth as well as depth.

Breadth of knowledge refers to the scope of what is known. An expert in a subject area will have a greater breadth of knowledge than will a novice in the same subject area. Past experience is likely to be a contributing factor to the increased breadth.

Depth of knowledge refers to the ability to extend existing knowledge and infer new knowledge. Again, experts have a greater depth of knowledge about a subject area than does a novice. Past experience is again a contributing factor.

To effectively solve real-world problems, an expert system must have **depth**. Real-world problems are often very difficult and complex to solve, so the knowledge possessed by an expert system must be capable of dealing with these problems.

Symbolic reasoning is a third characteristic of expert systems. When an expert systems solves a problem, it does so by manipulating symbols and not just by performing mathematical calculations or solving equations.

A symbol can be thought of as a string of characters that represents some real-world concept. For example:

brake system

manufacturer

0.95

all represent symbols. These symbols may be used in a symbolic structure to represent some real-world relationship. An example of such a structure might be:

(INADEQUATE brake system)

(SOLD BY automobile manufacturer)

(EQUAL (FAULT manufacturer) 0.95)

The fact that an expert system manipulates symbols does not mean that it does not perform mathematical calculations; such calculations are performed only as needed and are not the thrust of the systems' problem-solving techniques.

Finally, an expert system possesses **self-knowledge**. Self-knowledge is present when the expert system has knowledge about its knowledge. For example, most current expert systems have an *explanation facility*. This facility allows the system to explain to a user how and/or why a particular conclusion was reached.

The explanation facility is but a small part of the self-knowledge characteristic. In the future, expert systems will have the capability of reformulating their inference strategies to operate more efficiently and to reason new knowledge from experience. The further development of the characteristic of self-knowledge will allow expert systems to move closer and closer to performing like human experts. We will discuss the future in more detail in Chapter 9.

What is Knowledge?

When the term **knowledge** is used in AI work, it means the things that a computer program needs to behave intelligently. This information often takes the form of facts and rules for inferring new facts and rules. For example, we might have the following set of facts and rules from two knowledge bases. Note that new facts can be generated.

Fact: The car is out of gas.

Rule: IF the car is out of gas,
THEN the car will not start.

New Fact: The car will not start.

Fact: Can #7 contains green solution.
Can #4 contains blue solution.
Can #1 contains yellow solution.

Rule: IF the color of the solution is green,
THEN the solution is a mixture of yellow and blue solutions.

New Fact: Can #7 is a mixture of can #4 and can #1.

In the real world, facts and rules are not always entirely true or false. There may be some uncertainty about the validity of a fact or the accuracy of a rule. For example, you might hear a human expert say:

"I'm pretty sure this valve is the cause of the difficulty."
"It doesn't seem very likely that the brakes are defective."

or

"Nine times out of ten, the battery is the cause of the problem."

When this doubt occurs in a fact or rule, it is quantified in an expert system with the use of a number. These numbers are known as **certainty factors (CF)**. A certainty factor is an indication of the degree of certainty attached to some fact or rule. For example:

Fact: The car is out of gas (CF 0.80).

Rule: IF CF (car is out of gas) > = 0.80
AND the test error is greater than 0.02,
THEN the car will not start (CF 0.95).

Fact: Can #7 contains green solution (CF 0.9).

Rule: IF the can contains green solution (CF 0.9).
THEN the can is a mixture of only yellow and blue solutions (CF 0.85).

As you might suspect, an expert system must be sensitive to uncertainty in its reasoning strategies. We will explore this uncertainty and its effect on reasoning strategies in more detail in Chapters 4 and 5.

You may have noticed in the first examples in this section that facts and rules were used to generate new facts but were not used to generate new rules. The generation of new rules by the expert systems itself is, at this time, beyond the scope of current expert systems technology. The capability of an expert system to generate new rules on its own, without external assistance, is anticipated in the next decade but is not yet present in commercial systems. Hence, some expert systems workers prefer to call current expert systems knowledge-based systems or pseudo-expert systems, leaving the term expert system to the future. In this book, we will not be concerned with this distinction.

Expert Systems: Past and Present

From a historical perspective, expert systems have been around a relatively short time. Their development emanated from the efforts of AI researchers to achieve the goal of building computer programs that could 'think,' that is, solve problems in a way considered by human beings to be intelligent.

The early efforts at expert system development began in the 1950s with the work of Newell, Shaw, and Simon, who created a system called the General Problem Solver (GPS). About the same time and into the 1960s, Minsky and McCarthy also did significant work in expert system development. A third group, active in the 1960s and consisting of Ledburg, Buchanan, and Feigenbaum, worked on a system called DENDRAL which developed a structure of molecules using mass spectrometer data.

While the work of the three groups produced significant results, there was no solid breakthrough in achieving the original goal. The major problem was that a computer program designed to solve a wide variety of problems did not have the same power as a program designed to work with a more narrow domain.

The 1970s produced the realization by AI researchers that expert systems should be built with *narrow-scoped* problem domains. Researchers also came to realize that the quality of the knowledge possessed by the expert system was at least as important as the inference techniques used by the system.

These two realizations, along with advancements in microcomputer technology, were the real catalysts to advancements in expert system technology in the late 1970s and early 1980s. Expert systems had begun to move from the research environment to the commercial environment.

Today, there are a growing number of commercial expert systems being developed. This growth has been enhanced by the development and use of expert system development tools that do not require an expert system developer to have high-level language programming expertise.

With all of these advancements in expert systems technology, there is still much to be done. Current expert systems can be described as 'how to' systems. That is, all of the knowledge and control structures that a given expert system possesses must be programmed into the system initially. Today's expert systems do not have the capability of "learning" (adding to its knowledge base internally) as a human expert is able to do. Researchers are working on the problem, but no real breakthrough is expected for at least a decade or two; although, we may be surprised.

Components of an Expert System

Expert systems can be thought of as having three basic components: the knowledge base, the inference engine and the user interface. In this section, we will very briefly describe each of them; each component will be examined in greater depth in subsequent chapters. Figure 2.1 shows a block diagram of an expert system.

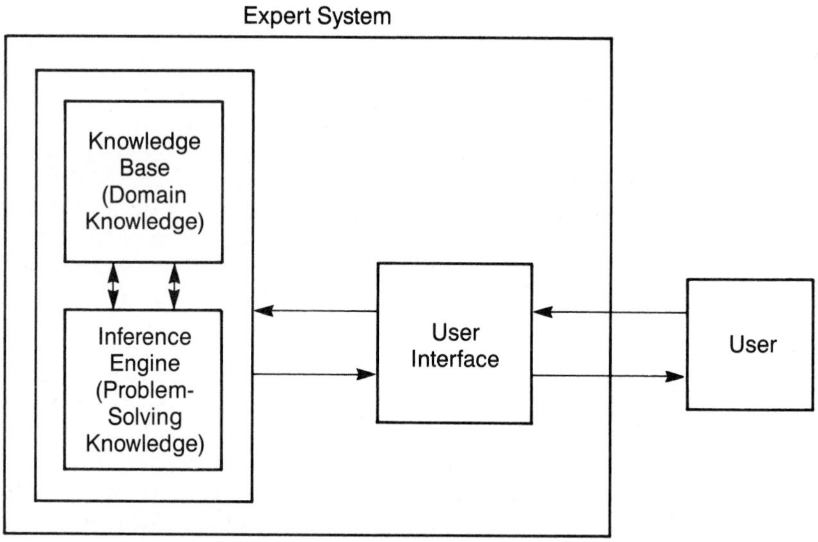

FIGURE 2.1 BLOCK DIAGRAM OF AN EXPERT SYSTEM

The Knowledge Base

The **knowledge base** in an expert system consists of the facts and rules (or other representation) which the system possesses about a particular problem domain. New facts and rules may be added externally at any time but, with current technology, only new facts (derived from the existing rules) may be added internally during program execution. More detail about the knowledge base is given in Chapter 5.

The Inference Engine

The **inference engine** in an expert system performs the task of deciding how and when facts and rules are to be applied to make decisions (solve the problem). The structure of the inference engine is independent of the knowledge base but may be the same for similar problem structures. More detail about the inference engine is given in Chapter 6.

The User Interface

The **user interface** in an expert system is the means of communication between a user wishing to solve a problem and the problem solver (expert system). It is vital that this communication be as meaningful and friendly as possible; otherwise, the expert system will neither be useful nor used. The user interface may be command driven, menu-driven, or icon oriented (graphical objects). User interfaces are discussed in detail in Chapter 7.

Expert System Development Tools

There are basically two types of expert systems development tools available today. These tools include knowledge engineering languages/systems and high-level programming languages.

Knowledge **engineering** languages/systems (also known as shells) are sophisticated expert system building tools. They can be classified as skeletal or general-purpose and are comprised of an expert system building language and an extensive support environment.

The advantage of the knowledge engineering language/system is that it is easier for the inexperienced expert system builder to apply. The **shell** essentially dictates how knowledge is to be represented and contains a pre-constructed inference engine for accessing the knowledge base. Its disadvantage is that, because its inference engine is already structured, the range of problems that can be solved in a given domain is limited to the constraints enforced by the shell. While the cost of good knowledge engineering shells can be relatively high (thousands of dollars), they probably do not take as much personnel and system development time, also a high-cost commodity. While the names of knowledge engineering shells are not as well known as those of standard high-level programming languages, there are a number of excellent ones available such as **VP-Expert**, and more are continually being developed.

High-level programming languages that are used for expert system applications include *symbolic-manipulation* languages such as LISP and PROLOG and *procedure-oriented languages* such as Pascal and FORTRAN. There are advantages and disadvantages to the use of these high-level programming languages.

The main advantage is that high-level languages allow a great deal of flexibility for the expert system builder. Because of this flexibility, an expert system built with these tools can usually solve a wider variety of problems within the same domain. The disadvantage is that these languages are more difficult to apply because they give little or no guidance as to how knowledge should be represented or how mechanisms for accessing the knowledge base should be designed.

Desirable Features of Expert Systems

There are several desirable features that expert systems should have. These features aid the user in operating the expert system as a tool. In this section, we will describe the features of dealing with uncertainty, explanation, ease of modification, transportability, and adaptive learning.

Dealing with Uncertainty

Whenever we set about to solve a problem, it would be very desirable if we could count on our knowledge (facts and rules) to be totally true or false. We could thus be certain that our derived solution was correct. Unfortunately, this desirable characteristic of our knowledge is seldom present. In reality, we must often deal with incomplete or less than accurate information.

One of the best features about an expert system is that it is capable of dealing with knowledge that is incomplete or not completely accurate. This allows us to obtain a solution even though we may not be one hundred percent confident of its correctness.

As we noted earlier in the chapter, an expert system deals with uncertainty through the use of certainty factors. We will discuss certainty factors and uncertainty in greater detail in Chapter 6.

Certainty factors are assigned to facts or rules in the knowledge base and indicate the degree of correctness of a fact or the accuracy of a rule. We again illustrate the concept of certainty factors with several examples in Figure 2.2.

As you can see from the figure, there are several methods for calculating the certainty factor of the THEN component. Figure 2.2(a) uses the greater of the two certainty factors given in the IF component while in Figure 2.2(b), the lesser value is used. In Figure 2.2(c), the final certainty factor is the average of the two certainty factors in the IF component. Thus, three different ways to specify the certainty factor are maximum, minimum, and average of the certainty factors of the input (A,B).

Other techniques for assigning a final certainty-factor value have been developed and used. However, there is no general agreement on which method is best to use.

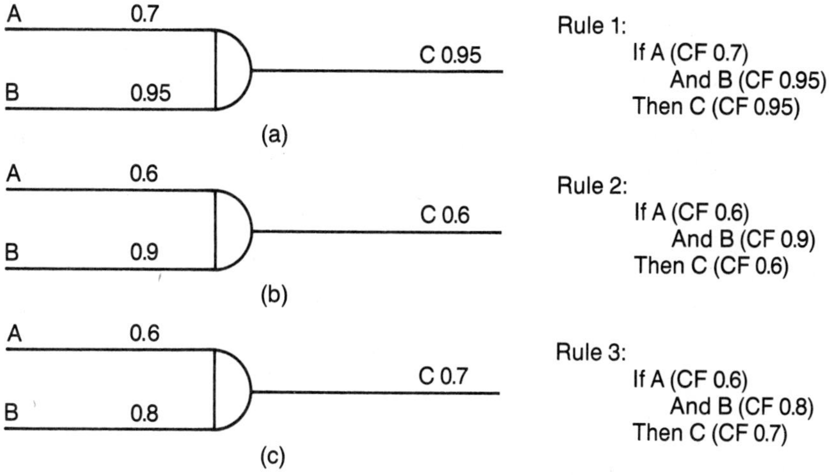

FIGURE 2.2 THREE METHODS OF DEALING WITH UNCERTAINTY

Another situation arises when several rules are chained together. In this case the certainty factor at the end of the chain will be affected by certainty factors of elements in the chain. This situation is illustrated, for example, in Figure 2.3.

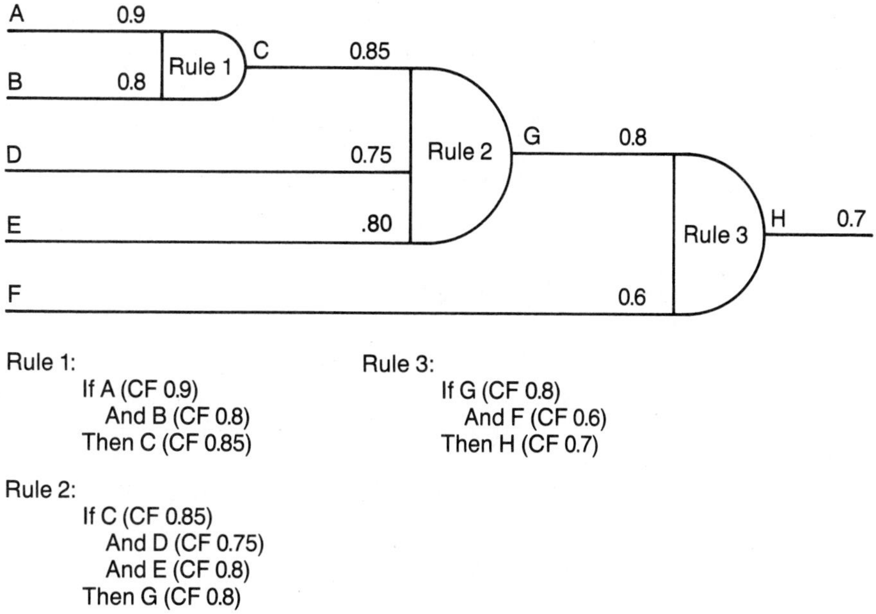

FIGURE 2.3 EFFECT OF CERTAINTY FACTORS ON AN INFERENCE CHAIN

All of these certainty factors in the chain were determined by using the average method.

Explanation

A second desirable feature of expert systems is the capability to explain how and why a decision or solution was reached. The user of the expert system is thus able to gain access to the reasoning behind the actions of the expert system. We can illustrate this capability with Figure 2.4.

Rule 1:
    If A
        And B
    Then C

Rule 2:
    If C
        And D
        And E
    Then F

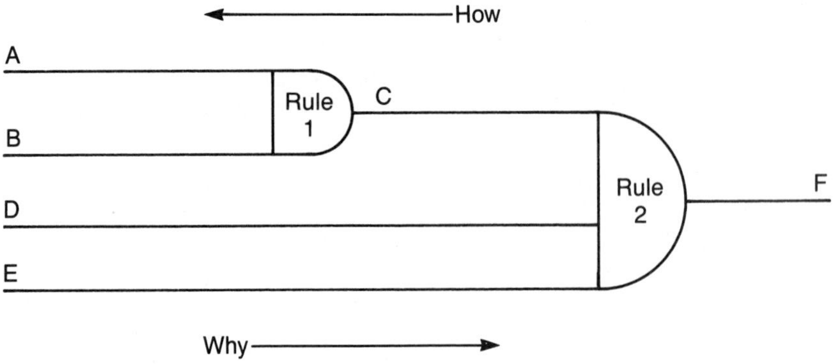

FIGURE 2.4 HOW THE EXPLANATION FACILITY IS IMPOSED ON AN INFERENCE CHAIN

The following dialogues might occur:

User: Why did you conclude F?

System: Because A and B gave me C and because C, D, and E gave me F.

User: Why did you conclude C?

System: I knew C since I knew A and B.

Ease of Modification

As new facts and rules become available or as existing facts and rules need modification, it is desirable that changes to the knowledge base be as easy to make as possible. Expert systems that have been developed using high-level languages such as

PROLOG or LISP are more difficult to modify or add to than expert systems which have been developed with shells. Shells generally have an editing facility which makes modifications relatively easy.

Transportability

An expert system is often developed to run only on one type of computer. This is not necessarily a desirable situation since the scope of usage may be limited. If the development process is such that more than one type of computer can be used to run the expert system, the end result will be a much higher level of usability.

Adaptive Learning

The **adaptive learning** feature is one that is possessed by few current expert systems. It involves the ability of the expert system to learn (add or modify facts and rules) on its own through experience. When this feature is available, the expert system will become much more powerful and move closer to the true emulation of human problem-solving capability. Researchers are actively working in this area, but it will be several years before this feature will be readily available. We will discuss this feature in greater detail in Chapter 9.

Applications of Expert Systems

We mentioned earlier that expert systems have been built for a number of applications. There are so many applications that an entire book could be filled with their descriptions. Perhaps the best way to give an overview of the different examples is to explore a generic classification scheme used by Frenzel [1987]. The classifications are shown in Table 2.1.

TABLE 2.1 GENERIC CLASSIFICATION OF EXPERT SYSTEM APPLICATIONS

CONTROL:	Intelligent automation
DEBUGGING:	Recommends corrections to faults
DESIGN:	Develops products to specification
DIAGNOSIS:	Estimates defects
INSTRUCTION:	Optimizes computer instruction
INTERPRETATION:	Clarification of situations
PLANNING:	Develops goal-oriented schemes
PREDICTION:	Intelligent guessing of outcomes
REPAIR:	Automatic diagnosis, debugging, planning, and fixing

An explanation of each type of application follows.

Control

Control is a very common application of computers. This application uses the computer to govern operation of a single component, several components, or the entire system. For example, a system that makes parts for an automobile, or tool and die, milling system could be controlled by a computer.

Many applications in this area involve the use of feedback data which is gathered by sensors. Examples of this kind of data might be temperature, water level, speed, or any other factor that might affect system performance.

Perhaps an algorithmic computer program could be used with these applications. Still, there will be times when an expert system would be a good choice if, say, an algorithm does not exist. The expert system is also useful when a decision about system performance needs to be made based on feedback data.

Debugging

In **debugging** applications, a system is found to be operating at less than an expected or specified level. An expert system may be used to locate the source(s) of the difficulty and then determine a solution to correct the difficulty.

Design

Design applications may involve the use of an expert system to collect information about constraints (specifications) relative to a particular product. The system then can be used as the design tool or to assist another design tool.

Expert systems have been used by several companies in the design of electronic and computer equipment and entire computer systems. They have also been used to supplement CAD/CAM systems in appliance and automobile manufacturing.

Diagnosis

It is probably fair to say that more successful expert systems have been built for **diagnostic** applications than for any of the others. In this type of application, the expert system is used to locate the source(s) of the system difficulty. It differs from an expert system that debugs in that the diagnostic expert system does not deal with the problem of corrective action.

These expert systems have found wide use in manufacturing applications and the detection of system faults. The medical profession has begun to use expert systems to aid and verify the diagnostic process.

Instruction

Computers have been used in **instruction** applications for some time. A student sits down with a computer program and follows a certain format as he or she attempts to learn a given concept or skill.

A major problem with computer-assisted instruction (CAI), and techniques known by other names, has been the lack of instructional strategy flexibility. The strategy(ies) embedded in the computer programs may not optimize the student's learning situation.

An expert system could correct this problem of optimization by determining the nature of the background knowledge brought to the learning situation by the student. It can then prescribe a possible strategy and, with feedback from the student, make alterations in the presentation of the material. In this sense, the expert system could be said to be like a debugging expert system except that its corrective action and diagnostic components possibly would be much more complex.

Interpretation

Interpretation applications involve the collection of various forms of input data and then inferring a meaning or situation based on that data. It is designed to help the user understand or clarify what has been recorded. Certain expert systems have been built that analyze military intelligence information. Others have been used for image or signal analysis.

Planning

Applications involving a variety of **planning** techniques are those that plan a method or strategy for achieving some desired goal. Planning is necessary in the solution of complex problem situations. With the appropriate knowledge and input, an expert system can perform the planning phase quite well. Some examples of planning applications include military tactics, project management, scheduling, and problem-solving strategies.

Prediction

Predictive applications involve the use of input to infer possible outputs. A prediction expert system may examine all possible outputs and then choose the one that best fits the input. As input is varied, a user can determine what changes will occur in the output. Among others, weather forecasting is an example of a predictive application.

Repair

Repair applications involve an extension of debugging applications. A repair expert system takes the prescribed solution generated by a debugging expert system and implements it. A repair system, of course, must have access capability to the tools needed for repair. It is fairly easy to see that a repair system must have diagnostic, debugging, and planning capabilities. Examples of applications involve fault-tolerant systems which actually may or may not be able to repair the difficulty; if not, the system is kept operational until repairs can be made by external sources.

Some Examples of Expert Systems

As we indicated in the last section, expert systems have been used for a wide variety of applications. There are many examples of successful expert systems and, in this section, we will briefly describe some of the more well-known systems.

MYCIN System

MYCIN is perhaps the most well-known of the expert systems currently in use. The system was developed in the mid-1970s by Edward Feigenbaum at Stanford University. The purpose of the system was to medically diagnose a bacterial infection and prescribe antibiotic treatment. The system has proven to be very effective in assisting physicians who have had little or no experience with such infections. It has also assisted physicians as a check against the accuracy of their diagnostic/prescriptive process, although it has never been turned into a commercial success.

XCON/XSEL System

XCON/XSEL is an expert system that was developed jointly by Digital Equipment Corporation (DEC) and Carnegie Mellon University in the late 1970s. The purpose of XCON/XSEL is to configure a computer system in the DEC VAX 11/780 series to meet specific customer orders. Large computer systems such as the VAX have a great number of different component parts designed to perform different tasks. There are thousands of combinations of these parts; each combination representing a unique computer system tailored to a specific customer. XCON/XSEL takes the given customer system specifications and produces a plan for assembling the final system.

DELTA System

DELTA is an expert system designed and developed by the General Electric Company to assist maintenance personnel in locating difficulties with electric diesel locomotive engines. These engines are very complex, and the task of troubleshooting problems is at best difficult. DELTA has proven to be extremely helpful to the maintenance personnel in performing the diagnostic function on the engines.

DENDRAL System

DENDRAL is an expert system also developed at Stanford University in the late 1970s. The system has knowledge of molecular structures and chemistry and is used to help identify the molecular structure of unknown chemical compounds. This assistance is very helpful to researchers as they work with existing unknown compounds for a variety of applications.

PROSPECTOR System

PROSPECTOR is an expert system designed by the Sheffield Research Institute in the late 1970s and early 1980s. The system was developed to assist geologists in the location of ore deposits. The assistance is in the form of analyzing data input by a geologist and making a recommendation as to what the likelihood of a particular ore deposit is at a given site. In addition, PROSPECTOR can also suggest further explanations, tests, or the need for more data collection. To date, PROSPECTOR has been credited with the location of several large and valuable ore deposits in the United States.

YESMVS System

YESMVS is an expert system designed by IBM in the early 1980s. It was developed to help computer operators monitor and control the MVS (multiple virtual storage) operating system. Among the other features, YESMVS runs in real time, monitors system operation, schedules large batch jobs, and alerts the operator about possible network link problems.

ACE System

ACE is an expert system designed and developed by A.T.&T. Bell Laboratories in the early 1980s to perform troubleshooting on large telephone cable systems. The system analyzes maintenance activity data and generates reports referring to the physical location of the problem and characteristics about the cable network or the problem spot. ACE does not interact directly with a user. Instead, it interacts with **GRAS**, which is a database management and report-generation system. The system has proven especially successful in its implementation by Southwestern Bell in Denver, Colorado.

It should be fairly clear from these brief descriptions that expert systems have a wide variety of capabilities and applications. Added examples are being produced almost daily by industrial companies, research organizations, and universities. A source for further information about each of the example expert systems is given in Assignment 8 at the end of this chapter.

Advantages and Limitations of Expert Systems

It has been demonstrated by existing expert systems, such as XCON/XSEL, that an expert system is capable of performing at or near the level of a human expert. This is important for several reasons. First, human expertise is fragile; it could be immediately lost by an organization through resignation, retirement, or death. An expert system is much more permanent. Second, human expertise is costly in terms of time and money. While initial development costs are high, it is usually less expensive to maintain the expert system, depending on the personnel used for this task. The expert system is portable and is easily shipped to remote locations for use. The latter point is especially important if human expertise is needed in more than one geographical location at the same time. Third, an expert system is easy to document, and its results are consistent. This is not always the case with human expertise.

There are limitations to expert systems, however. First, they cannot currently learn from experience as can a human expert. An expert system can generate new facts but, at this point, it is essentially incapable of generating new rules. Second, the knowledge acquisition process is a limitation. It is not an easy matter to extract knowledge from a human expert. The process of knowledge engineering is still not well understood, but its state is improving. Third, expert systems are appropriate for solving only certain kinds of problems. Problems with solutions that are not generally agreed upon by human experts are not likely to be good candidates for expert systems. Fourth, input into an expert system must have the same representation as the current knowledge base. Human experts are capable of dealing with different forms of knowledge representation, where expert systems are not.

Case Study: WPHELP

Throughout this book we use the case study WPHELP to reinforce the theory and concepts of an expert system. WPHELP is a software program that runs on IBM PCs and compatibles. The purpose of this expert system is to assist a small business manager in selecting software to process documents (letters, memos, reports, and so on) for the office. A business person can use WPHELP to obtain advice and guidance on selecting word processing software to fit the office needs of the company.

In today's office, it can cost as much as $20 to process a business letter using a typewriter. If a mistake is made, the letter must be retyped or corrected with fluid or ribbon. If two hundred form letters are to be mailed, then two hundred letters with different addresses must be individually typed. A *word processing* software program can eliminate these problems and reduce both the time and money involved. A user of a word processing program can operate a keyboard to type documents, and then save the documents to a floppy or hard disk. The advantage is being able to retrieve, revise, and save again. A document with three misspellings can be corrected without having to retype the entire document. Moreover, it is possible to create a list of addresses, say 200 customer addresses (which can be used again and again), to create one form letter (typed only one time), and to have the microcomputer program print out letters with individual addresses. Clearly, time and money can be saved in the office with the use of word processing software.

WPHELP can be categorized as a DESIGN system. The expert system helps a business person plan and develop the goals for document processing for the specified business.

The system helps the user clarify and prioritize word processing needs. WPHELP, after communicating with the user through the user interface, suggests a list of possible software packages with possible steps for maximizing the resources for the office. Since WPHELP does help to interpret the word processing needs and to predict the needed outcomes in terms of software, it can be also classified as **Interpretive or Predictive.**

With over 300 different packages ranging from $5 to $10,000 from which to choose, today's business person does not have the time and resources to research all possible word processing systems. WPHELP is designed to help the typical manager running a small business employing up to 20 people to clarify and plan for word processing in the office.

Processing documents is a vital step in maintaining a business. Hence, the advantage of WPHELP is its reliable advice for determining word processing needs. On the other hand, WPHELP has some limitations as an expert system. The nature of microcomputer hardware and software changes so fast that expert system software has to be continually updated. Rules that were true one year ago may not be true today. Constant maintenance and updating the knowledge base are crucial. Though the domain of knowledge is limited to word processing on IBM-compatibles for a small office, the document processing needs could still vary considerably. Then WPHELP might advise a user to investigate another type of software.

However, even with these limitations, the advantages of WPHELP make it a viable business expert system and a useful educational case study for this text.

Key Points

- An expert system is a computer program that emulates the behavior of human experts who are solving real-world problems associated with a particular domain of knowledge.
- Knowledge engineering is the process of extracting knowledge and methods for solving problems from a human expert and then using what has been extracted to create an expert system.
- An expert system manipulates knowledge while a conventional computer program manipulates data.
- An expert system uses inferential processes and heuristics (rules of thumb), whereas a conventional computer program uses sequential processes and algorithms.
- An expert system cannot guarantee a problem solution while a conventional computer program does guarantee a solution.
- In AI terms, knowledge is information needed by a computer program to behave intelligently. This information may take the form of facts and rules for inferring new information.
- Not all knowledge is entirely true or false. This uncertainty is quantified in an expert system with probability numbers called certainty factors (CF) or confidence ratios.

- Expert systems development work began in the 1950s but did not really move from the research environment to the commercial environment until the late 1970s and early 1980s.
- Current expert systems can be classified as "how to" systems with knowledge and inference strategies preprogrammed into the system. Future systems will be able to "learn on the fly."
- An expert system consists of three basic components:
  - Knowledge base
  - Inference engine
  - User interface
- The knowledge base contains the knowledge (facts and rules) that the expert system possesses about a particular problem domain.
- The inference engine performs the task of deciding how and when facts and rules are to be applied to make a decision (solve the problem).
- The user interface controls communication between the user and the expert system.
- There are two types of expert system development tools:
  - Knowledge engineering languages/systems (shells)
  - High-level programming languages
- Shells are easier to use by inexperienced expert system builders but are not as flexible relative to the range of potential problems to be solved because the inference engine is pre-constructed.
- High-level programming languages offer greater flexibility relative to the range of problems to be solved but are more difficult to use because the inference engine must also be constructed and decisions about how knowledge is to be represented must be made.
- Expert systems have several desirable features:
  - Ability to deal with uncertainty
  - Explanation facility
  - Easy modification
  - Transportability
  - Adaptive learning
- Expert systems have been used for many types of applications including control, debugging, design, diagnosis, instruction, interpretation, planning, prediction, and repair.
- There are examples of expert systems in a wide variety of applications. Among others, MYCIN, XCON/XSEL, DELTA, DENDRAL, PROSPECTOR, YESMVS, and ACE have had notable success.
- Expert systems have several advantages:
  - The knowledge base is (usually) permanent and easy to maintain
  - The system is relatively inexpensive to maintain and can be used in several locations at the same time
  - The system is easy to document and produces consistent results
- An expert system has several limitations:
  - The system cannot learn from experience
  - The knowledge acquisition process is not well understood
  - Not all problems are candidates for expert systems
  - All knowledge put into the expert system must be represented in the same form

- WPHELP is an expert system to be used throughout this text and:
  - Is designed for business managers who run a small office with up to 20 workers
  - Helps a manager clarify word processing needs and suggests possible software solutions to meet these needs
  - Has the advantages of low cost and productivity
  - Has the disadvantages of constant revision because of changing technology, emerging new products, and varying market conditions

Exercises

1. What is an expert system? How does it differ from a conventional computer program? How is it similar to a conventional computer program?
2. How is knowledge defined in AI terms?
3. Trace the history of expert systems. What were the significant factors that caused the current form of expert systems to be realized?
4. Describe the three components of an expert system.
5. Describe the two types of expert system development tools. What are the advantages and disadvantages of each type?
6. What are the desirable features of an expert system? How do these features enhance an expert system?
7. List the major advantages and limitations of an expert system.
8. Using the classification scheme of Table 2.1, propose an expert system of that type that would be useful to your organization.

PROPOSED EXPERT SYSTEM

TYPE	____________
CONTROL	____________
DEBUGGING	____________
DESIGN	____________
DIAGNOSIS	____________
INSTRUCTION	____________
INTERPRETATION	____________
PLANNING	____________
PREDICTION	____________
REPAIR	____________

9. Since WPHELP helps a user to select word processing software, define word processing.
10. List types of documents that a small business office might need to produce.

Assignments

1. The July 14, 1986, edition of Computer World contains a chart and summary of expert system development tools. From this article, list the major criteria for comparing and contrasting expert system development tools. Using your own judgment and environment, divide the selection criteria into three categories: essential, desirable, and expendable. Can you explain or justify your decision?
2. Write for information on five expert system tools that could be used in your environment. (Use the reference in Computer World or any better survey you find.)
3. You have read how knowledge is defined in AI terms. Compare and contrast this view of knowledge with the view of knowledge in the fields of psychology, education, and business.
4. Investigate in greater depth the projects of the three groups of early pioneers in expert system development. What specific contributions did each group make to expert systems development? What impact of each group's work has been realized in today's expert systems?
5. Beginning in November, 1985, Texas Instruments has sponsored four (free) satellite symposiums on knowledge-based systems (expert systems). This company consequently put together some valuable reference tools including videotapes, slides (with script), system demonstration disk, and so on. Contact Texas Instruments for availability, prices, and future satellite symposiums. A mailing address is:

   Texas Instruments
   AI Satellite Symposium
   P.O. Box 181153
   Austin, Texas 78718

6. The Summer 1988 *IEEE Expert* has an interesting article entitled "Expert Systems in Japan." The article gives a chart of 121 expert systems which have been developed for Japanese businesses. The chart lists the company name, application, development level, tools used, and name of the expert system. Summarize this article.
7. The Fall 1987 issue of *IEEE Expert* is dedicated to expert systems for financial applications. The issue includes expert systems on financial risk assessment, financial decision making, financial planning, marketing advisory system, and credit card application assessment. Summarize each article and rank order the expert system in terms of "future dollars saved."
8. In the text, we briefly described some examples of working expert systems. In this assignment, you are to choose one or more of the examples and do an in-depth study of the characteristics and functions of each expert system. To help you in this assignment, we have included a source of information for each expert system; you may find or be aware of other references.

MYCIN
Buchanan and Shortliffe, eds. *Rule-Based Expert Systems*, 295–301, 571, 596. Menlo Park, CA, Addison-Wesley, 1984.

XCON/XSEL
McDermott. "Domain Knowledge and the Design Process." *Design Studies*, vol. 3, no. 1, January 1982.

DELTA
"DELTA/CATS-1". *The Artificial Intelligence Report*, vol. 1, no. 1, January 1984.

DENDRAL
Buchanan and Feigenbaum. "DENDRAL and METADENDRAL: Their Applications Dimension." *Artificial Intelligence*, vol. 11, 1978.

PROSPECTOR
Waterman. *A Guide to Expert Systems*, 41–60. Menlo Park, CA Addison-Wesley, 1986.

YESMVS
Gresnerietal. "YESMVS: A Continuous Real-Time Expert System." *Proceedings of the American Association for Artificial Intelligence*, 1984.

ACE
Wright, et al. "ACE: Going From Prototype to Product with an Expert System." *Conference Proceedings of the Association for Computing Machinery*, October 1984.

9. The forerunner of the expert system development tool (shell) was EMYCIN which derived from MYCIN. Following is a brief description: EMYCIN is an example of an expert system development tool discussed earlier in this chapter. It is essentially MYCIN System with the knowledge base removed. The development of EMYCIN is important because it demonstrated that a shell could be created that contained only the inference engine and the user interface. The shell could then have a number of knowledge bases inserted into it, each knowledge base creating a unique expert system. There are a number of expert system shells available today, and they have grown in popularity for expert systems development by relatively inexperienced knowledge engineers.

   Prepare a more detailed description of EMYCIN, as you did for Assignment 8. Here is a reference to get you started. Buchanan, B. and Shortliffe, E. Eds. *Rule-Based Expert Systems*, Menlo Park, CA, Addison-Wesley, 1984.

3

KNOWLEDGE REPRESENTATION

As we mentioned in the previous chapter, an expert system contains knowledge about a particular problem domain. This knowledge represents the system's source of intelligence and is used by the inference engine to reason and draw conclusions and solutions about a particular problem in the problem domain.

The process of collecting and organizing the knowledge is perhaps the most important and difficult task involved in the creation of an expert system. We will discuss techniques for accomplishing this task in greater detail in Chapter 5. For the present, we wish to examine how the knowledge can be represented so that it can be stored and used in a computer.

Characteristics of Knowledge

To gain a better understanding of what is meant by knowledge, we think that it is useful to distinguish among three terms that are sometimes carelessly used interchangeably: data, information, and knowledge.

Data represents facts, such as raw figures (numbers) or measurements. The following are examples of data:

eight people

12 degrees

Data, by itself, may or may not answer a user's question.

Information is the refinement and use of data to answer a specific user question. Examples of information might include:

We can get six people in the car.

It is 32 degrees outside and the rain is turning into ice.

In addition, information can be described as organizing the data (numbers, words) so that it is meaningful to the user.

Knowledge can be thought of as refined information. It tends to be more general but also may be incomplete or fuzzy. It is more than what would be found in a conventional database. Knowledge can, of course, include facts and information and may also include concepts, procedures, models, and heuristics that can be used in problem solving and inference systems. Knowledge can be regarded as information in context that is organized so that it is readily available for solving problems, perceptions, and learning.

Knowledge varies widely in both its content and appearance. It may be specific or general, exact or fuzzy, or procedural or declarative. In the next section, we will discuss some common methods for organizing and representing knowledge: production rules, semantic networks, frames, and predicate calculus.

Knowledge Representation Models

Over the years, a number of knowledge representation models have been developed. These models have used several diverse approaches to the problem of representing knowledge, but there are two common characteristics of the models. First, each model can be programmed with one or more existing high-level computer languages, or expert system shells, and the results stored in computer memory. Second, the models are designed so that their contents (facts or other types of knowledge) can be used in a reasoning process. It may be helpful to think of each model as a data structure that can be manipulated by the inference engine in search and pattern-matching activities.

Knowledge representation models are usually classified as either *declarative* or *procedural*. A model is said to be declarative if it is used to represent facts or assertions. A procedural model is one that is used to represent actions or procedures.

Declarative models include semantic networks, frames, and predicate calculus (logic). Procedural models include production rules. Other models exist as we pointed out earlier but the models discussed in this section represent those most often used in the expert system and development process. The following chart summarizes these models.

Knowledge Representation Model	Type
Production Rules	Procedural
Semantic Networks	Declarative
Frames	Declarative
Predicate Calculus (Logic)	Declarative

The remainder of this section discusses each of these knowledge representation models or data structures in more detail.

Production Rules

Production rules (often referred to as simply rules or productions) are the most popular form of knowledge representation used in expert systems. This is because rules are relatively easy to understand and create. Rules are a good way to represent recommendations, directives, or strategies when the knowledge to be represented consists of the results of a great deal of experience in solving problems in a particular area or domain.

Rules consist of two parts, an IF and a THEN. These two parts establish a relationship which is the heart or purpose of the rule. Several pairs of terms are used to describe this IF-THEN relationship. These pairs are illustrated in the following charts.

IF	THEN
antecedent	consequent
situation	action
premise	conclusion

Also, the symbol → may be used in place of IF-THEN.

IF		THEN
antecedent	→	consequent
situation	→	action
premise	→	conclusion

Typical rules in a rule-based expert system might look like the following:

Rule 1: IF the number of widgets is less than 60, THEN place a reorder to be delivered in 24 hours.

Rule 2: IF the battery is dead, THEN the car will not start.

These two examples represent the *situation-action* and the *premise-conclusion* forms of a rule respectively. In these examples, the action or conclusion in the THEN part is performed or concluded if the situation or premise in the IF part is true or meets certain specified criteria. We will discuss specified criteria in more detail later in this chapter and in Chapters 4 and 6.

Rules may make use of the conjunction AND or the logical OR. This use is illustrated in the following rules:

Rule 3: IF (the board appropriates the money)
AND (delivery can be assured in less than 30 days),
THEN (purchase the laser printer).

Rule 4: IF (the contractor does not meet the completion deadline),
OR (there is a cost overrun),
THEN (the contract is void).

In Rule 3, the IF part uses AND to connect the two statements (situations). For the action of ordering the laser printer to be executed, both situations (board appropriates the money and assured less than 30-day delivery) must be true.

In the second example (Rule 4), the rule states that the contract is void provided either the deadline is missed or there is a cost overrun. It is also possible both situations have occurred (past deadline and cost overrun) and the contract would be voided.

Rules may contain any number of statements connected by AND or OR in the IF part. For an "AND" rule to be true, all of the statements connected by AND must be true. For an "OR" rule to be true, at least one of the statements connected by OR must be true. The other statements may or may not be true.

To accurately represent the knowledge in a particular domain, it usually takes a relatively large number of rules. This is because the rules contain the details of the knowledge. The number of rules will vary proportionately to the complexity of the knowledge. The rules are usually interrelated with each other. For example, the action or conclusion of the rule may be the situation or premise of another rule. The final action or conclusion may involve a chaining of rules; more will be said about chaining in Chapters 4 and 5, but an example here will illustrate the point:

Rule 5: IF (the customer has an account)
AND (the account has not been used for 90 days),
THEN (mark the account as "inactive").

Rule 6: IF (the account is inactive),
THEN (call the customer to re-establish the business connection).

Rule 7: IF (the customer indicates unwillingness to do further business),
THEN (delete the customer from the database).

In the example, the three rules are interrelated. Rule 6 is invoked only if Rule 5 is sequence of actions. As we shall see later, this chain may be traversed in either a forward or backward manner.

Semantic Networks

A second method of representing knowledge that has been around for several years is the **semantic network** (also known as a **semantic net**). This method is based on a network structure and is usually viewed conceptually by graphic means. A semantic net is described by points (*nodes*) connected by directed links (*arcs* or *arrows*) that show hierarchical tree relations between nodes. **Nodes** represent objects, concepts or events. **Arcs** can be defined in a variety of ways that are dependent on the type of knowledge they connect.

To illustrate the use of nodes and arcs, consider Figure 3.1. In the figure, Mary, Jack, threw, red, ball, and ball-1 are all represented by nodes. Arcs between the nodes show some type of relationship between the two nodes.

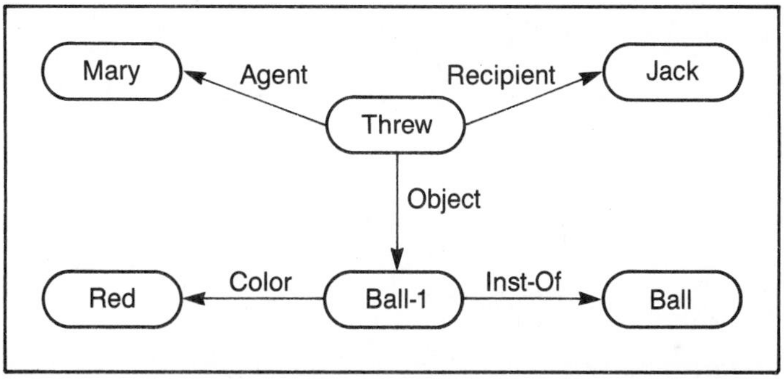

FIGURE 3.1 A SEMANTIC NET REPRESENTING THE ENGLISH SENTENCE "MARY THREW JACK THE RED BALL."

As we indicated, the kinds of relationships represented are dependent on the type of knowledge. For example, links between nodes in natural language applications use relationships such as agent, object, and recipient. Links representing hierarchies use relationships such as "is a" (is-a), "has part" (has-part), or "instance of" (inst-of). Examples of these relationships are shown by the semantic net in Figure 3.1; this net represents the English sentence "Mary threw Jack the red ball." This sentence describes an event.

Let's examine Figure 3.1 more closely. The sentence represents an event where an action (threw) occurred between entities (Mary, Jack) concerning an object (ball-1). The action, entities, and the object are represented in separate ovals. Further, an attribute (red) and a class descriptor (ball) are also shown in separate ovals. Directed links connect pairs of ovals and are labeled with the appropriate relationship. The directionality of the link is not arbitrary. The action's agent is Mary, the action's recipient is Jack, and the action's object is ball-1. In addition, the ball-1's color is red, and ball-1 is a member of (inst-of) the set (class) of objects named ball.

It may seem curious that the object is ball-1 when ball was used in the sentence. The object ball-1 represents a particular ball in the class of all balls and so the relationship is an instance of (inst-of) between ball-1 and ball indicates a hierarchical relationship. However, in the sentence, just the word ball was used.

It also may seem that this distinction between ball-1 and ball is unimportant. After all, we human beings know the difference because we have common sense, which is not a property of computers. The computer may have in its memory many objects named ball. If asked to search for a ball, which ball should it look for? There also may be two red balls (a big and a small one). Hence, there is a need to use a more specific label than just ball or red ball. The label ball-1 gives us the specificity we need.

One of the appealing features of a semantic net is that it can show the inheritance of properties. That is, if whatever is represented by a node is part of a hierarchy, then all properties of the higher level node are also properties of any connected node at a lower level. For example, consider Figure 3.2.

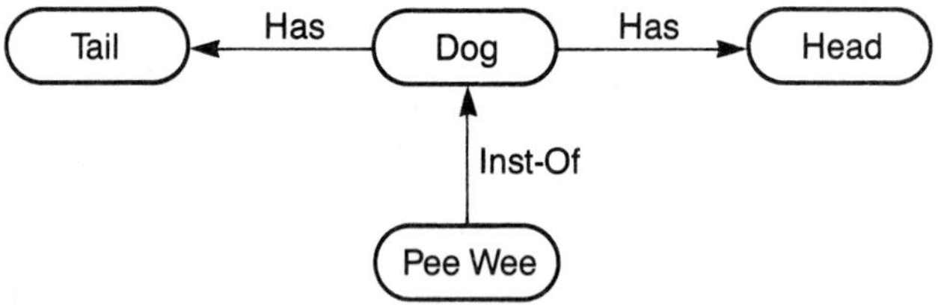

FIGURE 3.2 INHERITANCE OF PROPERTIES

Since Pee Wee is an instance of a dog, Pee Wee inherits the properties of having a head and a tail. We could not have a color description of dog, as we had a color description of ball-1 in Figure 3.1, because not all dogs are the same color. We could, however, have a color descriptor for Pee Wee.

Let us now examine the notion of ***hierarchical representation*** in greater depth. To do this, consider Figure 3.3. Note that the figure does not show all possible properties or hierarchies.

Several things are illustrated by this figure. First, there is inheritance of properties. We can infer that Pee Wee, Sport, and Skoonie can all move and that they each have a tail and a head. Since Pee Wee is a dog, he has all of the characteristics (attributes) associated with a dog including the ability to bark. The net also tells us that Pee Wee is small and is apricot in color.

A new relationship, ''isa'', is shown in this figure. The isa relationship is similar to the inst-of relationship, but a distinction is made by AI workers. To understand the difference between the use of isa and inst-of, it is convenient to make an analogy to the relationship of element and subset as they relate to the concept of set. Inst-of is a specific instance of (member) a class (as element is related to set). On the other hand, isa represents a subclass of a larger class (as subset is related to set). That is why, in Figure 3.3, Pee Wee is an instance of the class of dog and the class of dog is an (isa) subclass of the class of higher animal.

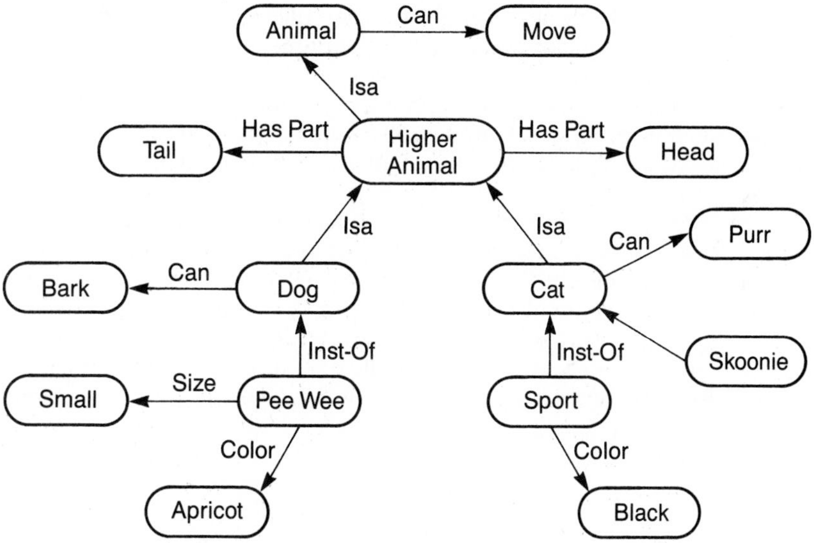

FIGURE 3.3 A SET OF HIERARCHICAL RELATIONSHIPS

One of the main advantages of the use of semantic nets is that almost any object, attribute (characteristic), or concept can be defined and relationships created. But there is a trade-off for this flexibility. There are no standard guidelines for forming semantic nets, so their form can vary from system to system. In contrast, prediction rules have a standard format.

The amount of detail included in a semantic net is dependent on the type of problem to be solved. General problems require less detail than do more specific problems. For example, in Figure 3.3 even more descriptors about animals, dogs, or Pee Wee could be added so that very specific questions from a user could be answered. In Figure 3.1 more information about Mary and Jack (age, physical condition, and so on) could be added so that desired questions could be answered. Clearly, semantic net representations can become very complex.

It should be noted that the graphic model is not how a semantic net is represented in a computer's memory. The objects and relationships are stored in a form dictated by the language used by the computer using some data structure. A program for accessing the semantic net starts at some point (node) and uses various search and pattern-matching techniques to locate the answer to the question (problem).

Frames

A **frame** is a third technique for representing knowledge. It is a way of organizing knowledge into a collection or *bundle* where the knowledge contained in the frame is common to the concept, object, or situation. For example, in Figure 3.3, all of the knowledge about dogs might be collected in one frame, and all of the knowledge about cats might be collected in another frame.

Frames are often used in conjunction with other forms of knowledge representation such as production rules and semantic nets. We might have a frame of rules about a particular concept and a frame of rules about another concept.

Why is it necessary to use frames? Recall that an expert system must use search techniques on its knowledge base to obtain the necessary knowledge to solve a given problem. If the knowledge base is very large, the search may take a great deal of time to locate what is needed. In the process, the search technique, because it is systematic in nature, may search through knowledge that is not relevant. If we are searching for knowledge about automobiles, then we do not want to search for knowledge about airplanes or trains. Human beings have the capability of knowing the difference between automobiles and airplanes, for example, but computers do not. The capability of differentiation is given to expert systems through the use of frames.

A frame consists of two parts: a name and a set of attributes associated with the name. Each attribute occupies a place in the frame called a slot; each slot has a slot name. Each attribute may have a value, and these values are known as fillers. As an example, consider Figure 3.4.

Slot Name	Filler
Frame name	Immediate family
Father	John
Mother	Sue
Sister — 1	Judy
Sister — 2	Jill
Brother	Nil

FIGURE 3.4 EXAMPLE OF SLOTS AND FILLERS

This example shows the names of the members of the immediate family for some person. In this case, the person has a father, mother, two sisters, and no brothers.

It is often the case that a frame may be associated with a class of objects or a category of situations. For example, a "trip" frame may contain slots for useful information about a trip: when, where, length of time, mode of transportation, and cost. Associated with this frame may be other frames which represent specific trips. Consider Figure 3.5.

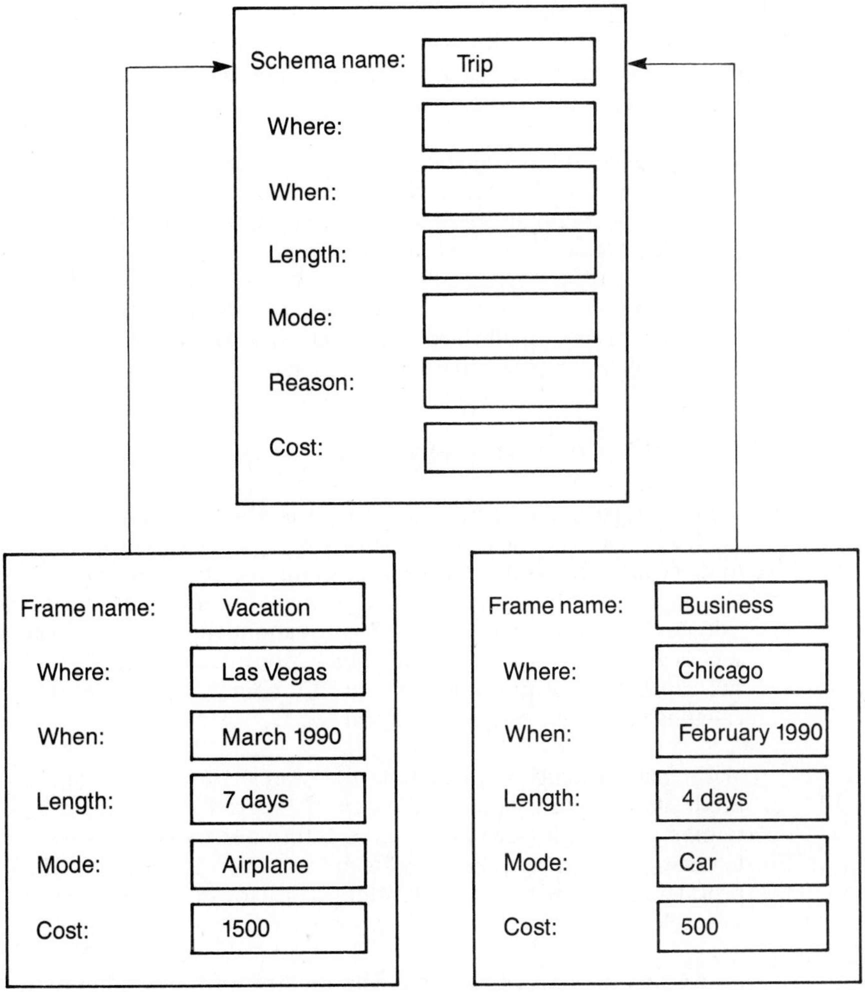

FIGURE 3.5 AN EXAMPLE OF A SCHEMA AND TWO INSTANCES OF TRIP

Each slot can have any number of procedures attached to it. These procedures perform specified tasks for the slot. The most common types of procedures are "if-added", "if-deleted" and "if-needed". The if-added procedure executes when new information is to be added to the slot. In the trip 1 frame of Figure 3.5, the where slot may need a new value each time we take a new vacation.

The if-deleted procedure executes when a value is to be deleted from a slot. Suppose that we change our mind about where our vacation trip in Figure 3.5 is to be. The value Las Vegas is then deleted here. Of course, this change may necessitate a change in values of the other slots.

The if-needed procedure executes when a value is needed for an empty slot. From our example in Figure 3.5, we might leave the value of the cost slot empty since the cost value is dependent on the values for the where, when, length, and mode slots. When we have made decisions about these values, the procedure can then calculate a value for the cost slot.

By themselves, frames are good for representing *declarative knowledge* as opposed to procedural knowledge. However, they can be used with other forms of knowledge representation that are used with procedural knowledge such as production rules. In this case, frames are used to represent classes of rules where each class of rules represents a related set of rules. This technique is being employed in expert systems which have a large number of rules because it makes searching much more efficient. Instead of searching all rules, the expert system proceeds to a frame containing the rules needed to solve a particular problem.

Propositional and Predicate Logic

We now turn our attention to a fourth method of knowledge representation. The method is called **predicate logic** or **predicate calculus**. Predicate logic allows us to determine the truth of assertions about objects, concepts, or events by using the techniques of propositional logic (calculus). But, unlike propositional logic, predicate calculus allows us to describe attributes about the objects, concepts, or events. We will begin our discussion by examining propositional logic and then extend to the full capabilities of predicate calculus. Of course, both predicate and propositional calculus are based on mathematical logic.

Mathematical logic is appropriate for representing knowledge in many situations. Predicate calculus is sometimes used in expert systems and is highly regarded by a number of people because of its structure and power relative to dealing with inferencing. It is, in fact, the basis for the computer language PROLOG which has been prominent in expert systems development. However, as we shall see, it is not as easy to implement as production rules, semantic nets, or frames.

As we mentioned in Chapter 2, the method of knowledge representation used in an expert system is closely tied to the inferencing technique used. Since inferencing with predicate calculus is well understood and developed, some system developers believe that it should dictate the knowledge representation method used. However, this is not a widely held view.

Propositional calculus. A **proposition** is a statement that is either true (T) or false (F). As such, it is a premise that can be used to derive new propositions or inferences. Rules are then used to determine the truth value (T or F) of the new proposition.

It is common practice in propositional logic to represent propositions with alphabetical letters. This is done to simplify the notation since connectives are used in the declaration of the propositions. So, we might have the following:

P = Our newspaper is published Sunday through Friday.

Q = Today is Saturday.

R = Our newspaper is not published today.

By themselves, these propositions are not very useful.

These propositions can be combined using logical connectives to form new propositions which can be used in more complex problem-solving situations. The most commonly used connectives are AND, OR, NOT, and IMPLIES. We illustrate these forms and then summarize the results in the form of a truth table.

NOT Q is the negation of Q.

From the example:

Q = Today is Saturday.

NOT Q = Today is not Saturday.

If Q is true, then NOT Q is false and if Q is false then NOT Q is true.

When the connective AND is used, the new proposition formed is true when both original propositions are true. For example:

J = The ball is green.
K = The ball has white stripes.
L = J AND K.
The ball is green and has white stripes.

If either J or K is false (or if J and K are both false) then L is false.

The connective OR forms a new proposition which is true when at lease one of the two original propositions is true. Using the J and K example:

M = J OR K
= The ball is green or has white stripes.

The OR used in this case is the inclusive form of OR. The proposition formed by the exclusive OR (XOR) is true when either proposition is true but not both are true. The XOR connective is useful in digital circuit logic but is not often used in propositional logic. The use of the IMPLIES connective means that if proposition C is true, then proposition D is true where we know that C implies D. This also can be written as:

$$C \rightarrow D$$

Consider the truth values for E where E = C IMPLIES D. By definition, E is evaluated logically as NOT C OR D. Hence, the only time that E is false is when C is true and D is false, otherwise E is true. Let's look at an example, where:

C = It is raining at noon.

D = The baseball game is canceled.

E = C → D

The possible cases are the following:

1. C and D are both false.
   This can be stated as:
   If it is not raining at noon, then the baseball game is not canceled.
   E is true in this case.
2. C is false and D is true.
   This case can be stated as:
   If it is not raining at noon, then the baseball game is canceled.
   E is again true since the baseball game could be canceled for other reasons.
3. C is true and D is false.
   This can be stated as:
   If it is raining at noon, then the baseball game is not canceled.
   In this case, E is false since we have already said (from C→D) that if it is raining, then the game is canceled. This is the only time that E is false.
4. C is true and D is true.
   This case can be stated as:
   If it is raining at noon, then the baseball game is canceled. Clearly, E is true.

We can summarize all of the connectives and their results in Table 3.1 using statements A and B.

TABLE 3.1 TRUTH TABLE

A	B	NOT A	A AND B	A OR B	A → B
T	T	F	T	T	T
F	T	T	F	T	T
T	F	F	F	T	F
F	F	T	F	F	T

We can now extend our discussion to more complex situations in predicate calculus by using these ideas from propositional calculus.

Predicate Calculus. Propositional calculus is adequate for some problem solving situations. However, it suffers from the fact that propositions cannot be broken apart; that is, the proposition must be treated as a whole. This state of affairs is not satisfactory for dealing with most real world situations where finer detail is needed.

Predicate calculus allows a proposition to be broken into two basic parts: arguments (objects) and predicates (assertions about or characteristics of objects). It also allows the use of variables and functions of variables. It makes use of symbolic logic statements and allows the use of all properties of propositional calculus. These characteristics of predicate calculus make it much more powerful than propositional calculus and, hence, a more desirable knowledge-representation method.

Here are some examples of how predicate calculus can be used with several propositions.

Proposition: Jack threw the ball.
Predicate calculus: THREW (Jack ball)
Proposition: The airplane is on the ground.
Predicate calculus: ON (airplane ground)

In the first example, "THREW" is the predicate and the arguments are "Jack" and "ball". In the second example, "ON" is the predicate and "airplane" and "ground" are the arguments. It is not coincidental that there is an order associated with the arguments.

Predicates can also have only one argument. Here is an example:

Proposition: The apple is red.
Predicate calculus: RED (apple)

An alternative form of the predicate calculus is sometimes used. From the examples, this form may appear as the following:

(threw Jack ball)
(on airplane ground)
(red apple)

One of the characteristics of predicate calculus is that **variables** may be used. A variable is represented by a letter of the alphabet and it can take on a number of specified values, all of which must make the proposition true. For example, if we encountered the expression:

red(X)

then any name that can be substituted for X must have the color red as a property.

The power of variable usage is that of generalization. A proposition that can be stated in general terms is more useful than one that can be stated only for a specific case.

Predicate calculus also makes use of quantifiers. A quantifier is represented by a symbol that states the range of a variable. A universal quantifier is one that states that a proposition containing a variable is true for all possible values of the variable. An *existential quantifier* states that a proposition is true for at least one value of the variable. For example:

All Hoosiers are U.S. citizens.

(A Hoosier is a (legal) resident of Indiana.)

Using the universal quantifier, we have:

(for all x)[Hoosier (x) → U.S. citizen (x)]

This last expression says that if x is a Hoosier, then x is a U.S. citizen.

The *existential qualifier* (there exists) is used with a proposition such as the following:

Some dogs like cats.

Using the existential qualifier, we have:

(there exists x)[dog (x) → likes (x,cats)]

This expression says that there exists at least one x such that if x is a dog, then x likes cats.

We can use the predicate calculus to deduce certain facts. Suppose we want to show that Tweety is yellow, given that Tweety is a canary and all canaries are yellow. This task can be done with the following expression:

(for all x) [(canary (x) → yellow (x) AND canary (Tweety)]
IMPLIES yellow (Tweety)

We will discuss the deduction technique used here in greater detail in Chapters 4 and 6.

Case Study: Knowledge Representation in WPHELP

Now let's turn our attention to knowledge representation in our expert system WPHELP. As you recall, this expert system advises a small business on what word processing packages to buy to meet determined word processing needs.

An overview of the factors affecting the selection of a word processing package is timely. Since this is an illustrative expert system, we will simplify the number and complexity of the factors involved. Let's assume that two factors are critical in the selection of a word processor for the office. First, the type of documents produced by the office must be identified. Typing a memo is quite different from producing a complete book on a word processor. Reports, letters, charts, and so on, all have different word processing needs. A second important factor is cost. Five dollars versus 500 dollars is definitely a consideration to any small business. Even though there are other factors, such as training of office workers, compatibility with other software packages, availability of telephone assistance, and so on, we will consider the selection of a word processor to rest mainly on identifying the functionality required by the office and the price allocated by budgetary concerns.

The knowledge can be represented in four different ways: production rules, semantic nets, frames, and predicate calculus. We will attempt to sketch out the representation of the WPHELP knowledge in each of these four ways.

Production rules (or rules) express the knowledge in a series of if-then or if-then-else rules. Our WPHELP knowledge base might consist of the following variables and rules as shown in Figures 3.6 and 3.7.

Variables	Meaning	Values of Variables
Functionality	Degree of complexity of desired document	Simple, Complex
Cost	Amount of money budgeted or available for purchasing a word processor	Low, High
Word Processor	Software package or program to produce documents	A, B, C

FIGURE 3.6 VARIABLES FOR WHELP

Rule: 1
IF (functionality is simple)
AND (cost is low or high),
THEN (select a word processor equal to A).

Rule 2:
IF (functionality is complex)
AND (cost is low),
THEN (selecting a word processor is not possible).

Rule 3:
IF (functionality is complex)
AND (cost is high),
THEN (select word processor B or C).

FIGURE 3.7 RULES FOR WPHELP

The rules for WPHELP can be summarized as shown in Figure 3.8.

Functionality	Cost	Word Processor
Simple	Low	A
Simple	High	A
Complex	Low	None possible
Complex	High	B or C

FIGURE 3.8 A TABLE FOR WPHELP

The rules and relationships can be expressed in a tree or branching structure as shown in Figure 3.9.

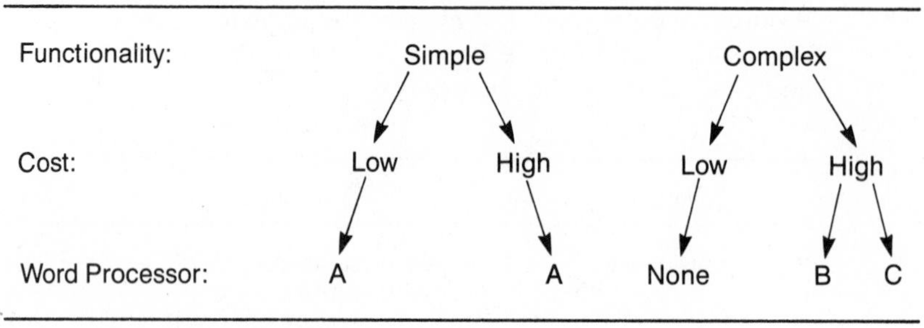

FIGURE 3.9 TREE FOR WPHELP

The values of the functionality and cost variables determine which rules are used to select a word processor. Again, for simplicity of understanding, only selected rules and variables are being considered at this time.

The second method of knowledge representation, the semantic net, uses nodes and arcs to display relationships and variables. A possible semantic net for WPHELP is given in Figure 3.10.

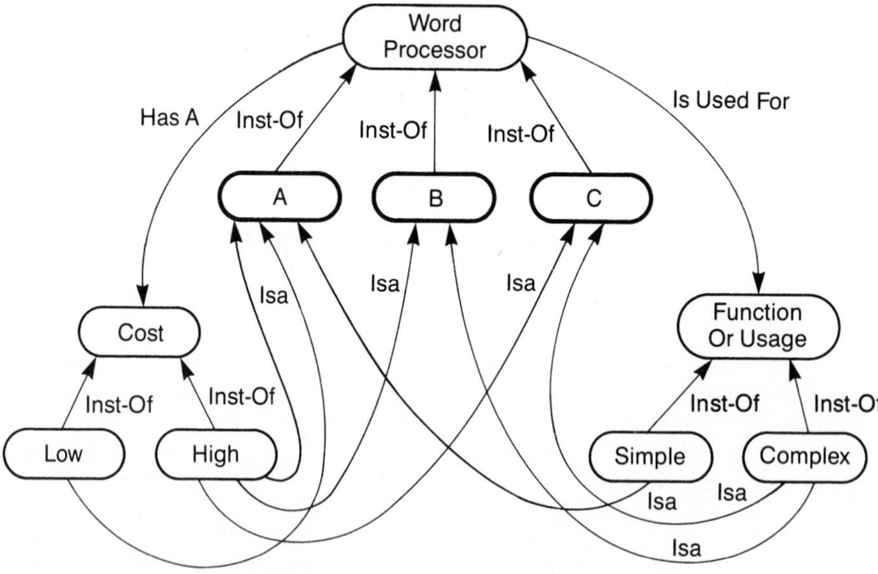

FIGURE 3.10 SEMANTIC NET FOR WPHELP

The variables are pictured by the darkened nodes (ovals) and the values (or instances) are indicated by the lighter nodes (ovals). The isa relationship could be broadened from "is a" to other equivalent words. For example, "A is a Low" could be interpreted as "Word processor A is a low-priced word processor."

Using the third method of knowledge representation, frames, we could represent the knowledge base of WPHELP as shown in Figure 3.11 as a schema with frames.

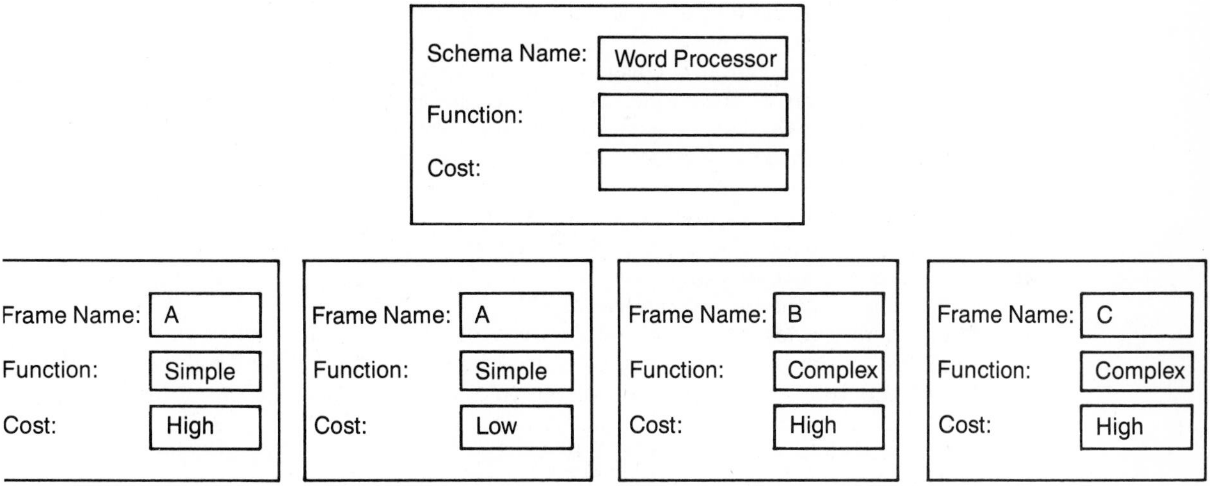

FIGURE 3.11 FRAME REPRESENTATION FOR WPHELP

In this arrangement information about each word processor is grouped together into a separate frame. The schema is the outline, or template, for the information in each of the three word processor frames (A, B, C).

In the fourth method, predicate calculus, we could state the same information in the following mathematical structures:

F: Functionality
C: Cost
WP: Word Processor
Given: F and C
Find: WP

SELECTION (C, F) = WP

In this statement, SELECTION is a function or operation that is dependent on the variables C and F.

Thus, we have expressed the knowledge base of WPHELP with production rules, semantic nets, frames, and predicate calculus. This case study will use rules, the most common method, in subsequent chapters.

Key Points

- Three terms — data, information, and knowledge — should not be used interchangeably.
  - Data is facts, words, numbers, or measurement.
  - Information is data organized to answer questions.
  - Knowledge is refined information.
- There are models which represent the structure or organization of knowledge.
  - Each model can be transferred into digital data stored in a computer and accessible through a language or expert system tool.
  - The contents of the model can be used in the reasoning process.
- Models of knowledge representation in an expert system may be either declarative (facts or assertions) or procedural (actions or procedures).
- There are four common models of knowledge representation:
  - Production rules (procedural model)
  - Semantic networks (declarative model)
  - Frames (declarative model)
  - Predicate calculus (declarative model)
- Production rules, the most popular type of model, infers a set of rules of IF–THEN relationships. The symbol → may be used instead of IF–THEN, to represent the same rules. The parts of the rule are known as follows:
  - IF antecedent THEN consequent
  - IF situation THEN action
  - IF premise THEN conclusion
- The THEN part of a rule is considered valid (True) when the IF part is valid (True).
- The IF–THEN parts of a production rule may contain compound statements with AND or OR.
- The second model for knowledge representation, semantic networks (nets), is a graphic scheme where points (nodes) are connected by directed links (arcs or arrows) that show hierarchic (tree) relations between points.
- Common relationships in semantic nets are is a (is-a) and has part (has-part). Other relationships indicate the characteristics of a node (thing).
- Semantic nets are a very flexible tool for knowledge representation, but there are presently no standards for the symbols used in the nets. The net can vary depending on the type of knowledge and the degree of desired detail.
- A third method for knowledge representation is frames. This method organizes, bundles, or clusters knowledge in frames or partitions. For example, all knowledge about dogs could be in one frame and all knowledge about cats in another frame.
- Partitioning, or grouping, knowledge into frames can make computer searching easier and more efficient.
- A frame has a name and a set of characteristics or attributes (of the named object or thing). The divisions or places in a frame for attributes are called slots. The value of the attribute is given as the "filler" to the attribute.
- The fourth model for knowledge or representation is predicate calculus or predicate logic.
- Predicate calculus includes propositional calculus, which is all statements (A,B,C, and so on) are either true or false, but not both.

- Predicate calculus allows a statement (proposition) to be broken into two parts: arguments (objects) and predicates (assertions about or characteristics of objects). It also allows for the use of variables and functions of variables.
- Predicate calculus uses quantifiers:
  - for all
  - there exists at least one
- How these models for knowledge representation — production rules, semantic nets, frames, and predicate calculus — are converted into usable computer code has not been explained here. The logical representation of the knowledge, not the physical implementation, has been the theme of this chapter.
- The knowledge base of WPHELP, the expert system on selecting a word processor, can be expressed in any of the four given methods; however, the production rule method will be emphasized in this text.

Exercises

1. Organize the following character string into information.
   therearefourmodelsforknowledgerepresentation
   productionrulessemanticnetsframespredicatecalculus
2. Name the four common models for knowledge representation.
3. Given the statement:
   If today is Tuesday and the temperature is above 60 degrees F, then I will go fishing.
   Answer the following:
   What is the antecedent?
   What is the consequent?
   Using the form: If A and B, THEN C, What is A? B? C?
   At this moment in time, what is the truth value of:

   A ______________________________

   B ______________________________

   A AND B ______________________________

   C ______________________________

   If (A AND B), THEN C ______________________________
   Would this production rule be a good rule in an expert system concerning your hobbies? Why?
4. State four production rules that apply to your business or educational institution.
5. Given the semantic net, fill in the names or values of the nodes in Figure 3.12 (Select your favorite car and write it in the car node).

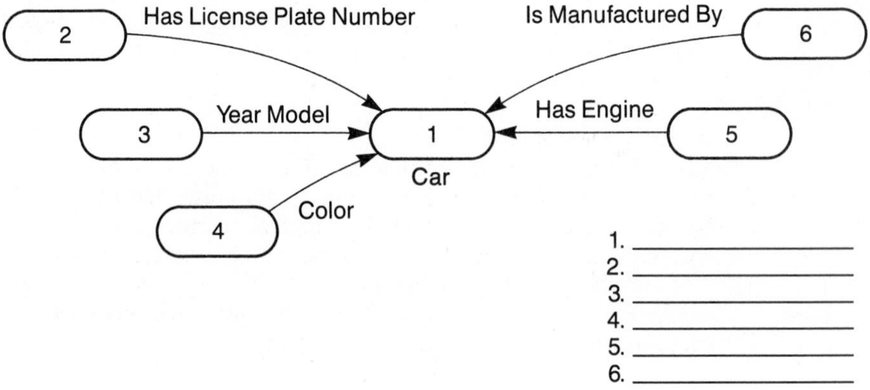

FIGURE 3.12 SEMANTIC NET FOR CAR

6. Given the attribute values in Figure 3.13 fill in the possible relationships on the five arcs.

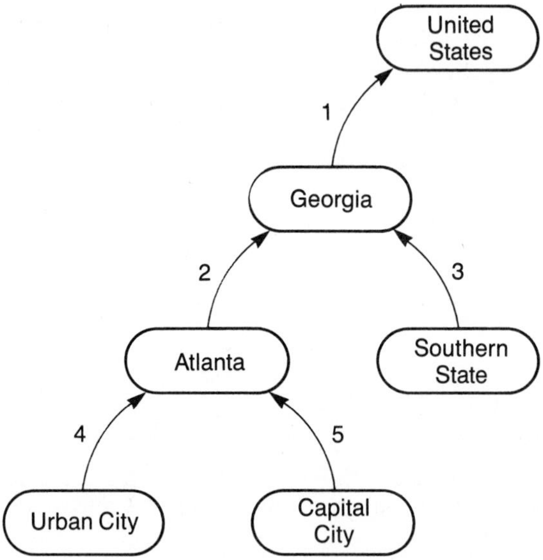

1. ____
2. ____
3. ____
4. ____
5. ____

FIGURE 3.13 SEMANTIC NET FOR ATLANTA

7. Convert the information in Exercise 5 to the following frame:
   Frame name

   ____

   License plate number

   ____

   Year of model

   ____

   Color

   ____

   Type of engine

   ____

   The manufacture could be an attribute, but the chosen representation has the manufacturer in a higher frame (because many manufacturers make more than one type of car).

8. What procedures would be relevant to the frame in Exercise 7?

9. Fill in the following table.

A	B	NOT A	NOT A AND B	A OR NOT B	B → A
T	T	F			
T	F	F			
F	T	T			
F	F	T			

10. Convert the following predicate calculus propositions to English sentences.

    a. DROVE (Mary car)

    ____

    b. ON (back, floor)

    ____

    c. BANANA (yellow)

    ____

    d. BLUE (x)

    ____

    e. (for all y) [(Buick (y) → CAR (y)]

    ____

11. Using the rules from WPHELP, rewrite rule 1 by splitting it into two separate rules.
    IF functionality is simple and cost is low,

    THEN ______________________________
    IF functionality is simple and cost is high,

    THEN ______________________________

12. Using the definitions of variables given in the case study WPHELP, circle the correct classification, simple or complex.

Document	Simple	Complex
a. Memo	S	C
b. Book of 1,000 pages	S	C
c. One-page business letter	S	C
d. Two-column newsletter with pictures	S	C
e. German to French dictionary	S	C

Assignments

1. Using the WPHELP expert system, increase the possible values of functionality to:
   Simple
   Standard
   Complex
   Using the following chart, rewrite the production rules for the expert system.

Functionality	Cost	Word Processor
Simple	Low	A
Standard	Low	B
Complex	High	C

2. a. List five factors other than cost and functionality, that could affect the selection of a word processor.
   b. Now transform these factors into heuristic (rule of thumb) IF–THEN rules.
3. Give five heuristic IF–THEN rules that save you time (in your job or at school).
4. List five heuristic IF–THEN rules for finding a job.
5. Itemize five heuristic rules for purchasing a used car.
6. Give five heuristic IF–THEN rules for excuses that a college student might use for late assignments.
7. Short overviews of nets, frames, and logic are given in two articles: "An Overview of Knowledge Representation" and "Knowledge Representation" in the July/August issue of *PC AI*.
   Read and summarize either or both article(s).

8. Another good source of understanding knowledge representation is an article by B. Buchanan and E. Shortliffe: "Production Rules as a Representation in a Knowledge-Based Consultation System," *Artificial Intelligence.* February 1977. Read and report on this rule-based system.

9. Frame-based systems are used in MIS and Finance. For a detailed description of a frame-based system, INVEST, for advising financial investments, read and report on the article "INVEST: An Expert System for Financial Investments" in the Summer 1988 issue of *IEEE Expert.*

10. A similarity network is a relatively simple knowledge representation that stores information by its resemblance to surrounding information. Such a network provides an intuitive way for retrieving and manipulating information, which in turn establishes a foundation for constructing valuable and practical expert systems. Similarity networks enhance rather than replace existing knowledge representations. For a more detailed explanation of similarity networks, read "Similarity Networks: A Knowledge Representation for Information Analysis and Retrieval" in the July/August, 1988, issue of *PC AI.*

11. For more detailed reading on knowledge representation, utilize *Byte,* November 1986. The special theme on representing knowledge includes the following:
    "Finding Rules in Data" by Beverly Thompson and William Thompson
    The ID3 algorithm lets you obtain knowledge directly from a set of data.
    "A Bit-Mapped Classifier" by Peter W. Frey
    This unconventional expert system is based on pattern recognition.
    "Predicting International Events" by Philip A. Schrodt
    Modeling political knowledge and making short-term forecasts with a Holland classifier are presented.
    "Handling Conflicts in Data" by Clara Y. Cuadrado and John L. Cuadrado
    A decision support system in PROLOG helps managers make the right choice.
    "The Art of Deduction" by J.C. Edmond and A. Paulissen
    Watson, an AI program in PROLOG, plays the mystery game CLUEDO.
    "Rule-Based Programming" by Leonard Moskowitz
    A look at OPS5, the production-system language popular with AI researchers.
    "Machine Learning" by Angelos T. Kolokouris
    Teaching computers to learn with a language that grows.

    Report on any two articles that interest you.

4

REASONING

As we have seen in the previous chapter, the knowledge possessed by an expert system is essential to the performance of the system in some given problem-solving situation. The knowledge must be organized and represented in such a way that it can be stored in the computer's memory and later retrieved as needed. The knowledge base, by itself, is not sufficient to solve problems. However, it is in a form that can be used by an expert system in the problem solving process.

To use the knowledge it possesses, an expert system must have an inferencing mechanism that it can use to access the knowledge, reason about it, and draw conclusions or generate solutions. This can be done by using search and pattern matching techniques. The inference mechanism searches the knowledge base looking for appropriate knowledge to deal with the problem at hand. Pattern matching techniques are used to match a desired goal or to determine if the criteria associated with a particular hypothesis can be satisfied.

In this chapter, we will discuss several important concepts related to reasoning. We will examine methods of reasoning including search, inferencing strategies and the relationship between uncertainty and reasoning. Finally we will discuss two reasoning control strategies, forward and backward chaining, which are the primary control strategies used in expert systems.

Methods of Reasoning

Search

We are all familiar with the concept of search. We search for answers to questions using books or databases, for objects that we need or have misplaced, and in a number of other everyday activities. Computers use search to locate data. Search implies moving around and looking at or listening to things and making judgments about the pertinence of our findings to what we are trying to locate.

The search techniques we use as human beings are often systematic with a predetermined search plan. Often, however, our search techniques are rather haphazard with the result that they are not very efficient.

Computers can be programmed with search techniques or algorithms that are quite efficient. In expert systems, one or more search algorithms are used on the knowledge base to locate knowledge to *potentially* solve the problem. These search algorithms do not solve the problem but provide the means for the expert system to find the solution.

Search is essentially a trial and error technique. Unlike an algorithm, or formula, which solves a problem directly, it is more random and less organized in finding answers or solutions. This should not be surprising or troublesome because we, as human beings, use search techniques when we are solving problems. We search our memory for relevant knowledge that we need in a particular situation. Our search techniques are not always successful and we must turn to other sources (people, books, databases, and so on) for help.

Like knowledge-representation techniques, search has been a major focus of work by people in the fields of AI and expert systems. A number of search methods have been used with knowledge bases in expert systems. Before we discuss some of these methods, we wish to examine some fundamental elements of problem solving involving the use of *states*.

The Essence of Problem Solving

The general purpose of problem solving is to move from a problem (initial) state to a goal (solution) state. This movement is done through the use of procedures or operations.

Problem states define the problem situation and the existing conditions. The initial problem state is a statement of the problem and preexisting conditions. Beginning with the initial state, a problem solver devises a plan for reaching the **goal state**. The plan may be a single procedure that allows direct movement from the initial state to the goal state. However, this is not usually the case, particularly in complex problems. In these situations there will be movement through a hierarchy of **intermediate problem states** to the goal state; each problem state along the way representing a partial solution or a part of the goal state.

Let us illustrate these points using the game of tic-tac-toe. The initial state is the empty 3 × 3 grid. The preexisting conditions include two players wishing to play the game and some way (pen, pencil) for recording player moves on the grid. A goal state is represented by the grid form when one player has three Xs or three Os in a row; each player has a different goal state.

Since each player can only make one mark at a time, it is not possible to go directly from the initial state to a goal state. In this case, there will be a series of intermediate problem states where a new intermediate state is reached after each player makes a mark. Note that the set of intermediate problem states will vary from game to game. The procedure for moving from one state to the next is that each player makes a mark.

It is possible that the goal state cannot be reached with the devised plan. In the case of the tic-tac-toe game, the intermediate problem state can occur where neither player can make a mark that will allow movement to the desired goal state. The alert player will alter the plan if the same problem situation occurs in the next game.

A few comments need to be made about the planning process. It is often necessary to revise a plan as movement is made from one intermediate problem state to another. In our game example, each player may have devised an initial plan or strategy. However, after each turn, each player must examine the consequences of the last action and possibly revise the original plan. If a revision is made, it is usually based on several anticipated intermediate problem states closer to the desired goal state. The player may reason "If I make this move now and these moves the next two times, I can get into a position where my opponent cannot win."

Our discussion can be summarized with Figures 4.1 and 4.2. In Figure 4.1, there is movement from the initial state to the goal state through a series of intermediate states. The control strategy defines procedures (operations) that determine how the movement is made from state to state. From our tic-tac-toe example, the initial state was the empty grid, the goal state was a grid of either three Xs or three Os in a row, and the intermediate states were the grid form after each player had a turn. The **control strategy** defines how the game moves from one state to the next.

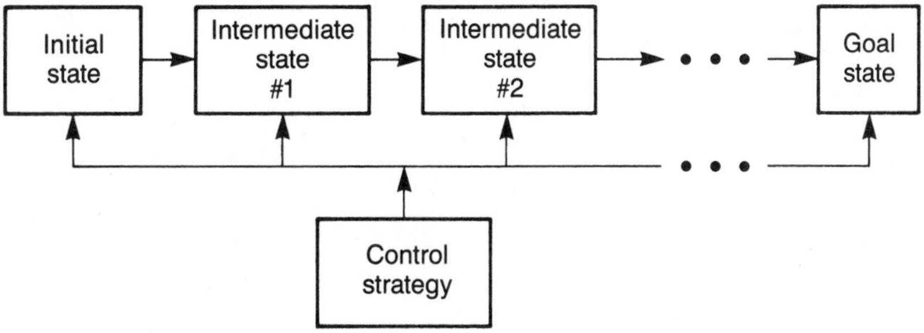

FIGURE 4.1 RELATIONSHIP AMONG INITIAL STATE, INTERMEDIATE STATES, GOAL STATE AND CONTROL STRATEGY

Figure 4.2 illustrates the relationship between the control strategy and the operators. The control strategy calls on an operator (or operators) to move from one state to another. Information about the states is stored in the database; this information includes the initial state, goal, current state and previous state transitions.

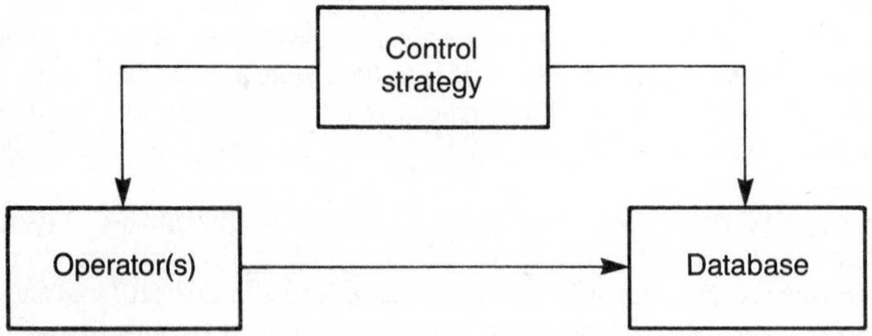

FIGURE 4.2 THE ESSENCE OF CONTROL STRATEGY

State and Search Space

To extend our discussion of problem solving, it is often helpful to use a graphical method to visualize the problem and possible solutions. This graph is sometimes known as a **state graph**.

We can illustrate this notion of problem visualization with a state graph by thinking of the graph as a map of how to go from a starting point to a destination (goal). This map is illustrated in Figure 4.3.

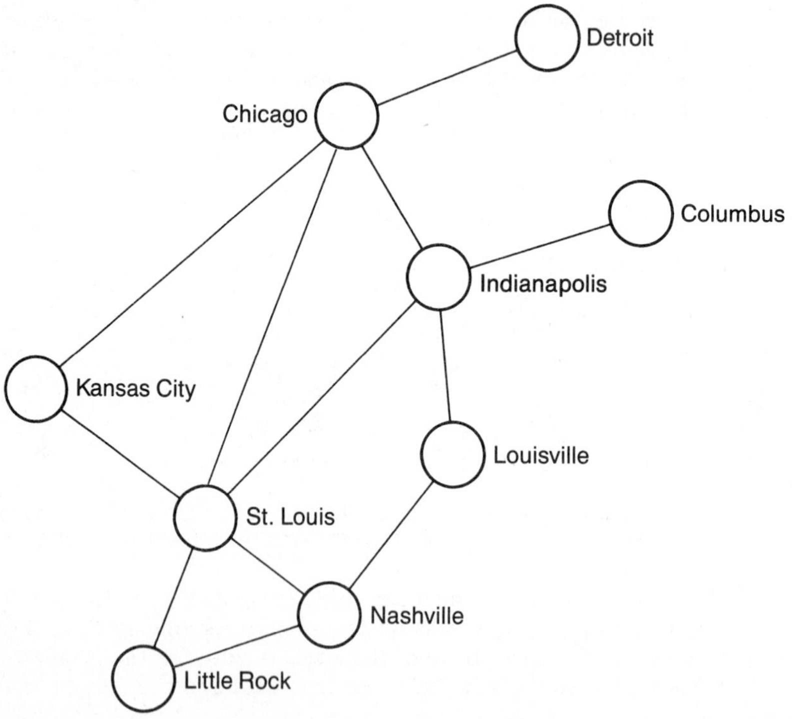

FIGURE 4.3 A STATE GRAPH

The cities in the graph are nodes that must be traveled through on the way from a starting point, say Chicago, to a destination point, say Nashville. There are several ways to travel between Chicago and Nashville, and the route will depend on several factors. If the least mileage is the criteria, then we would take one route. If stopping to see friends or relatives along the way is important, then we might choose another route. Of course, we may change our mind part way through a particular route; this change could be caused by road conditions or other constraints.

Relating this example to problem solving, the nodes represent the problem states (initial, goal, intermediate). The links between the nodes represent the transition (operator or procedure) for moving from one state to the next. Distance between states may be a constraint; the distance can be thought of as a measure of the complexity of interstate movement.

As we have pictured it, it is very difficult to represent a state graph in computer memory. For this reason, we can think of this representation as conceptual or implicit with its actual representation embedded in some computer language that we are using.

The state space representation can be altered using a data structure known as a *tree* in general and as a *search tree* in particular. (There are other kinds of trees, but they are beyond the scope of this writing.)

A **search tree** shows all possible paths from the initial state node to other nodes. Some of the paths may not lead to the goal node. A search tree for our travel example is shown in Figure 4.4. There are several things to note about this figure, and we will also use it to introduce some terminology about tree structures.

First, several nodes are repeated in the search tree. This is because there may be more than one path through a particular *node* (city). For example, St. Louis appears on three different paths.

A second point to notice is that not all paths lead to the goal (Nashville). There is a path that leads to Detroit, one that leads to Columbus and several that lead to Little Rock. While these paths are not successful (they do not lead to the goal), they are nonetheless paths that have been defined and must be considered in a search process.

A third point to note is that the search tree is divided into levels with one or more nodes on the same level. The reason for the use of levels will become clear in our later discussion of search methods. A final point to note is that the lengths of the links between the nodes is some unit distance and is not reflective of actual distance. The choice of the cities (nodes) for each path is arbitrary; choosing additional cities along any path would change the appearance of the graph. The choice of cities is also arbitrary in the sense that there are other possible nodes (cities) and paths from Chicago to Nashville. But at least you get the idea conceptually of a search tree. In an actual problem-solving situation, it would be important to make an exhaustive list of possible intermediate states based on the given conditions.

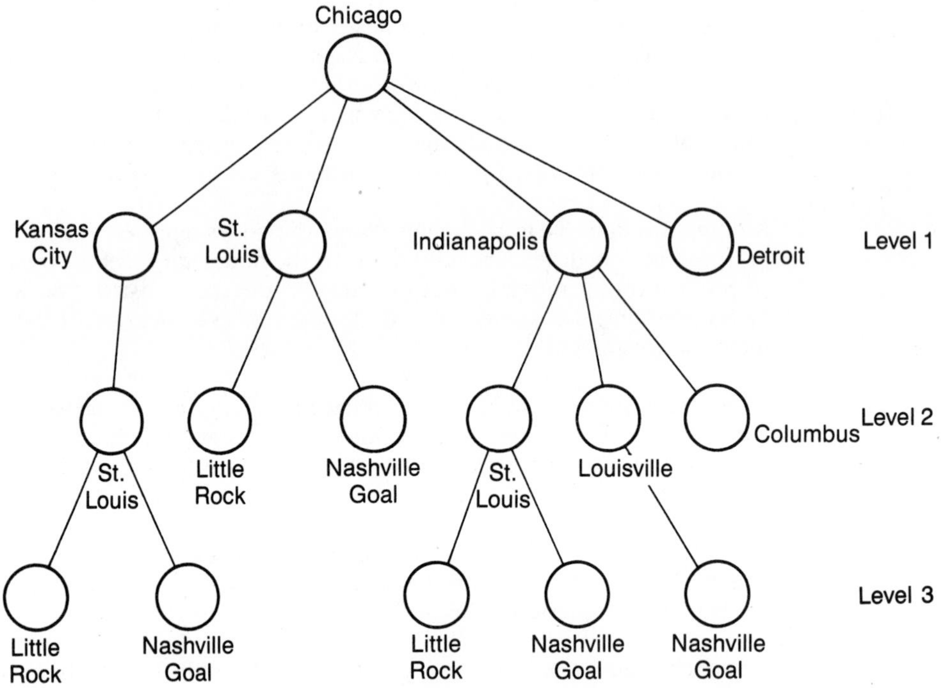

FIGURE 4.4 EXAMPLE OF A SEARCH TREE

As we mentioned earlier, there are a number of terms associated with trees. Many of the terms are in the context of what we know as a family tree, and so they should not seem strange.

The entry node for a tree is called the *root node*. In Figure 4.4, Chicago is the name of the root node. There are *branches* (links) from the root node to nodes on the next level, and these nodes are known by several descriptors including child, successor, or descendant. For example, Indianapolis is a child of Chicago, Louisville is a child of Indianapolis, and Nashville is a child of Louisville. In the other direction, Louisville is a parent or antecedent of Nashville, Indianapolis is a parent of Louisville, and so on. The end of any path is called a *leaf node*. In our example, Detroit, Columbus, Nashville, and Little Rock are all leaf nodes.

It may seem strange that St. Louis is a child of both Chicago and Indianapolis. This occurs because of the nature of the search tree and is not characteristic of trees in general.

Search Methods

There are basically two methods of search. One method is known as *systematic* or *blind search* and the other is known as *heuristic search*. Both methods are used in AI and expert systems.

Strictly speaking, there is another search method that is known as *random search*. As human beings, we all have used this method, usually with less than spectacular results. Because of its inherent likelihood of failure and inefficiency, it is not a viable method for AI and expert systems work.

As we shall see, heuristic search is, in a sense, a specialized form of systematic search. It is systematic search that has the benefit of some sort of guidance.

Systematic search is a set of procedures used to search a state space. The procedures vary but all have the common characteristic of searching the entire state space, or searching until the first occurrence of the goal node is found. These procedures are complete; that is, they do not miss a single node. At the same time, there is inherent inefficiency in these procedures. A great deal of time can be wasted before the goal node is found. However, even with these limitations, it may be the only tool we have to use, and it is certainly better than a random search.

A number of systematic search algorithms have been developed for AI and expert systems work. We will examine four of them: depth-first, breadth-first, forward, and backward. The underlying approaches of these four are the basis of most of the others.

The first systematic search method is **depth-first search**. This method begins at the root node and proceeds down each path from the root to a leaf node searching for the goal. When it reaches the end of the path and there has been no success, the algorithm backtracks to an unsearched node and starts down the next path. This algorithm is illustrated by Figure 4.5.

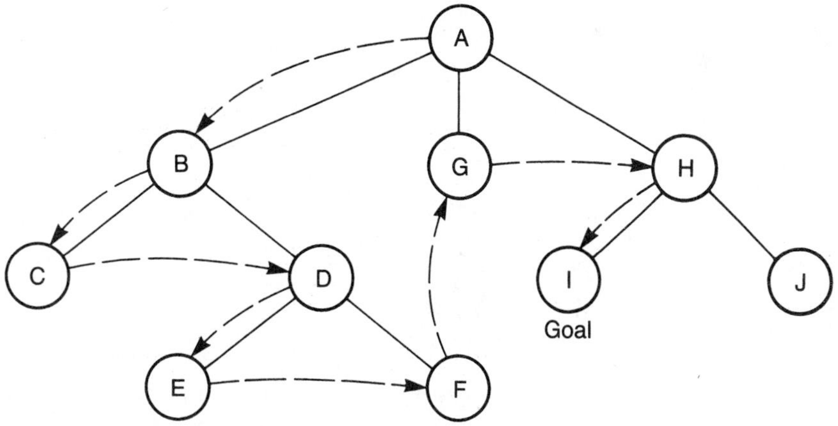

FIGURE 4.5 DEPTH-FIRST SEARCH

The search begins at A and continues until it reaches the goal node I. At each node, the algorithm checks to see if it is the goal node. If the goal node is found, the search terminates. If the goal is not found, the algorithm proceeds along the same path or goes to the next path.

In our example in Figure 4.5, the algorithm would move from A to B, B to C, over to D (B and A have already been determined to be unsuccessful), and then to E and F. Next G is searched and then H. Finally, I is found to be the goal and the search terminates. The algorithm does not re-search nodes previously found to be unsuccessful.

The amount of search needed is directly dependent on where the goal-node is located. In general, the goal node location cannot be determined in advance, and so the algorithm cannot be made more efficient.

The second systematic search method is **breadth-first search**. As with depth-first search, this method also begins at the root node. However, instead of proceeding down to the end of the left most path, the algorithm proceeds to the first level of nodes below the root node and then searches all nodes at that level. It then proceeds to the next level and searches all nodes on that level. The process continues until the first occurrence of a goal node or until every node has been found to be unsuccessful.

The breadth-first search algorithm is illustrated in Figure 4.6. The search begins at A and then proceeds to B as before. At this point, the search proceeds to G and then to H. Having had no success (finding the goal node), the algorithm moves to the left most node on the next level, which is C. It then proceeds to D and then reaches I, which is the goal state.

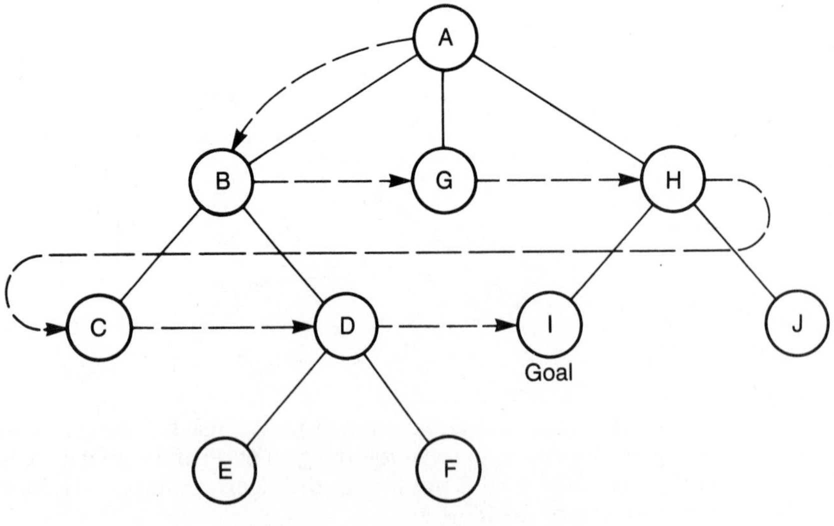

FIGURE 4.6 BREADTH-FIRST SEARCH

As with depth-first search, breadth-first search is complete but relatively inefficient. The amount of search needed is again dependent on the location of the goal node, which is usually not predetermined.

There is really no good way to compare the performance of breadth-first search to that of depth-first search. Both methods work but suffer from the limitations described such as inefficiency and time.

Recall, for a moment, our earlier discussion of state space and how we moved from the initial state to the goal state. As we searched for a path to the goal state, we were using a third systematic search technique known as **forward search** or **forward chaining**. We can think of it as moving forward from the initial state to the goal state and we could use the same search tree as in Figure 4.4.

There is no reason why we cannot search for the initial state by starting at the goal state. This technique is the fourth form of systematic search and is called **backward search**. To illustrate this, we can redraw Figure 4.4 to reflect the movement from goal state to the initial state. **Backward chaining** is illustrated in Figure 4.7.

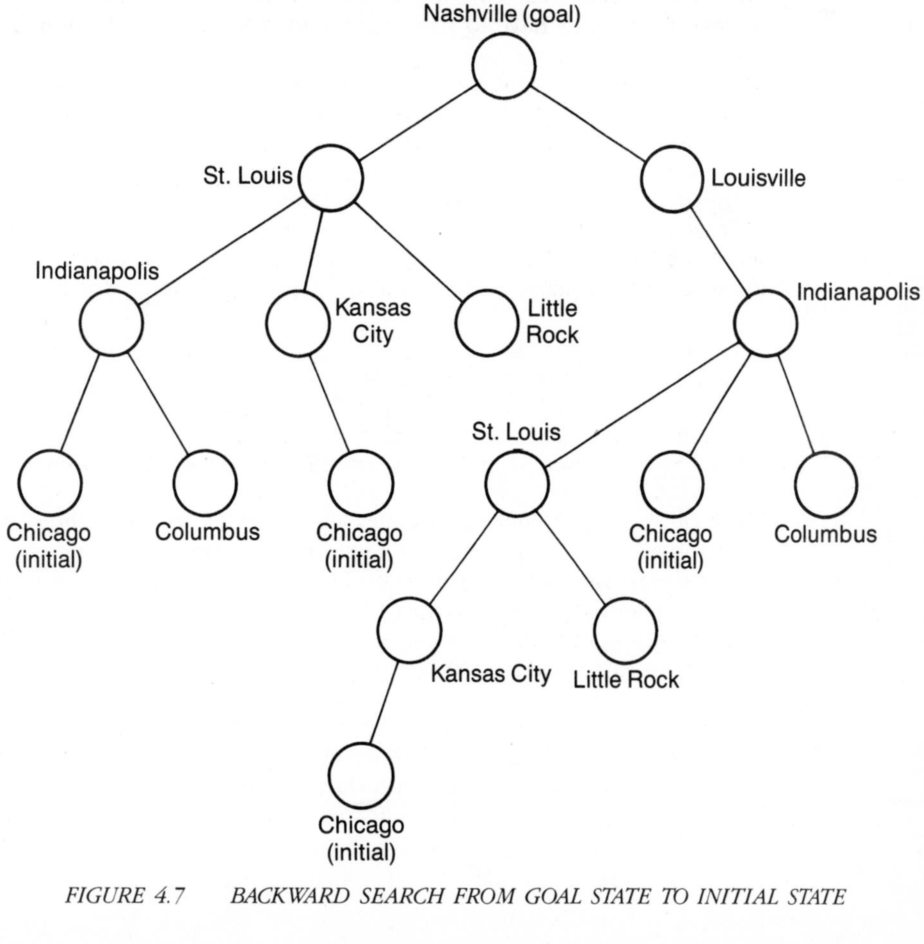

FIGURE 4.7 BACKWARD SEARCH FROM GOAL STATE TO INITIAL STATE

The search tree in Figure 4.7 also could be used with either the depth-first or breadth-first search methods. In this case, we are again searching from the root to a leaf. The difference is that the positions of the goal and initial states have been interchanged.

It should also be noted that a search can begin from any node in a search tree. It can then proceed forward (toward the goal state) or backward (toward the initial state).

We have seen in the last section that systematic search will locate the goal node if it exists. This type of search is sometimes referred to as ***blind search*** because the search process has no idea where the goal node is until it is located and in fact, is not concerned. As we saw before, this type of search technique can be very inefficient from a time perspective.

The problem of inefficiency is often referred to as "cost." We are all familiar with the notion of cost although we usually think of it in terms of money. However, cost can be measured in other ways. It may be measured in terms of time or distance units, for example. The cost will be less if the solution is found in less time, or will be less if we don't have to travel so far to reach the destination (goal).

There must be ways to reduce the cost of search. Fortunately, there are and we can classify these techniques as heuristics. Heuristics may either be general in nature or be associated with a specific problem domain.

Heuristics refer to guides or hints or rules of thumb. That is, if we have several alternative paths to choose from in a search tree, a heuristic gives us a hint about which path may be most likely to lead to the goal node, and thereby make our searching easier in the sense of less time (or whatever criteria) spent and perhaps even less frustration.

To illustrate the concept of heuristic, let us return to our childhood for a moment. Our parents would hide some little gift or surprise for us in the house. We had to search for it. Our parents would give us hints such as "warmer" or "colder" as we moved either closer to or farther away from our sought treasure.

From our own personal experience, we can think of many times where we have used some heuristic to search for a solution to a problem. Often, the heuristic that we used was based on our past experience with the same problem or one that was closely related. We also remember that the heuristic we chose did not always work. What we thought would work to solve the problem sometimes didn't, and we lost time and effort backtracking to try other techniques.

The point is, heuristics are not a guarantee of finding a solution to a problem on the first try or locating the goal in the most efficient manner. In the long run, however, the use of heuristics is likely to produce desired results more quickly. And, as we learn from experience, we will improve our set of heuristics and add new ones.

The use of heuristic in many cases involves the use of some type of mathematical evaluation. The evaluation may involve the use of a formula or some value to determine the desirability of moving to the next state (node) in the search for the solution (goal) to the problem. This mathematical evaluation is often performed by an evaluation function. Let us illustrate with some examples.

Suppose we wish to travel by car from city A to city B. We have several alternative routes. In deciding on which route to take, we may sit down with a road map and calculate the total distance for each route. Based on this evaluation, we can determine the shortest route, mileage-wise, from A to B. Alternatively, the shortest route may require the use of substandard roads or lots of traffic. We may decide that another route that is longer in miles but shorter time-wise would be a better choice. In this case, our evaluation was done apriori for the entire path to our destination.

As a second example, let us return to our game of tic-tac-toe. Is it possible to use some sort of evaluation technique to determine our next move?

The answer is "yes." To do this, we can assign values to particular moves. We are interested in maximizing our chances of winning and minimizing our opponents chances of winning. This technique has been known as Minmax.

Suppose we are in the middle of a game and the current board configuration appears as shown in Figure 4.8; we can build a game tree of possible moves using this configuration as the root node for the tree. A partial game tree is shown in Figure 4.9. For purposes of our discussion, player A will represent our interests in the game and player B will represent our opponent's interests. Of course, when the game first began, player A could have plotted a strategy that would have won the game (three Xs in a row). But player B likely would not have cooperated; after two or three moves a "wait and see" strategy might be used by player A. Then a reevaluation of the original strategy would have been necessary.

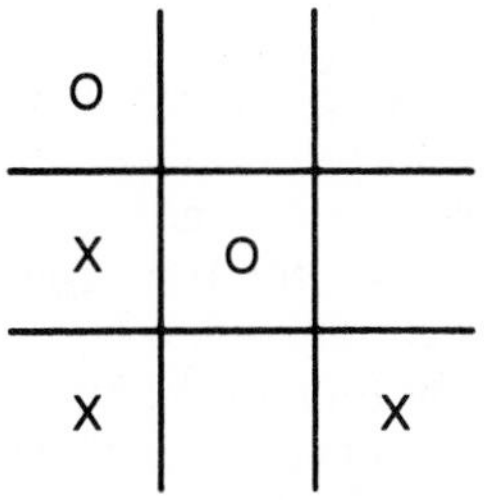

FIGURE 4.8 CURRENT TIC-TAC-TOE BOARD CONFIGURATION

In Figure 4.9, node 1 represents A's move. Then the next level of nodes (2,6, . . .) would represent B's possible move. The bottom level (nodes 3,4,5,7,8,9, . . .) represent A's possible moves and so on.

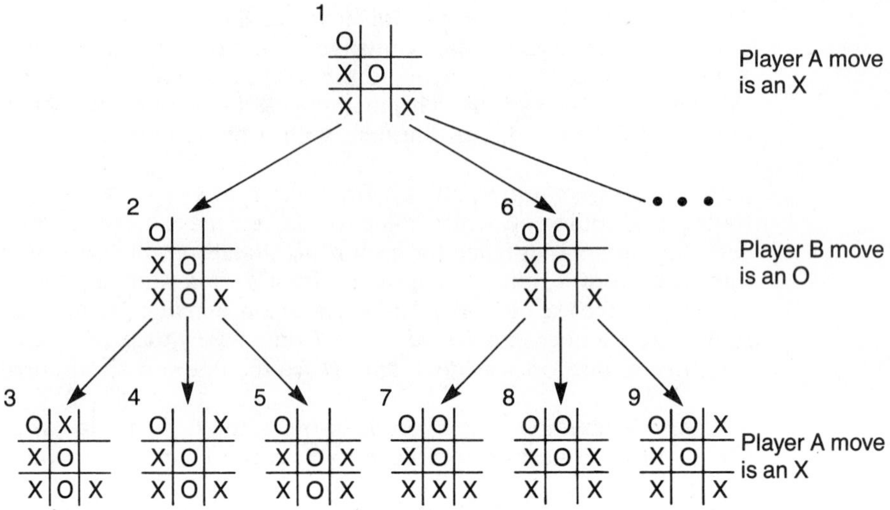

FIGURE 4.9 PARTIAL GAME TREE FOR TIC-TAC-TOE

Suppose player A decides to use the following evaluation function.

$$100A + 10B + C - (100D + 10E + F)$$

Where

A = number of current rows with 3 Xs

B = number of current rows with 2 Xs

C = number of current rows with 1 X

D = number of current rows with 3 0s

E = number of current rows with 2 0s

F = number of current rows with 1 0

Note that the use of "row" may represent a row, column, or diagonal and that, to be counted, the rest of the row, column, or diagonal must be blank.

Using the evaluation function, player A calculates that the value of nodes 3 through 5 are 1,0, and -1, respectively and the values of nodes 7 through 9 are 91, 0, and 10, respectively.

In analyzing the results, player A recognizes that the consequence of his or her move of node 1 has a maximum value of 1 considering node 3. Nodes 7 and 9 have higher values, but player B probably will never choose node 6; hence, the path to nodes 7 and 9 is blocked.

Reasoning Strategies

Now that we have examined the notion of search, we are ready to look at **reasoning strategies**. Whenever we think of reasoning, we think of logic.

Logic can be described as the scientific study of the process of reasoning and the system of rules and procedures used in the reasoning process. As such, it is of interest to us in our study of expert systems as they are used to solve problems. We now wish to examine the two basic types of reasoning strategies: deduction and induction.

Deduction

Deduction is the process of taking known general principles and applying them to specific instances to infer some sort of conclusion. For example, we know that the interest on a loan is given by the product of the principal, interest rate, and duration of the loan. We can deduce what our interest would be for a given principal, interest rate, and duration.

Not all general principles can be quantified or are generally accepted. It may be an assertion or belief that we think to be true. For example, we may assert that if our (body) temperature is over 100 degrees, then we will not go to work today. Someone else might not use these parameters.

To use deduction, we must be able to state the situation using *major* and *minor premises*. For example, in the situation just described, we have

Major premise:	IF my temperature is over 100 degrees, I will not go to work today.
Minor premise:	My temperature is 100.6 degrees.
Deduction:	Therefore, I will not go to work today.

As a second example, suppose that our company will not ship parts unless they have been quality tested. Our process of deduction would appear as the following:

Major premise:	All parts must be quality tested.
Minor premise:	At least one part has not been tested.
Deduction:	The lot (of parts) cannot be shipped.

In both cases, the deduction (conclusion) is valid if both the major and minor premises are true.

It may be the case that a major premise can have several minor premises. In this case, all of the minor premises must be true in order to arrive at a valid deduction.

This requirement is, unfortunately, a limitation of deductive reasoning. In real life, in a complex situation, not all minor premises may be known to be true with 100% accuracy. In this case, a valid deduction cannot be made.

Induction

Like deduction, **induction** uses facts to infer conclusions. However, unlike deduction, the conclusions do not have a general principle or assertion as its basis.

Conclusions are inferred from only known facts. For example, suppose we have the following facts (premises)

Premise: Defective spark plugs cause poor engine performance.

Premise: Defective alternators cause poor engine performance.

Premise: Dirty crankcase oil causes poor engine performance.

Conclusion: Defective spark plugs, defective alternators, and dirty crankcase oil are the causes of poor engine performance.

This example represents some interesting facts. First, induced conclusions may not be entirely accurate. In our example, we know that there are certainly other causes of poor engine performance. As more facts are added to the inferencing process, the conclusion will increase in accuracy. The conclusion will be most accurate if all possible premises are known to be true, which is usually impossible. Hence, inductive reasoning must deal with uncertainty in obtaining conclusions.

Second, the inferred conclusion is changeable. As new facts are known, the conclusion will change.

We human beings use inductive reasoning on a daily basis. From a few examples or facts, we infer generalizations about things and people. As an example, we may think that a particular spreadsheet software package is the best one to use. This package was the first one we learned and we have used it for several years. We have tried other packages but none seem as good. Similar new packages may appear on the market; but we are convinced that there is none better than ours, and we won't even consider anything new.

As another example, when we were growing up, our parents always owned a certain brand of appliance or car. When it came time to buy our first appliance or car, the brand our parents bought must have been the best so we purchased that brand.

Sometimes we are correct but often we are not, with a resulting loss in quality or life. There will, in general, always be a certain degree of uncertainty.

Abduction

A third type of inferencing strategy is **abduction**. Like deduction, it also makes use of major and minor premises. Recall from the prior example:

Major premise: IF my temperature is over 100 degrees, THEN I will not go to work today.

Minor premise: I did not go to work today.

Conclusion: My temperature was over 100 degrees.

Unlike deduction, abduction is not a legal form of inference. From our example, there may have been other reasons why we did not go to work today such as the car would not start or we needed a mental health day.

In spite of the fact that abduction is not a valid inference technique, it is still very useful and sometimes necessary. It is useful in diagnostic types of expert systems because it can generate possible explanations. But, it must be carefully used.

For example, suppose we know the following rule:

IF the car is out of gas,

THEN it will not start.

We find that the car will not start. We cannot definitely conclude that the car is out of gas. There may be some other explanation, but our abduction, the car is out of gas, gives us a plausible explanation that we can easily check out. Since there are a number of possible explanations, we have to start somewhere and our abduction acts as a kind of heuristic; it gives us a place to start.

Uncertainty and Reasoning

Uncertainty is very much a part of our reasoning process whether we use deduction or abduction. In the case of deduction, it is often impossible to know all of the possible facts needed to reach a desired conclusion. We must decide at what point we are willing to make a deduction, short of all possible information. As we pointed out in the previous section, a similar problem exists in the use of inductive and abductive reasoning.

Expert systems are designed to deal with incomplete or uncertain knowledge. The system may ask the user for input and receive the reply that he or she does not know the answer. The expert system must then take this lack of knowledge into account in its inferencing process. The system will still come up with an answer to the problem, but it may be qualified or be different than anticipated.

Such is not the case with algorithmic systems. If data is incomplete or missing, the algorithmic system will come up with inaccurate results or no results at all. It cannot deal with incomplete or uncertain data.

Certainty Factors

Uncertainty is handled by some expert systems through the use of **certainty factors** which are also known as **confidence factors**. These factors are a measure of the degree of the uncertainty about the knowledge involved.

Certainty factors should not be confused with probability numbers. We will discuss this point in greater detail in Chapter 6.

Certainty factors reflect confidence or belief rather than a probability. For example, what does it mean when the weatherperson says that the chance of snow is 50%? It does not really mean that a probability of 0.5 has been assigned to the chance of snow. What it means is that, on days with similar weather conditions, it snowed 50% of the time. The weatherperson is 50% confident that it will snow, but this confidence is based upon past statistics.

To further illustrate this point, a set of certainty factors does not have to contain numbers between 0 and 1 although these numbers are certainly valid. Certainty factors could come from a set of, say, -100 to +100 where +100 refers to absolute belief and -100 refers to absolute disbelief. Numbers in between -100 and +100 refer to the relative degrees of believability.

Certainty factors are almost always assigned by experts and are based on their intelligent judgment. These certainty factors can change as new knowledge is gained. But, at any point in time, they are static values.

Certainty factors can be associated with either premises (IF) or conclusions (THEN). Here are some examples:

> IF the car has a defective battery (CF = 0.6),
>
> THEN the car will not start.
>
> IF it rains today,
>
> THEN the game will be canceled (CF = 0.8).

These rules establish what is known as a *threshold level*. That is, it is decided beforehand what CF value is needed by a rule to be fired (executed). This level is established by the knowledge engineer (system developer) in consultation with the expert(s). This threshold value will, of course, vary from rule to rule.

We also must consider the effect of threshold values when several rules are combined (chained) together. Techniques such as averaging are often used, but there is no general agreement among workers in the field as to which technique is best. It is also obvious that the validity of any threshold value will be tested during system usage.

There will be times when a rule will have multiple premises. What the aggregate effect of the certainty factors assigned to each premise is not standard among expert system developers. For example, consider the rule

IF A (CF = 0.6)

AND B (CF = 0.3)

AND C (CF = 0.8),

THEN D

What certainty factor should be assigned to D? Some would argue that the confidence is as good as the highest certainty factor of the premises, which is 0.8. Others would argue that D should not have a certainty factor greater than the lowest of the premise certainty factors, which is 0.3. Still others would say that the certainty factor of D should be the average (0.57) or the median (0.6). In any case, the decision must be made by the knowledge engineer and the expert(s).

A similar problem occurs when there is a chain of rules as was mentioned earlier. Again, there are no generally accepted guidelines, but suffice it to say that if there is an error (relative inaccuracy) for one or more rules in the chain, then the inaccuracy will be compounded as the various rules move through the chain.

Clearly, while the ability to deal with uncertainty is a major advantage of expert systems, it can also be a major disadvantage if not thoroughly considered by the knowledge engineer and the expert(s). The alternatives must be clearly studied and a defensible conclusion must be reached relative to dealing with uncertainty for the system to maintain its creditability.

Fuzzy Logic

One of the more interesting techniques for dealing with the whole question of uncertainty is **fuzzy logic** [Zadeh 1988]. Fuzzy logic is a way of dealing with ambiguous criteria or values.

For example, we may say that "the girl is tall." What do we mean by tall? Is 5 feet 6 inches tall? Is 6 feet 2 inches tall? A particular height is tall to one person but is not tall to another. It depends on one's relative definition of tall.

Fuzzy logic represents an attempt to define such ambiguous terms as tall, short, heavy, and so on. It defines such a term as a range with a probability associated with that range. We can then assign a probability to that range that indicates whether tall is in the specified range. If ambiguous terms such as tall can be more quantitatively defined, then they can be more readily and reliably used.

Representing ambiguous terms is very complex and difficult. For this reason, fuzzy logic currently is not widely used in AI and expert systems. This may or may not change as work in fuzzy logic continues.

Reasoning Control Strategies

Earlier in this chapter, we discussed the notion of a control strategy relative to the movement from one state to another in a problem-solving situation. This control strategy determines how a search is conducted as it attempts to find an occurrence of the goal state.

Expert systems make use of control strategies in their reasoning process. These strategies are used to search the knowledge base for the occurrence of facts and/or rules which can be used to obtain a problem solution.

The two most popular control strategies used in expert system development work are *forward chaining* and *backward chaining*. As we shall see in this section and in later chapters, both control strategies are very powerful and relatively easy to implement.

Forward Chaining

From our earlier discussions in this chapter, there are two ways to deal with a search space for a given problem. One way is to consider given facts and move forward to reach a solution to the problem. Rules are used in this forward movement; the rules generate new facts which can be used with other rules. This is known as **forward chaining**.

To illustrate forward chaining, consider the following example of initially known facts and rules.

Initial Facts: A,B,C,D,E

Rules

1. IF A AND B THEN F
2. IF C AND D THEN G
3. IF F AND G THEN H
4. IF E AND H THEN I

There are several things to notice about this example as pictured in Figure 4.10. Rules 1 and 2 contain information about given facts (initial facts A,B,C,D and E). Rule 3 deals with facts F and G which are not initially known, while Rule 4 is concerned with one initially known fact (E) and one unknown fact (H).

Forward chaining works like this. Since we know A and B, Rule 1 allows us to know F so that F is now a known fact. Since we know C and D, Rule 2 allows us to now know G. Since we know know F and G, Rule 3 is used and now we know H. Since we now know H and we already know E (initial fact) we now know I from Rule 4. Let us suppose that I is the solution/conclusion to the problem; so we need go no further. We have used a chain of rules and facts to find out what we wanted to know.

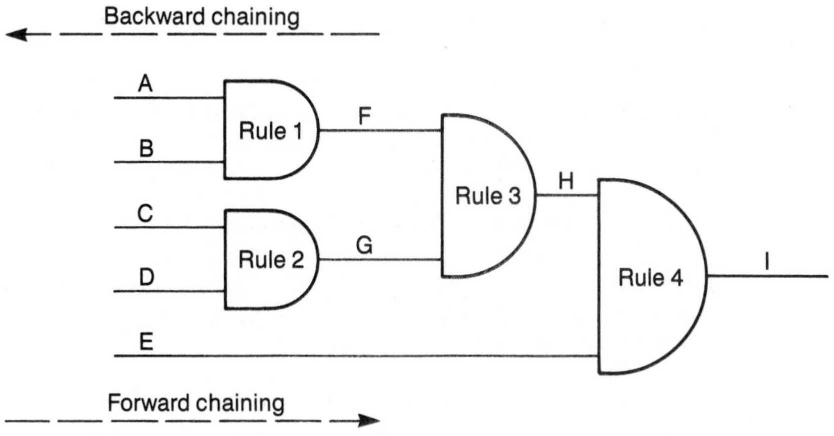

FIGURE 4.10 FORWARD AND BACKWARD CHAINING

In our example, the chain was able to be completed. This will not always be the case. Suppose we had not known E initially. The fact E was not derivable from any of the given rules. In this case, our chain would have been broken and we could not have known I. The point is, that just because we have a mechanism (chain) for determining I, we cannot guarantee that we can determine I, unless we somehow manage to find fact E or we generate another rule which will have I as a conclusion but have different premises than Rule 4.

Backward Chaining

The other way we use facts and rules to obtain a conclusion (solution) is known as **backward chaining**. Here we move backward from what we finally want to know to see if we have the necessary initial facts.

Let's use our previous example of initially known facts and rules of Figure 4.10. We begin by supposing that we know I, which is our conclusion/solution. To know I, we need to know E and H through Rule 4. We initially know E. To know H, we need to know F and G by Rule 3. To know F, we need to know A and B via Rule 1, and to know G, we need to know C and D from Rule 2. As it happens, we know A,B,C,D and E (initial facts). Hence, we can verify that we know I; we worked backward through the rules and facts.

Of course, our chaining could have broken down. Again, suppose we did not know E. Our chain would have stopped with Rule 4 and we could have gone no further. Given this set of rules, there was no way to know I.

Case Study: Reasoning Strategies for WPHELP

Let's incorporate some of the concepts from this chapter into our case study of WPHELP, the expert system for selecting a word processor. We will refine the fuzzy concept of functionality, use forward and backward chaining for deductive reasoning, and explore certain factors for our rules.

The concept of simple or complex functionality is indeed a little nebulous and needs to be refined. Just how do we know if a particular word processing document is simple or complex? In order to clarify the fuzzy notion of functionality, let's use a more precise and descriptive characterization of the types of documents that could be produced with a word processor.

We will assume that there are four types of basic classifications of word processing documents: Type 1, Type 2, Type 3 and Type 4. A Type 1 document is a simple sequential list of words like a letter, memo, or rough draft of a book chapter. A Type 2 document has all the features of a Type 1 document with the addition of page numbering, titles, headers, or footers. An example of a Type 2 document would be a report, term paper, or book chapter of text only. If a Type 2 document requires a structured layout, then we will classify it as a Type 3 document. Examples of Type 3 documents would include resumes, charts, and multiple-margined reports. Centering, italics, and form letters with insertion capability from a database would be in this category. A Type 3 document is labeled a Type 4 document whenever a typographical layout is needed. This implies the need for different-sized characters and different fonts (styles of lettering). Type 4 documents are newsletters, advertisements, and brochures. If we allow for the mixing of text and illustrations (graphics) in the same document, we might be using desktop publishing. Examples of each type of document and the characteristics of each type are summarized in Figures 4.11 and 4.12, respectively.

Document	Examples of Document Types
Type 1:	sequential text letters memos rough drafts
Type 2:	paginated text reports term papers book chapters
Type 3:	structured layout of text resumes charts multiple-margined documents form letters with insertion capability from a database

(continued on page 81)

Type 4:	typographical layout newsletters advertisements, brochures reports with different text sizes and types of characters

FIGURE 4.11 EXAMPLES OF DOCUMENT TYPES

Document	Characteristics
Type 1:	simple, sequential text
Type 2:	page numbering, headers, footers, titles
Type 3:	multiple margins, centering, italics
Type 4:	different fonts, superscripts, integrated graphics, desktop publishing

FIGURE 4.12 CHARACTERISTICS OF DOCUMENT TYPES

Let's now expand the rules for WPHELP by including two new rules which link type to functionality. If the needed document is Type 1 or Type 2, then the functionality is simple. If the needed document is Type 3 or Type 4, then the functionality is complex. The rules for our expanded expert system with certainty factors between 0 and 1 (in parentheses) are given in Figure 4.13.

Rule 1: IF functionality is simple
AND (cost is high or low) (0.90),
THEN select word processor A.

Rule 2: IF functionality is complex
AND cost is low (0.90),
THEN selecting a word processor is not possible.

Rule 3: IF functionality is complex
AND cost is high (0.95),
THEN select word processor B or C.

Rule 4: IF the document is Type 1 (0.85)
OR Type 2 (0.90),
THEN the functionality is simple.

Rule 5: IF the document is Type 3 (0.90)
OR Type 4 (0.95),
THEN the functionality is complex.

FIGURE 4.13 EXPANDED RULES FOR WPHELP

These five rules can be expressed as search trees as shown in Figure 4.14, with the goal states (word processor A, B, or C) as the root and the initial states Type 1, Type 2, Type 3, Type 4, Low, and High as the leaves of the trees. Intermediate states are simple and complex.

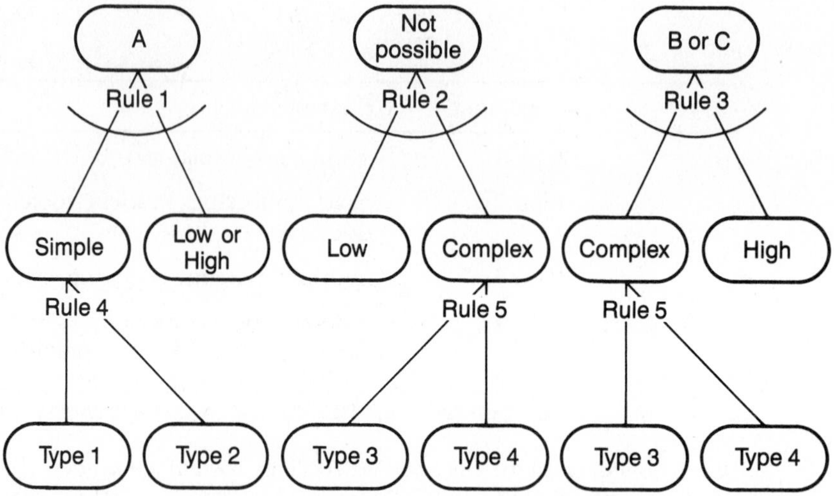

FIGURE 4.14 SEARCH TREE FOR WPHELP

If two child nodes from a parent node have an arc connecting the links, then the diagram is interpreted as an AND rule such as

IF child1 AND child2, THEN parent node.

If there is no arc connecting the links, then an OR is inferred as

IF child1 OR child2, THEN parent node.

For example, Rule 3 in Figure 4.14 is

IF complex AND high, THEN B or C.

An OR condition is expressed in Rule 5 with

If Type 3 OR Type 4, THEN complex.

Even though "Not possible" is not a desired goal state, it is shown so that each rule is included in the tree.

In Figure 4.14, we can visualize forward and backward chaining as control strategies. If we start with facts (initial states) at the bottom of any of the trees and "climb" upward to its root, we are using forward chaining. For example, if we know that the document is Type 2 and the cost is low, then Rule 4 would be true because of the OR and Rule 1 would be true because both premises (simple and low) are true. Hence, the goal, A, is reached. Forward chaining is *traveling towards* a goal state.

The opposite approach, backward chaining, can also be illustrated with Figure 4.14. Assume the goal state as A. For A to be true, both simple and low must be known to be true. Simple is true if the document is known to be Type 1 or Type 2. In this diagram with the goal at the top (root), backward chaining is searching down the tree, whereas forward chaining is searching up the tree.

These concepts also can be illustrated in a left-to-right format that is shown in Figure 4.15.

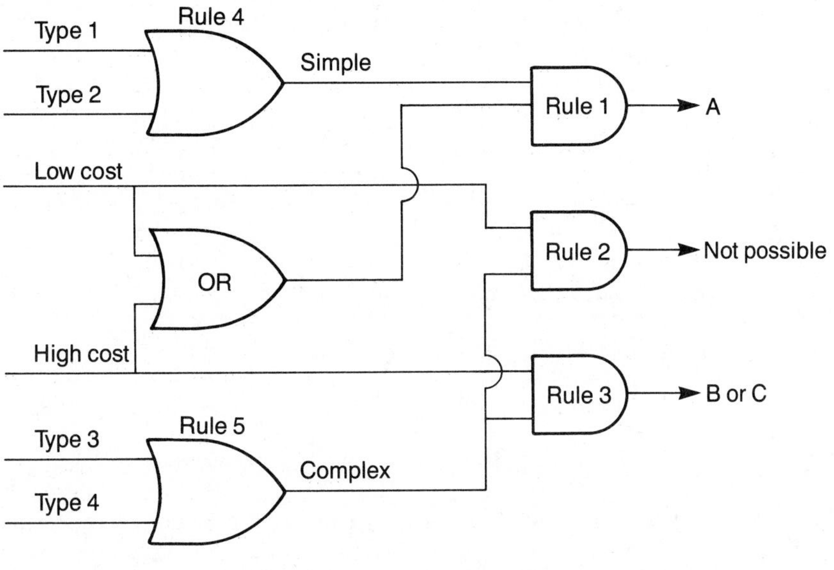

FIGURE 4.15 LEFT TO RIGHT DIAGRAM OF RULES FOR WPHELP

An AND is shown as a half-circle and OR is shown as a triangle. The inputs are to the left of the rule and the output(s) are to the right. For example, Rule 4 would be interpreted as:

IF TYPE 1 OR TYPE 2, THEN the task is simple. Initial states are on the far left and goal states are on the far right. Hence, searching from left (initial state) to right (goal state) is reaching conclusions by forward chaining. Moving from the right (state) to the left (initial state) is backward chaining. Sometimes in searching, we are not able to move *across the diagram*, hence a goal state cannot be reached. Regardless of the visual orientation of the rules, always determine the goal state (THEN) from the initial state (IF).

Moving on to certainty factors (CF) with our expanded rules, Figure 4.16 shows the search trees for WPHELP with the certainty factors from the rules in Figure 4.13. The initial states have been assigned certainty factors between 0 and 1 (in parentheses). For example, Type 1 (0.85) means that we are 85% certain that the classification scheme for Type 1 documents is correct. The question now is, how do we determine certainty factors for the THEN part of rules? We will discuss this question in the Case Study in Chapter 6.

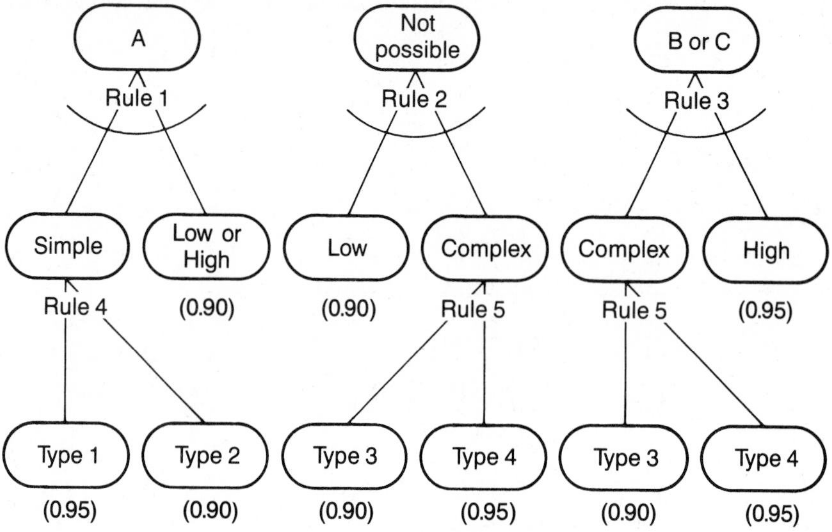

FIGURE 4.16 CERTAINTY FACTORS FOR WPHELP

In this section, we have refined the fuzzy concept of functionality, depicted forward/backward chaining in search trees and gate diagrams, and explored certainty factors for the WPHELP expert system. In the next chapter, we will concentrate on the knowledge base instead of the reasoning mechanisms.

Key Points

- Search and pattern matching techniques are needed to search the knowledge base of an expert system.
- The general purpose of problem solving is to move from a problem (initial) state to a goal (solution) state. This is accomplished by procedures or operations.
- In moving from the initial state to the goal state, an intermediate state can occur.

- The control strategy of an expert system determines how a move is made from one state to another state.
- Information about states (initial, goal, current, and previous) is stored in a database.
- A state graph is a visualization of the alternative moves from state (node) to state.
- The links in a state graph represent the transition (operator or procedures) for moving from one state to another.
- One way to represent a state graph (in a computer's memory) is to use a search tree structure.
  - Nodes may be repeated in a search tree.
  - Not all paths lead to the goal (node).
  - The search tree is divided into levels.
  - The length of the links between nodes is not reflective of actual distances.
- Search-tree terminology includes:
  - Root node — The entry or top node
  - Branches — Links from the root node to nodes at the next level
  - Child —The node at the end of one link (Also called successor or descendant)
  - Parent —The node above the link to a child node (Also called an antecedent)
  - Leaf — A node at the end of a path
- In search trees, the root node may represent either the goal state or the initial state.
- There are two types of search methods used in expert systems: Systematic (blind) Heuristic (guided by hints)
- Four common algorithms for systematic searches are: depth-first (down from the root) Breadth-first (across each level) Forward (from initial state to goal state) Backward (from goal state to initial state)
- An example of a heuristic search is a game tree for tic-tac-toe. Mathematical or evaluation functions can guide players in sequential moves.
- Three basic types of reasoning are deduction, induction, and abduction.
  - Deduction is applying known principles (major and minor premise) to specific instances to reach a conclusion.
  - Induction is inferring conclusions from known facts.
  - Abduction is a form of inference that is not valid that may generate possible explanations.
- Uncertainty of either premises or conclusions can be expressed as certainty or confidence factors.
- The threshold level of a rule is the predetermined certainty value assigned to the premise or conclusion in a rule.
- There is no general agreement on how to assign a certainty factor to a conclusion derived from multiple premises with certainty factors. Methods include:
  - Highest
  - Lowest
  - Average
  - Median
- Fuzzy logic is a method for dealing with ambiguous criteria or values.
- Knowledge engineers determine the search strategies, reasoning methods, and certainty factors in an expert system.
- The case study WPHELP was expanded to more precisely define functionality. The five rules were expressed in a search tree and a gate diagram. Reasoning strategies and certainty factors were discussed.

Exercises

1. What is the control strategy for moving from an initial start state (off) to the goal state (on) for turning on a light in your home?
2. Using Figure 4.7, answer the following:
   Name the root node ____________________
   Name the level one nodes ____________________
   Name the level two nodes ____________________
   Name the level three nodes ____________________
   Name the leaves of the tree ____________________
   Name the children of the Nashville node ____________________
3. Given the tree in Figure 4.17, answer the following:
   Name the root node ____________________
   Name the level one nodes ____________________
   Name the level three nodes ____________________
   Name the leaves of the tree ____________________
   Name the children of node B ____________________
   Name the parent of node I____________________
   Name the successor(s) of node D ____________________

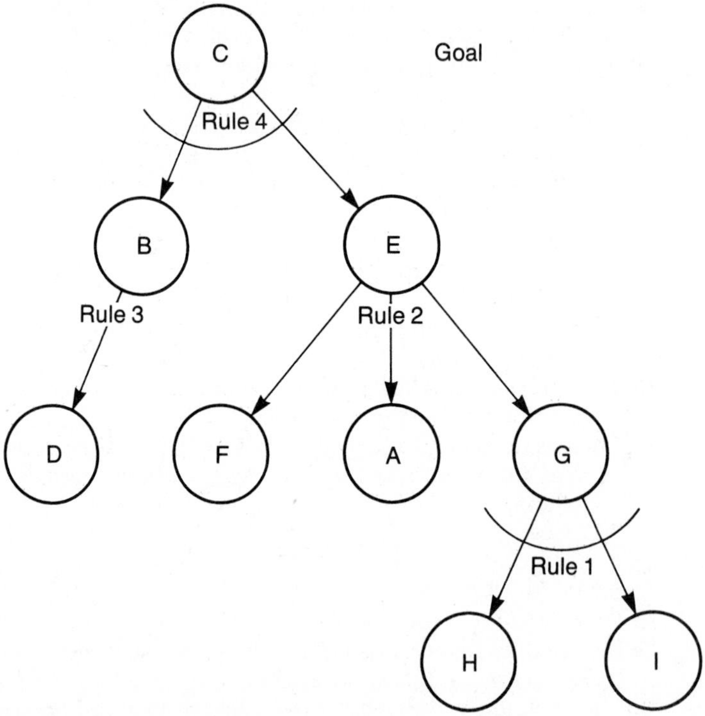

FIGURE 4.17 SEARCH TREE

From the same tree, list all the nodes after a
Depth-first search ______________________
Breadth-first search ______________________
If the goal state were C, which search method, depth-first or breadth-first, would be more efficient?

4. Given the search tree in Figure 4.17, write the IF-THEN rules using AND/OR. Assume that the goal state is the root node and that initial states are the leaves.
5. Using Figure 4.10, write the four IF-THEN rules expressed in the diagram.
   Rule #1:______________________
   Rule #2:______________________
   Rule #3:______________________
   Rule #4:______________________
6. What certainty factor (between 0 and 1) would you give if:
   a. Your car didn't start on a morning where the temperature is -40 degrees F?
   ____
   ____
   b. You call a friend on the telephone; it rings ten times and no one answers; hence your friend is not at home?
   ____
   ____
   c. You want to buy a microcomputer on a budget of $100?
   ____
   ____
7. Verify the computation on nodes one through nine for the partial game tree for tic-tac-toe in Figure 4.9.
8. What are the deductive conclusions from the stated premises?
   a. Major premise: IF today is Tuesday, THEN tomorrow is Wednesday.
   Minor premise: Today is Tuesday,
   Conclusion: ______________________
   b. Major premise: IF A=B AND C=D, THEN F<G.
   Minor premise: A=B
   C=D
   Conclusion: ______________________
9. Given the information below, what would be your inductive or inferred guess for the next element in each list?

List	Next Element
a. Red,Green,Blue,Red,Green,Blue,Red,Green	______
b. 1,2,3,4,5,6,7,8,9,10,11,12,13,	______
c. 1,1,2,3,5,8,13,21,34,	______

10. What certainty factors between zero (not possible) and 1 (certain) would you assign to the following
   a. IF my car is orange,
   THEN the car will be hard to resell (CF=__________).
   Why? ______________________

b. IF Miami beats Notre Dame in next year's football game
(CF=__________),
THEN Miami will go to a bowl game.
Why?

c. IF inflation increases next year,
THEN interest rates on mortgages will rise
(CF=__________).
Why?

Assignments

1. Complete the following search-tree problem. A microcomputer program controls a robotic arm which can reposition blocks X, Y, and Z one at a time. See Figure 4.18.

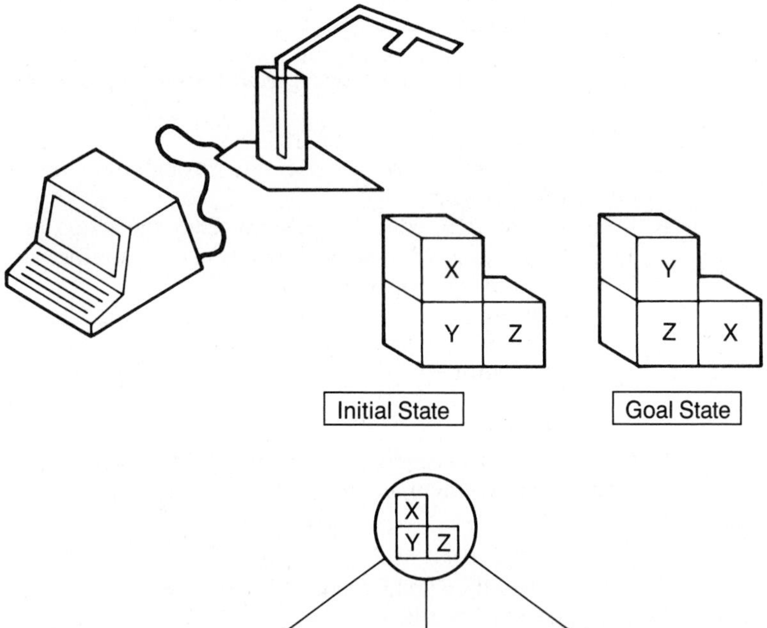

FIGURE 4.18 ROBOTIC-ARM PROBLEM

a. Complete the search tree in Figure 4.18 for the robotic arm to move the blocks from the original state (root) to the goal state.
b. Change the goal state to ZYX and redraw the search tree.

2. Convert the rules in Figure 4.19 to a search tree and a left-to-right diagram. The following summary may be helpful: The seven rules given in Figure 4.19 are for advising a person to invest or not to invest — only three factors: insurance, marital status, and amount of savings — are considered. The rules utilize the following variables:

Status:	Single or married
Savings:	Satisfactory of unsatisfactory
Insurance:	Adequate or inadequate
Action:	Invest or not invest

The expert system must have the value of the saving accounts and the monthly wages in order to advise on whether to invest or not.

Rule 1: IF status is married
AND savings is satisfactory
AND insurance is adequate,
THEN action is to invest.

Rule 2: IF status is single
AND savings is satisfactory
AND insurance is adequate,
THEN action is to invest.

Rule 3: IF savings is not satisfactory
OR insurance is not adequate,
THEN action is not to invest.

Rule 4: IF status is married
AND savings is six times monthly take-home wages or more,
THEN savings is satisfactory.

Rule 5: IF status is married
AND savings is less than six times monthly take home wages,
THEN savings is not satisfactory

Rule 6: IF status is single
AND savings is four times monthly take-home wages,
THEN savings is satisfactory.

Rule 7: IF status is single
AND savings is less than four times monthly take-home wages,
THEN savings is not adequate.

FIGURE 4.19 RULES FOR INVESTMENT EXPERT SYSTEM

3. What is the action (goal state) from the expert system in Assignment 2 for each of the following (initial states)?

Initial State	Goal State
a. Married Adequate insurance $10,000 in savings Monthly wages: $1,700	____________
b. Single Adequate insurance $10,000 in savings Monthly wages $1,700	____________
c. Single Adequate insurance $20,000 in savings Monthly wages $4,000	____________

4. Expand the rules in the investment system in Assignment 2 to be more precise about insurance. Assume that a single person needs insurance of at least five times his or her annual salary and a married person needs at least eight times his or her annual salary.
5. Using the investment expert system, do you think monthly wages (gross) or take-home wages should be used as predictors? Why?
6. List several additional factors that should be included in a comprehensive expert system advising a person to invest or not invest.
7. To obtain a more in-depth understanding of inductive reasoning, read Chapter 4, "A Theory and Methodology of Inductive Learning" from *Machine Learning* by R. S. Michalski (and others), Morgan Kaufmann Publisher, Inc., Los Altos, CA.
8. Fuzzy logic is an important part of expert systems. Report in detail about the principles underlying fuzzy query processing (asking questions) from "Fuzzy Data Retrieval," an article in the July 1988 issue of *AI Expert*.

5

THE KNOWLEDGE BASE

We have examined a number of general concepts associated with artificial intelligence and expert systems so far, and we are now ready to discuss in greater detail the component parts of an expert system. They are the knowledge base, the inference engine, and the user interface.

In this chapter we will examine the creation and maintenance of the knowledge base. Questions of whether a given problem is an appropriate candidate for an expert system, the choice of an appropriate development tool, the role of the human expert and how his or her knowledge is to be acquired, and finally, the need for organizing the knowledge base will be explored.

Is the Problem Appropriate?

The question of whether a problem is **appropriate** for expert system development is a difficult one at best. There are no specific criteria that generally can be applied to a problem that will answer the question. We discussed some generic types of problems that are probable candidates for expert systems development in Chapter 2. But, these classifications are general; they give us a place to start but more specificity is needed.

There are, however, basic questions that must be answered before using an expert system in an organization. Waterman [1986] suggests that three questions need to be answered. Their role is illustrated in Figure 5.1.

1. Is expert systems development possible for the problem solution?
2. Is expert systems development justified for the problem solution?
3. Is expert systems development appropriate for the problem solution?

To determine whether a given problem is appropriate for expert system development, all three questions must be answered in the affirmative. Each of the questions can be answered by considering a series of subquestions. This will be the focus of our discussion in the next several paragraphs.

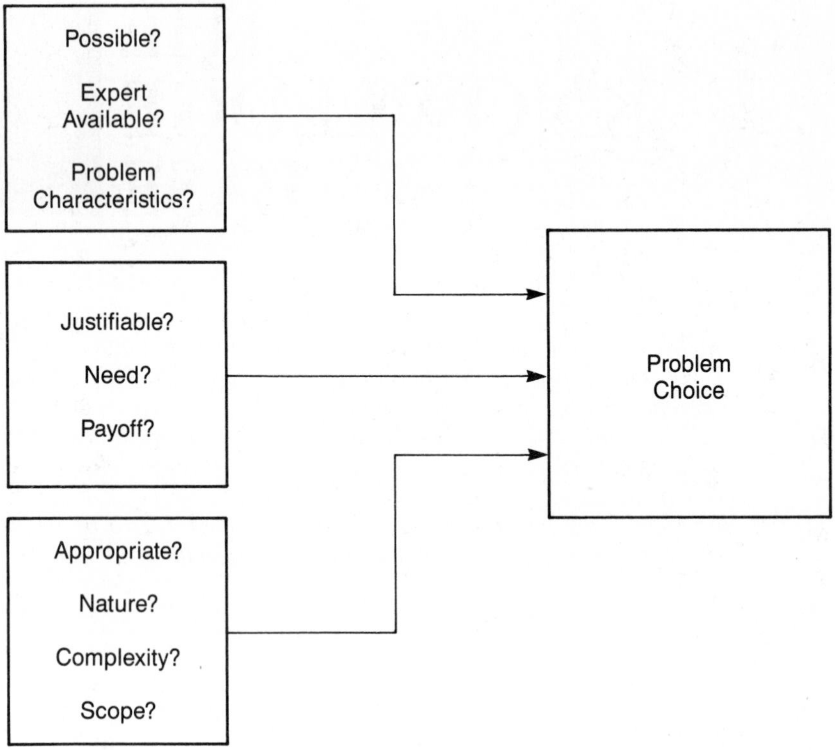

FIGURE 5.1 QUESTIONS RELATIVE TO PROBLEM APPROPRIATENESS

Relative to the questions of ***possible***, we need to consider both the expert who will serve as the model for the expert system and certain characteristics of the problem that make it possible to use expert system development.

The ***availability*** of a true expert is an initial key consideration. If one does not exist, the question of the use of an expert system is a mute one. If such an expert does exist, does he or she have an interest in helping develop an expert system? Finally, do other true experts exist who disagree with the initially designated expert? If so, then the attractiveness of the given problem as a candidate for expert system development diminishes considerably, if not completely.

What about the ***characteristics*** of the problem? It must deal with the cognitive skills of the expert. Skills that are physical cannot be performed by an expert system. If a problem deals with both cognitive and physical skills, then the cognitive part might be used in the expert system development. For example, the XCON/XSEL expert system configures VAX computer systems specific customer orders. It can advise how the computer system will be arranged, but XCON cannot go to the customer site and put the cables and wiring into the system; these tasks must be completed by the human expert.

Some problems may be too difficult to consider. That is, if an expert takes days, weeks, or even months to solve the problem, then it is really not possible to develop an expert system for that problem.

Finally, problems that require on-the-job experience or common sense are not likely candidates for development purposes. It is just too difficult to create an expert system that requires direct experience or common sense. However, this state of affairs may change in the future.

The second question deals with the problem of *justification* for purposes of obtaining needed resources such as time, personnel, and money. Justification is always a major hurdle in any organizational structure for any type of project.

Justification usually involves two questions: Is there a need? and What is the payoff? The question of *need* revolves around how the expert system will be used or implemented. If the knowledge possessed by the expert exists in no other individual (or there are very few such individuals), then a need can be demonstrated on several grounds. First, retirement or even death could cause an organization the loss of the expert's knowledge. Or, if the expert's knowledge is needed in several places at the same time or in a physically dangerous environment (such as a fire or nuclear explosion), then the development of an expert system can be justified. Multiple copies of a completed expert system can be made and distributed in either case.

There are two schools of thought relative to the *payoff* question. Some would argue that the largest possible payoff to the organization should be the determining factor, such as saving the organization from demise. This is a noble goal but is also a big gamble. If the expert system development project succeeds, then all is well. However, if it fails then the results can be very damaging with possible considerable loss of time, personnel, and money.

The other school of thought takes a more conservative approach. Build one or more expert systems that solve smaller problems. While the total payoff (or individual system payoff) may be somewhat smaller, the amount of resources committed by the organization will probably be much less. A failure at this point will not cause as much impact on the organization. The choice of a large or small payoff will depend directly on the attitudes of the organization's management.

We wish to note, at this point, that the problem of justification in an organization is not unique to expert systems. The methods used in the justification process also apply to other proposed projects. For more details on methods of justification, we suggest that you consult a systems analysis text such as *Systems Analysis and Design* by James C. Wetherbe (West Publishing Company, 1988).

The final question pertinent to problem selection relates to the *appropriateness* of the problem. This question deals with the complexity, and scope of the problem; some aspects of the nature, complexity and scope were considered in the question of whether it was possible to use expert system development.

The *nature* of the problem would require the use of symbolic manipulation and heuristics. If these are not required, then the problem likely could be solved with a conventional algorithmic program, and there would be no need to develop an expert system. This does not mean that symbolic manipulation and heuristics must always be used but it means that their use should be the primary focus needed to solve the problem.

The issue of *complexity* was referred to earlier with the discussion of problem difficulty. A problem should not be too trivial. Even if it takes only a few seconds to solve, it still can be considered for expert system development. The difficulty is finding a good criteria to make this judgement, since the use of time to generate a solution as a criteria could be misleading. A possible heuristic (not to be taken too literally) might be "If the problem appears too easy, then it may be about right."

We have already discussed, in this section, issues concerning the scope of the problem. Its size and practical value (payoff) must be considered at this point.

To summarize, for a problem to be chosen for expert systems development, it must be possible, justifiable and appropriate. If the determination process is hurried or cursory, the end result is likely to be less than desirable.

Choosing the Development Tool

Once it has been determined that a given problem is acceptable for expert system development, a **development tool** must be chosen. Again a systematic approach is useful.

In Chapter 2, we classified expert system development tools as either high-level languages or as shells. Following are some of the features or characteristics of each class.

With **high-level languages**, the knowledge engineer has several possible options. There are a number of languages available such as LISP, PROLOG, FORTRAN, and Pascal. Most of these high-level languages are mature, and for some of them there are a number of support facilities available such as debuggers, graphics interfaces, and full-screen editors. These facilities are helpful to the programmer.

High-level programming languages have the advantage of flexibility. They are not constrained by the type of problem nor by the desires of the knowledge engineer. They will support different forms of knowledge representation; although some languages are better suited to particular representations than others. For example, PROLOG is best suited to a logic form of knowledge representation.

There also are some disadvantages to the use of high-level programming languages. For one, to use these languages requires sufficient skill and understanding. The structures of both the knowledge base and the inference engine must be created from scratch, utilizing personnel, time, and hence, money.

The class of tools known as **shells** has become increasingly popular in recent years. The shells provide an environment for creating an expert system that can be used by an inexperienced knowledge engineer. The shell requires only that the knowledge base be created; the structure of the inference engine has been already provided with the shell. A number of shells such as VP-Expert have been created with a number of support facilities that have made the use of the shell much easier.

Even with all of this popularity, shells have some disadvantages. The shell dictates the form of knowledge representation and the type of inferencing to be used. The human/machine interface is physically dictated although the knowledge engineer usually can control the content of the interface through available programming tools.

Shells are sometimes more expensive initially than high level programming languages; however, expert systems developed with shells usually take less time to complete so that overall development cost may be less. A particular shell usually can deal with only one type of problem, whereas high-level languages deal with a broader range of problems.

Which is better? There is no definitive answer. It depends on the application, the time allotted to the development of the expert system, and the skill level of the knowledge engineer. We will focus our attention on the actual choice of development tools in the remainder of this section.

The choice of which is the right tool is not always an easy one. Recognize that the initial choice of a particular development tool may need to be changed because it simply is not doing what the knowledge engineer anticipated. This perhaps is more of a potential problem for an inexperienced knowledge engineer, but not always, since expert systems design often involves scrapping the project and starting over.

There is also a potential problem in tool choice even with the experienced knowledge engineer. It is often the case that this individual has developed a preference for one particular tool or set of tools. It may be that there is not a good match between the preferred tool and the problem to be solved. There is a temptation at this point to alter the problem to fit the tool. This is not a desirable move and will many times result in less than satisfactory performance of the finished expert system.

What are the appropriate considerations in the choice of an expert system development tool? Waterman [1986] suggests that there are six considerations, and these are summarized in Figure 5.2.

The first of the considerations is *developmental constraints*. As we already pointed out, these constraints involve time, personnel, and money.

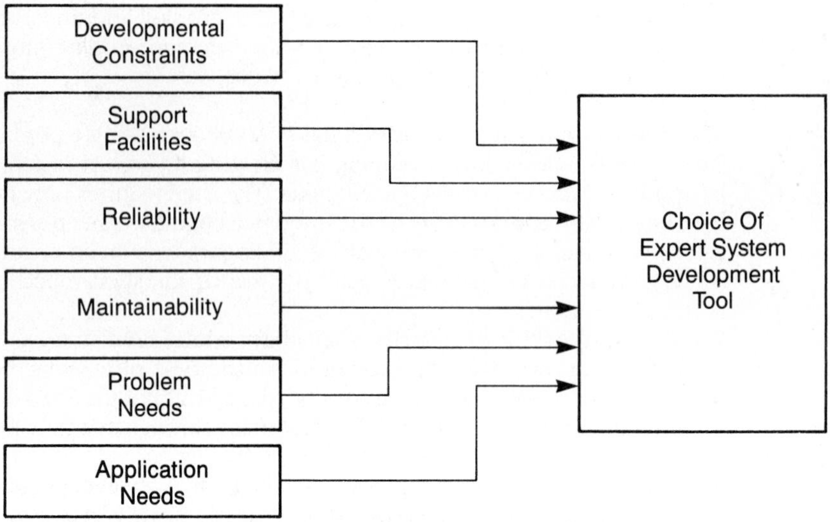

FIGURE 5.2 DEVELOPMENT TOOLS CONSIDERATIONS IN THE CHOICE OF AN EXPERT SYSTEM

The constraint of development time can be a major one. If the knowledge engineer has a specified time period in which to complete the work, then a tool must be chosen that can be easily learned and used (if not previously known to the system developer). The time constraint can cause the problem of the experienced engineer and the "preferred" tool.

Personnel can also be a constraint. Often a team approach is used in expert systems development because of the complexity of the problem to be solved. However, there is no linear relationship between the size of the team and the amount of time used to develop the expert system; that is, for example, doubling the size of the team does not cut development time in half. The knowledge engineer/team leader must be wary of the offer by management to increase the number of team members [Waterman 1986].

Money is the third development constraint. The development costs for an expert system are high. You cannot hurry the development of an expert system; simply increasing the number of people in the development effort will not alleviate the time factor.

The cost of personnel is high. If an outside knowledge engineer is used, he or she will be expensive. Good and experienced knowledge engineers are in short supply. If internal personnel are utilized, training is often required. If they are assigned to the expert system development team, they must be replaced in the organization.

Finally, the preliminary cost of the development may be high. A high-level language may cost less initially but will require a skilled programmer whose services could be expensive. An expert system shell also is likely to have a high initial cost.

A second consideration is *support facilities* which were described earlier in this section. An adequate set of support facilities will be a major asset to the development process.

Reliability is a third consideration. Beware of choosing a tool which is still in the experimental stage or is being revised, such as a Beta release. Companies that develop these tools are often in a big hurry to get the tool to the marketplace and so testing and other tool construction work is sometimes slighted. If possible, try to seek out the names of other people who have used the tool; a great deal of information about the performance of the tool can be gained from these sources.

Maintainability is a fourth consideration. Be sure the manufacturer of the tool will be available to deal with technical questions and/or problems with the use of the tool after you have purchased it. If possible, deal only with companies that have an established record of product service.

A fifth consideration is that of *problem needs*. These needs represent characteristics of the problem input and output. For example, what kind of data will be given to the expert system? Is the data easily accessible? The data might vary over time or be very costly to acquire. The output may be in the form of a summary report. Perhaps the problem must be broken into a series of subproblems whose solutions may or may not have an effect on the solution of the other subproblems. It is quite obvious that a clear understanding of the problem to be solved is a consideration in the choice of a development tool.

The final consideration is that of *application needs*. The type of application the expert system is being designed for and who the end users will be determine the application needs. We discussed a generic classification system for applications in Chapter 2; each application type has a set of needs, although these classes of problems are not mutually exclusive. Will the expert system be an assistant to the user or perform in an autonomous fashion? Again, a clear understanding of the application is an important consideration in the choice of the expert system development tool.

The weight given to these various considerations will vary depending on the person(s) making the choice. This set of considerations is not necessarily exhaustive but probably does represent the vast majority of factors to be considered. The point is that initial care in the choice of an expert system development tool for the given problem will go a long way to determine the eventual success (or failure) of the development efforts. The choice process should not be taken lightly.

Acquiring and Organizing the Knowledge

The key tasks for the knowledge engineer in the creation of the knowledge base are the *acquisition* and *organization* of the knowledge. The tasks must be accomplished in such a way that when the knowledge base is complete it can be used as effectively as possible.

In this section, we will examine some of the desirable characteristics of the knowledge engineer and several techniques which the knowledge engineer can use to acquire the knowledge. Finally, we will discuss how the knowledge engineer can organize the acquired knowledge for efficient use.

Acquiring the Knowledge

What kind of person makes a good knowledge engineer? Since most expert systems are built in cooperation with one or more human experts, the knowledge engineer must have good communication skills. He or she must be skilled in the arts of interviewing and listening and be able to translate the knowledge gained into a representation that can be understood by the computer. In addition, the person must be thorough and organized so that sessions with the experts are as productive as possible.

The Interaction Process. The key to the knowledge-acquisition process is the **interaction** between the knowledge engineer and the human expert. This interaction is represented in Figure 5.3. The knowledge engineer queries the expert to try to capture his or her knowledge and to determine what strategies he or she uses to solve a given problem. The query/response process should be, ideally, a flow of the expert's knowledge and strategies with minimal or nonexistent gaps.

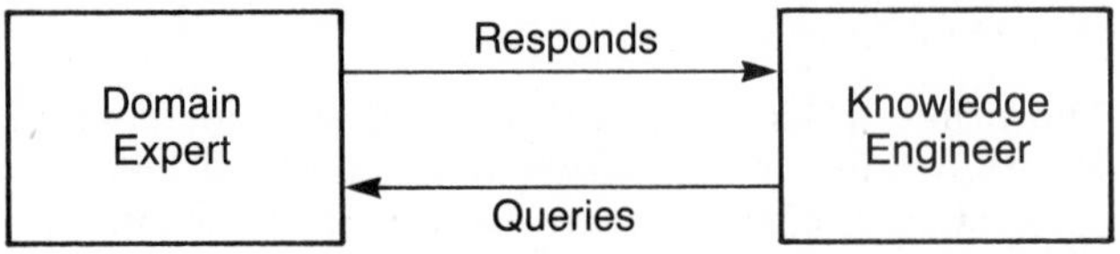

FIGURE 5.3 THE DOMAIN EXPERT/KNOWLEDGE ENGINEER CONNECTION

Prior to the initial session with the expert, the knowledge engineer must gain a basic understanding of the expert's area of domain and an understanding of the problem(s) to be solved. It is often difficult for an expert to express thoughts pertinent to subject domain. Because an expert has a deep knowledge about the subject, as he or she talks assumptions are made about the qualifications of the listener (knowledge engineer). If the listener is unprepared for the subject, what the expert says is likely to be meaningless, causing frustration during the communication process and possibly resulting in a waste of time as each tries to understand the other.

The knowledge-acquisition process usually involves more than just the use of the consultation. It also may involve the posing of sample problems to the expert for solution and discussion of that solution, similar to the use of what-if. Then problem situations are changed and again posed to the expert. A representative sample of problems given to the expert and the resulting analysis of the solutions may aid the knowledge engineer in the development of the knowledge base.

The Interview Process. While there are other techniques as we have mentioned, the **interview** is probably the technique most often used to acquire knowledge from the human expert. While there is an art to good interviewing, there are also some techniques that the knowledge engineer can use to make the process more effective.

The first goal of the knowledge engineer is to understand the structure of the expert's thinking. Understanding this structure will allow the knowledge engineer to maximize the transfer of knowledge from the expert to the knowledge base.

The key to understanding the expert's thinking structure is to use *introspective modeling*. Introspective modeling involves examining portions of the expert's previous experience. These portions are made up of such things as sensations and sensuous memories (by sight, sound, and so on), thoughts (such as visual images or auditory dialogue), and feelings (emotions such as fear, anger, happiness, and so on). It is not enough to simply transfer knowledge. At any given moment in time, the expert's thinking can be considered as a structure which can be explored. For example, we might ask the question: "What direction is Los Angeles from Chicago?" The response might come slowly or automatically. If the response was not immediate, it might have involved erecting a visual image of a United States map, marking the approximate locations of both cities and then answering the question. Knowing how the expert proceeded to answer the question may give insight to the knowledge engineer. While this technique is often helpful, it is not an ultimate one.

To this end, the knowledge engineer should frame questions such as, What was your thinking as you saw the accident? or Did you use past experiences to solve the problem? If confused, the knowledge engineer must review the expert's responses until they become clear; if the knowledge engineer has prepared prior to meeting the expert and has gained some understanding of the expert's thinking process, then confusion is less likely to occur. The knowledge engineer also must be objective in this process of eliciting knowledge from the expert and not let his or her biases affect what the expert has said.

It is probably obvious at this point that the interview process is based on verbal communication between the expert and the knowledge engineer. There is always the danger with verbal communication that words do not communicate the message. This is why we suggest a thorough understanding of the expert's thought processes and an initial understanding of the problem content.

The knowledge engineer also must be alert to the ambiguities of language. A statement by the expert, such as "This is the key to the problem," likely indicates gaps in the knowledge that can be bridged by the expert but are not obvious to the knowledge engineer; these gaps must be filled. Comparative words may be used by the expert. For example, "This is a better system" might be heard. The response is better than "what?"

A few words may disguise some very complex processes. An example of this is given by "The uncertainty of the test results indicates that we need to review the entire system and its control processes." This simple (on the surface) statement could turn out to be quite complicated.

Some words incorrectly imply universality. A statement such as "This technique will never work" is an example. The engineer wants to know, "Could a major modification be made so that it will work?"

Some words have unspecified references. An example of this difficulty is a statement such as "This component forms a protective shield." Again, the response is "Which component is this?"

Words can also imply causal relationships that do not exist. An example statement is "If we continue to run this much water through the system then we could have some expensive repair bills."

To summarize, the knowledge engineer must gain an understanding of the expert's thinking process. This is not an easy task, but the use of careful questioning techniques to elicit maximum knowledge and the possible use of introspective modeling can be very useful. Finally, the knowledge engineer must be continually aware of the potential impreciseness of language in the verbal communications with the expert.

Organizing the Knowledge

Periodically throughout the knowledge-acquisition process, the knowledge engineer must be concerned with how the knowledge is to be organized into a form suitable for the knowledge base. The process of **organizing the knowledge** involves the decision about how the knowledge is to be represented, verification of the knowledge, and validation of the inference chain. We will examine each of these areas in this section.

Representing the Knowledge. The acquired knowledge must be converted into a form that can be understood by the expert system. In Chapter 3, we discussed several methods for **representing knowledge**.

The choice of the method of representation depends on the application for which the expert system is designed and the choice of the system development tool. Recall from our discussion in Chapter 3 that procedural knowledge is best represented by production rules and that declarative knowledge is best represented by semantic nets, frames, or predicate calculus. Many applications have a mixture of these two types of knowledge, and so a choice of representation is not hard and fast. Many applications tend to be procedural in nature and so the use of rules has been predominant. Rules have also been favored because of their ease of creation and interpretation.

The particular development tool to be used also has a pronounced effect on the elected knowledge representation model. Ideally, the tool should be decided on after the representation model has been chosen. For a variety of reasons, which we have previously discussed, this is not always the case.

If a high-level programming language is going to be used then, conceivably, any of the four models of knowledge representation discussed in Chapter 3 could be used. Some languages lend themselves to specific representation models such as PROLOG and predicate calculus.

Most expert system shells use the rule as the form of knowledge representation. Some people view this as a limiting factor in the use of a shell, but there is little question about the value and impact that the shells have had. A number of significant expert systems such as COMPASS [Goxal et al 1985] and LITHO [Bonnet and Dahen 1986] have been built with shells, and this will continue to be the case for some time to come. At this point in the evolution of expert system research and development, it is not generally feasible to mix different knowledge representation models in the same expert system. The only exception to this statement has been the organization of the rule-based system into a frame representation so that search techniques can be made more efficient.

Verification. The importance of **verification** cannot be overemphasized. It is the process of ensuring the accuracy of the acquired knowledge that gives creditability to the expert system for its knowledge.

Verification must be performed in a systematic and meticulous fashion; it is a determining factor in communication between the knowledge engineer and the human expert.

As the knowledge is acquired, the knowledge engineer must organize it so that meaning can be derived from it. This derived meaning must be verified with the expert for its accuracy.

Verification is best achieved on a periodic basis. If inaccuracies occur, they can be corrected before they become a major problem.

The verification process also can assist in locating gaps in the knowledge base. It is relatively easy for these gaps to occur, so the knowledge engineer must be sensitive to this potential problem.

Validation. Equally important to the verification process is the **validation** process. Validation is used to check the accuracy of inference chains that may be used on the knowledge base; the question being, Does the expert system give appropriate and correct results?

Validation also is best accomplished at the beginning of the development process and on a periodic basis. In consultation with the expert by submitting test problems for solution, the validation process is most effective. The results should be valid and also consistent.

Validation also can assist in locating gaps in the knowledge base. If the inference chain produces invalid results (or no results at all), then the validation process can assist the knowledge engineer in locating and repairing troublesome spots.

The systematic use of the validation process in the creation of the knowledge base will keep small difficulties from becoming large ones. The end result should produce an expert system that is much more likely to perform to predetermined specifications.

Updating and Maintaining the Knowledge Base

Once created, no knowledge base should be considered static. As new knowledge becomes available, the knowledge base will need to be updated. Further, new problems may be posed to the knowledge base that either use the new knowledge, existing knowledge, or a combination of the two.

The process of adding new knowledge or correcting existing knowledge in the expert system must be carefully monitored to maintain verification and validation standards. Failure to do so may result in a performance level that is less than acceptable.

If a problem is encountered because of the addition to or a change in the knowledge base, the "quick-fix" method, while tempting, may create an even larger problem. The system must be thoroughly tested during the updating process to ensure that changes are implemented without degradation of system performance.

Maintenance of the knowledge base is also an important consideration. No matter how thoroughly the knowledge base has been tested, errors will occur that must be corrected. As new knowledge is added or changed, the system may experience performance degradation that may be caused by a lack of computer memory or resulting inefficiency in the search techniques used on the knowledge base. In a rare situation, the knowledge base may need to be redesigned to correct these complex problems. However, the point is that the knowledge base will always need some maintenance services.

While the knowledge engineer is the one who creates the knowledge base, the responsibility for the updating and maintenance is often delegated to an individual or group of individuals within the organization. This individual or group must be interested in and accept the potential role of maintaining the expert system. As the reins of control pass from the knowledge engineer to others, appropriate and adequate documentation also passes. We will say more about documentation in Chapter 8.

Case Study: WPHELP

To this point, we have concentrated on details and the development of rules for our example expert system. The data to be used by the WPHELP system in making its choice of an appropriate word processing package is to be input by the user during a session with the expert system.

It is also possible to input data to be used by the knowledge base from a database or a spreadsheet. Large volumes of data can be input efficiently without requiring the user's time. We will discuss these possibilities, but we will not attempt to write any rules for WPHELP.

There are several advantages of using a database in conjunction with an expert system. The database can provide to the expert system a great deal of data in a very short period of time. This means that an expert system with many rules can perform its function in a relatively short period of time. In addition, the user is freed from the tedious task of entering large amounts of data; a task that can be very time consuming. Accuracy of data entry is guaranteed with the database; the user may make errors as the number of data entries increases.

The use of the database does not necessarily eliminate the problem of dealing with uncertainty (incomplete or missing data) for the expert system. The database itself may have incomplete or missing data. There also is the problem of updating the database which is especially important in dealing with fast-changing data.

WPHELP might use a database in several ways. First, considerable word processing product information might be contained in the database. This would allow the use of a larger number of rules to better assist in the final product choice. For example, the variable of cost could have a number of values other than low and high.

Spreadsheets can also be effectively utilized with an expert system. The accounting information in a spreadsheet can be used to make financial decisions where a number of calculations are needed as new data becomes available. As with databases, spreadsheets can provide large amounts of data in an efficient manner and free the user from data entry. It also provides the opportunity to use the what-if capability that exists in most expert systems. The what-if facility allows the user to see what would happen if the figures in the spreadsheet were changed. As with databases, spreadsheets also may have incomplete or missing data, but the expert system can deal with this problem.

WPHELP could make use of a spreadsheet in its choice of a word processor. Budget information about the cost of the package and its effect on the business could be stored in the spreadsheet. Also, if the word processing applications for the business need special equipment such as monitors, screens, or printers, the financial effect of the equipment could be analyzed; amortization and depreciation of the equipment as well as employee training costs could be determining factors in the final product choice.

Key Points

- Determining whether a given problem is appropriate for expert system development is a difficult one since there are no established criteria.
- Problems are unique and often complex so that only one or more parts of the problem may be candidates for expert system development.
- While not all expert systems are developed in an organizational setting, those that are must have access to organizational resources.
- For a problem to be a candidate for expert systems development, its solution must be possible, justifiable, and appropriate.
- For a problem to be considered for expert system development:
  - Genuine expertise must exist
  - The problem must involve only cognitive skills

  - The problem cannot be too difficult to solve in terms of time
  - The problem cannot require on-the-job training or common sense to obtain a solution
- To justify expert system development:
  - There must be a need within the organization
  - There must be a recognized and appropriate payoff to the organization
- For expert system development to be appropriate:
  - The problem should require the use of symbolic manipulation and heuristics
  - The problem must not be too difficult to solve
- High-level programming languages are good expert system development tools because they are flexible. However, they require a great deal of programming skill and are generally difficult to use for an inexperienced knowledge engineer.
- Shells as expert systems development tools are easier to use than high-level languages and are appropriate for inexperienced knowledge engineers. However, the shells are less flexible and usually dictate the knowledge representation, the inferencing strategies, and the format of the user interface.
- The choice of an expert system development tool should be based on the following:
  - Developmental constraints
  - Support facilities
  - Reliability
  - Maintainability
  - Problem needs
  - Application needs
- The key tasks for the knowledge engineer in creating a knowledge base are the acquisition and organization of the knowledge.
- A good knowledge engineer must:
  - Have good communication skills
  - Be skilled in the arts of interviewing and listening
  - Be thorough and organized
  - Be able to interpret the acquired knowledge and convert it into the appropriate knowledge representation
  - Acquire adequate background knowledge before consulting with the expert
- The key to the knowledge-acquisition process is the interaction between the knowledge engineer and the human expert.
- The first goal for the knowledge engineer in the interview process is to understand the structure of the expert's thinking.
- Introspective modeling may be very helpful to the knowledge engineer in understanding the expert's thinking process.
- Verbal communication between the human expert and the knowledge engineer must be thorough and meaningful.
- The knowledge engineer must be continually aware of the potential impreciseness of language during verbal communication in the interview process.
- Organizing the knowledge involves decisions about how the knowledge is to be represented, verification of the knowledge, and validation of the inference chain.

■ The processes of updating and maintaining are very important to the continued successful performance of the expert system. These tasks are often performed by someone other than the knowledge engineer so that appropriate and adequate documentation about the expert system must be provided by the knowledge engineer.

Exercises

1. What are the factors involved in determining whether a problem is appropriate for expert systems development?
2. What factors must be considered in the choice of an expert system development tool?
3. What difficulties can occur during the interaction between the human expert and the knowledge engineer?
4. What are the different techniques for acquiring knowledge? Give one advantage and one potential problem with each technique. How could the potential problem be solved or avoided?
5. What is meant by introspective modeling? How does its use aid in the interview process?
6. What is meant by verification of the knowledge base? What is meant by validation of the inference chain? Why are these two tasks important to the expert system?
7. What is meant by the art of listening? Why is listening important to a knowledge engineer?
8. What potential problems are caused by the processes of updating and maintaining the knowledge base? How can these problems be solved?
9. Contrast the use of high-level programming languages and shells as expert system development tools.
10. What factors must be considered in the choice of a development tool? Explain what is meant by each factor.
11. Describe the interaction process between the knowledge engineer and the human expert.

Assignments

1. We have said in the chapter that the knowledge engineer must have good communication skills. It also has been said that college graduates entering the business world must have good communication skills. Are these two sets of communication skills the same? How are they different?

   To assist you in developing your business answer, ask three people in your local business community who have the responsibility of hiring college graduates. Use these opinions to form a consensus of a list of good communication skills. What skills seem to be most important? Why?

After the list of communication skills has been developed, look at the list of courses in your department's curriculum. Where is emphasis placed on the development of each of the skills? Are there skills that seem to be neglected? If so, how might they be included?

2. Talk to a top-level management person at one or more of the local businesses in the community about problems that the business is trying to solve. Make a list of the problems and make a judgment about whether each problem is a candidate for expert systems development. If a problem is not a candidate, why not?
3. Identify at least one problem on your campus that could be solved with the aid of an expert system.
4. Find product descriptions for three expert system development tools that are rule-based. Good sources of information for these descriptions and/or addresses are magazines such as *BYTE, PC AI,* and *AI Expert.* How do the products seem to compare (from the descriptions) to the criteria for selecting a tool? What appear to be the strengths and limitations of each shell? You may choose your desired application. If necessary, write to the company for further information using your school or company letterhead. See also Assignment 4 in Chapter 6 and Assignment 1 in Chapter 8.
5. The purpose of this assignment is to build a small knowledge base using rules. In addition to writing out the rules, show the knowledge base as either a search tree or a left-to-right diagram; the format for both of these illustrations was discussed in Chapter 4. Do not assign certainty factors. Use the criteria specified in the description of each problem. What would be your source of expertise for each problem?
   a. The problem is to find student or personal housing for the next term. Factors to be considered include:
      1) distance from the main classroom building or from your job
      2) type of housing
      3) number of people

   Add any additional factors that you would like to consider.

   b. The problem is to determine what you are going to do for your next vacation. Factors to be considered include:
      1) when
      2) number of days
      3) cost
      4) main activity during the vacation
      5) number of people

   Add any additional factors that you would like to consider.

   c. The problem is to pick an ideal partner for a date. Factors to be considered include:
      1) type of activity
      2) cost
      3) hobbies
      4) personality
      5) likes and dislikes

   Add any additional factors that you wish to consider.

d. The problem is to decide what kind of car to purchase. Factors to be considered include:
   1) gas mileage
   2) mileage from school or work to home
   3) number of possible passengers
   4) cost

   Add any additional factors that you wish to consider.

6. A number of approaches to the interviewing process have been developed. These approaches are often discussed in books on systems analysis and design such as *Systems Analysis and Design* by Wetherbe, (West Publishing Company, 1984) and in journals such as *Audobon Information Management Services, MIS Quarterly,* and *Management and Information*. What are the major techniques? What are the characteristics of each? Could these techniques be used by a knowledge engineer in expert systems development? Why?

6

THE INFERENCE ENGINE

In the previous chapter, we examined in some detail the process of creating the knowledge base. We now wish to turn our attention to issues involved in creating the inference engine. *Our discussion here uses Chapter 4 as the basis and expands on these topics covered therein. Also in this chapter, we will deal with the two areas with which most, if not all, expert systems must deal with: uncertainty and/or inexact reasoning because of the nature of the knowledge in the knowledge base. In this chapter, we will deal with these two areas.*

Uncertainty

Uncertainty can be considered as the lack of adequate information needed to make a decision. Uncertainty is a problem because it may prevent us from making the best decision and, at worst, it can cause us to make a bad decision. In the business world, uncertainty may mean financial loss or less than appropriate profit.

As human beings, we have become experts, at least to some extent, in dealing with uncertainty. If we could not do so, we would not survive. For example, we are confronted with uncertainty about job, school, weather, traffic, and so on. We become experts at maximizing our performance, how to select easy classes, what to do if the weather is inclement, and how to drive under adverse traffic conditions. In order to deal with uncertainty, we must reason under uncertainty.

Recall our discussion in Chapter 4 of methods of reasoning. The **deductive** method of reasoning is also referred to as **exact reasoning** because it deals with exact facts and exact conclusions. Some expert system applications permit the use of exact reasoning, and it is relatively easy to find the best conclusion.

Unfortunately, when some of the data are not exact, the problem of finding the best conclusion becomes more complex. The number of possible conclusions increases and the additional task of determining which conclusion is best arises. Several methods for dealing with this task have been developed, and it is up to the expert system designer to determine which method is appropriate for the given application.

Sources of Uncertainty

There are a number of reasons why the knowledge which we have at hand may seem uncertain to us. Sometimes the sources of uncertainty can be easily eliminated, but many times they cannot be resolved and so we must live with them. Clearly, we want our expert system to be able to deal as effectively as possible with uncertainty; this feature must be taken into account in the design of the inference engine.

Sources of errors that create uncertainty in knowledge can be classified as follows [Giarratano and Riley 1989]:

1. Ambiguity
2. Incompleteness
3. Incorrectness
4. Measurement
5. Systematic
6. Random
7. Reasoning

Ambiguity errors occur when a statement can be interpreted in more than one way. For example, the statement *Sell the bad stock* is ambiguous. Which company's stock should be sold?

The **incompleteness** errors occur when some piece of knowledge is missing. The statement *Turn the valve* is incomplete. Which way should the valve be turned?

Errors of **incorrectness** occur when some piece of knowledge is wrong. This could be caused by human error or equipment malfunction. It also could occur in the case of a hypothesis which is an assertion about something or the consequent of a rule. An example of a hypothesis is: This key will open the door. One type of incorrect knowledge is called *false positive* which means accepting a hypothesis which is not true. There is also the case of *false negative* which means rejecting a hypothesis which is true. From our example, if the key will not really open the door, then accepting the hypothesis gives a false positive error (known to statisticians as a *Type I error*). On the other hand, if the key will really open the door, then rejecting the hypothesis gives a false negative error (known to statisticians as a *Type II error*).

Errors of **measurement** occur when a numerical fact is reported about a person or object. These errors are caused by mistakes in precision and accuracy. Although the terms precision and accuracy sometimes are carelessly used interchangeably, they are quite different. For example, suppose we wish to measure a person's height. We could do it with a centimeter rule or a meter ruler. Since it is quite unlikely that the person's actual height falls exactly in a gradation mark on either ruler, we would have to estimate the height based on visual inspection of the two rulers. Our estimation would be more precise with the centimeter ruler because the distance between gradations is less, making it easier to estimate. Accuracy would come into play if we used two centimeter rulers where the gradations on one ruler were marked incorrectly. Hence, one ruler (correctly marked) would be more accurate than the other ruler (incorrectly marked).

Systematic errors are errors that are made consistently. For example, if we use an incorrectly marked centimeter ruler, we will always get an inaccurate measurement.

Random errors sometimes occur when electrical equipment is used to give, say, a measurement, and the equipment is not reliable. That is, sometimes the equipment gives the correct reading and sometimes it doesn't; we never really know.

Finally, errors can occur in the **reasoning** process. These errors can be inductive or abductive; these two forms of reasoning were introduced in Chapter 4.

Recall that induction reasons from the specific to the general case. For example,

> We have never had a customer complaint about our service.
>
> Therefore, we will never have a customer complaint about our service.

We really would not be very confident that there will never be a complaint about our service since it is likely that eventually there will be someone who will complain. There is a good likelihood of error if we accept our conclusion.

Consider another example.

> The car will not start.
>
> Therefore, the battery is dead.

We would have little confidence in this conclusion. But, suppose we had more information.

> The car will not start.
>
> The headlights will not come on.
>
> Therefore, the battery is dead.

Now we would have more confidence in our conclusion but still could not be completely sure that the battery is dead.

The point is that the addition of more specifics raises our level of confidence in the conclusion.

Human experts tend to make use of inductive processes in making their judgments. They have the capability of altering their conclusions as new knowledge becomes known to them. Human experts are usually quite good at this process; if they were not, they would not be experts for long! However, human experts are not infallible, and they can and do make errors.

At this point in time, it is extremely difficult to program a computer to use inductive processes. Hence, most current expert systems are not able to generate new conclusions on their own; new conclusions must still be preprogrammed.

Errors als can occur in the abductive process. Recall that abduction uses the form of reasoning

p implies q

q

therefore p

This type of reasoning is illustrated by this example:

If the battery is dead, then the car will not start.

The car will not start.

Therefore, the battery is dead.

We know that there may be many reasons for the car not starting. So our confidence in the conclusion would not be very great.

While abductive reasoning has a good possibility of error, it is nevertheless useful in diagnostic expert systems. It must be used carefully, however.

Uncertainty and Rules

Since most expert systems are rule-based, it is appropriate to examine in greater detail the effect of **uncertainty** on the rules in the expert system. Giarratano and Riley [1989] note that there are three basic areas of uncertainty pertaining to rules, and these are illustrated in Figure 6.1.

Uncertainty can occur in individual rules. Recall that a rule is made up of an *antecedent* (IF part) and a *consequent* (THEN part). As we discussed in the last section, there are various different sources of errors that can occur either in the antecedent and/or the consequent. Reasoning errors can occur in the rule as a whole. Uncertainty factors can affect the evidence in both the antecedent and the consequent. Finally, there is uncertainty involved in determining how the knowledge should be combined in the antecedent. Should AND be used exclusively? Should OR be used exclusively? Should there be a combination of AND and OR? These decisions must be made by the knowledge engineer as the rules are formulated.

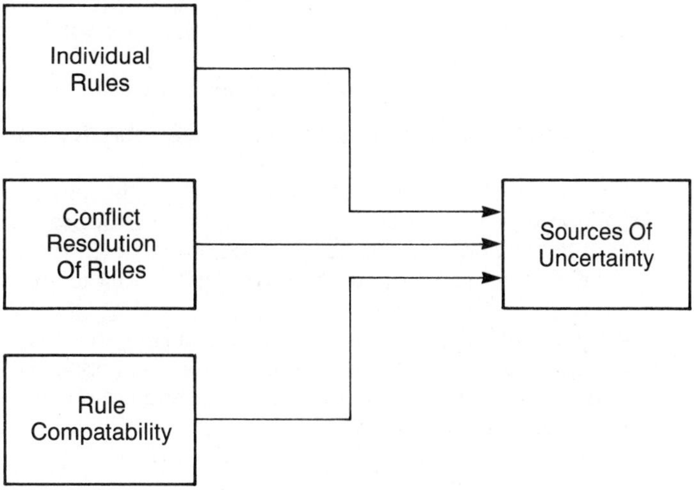

FIGURE 6.1 SOURCES OF UNCERTAINTY IN RULES

As the knowledge engineer formulates the individual rules, each rule must be verified for correctness. At this point, the knowledge engineer tries to minimize the inherent uncertainties described above.

Even if each individual rule can be verified, there is no guarantee that the inference chain will give valid results. Uncertainties exist as inference chains are formulated. These uncertainties involve situations where there is conflict between rules or when rules are found to be incompatible. *Conflict resolution* is used to deal with conflicts between rules and is also a source of uncertainty.

The knowledge engineer may establish an *explicit* priority which determines the order in which rules are executed or fired. A problem can occur if the established priorities are not optimal or even correct.

Implicit rule priority can also be a problem. If the antecedents of two rules are both satisfied simultaneously, the inference engine must decide which rule is to be fired first; strategies such as specificity (number of conditions, more conditions implies more specificity) of the antecedents or order in which the rules were entered are possible resolutions of the conflict. In the case of antecedent specificity, consider an example:

Rule 1: IF there is a fire, THEN use a fire extinguisher.

Rule 2: IF there is a fire and it is burning grease, THEN use the fire extinguisher.

In this case, Rule 2 is more specific in its antecedent than Rule 1; so Rule 2 would fire first. This order assumes that it is known that there is a fire and that it is from burning grease. If it is only known that there is a fire, then Rule 1 would be fired. We will discuss conflict resolution in greater detail later in this chapter.

Incompatibility of rules is also a source of uncertainty. This can occur, for example, if two rules exist that are contradictory. Suppose we have these rules:

Rule 3: IF there is a fire on the assembly line, throw water on it.

Rule 4: IF there is a fire on the assembly line, don't throw water on it.

These two rules are obviously contradictory. But, closer inspection indicates that the action depends on the type of fire. Water is appropriate for extinguishing one type of fire but not appropriate for other types of fires. If the antecedent were more specific such as in Rule 2 above, then the contradiction would not exist.

Rule incompatibility and rule conflict resolution are much more of a problem with large knowledge bases where there are a great number of rules. Careful testing by the knowledge engineer to validate the inference chains is necessary to minimize as much uncertainty as possible.

Dealing with Uncertainty

Over the years, there have been a number of methods developed for dealing with uncertainty in some quantifiable way. There is no general consensus among AI researchers as to which method is best since it depends on the class of applications being developed. All agree that uncertainty cannot be ignored.

It appears that *classical probability theory* is the best way to deal with uncertainty, and there is a group of people who subscribe to its use. When classical probability is used, a formula known as *Baye's Theorem* is often used. If it were applied to a medical diagnosis situation, it would be done as follows:

P(D given S) = [P(S given D) P(D)]/P(S)

where

D is the disease.

S is the set of symptoms exhibited by the patient.

P(D given S) is the probability that the patient has the disease D, given that the patient has symptoms S.

P(S given D) is the probability that the patient will exhibit symptoms S, given that disease D is present.

P(D) is the prior probability that the patient has the disease D before any symptoms S are known.

P(S) is the prior probability that the patient has the symptoms S before the disease D is known.

If all of these probabilities were known on the right side of the equals sign, then it would be quite easy to calculate P(D given S). However, in reality it usually would be impossible to obtain the needed probabilities in this medical situation, so Baye's Theorem is of little or no use. While classical probability theory is not useful in a medical diagnosis expert system, for example, it has been successfully used in a geological expert system called PROSPECTOR.

Another major problem with the use of classical probability in the medical diagnosis expert system was discovered by the developers of MYCIN. They found that, while physicians were quite willing to assign a probability to a patient's having a disease, they were not willing to assign a probability to the patient's not having the disease.

Let's examine this point in more detail. In classical probability,

P(event will occur) +

P(event will not occur) = 1

For example, if we roll a single die,

P(rolling a five) = 1/6

P(not rolling a five) = 5/6

(We could get a one, two, three, four, or six.) The sum of the two probabilities is 1.

P(five) + P(not a five) = 1

It then follows that

P(five) = 1 − P(not a five)

In the MYCIN situation, the physicians (experts) were willing to say that given a particular set of symptoms, the probability that the patient had a particular disease was, for example, 0.8. They were not willing to say that given the same symptoms, the probability that the patient did not have the disease was 0.2.

What the MYCIN knowledge engineers found was that the judgments of the experts were based on belief and disbelief. From these findings, the MYCIN group developed the notion of certainty factors and made use of them in MYCIN [Giarratano and Riley 1989, Buchanan and Shortliffe 1985]. A number of expert systems and expert system shells have made use of the certainty factor structure used in MYCIN, and others have used variations on the MYCIN model.

Certainty Factors

MYCIN knowledge engineers developed the **certainty factor** as a way of combining a measure of belief with a measure of disbelief relative to a given hypothesis H and observable evidence E. The certainty factor was originally defined as

$$CF\ (H,E) = mB\ (H,E) - mD\ (H,E)$$

where

CF (H,E) is the certainty factor for the hypothesis H with evidence E.

mB (H,E) is the measure of belief in H given E.

mD (H,E) is the measure of disbelief in H given E.

In the MYCIN model, mB and mD were defined as probabilities that were assigned by the physicians (experts) and so the values of both mB and mD could range between 0 and 1. Hence, the value for the certainty factor could range between 1 ($mB=1$ and $mD=0$) and -1 ($mB=0$ and $mD=-1$).

A positive certainty factor ($mB > mD$) means that the given evidence supports the hypothesis. On the other hand a negative certainty factor ($mB < mD$) indicates that the evidence does not support the hypothesis. If there is a zero value for the certainty factor, then one of two situations has arisen. Either both mB and mD are 0 (there is no evidence) or mB and mD have the same nonzero value (the belief is canceled out by the disbelief).

The original MYCIN definition of the certainty factor presented some interesting difficulties. A piece of disconfirming evidence (mD) could have a drastic effect on the certainty factor for a particular hypothesis. For example, suppose that $mB = 0.85$ and $mD = 0.60$. Part of the MYCIN method involved the setting of a *threshold (minimum) value* for the firing of a rule. In order for a rule to be fired, the certainty factor of the hypothesis had to exceed the threshold value. Suppose that the threshold value was 0.25. The rule in our example would not be fired since the certainty factor was not greater than the threshold value.

To lessen the possible effect of such a situation, the MYCIN definition was changed in 1977 to

$$CF\ (H,E) = (mB-mD)/(1-\min[mB,MD])$$

In our, previous example, the effect of the change in the definition can be readily seen. Under the original definition, the certainty factor was calculated to be $0.85-0.60=0.25$. Under the new definition, the certainty factor would be

$$\begin{aligned} CF &= (0.85-0.60)/(1-\min[0.85,0.60]) \\ &= 0.25/0.40 \\ &= 0.625 \end{aligned}$$

The new definition thus softened the effect of a piece of disconfirming evidence.

Since the certainty factor concept was developed, a number of expert systems and expert system shells have adopted a variety of conventions for representing certainty factors as numbers. For example, VP-Expert has confidence (certainty) factors (CNF) that range from 0 to 100. These numbers represent percentages as a measure of confidence (belief) with 100 representing 100% confidence (total belief) equivalent to the MYCIN certainty factor of 1. The confidence factor of 0 represents 0% confidence (total disbelief), which is equivalent to the MYCIN certainty factor of -1. Thus, a CNF of 65 means that a confidence of 65% has been assigned. Another expert system shell, EXSYS, has three different schemes for representing certainty factors: -100 to 100, 0 to 10 and 0 to 1. In both VP-Expert and EXSYS, the initial values are assigned subjectively by the expert or the knowledge engineer.

The MYCIN knowledge engineers also noted that there was an extension to the definition. Given the rule

IF E THEN H

then

CF (H,E) = CF (E) CF (H)

where

CF (H,E) is the certainty factor of the hypothesis H given the evidence E.

CF (E) is the certainty factor of the evidence E.

CF (H) is the certainty factor of the hypothesis H.

If the evidence is certain (CF=1), then CF (H,E) = CF (H), which is intuitively what we think should be the case. For example, if we have the rule

IF E THEN H (CF = 0.75)

then

CF (H,E) = 0.75

Note that if no certainty factor is specified for E, it is assumed that CF (E) = 1. The same assumption is also made for H; in our example, CF (H) was specified to be 0.75.

As we have mentioned in Chapter 4, both the antecedent and the consequent of a rule have certainty factors associated with them. The certainty factors may or may not be specified; if they are not specified, then they are assumed to be one.

So far, we have looked only at certainty factors as they apply to the consequent (hypothesis) of a rule. The MYCIN model also considers certainty factors applied to antecedents. We have two possible situations, either there is a single piece of evidence in the antecedent, or there are multiple pieces of evidence whose certainty factors must be combined.

Consider, first, the situation where there is a single piece of evidence in the antecedent.

What is the effect if we have uncertain evidence (CF < 1)? What could be said about the certainty of H?

The MYCIN model solved this problem by using the relation

$$CF(H,e) = CF(H,E)\ CF(E,e)$$

where

CF(H,e) is the certainty factor of the hypothesis based on uncertain evidence e.

CF(H,E) is the certainty factor of the hypothesis based on the evidence E.

CF(E,e) is the certainty factor of the evidence E.

For example, IF

$CF(H,E) = 0.8$ and $CF(E,e) = 0.5$, we have

$$CF(H,e) = 0.8 * 0.5$$
$$= 0.4$$

From an intuitive point of view, the result should not seem surprising. If we are less than certain about the evidence, then we should be less confident about the certainty of the hypothesis which was originally based on certain evidence.

Now consider the situation where there are several pieces of evidence in the antecedent. These pieces of evidence are connected by ANDs, ORs, NOTs, or some combination thereof.

In the MYCIN model, when several pieces of evidence are connected by the logical operator AND, the final certainty factor of the antecedent is the minimum of the set of certainty factors contained in the antecedent. For example, the rule

IF E1 and E2 and E3 THEN H

has the pieces of evidence in the antecedent: E1, E2 and E3. If $CF(E1)=0.6$, $CF(E2)=0.7$, and $CF(E3)=0.5$, then the certainty factor of the antecedent is

$$\min\ [CF(E1),\ CF(E2),\ CF(E3)]$$

or 0.5. If $CF(H) = 0.9$ then the adjusted certainty factor for H is

$$0.5 * 0.9 = 0.45$$

which follows from our earlier discussion.

The logical operator OR operates in a similar fashion to the AND operator but uses the maximum value of the set of certainty factors in the antecedent. Consider the rule

IF E1 or E2 or E3 THEN H.

The certainty factor of the antecedent is given by

max [CF(E1),CF(E2),CF(E3)]

If CF (E1) = 0.3, CF (E2) = 0.6, and CF (E3) = 0.5, then the certainty factor of the antecedent is 0.6. As before if CF (H) = 0.7, then the adjusted factor for H is given by

0.6 * 0.7 = 0.42

In the case of the NOT logical operator, the certainty factor of the negative of a piece of evidence is the negative of the certainty factor. For example, if CF (E) = 0.6, then CF (not E) = -0.6.

The logical operators can be combined in the MYCIN model. Suppose we have the rule

IF (E1 and E2) or (E3 and not E4) THEN H.

The certainty factor of the antecedent would be given by

max [min [CF(E1)], CF(E2)], [min [CF(E3), -CF(E4)]]

If we have

CF (E1) = 0.4	CF (E3) = 0.5
CF (E2) = 0.7	CF (E4) = 0.6

then the certainty factor for the antecedent is given by

max [min [0.4, 0.7], min[0.5, -0.6]]
= 0.4

If CF (H) = 0.8 then the adjusted factor for H is given by

0.4 * 0.8 = 0.32

As with the range of certainty factor values, not all expert systems and expert system shells use the same techniques for calculating certainty factors as does the MYCIN model. The techniques used by other systems are similar but have some variances.

For example, VP-Expert, an expert system shell, assigns a confidence factor (CNF) to a rule in the same way as MYCIN. That is, for the rule

IF E THEN H

the confidence factor is given by

CNF(H,E) = CNF(E)CNF(H)

While confidence factors are entered in VP-Expert as whole numbers, the system converts them to decimal form for purposes of calculation.

VP-Expert also uses the MYCIN technique for dealing with multiple pieces of evidence in the antecedent where AND is used. For example, the confidence factor for the antecedent in the rule

IF E1 AND E2 AND E3 THEN H

would be calculated as

min [CNF(E1),CNF(E2),CNF(E3)]

VP-Expert uses a different technique than MYCIN for calculating the confidence factor of an antecedent that makes use of the logical operator OR. For the rule,

IF E1 OR E2 THEN H

V-Expert uses the formula

CNF(E1) + CNF(E2)-[CNF(E1) * CNF(E2)]

For example, if CNF (E1) = 70 and CNF (E2) = 60, a confidence factor of 88 would be assigned to the antecedent.

$$0.70 + 0.60 - [(0.70) * (0.60)]$$

$$= 1.30 - 0.42$$

$$= 0.88$$

Recall that the CNF of 88 means 88% confidence or 0.88 confidence.

VP-Expert also treats the combination of the operators AND and OR in the antecedent. For example, in the rule

IF E1 OR E2 AND E3 THEN H

VP-Expert separates the antecedent into two statements for purposes of calculating the CNF. The antecedent

E1 OR E2 AND E3

is treated as

E1 AND E3 OR E2 AND E3

This expression would be translated to

min[CNF(E1),CNF(E3)]

OR

min[CNF(E2),CNF(E3)]

If CNF1 = min[CNF(E1), CNF(E3)] and CNF2 = min[CNF(E2), CNF(E3)], then the expression becomes

CNF1 OR CNF2

which becomes

CNF1 + CNF2 − [CNF1*CNF2]

For example, suppose

CNF(E1) = 40, CNF(E2) = 50 and CNF(E3) = 60

then the antecedent

E1 OR E2 AND E3

becomes

min[0.40,0.60]

OR

min[0.50,0.60]

= 0.40 OR 0.50

= 0.40+0.50-[(0.40)(0.50)]

= 0.90-0.20

= 0.70

Recall that the confidence factors for VP-Expert range between 0 and 100. Hence, VP-Expert does not support the NOT logical operator since using it would require the use of a negative number as a confidence factor.

Resolving Rule Conflicts

Earlier in the chapter, we briefly mentioned that rule conflict had a certain amount of uncertainty associated with it. We now want to examine this problem in greater detail.

One of the responsibilities of the inference engine is to resolve conflicts between rules. Some sort of priority system must be present so that rules can fire in some order for purposes of execution; a conflict resolution scheme is critical since only one rule can fire at a time.

A number of **conflict resolvant techniques** have been developed. All expert systems and expert systems shells use one or more such techniques in the inference engine. Conflict resolution can be classified as shown in Figure 6.2.

Priority	Description
Explicit	Priority Assigned By The Expert Or Knowledge Engineer
Implicit	Priority Assigned By The Inference Engine

FIGURE 6.2 CLASSIFICATION OF PRIORITIES FOR RULES

Rules may be fired in the order set by explicit priorities. These priorities are attached to the rule and are assigned by the expert or knowledge engineer. This priority technique works best for smaller expert systems. It is relatively inflexible to changes in the knowledge base since the priorities are static.

Implicit priority techniques are more flexible, especially when more than one technique is employed in the expert system. If the first technique used does not resolve the conflict, then a second technique is employed and so on.

There are a number of implicit techniques that have been used. Among others are the following:

1. The use of certainty factors associated with the rules
2. The specificity of the rules' antecedents
3. The order in which rules were entered into the knowledge base
4. The order of rules in the knowledge base
5. The recency of fact entry into the knowledge base

The idea behind the use of certainty factors is that the rule with the higher certainty factor should be fired first. Recall that the certainty factor of the rule is calculated by multiplying the certainty factors of the antecedent (evidence) and the consequent (hypothesis). For example, suppose we have the following rules:

Rule 1: IF E1 (CF=0.8) THEN H1 (CF=0.9).

Rule 2: IF E2 (C1F=0.95) THEN H2 (CF=0.75).

The certainty factor for Rule 1 is

$$(0.8)(0.9) = 0.72$$

The certainty factor for Rule 2 is

$$(0.95)(0.75) = 0.76$$

So, Rule 2 would be fired first.

A second technique considers the specificity of the rules' antecedents. For instance, recall an earlier example:

Rule 3: IF the car will not start,
THEN the battery is dead.

Rule 4: IF the car will not start
AND the headlights will not work,
THEN the battery is dead.

If we know that the car will not start and the headlights will not work, then Rule 4 would be fired since its antecedent is more specific than that of Rule 3. If it is known only that the car will not start, then Rule 3 would be fired first.

The order in which the rules were entered into the knowledge base is a third conflict resolution technique. When the rule is entered into the knowledge base, it is marked with a timestamp or some other indicator. If there is a conflict, the rule that had been entered first would be given priority.

A fourth technique is to use the current order of the rules in the knowledge base. This technique differs from the previous one in that a new rule may be inserted between two other existing rules. This technique is the simplest one to implement because it requires no additional overhead from the inference engine such as calculation or reading of some indicator of entry order. With some of the previous techniques, a second conflict resolution technique may be needed, as in the case where two rules in conflict have the same certainty factors.

A final technique for our discussion is to use the recency of data entry into the knowledge base as a way of resolving rule conflicts. For example, if data used in the antecedent of Rule 5 was entered at 12:30 p.m. today and Rule 6's antecedent date was entered yesterday, then Rule 5 would fire before Rule 6. This technique is most often used in applications that are real-time where facts in the knowledge base are continually updated.

Case Study: WPHELP

One of the features of an expert system is its capability to deal with uncertainty. Many expert systems make use of certainty factors to perform this task. The certainty factors are initially assigned by the knowledge engineer and/or a human expert and represent a quantitative degree of belief (confidence) in a rule. How can we incorporate certainty factors into WPHELP? In the choice of a word processor, we must consider our confidence about the vendor who has produced the package we are considering. Some of the questions that should be considered, might be:

1. Does the vendor have a record of longevity in software development?
2. What kind of support does the vendor provide after the package has been purchased?
3. What is the quality of the documentation provided with the package?
4. What is the reaction of users of the package? Are they satisfied?

If we are very confident that the response to each question will be positive, then we might assign a high certainty factor (such as 95% or even 100%) to the choice of that package. If we are very confident in the positive response to three of the questions but somewhat uneasy about the other question, we might assign a certainty factor of 80% to the choice of the package. This certainty factor could be lower if we are uneasy about the response to a question that we consider to be much more important than the others. For example, the opinions of others who have used the package might be much more important to us.

If it seems to you that there is a lot of subjectivity involved in the assignment of certainty factors, then you have a good perspective of how difficult the process can be. It is very difficult to be totally objective. The use of subjectivity is common among human experts, but their subjectivity has been tempered by past experience. That is why they are called "experts."

Now, let's consider how certainty factors can be assigned to the antecedents of the rule. Recall (from the Case Study in Chapter 3) that functionality was described as simple or complex and that cost was described as low or high. Clearly, these descriptors can have different meanings. At what point does functionality change from simple to complex or cost from low to high? Also, a complex function to one person may be simple to someone else and vice versa. These perceptions can be reflected with certainty factors. If the functionality level of a task is somewhere between simple and complex, this can be reflected in the certainty factor. If we feel that the tasks will be more simple than complex, then we might assign a certainty factor of 40% to complex. But, it would not necessarily follow that we should assign a certainty factor of 60% to simple.

We might establish a minimum level (threshold) of acceptability for our certainty factor. That is, we may say that if we are less than 50% confident in the choice of a particular vendor, then the vendor will not be considered. This could also be true for our declaration of, say cost, where, if we are less than 50% confident that the cost is high, then we would use the value of low. This choice can affect the rules that we will finally consider because only rules with low as a value for cost would be considered.

In Module 6, we will look at some examples of the effects of certainty factors on rules, both individually and collectively. Mathematical calculations for the combining of certainty factors will also be explored.

Key Points

- Uncertainty can be considered as the lack of adequate information needed to make a decision.
- Deductive reasoning is referred to as exact reasoning.
- When facts are not exact, the number of possible conclusions increases causing a new problem, that of determining which conclusion is best.
- There are several sources of errors that cause uncertainty including:
  - Ambiguity
  - Incompleteness
  - Incorrectness
  - Measurement
  - Systematic
  - Random
  - Reasoning
- Uncertainty can occur in individual rules, the conflict resolution techniques used, or when rules are found to be incompatible.
- In individual rules, errors can occur in the antecedent and/or the consequent of the rule as well as in the rule as a whole.
  - The likelihood of both the antecedent and the consequent must be considered.
  - Techniques for combining the evidence (where more than one piece of evidence is available) can have an effect on the rule.
- Conflict resolution is used to determine the order in which rules are fired (executed).
- Conflict resolution strategies may be explicit (priorities assigned by the knowledge engineer) or implicit (priorities assigned by the inference engine using some algorithm).
- Rule incompatibility occurs when two rules have the same antecedent but have conflicting consequents.
- Rule incompatibility and rule conflict resolution are much more of a problem with large knowledge bases that have a great number of rules.
- A number of methods have been developed over the years to deal with uncertainty in a quantifiable way, but there is no general agreement among researchers as to which method is best.
- Classical probability theory has been used successfully in the PROSPECTOR expert system but could not be used in the MYCIN system.
- Certainty factors were developed by the MYCIN knowledge engineers to deal with the notions of belief and disbelief.
- The original MYCIN definition of the certainty factor for a given hypothesis H and give evidence E used the difference of the measure of belief (mB) and the measure of disbelief (mD).
- The MYCIN measures mB and mD were probability numbers assigned by the physicians (experts). Hence the certainty factor value could range between -1 and 1.
- A single piece of disconfirming evidence could have a significant effect on the certainty factor value. The MYCIN definition was changed in 1977 to soften the effect of the disconfirming evidence. The difference (mB - mD) was then divided by 1-min[mB,mD].

- A number of expert systems and expert system shells have adapted the MYCIN model for the certainty factor or have made variations in the definition.
- In the MYCIN model
  - The certainty factor of the hypothesis H given the evidence E is the same as the product of the certainty factors of E and H.
  - If the evidence is uncertain ($CF < 1$), then the certainty factor of the hypothesis is affected; the certainty factor of the hypothesis is now the product of the certainty factor of the antecedent and the original certainty factor of the hypothesis (conclusion). If no certainty factor is specified, it is assumed to be 1.
  - The value of the certainty factor of an antecedent, containing more than one piece of evidence connected by the AND logical operator, is the minimum of the set of the certainty factors of the pieces of evidence. If the pieces of evidence are connected by the OR logical operator, the certainty factor of the antecedent is the maximum value of the set of the certainty factors of the pieces of evidence.
  - The certainty factor of the negation of a hypothesis is the negative of the certainty factor of the hypothesis.
- VP-Expert is an example of an expert system shell that uses a different range of possible certainty factors than MYCIN. The calculation techniques for VP-Expert differ from MYCIN with respect to the OR and NOT logical operators and the combining of evidence in the antecedent where both the AND and OR logical operators are used.
- Rule conflict resolution techniques may be classified either as explicit or implicit.
- Explicit conflict resolution techniques use priorities that are established by the expert or the knowledge engineer while implicit conflict resolution techniques are established by the inference engine.
- Among others, implicit conflict resolution techniques include:
  - The use of certainty factors associated with the rules.
  - The specificity of the rules' antecedents.
  - The order in which rules were entered into the knowledge base.
  - The order of the rules in the knowledge base.
  - The recency of fact entry into the knowledge base.

Exercises

1. What is uncertainty?
2. What are the major sources of errors that cause uncertainty? Give an example of each.
3. What are the sources of uncertainty in individual rules?
4. What is the role of verification and validation pertaining to individual rules?
5. Why is there a need for conflict resolution between rules?
6. Contrast explicit and implicit rule conflict resolution.
7. Why is rule compatibility a source of uncertainty?
8. What were the major problems in the use of classical probability in the MYCIN expert system?
9. How were certainty factors originally defined in the MYCIN model?
10. How and why was the MYCIN definition of certainty factor changed in 1977?
11. How does VP-Expert define and use the certainty factor?

12. Using the MYCIN method, calculate the certainty factor for the hypothesis in each of the following rules.
    a. IF E (CF = 0.7) THEN H ______________
    b. IF E1 (CF = 0.4)
       AND E2 (CF = 0.75)
       AND E3 (CF = 0.70)
       THEN H ______________
    c. IF E1 (CF = 0.95)
       OR E2 (CF = 0.68)
       THEN H (CF = 0.75) ______________
    d. IF E (CF = 0.75)
       THEN H (CF = 0.9) ______________
    e. IF E1 (CF = 0.85)
       AND E2 (CF =0.65)
       OR E3 (CF = 0.75)
       THEN H (CF = 0.85) ______________
    f. IF E1 (CF = 0.65)
       AND NOT E2 (CF = 0.8)
       THEN H (CF = 0.40) ______________
13. Repeat Exercise 12 using the VP-Expert method, if possible.
14. Name and describe five implicit rule conflict resolution techniques.

Assignments

1. Consider the small investment expert system from Assignment 2 of Chapter 4.
   a. Describe, by tracing the execution of the rules, how forward and backward chaining would be used on the knowledge base. Assume that the order of the rules in the knowledge base is the order in which the rules would be checked.
   b. Repeat part (a) but with the order of the rules reversed. What differences, if any, do you find in the chaining processes?
2. In the investment expert system of Assignment 2 in Chapter 4, the measure of what is adequate insurance is rather vague. We can use certainty factors to help better define the levels of adequate. Consider the figures below.

Insurance Amount	CF
10,000–20,000	0.30
20,000–30,000	0.60
over 30,000	0.90

We can also apply certainty factors to the ratio of the take-home pay and savings. Consider the figures below.

Status	Savings-to-Pay-Ratio	CF
Single	4.00 to 5.00	0.30
	5.00 to 6.00	0.60
	over 6.00	0.90
Married	6.00 to 7.00	0.30
	7.00 to 8.00	0.60
	over 8.00	0.90

a. Assume the certainty factors for both married and single are 1.0. For each of the following sets of initial conditions, calculate the final certainty factor to invest using the inference chain for the knowledge base.

Set 1

Married
$25,000 insurance
$10,000 savings
$1500 monthly take home pay

Set 2

Single
$15,000 insurance
$20,000 savings
$4,000 monthly take home pay

Set 3

Married
$100,000 insurance
$50,000 savings
$5,000 monthly take-home pay

b. Repeat part (a) using the VP-Expert method.
c. Compare the results of your work in parts (a) and (b).

3. In Assignment 4 of Chapter 5, you were asked to investigate the characteristics of three expert system shells. Now, let's look in greater detail at the operation of the inference engine.
   a. How does the inference engine in each shell deal with uncertainty?
   b. How does each shell deal with rule conflicts?
4. In Assignment 5 of Chapter 5, you were asked to develop a small knowledge base to solve the given problem in each part. You were also asked to identify the source(s) of expertise that you used. Using your source(s), assign certainty factors to the rules in each knowledge base. (See also Assignment 1 in Chapter 8.)

7

THE USER INTERFACE

As we have previously mentioned, an expert system is composed of three basic parts: a knowledge base (rules and facts), an inference engine (reasoning mechanism), and a user interface. The user interface is the total communications medium between the participant and the expert system. This user interface could be typing answers to questions displayed on a computer screen or selecting icons (symbols) by touching a touch-sensitive screen with your finger. The user interface includes the entire communications scheme between the user and the expert system. This communication system includes the design of the computer screen, the use of external input/output devices, and the schema by which information flows between the user and the expert system. In this chapter we will present an overview explaining how useful interfaces are formed, exploring various types, providing guidelines for effective user interfaces, and finally, we will consider a user interface for the WPHELP expert system.

Overview of the User Interface

The **user interface** is the lifeline of an expert system. Just as a well-manufactured product is not useful or profitable without good marketing, a good expert system is not effective without an appropriate user interface. The user interface can determine whether an expert system is accepted and utilized by a given population. A microcomputer system that no one uses is worthless. Hence, to reap the benefits from a well designed and informative expert system, the user interface must be conducive to the easy and timely use of the expert system by the intended audience.

The user interface is the total communications channel between the participant and the expert system. If an expert system is perceived as a circle, then the *atmosphere* surrounding the circle is the user interface as shown in Figure 7.1.

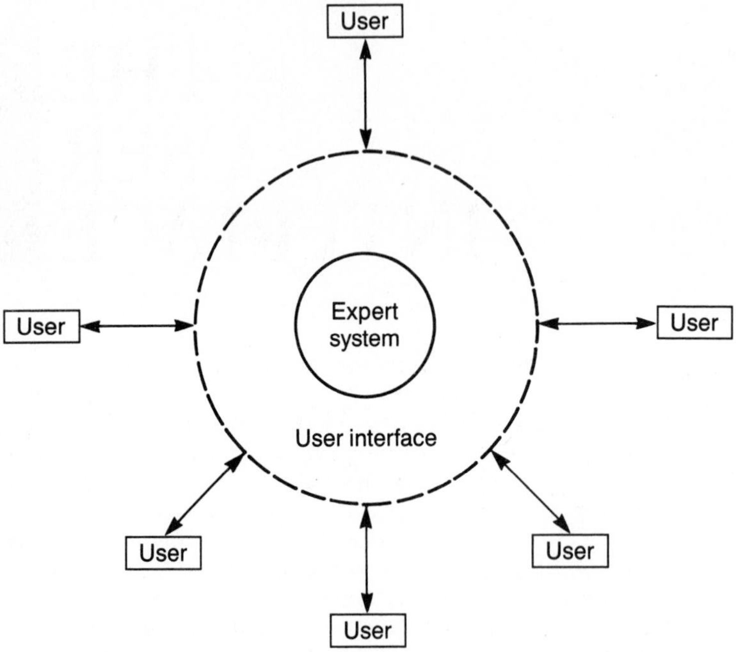

FIGURE 7.1 USER INTERFACE AS AN ATMOSPHERE

If the atmosphere is appropriate for the intended audience, then the users will be able to communicate effectively with the expert system. If the information doesn't flow through the atmosphere between the user and the expert system, then the system fails. This communication is considered to be not only the physical method of sending and receiving information from the expert system, but also the perceptual and psychological media. Just as water is composed of hydrogen and oxygen, the user interface is composed of physical, perceptual, and psychological components. The user's perceptual image of the system is critical to the overall success of the system. If the tasks, functionality, and benefits are not readily understood by the user, then the system will not be optimal. Moreover, from a psychological point of view, if the user perceives the system as confusing because of lack of proper instructions or thinks the system is hostile because of terse error messages or feedback, then the user interface is inadequate. A poorly designed user interface can cause an expensive and well-thought out expert system to fail.

Formation of the User Interface: Screen Design and Input Devices

User interfaces are man-made from three sources: the designer model, the user model, and the system model. A **model** is another name for image, schema, or configuration. You can think of a model as being a set of eyeglasses through which an image or schema of an object, event, or person is formed, as illustrated in Figure 7.2.

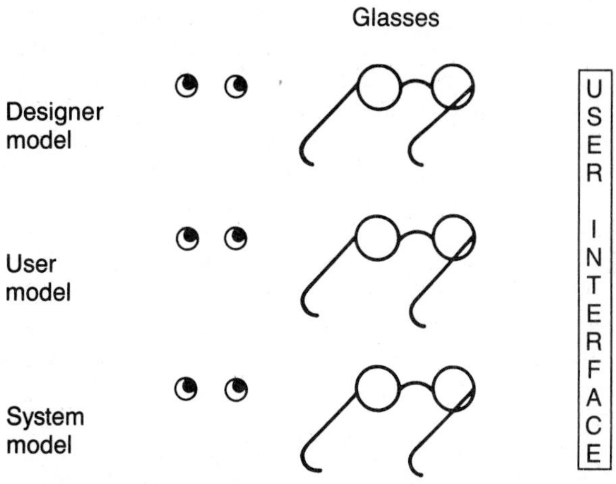

FIGURE 7.2 THREE MODELS (EYEGLASSES) FOR BUILDING A USER INTERFACE

Hence, the three models that help to build a user interface are like three sets of eyeglasses, one from the system designer, one from an individual user, and one from all users of an expert system. The **designer model** includes the view of the person(s) who are designing, writing, and implementing the system. If the designers are a team of content experts, knowledge engineers, programmers, and users, then the designer model is their composite view and understanding of the system. As the system is being formulated, this model can vary from team member to team member. If the designer is one person, then the designer model is that one person's mental configuration of the expert system. The second building block, **the user model**, is a single individual's view of the system. This model can change from user to user. The third building block, or **system model**, is the composite view by all users of the entire system. These three components are the pillars upon which the user interface is formulated.

An example is appropriate. A manufacturer was interested in improving maintenance and troubleshooting of shop floor equipment. An expert system designer and programmers were hired to create an expert system. The expert system on the shop floor was not successful, however, because the mechanics (or users of the system) had to communicate in terms that were not familiar to them. The vocabulary used by master mechanics was not incorporated in the user interface to the expert system. Hence, the user model and the system model were not identified correctly. The expert system interface was then rewritten to create an atmosphere more like the working vocabulary of the mechanics. This change made the expert system successful.

Another example of an inadequate user interface occurred in a mortgage advisement system. A mortgage firm, eager to help its advisors become more proficient, hired a team of designers to formulate a mortgage advisement system for its employees. After many months of work and considerable expense, the firm was confused as to why the mortgage advisors were not using the system. After a thorough investigation, the designers of the system found that the users viewed the new expert system as an eventual threat to their positions. Hence, the view of the designers did not match the system model or composite image from the mortgage consultants. After considerable training and reworking the *user interface*, the expert system was viewed as an assistant rather than a job replacement.

Underlying all three models which form a user interface are **tasks**. No user interface can be properly designed without understanding the overall, specific tasks to be accomplished. All three models must incorporate the same threads of task definition. If the expert system is only used by domain-specific experts (doctors, lawyers, airplane mechanics, and so on), then the tasks must be specific to that domain. If, however, the expert system is to be used by more general audiences (receiving advice on investments for example), then the tasks must be appropriate and defined for more general-purpose users. The nature, background, and knowledge of the intended user is crucial to understanding the tasks to be incorporated in the user interface.

Screen Design

There are many different types or styles of interface design in today's expert systems. Even though the user interface is not exactly the same as the design and type of interaction between a computer keyboard and display screen, we will discuss some common screen formats and types of interaction that have evolved. The more common screen layouts are: question and answer (teletype), menus (hierarchical, pull-down), icon-driven, and windows. Different types of interaction for any of the above types are achieved with keyboard, mouse, touch-sensitive screen, light pen, or voice.

Many of the currently used screen layouts have been ported from the trends in microcomputer software applications development. The past decade has seen a decrease in hardware costs, increase in memory size, development of graphics tools, and increased concern on user communications. This trend has centered on microcomputer software development but has also migrated to the mainframe software environment. The new range of applications with word processing, database, spreadsheet, and desktop publishing have offered rich and varied user interfaces which system designers are incorporating into expert systems. Even though a video display is not always required, we will restrict our comments to them because of their widespread use and availability in computer systems.

Questions and Answers (Teletype). Turning our attention to the design of a video display terminal (computer screen), let's take a look at each of the different types of screen layout. The simplest and earliest is called the **teletype**, or **question and answer**. The expert system, through computer software, displays a question on the screen. The user then types in a reply with the keyboard or other device. The computer software of the expert system takes the reply and incorporates the information within the knowledge base. This method is quite linear and is shown in Figure 7.3.

City College
Course Advisement
Expert System

1. What is your name?

   Jean Kirkland

2. What is your major
   here at City College?

   Business

3. How many semester hours
   have you earned?

   75

Computer: Regular type
User reply: **Boldfaced type**

FIGURE 7.3 QUESTION AND ANSWER TYPE SCREEN DESIGN

This type of screen organization in a user interface can be more than adequate for certain expert systems. The advantage is that it is easy to design and implement in software; the disadvantage is that it allows the user to retype or re-enter incorrect or misspelled answers.

Menus. A **menu-driven** interface displays a list of choices to the user as shown in Figure 7.4. The user's selection could lead to another menu of choices. Users of information and database systems are quite familiar with menu-driven interfaces.

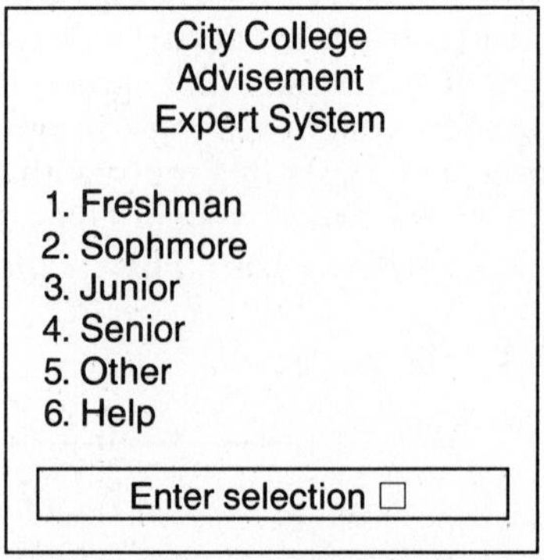

FIGURE 7.4 MENU TYPE SCREEN DESIGN

One issue with menu-driven user interfaces is the determination of the optimal number of displayed items on one menu screen (breadth of a menu) versus the optimal number of levels of submenus (depth of a menu). See Figure 7.5.

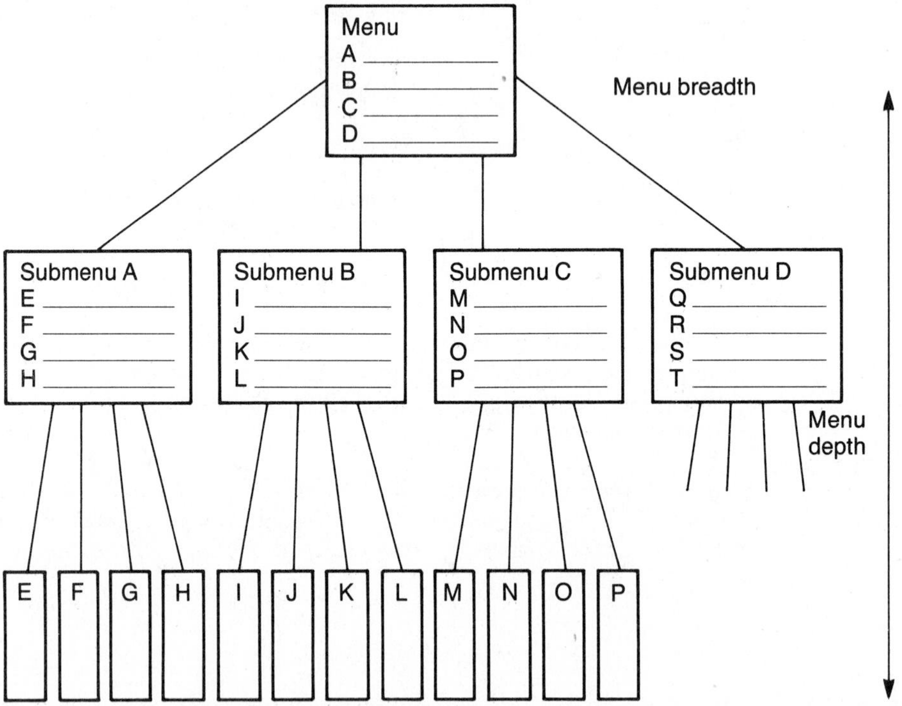

FIGURE 7.5 MENU BREADTH AND MENU DEPTH

Users like to get to specific information as soon as possible, yet, too many choices in one menu (breadth) leads to a crowded and confusing organization of information. This ***breadth-depth*** menu structure can be designed in hierarchical and pull-down menu formats. Both formats display the same logical menu structure information as shown in Figure 7.5, but the arrangement of the item on the screen is different.

Hierarchical. The **hierarchical** format for a menu structure displays the menu choices arranged horizontally, as shown in Figure 7.6, in a band called a ***menu bar.*** The user moves across the menu bar (A to B to C to D) by moving a cursor or highlighted box around the item. When the locator box is on A, the submenu for A is displayed for possible selection of E, F, G, or H. As the locator box is moved from A to B, the submenu A disappears and submenu B becomes visible. This interface is common to many spreadsheets users. The well-known spreadsheet package Lotus 1-2-3 employs this hierarchical type of menu interface. It is possible to move left or right in the menu bar and also possible to have submenus in horizontal format under submenus.

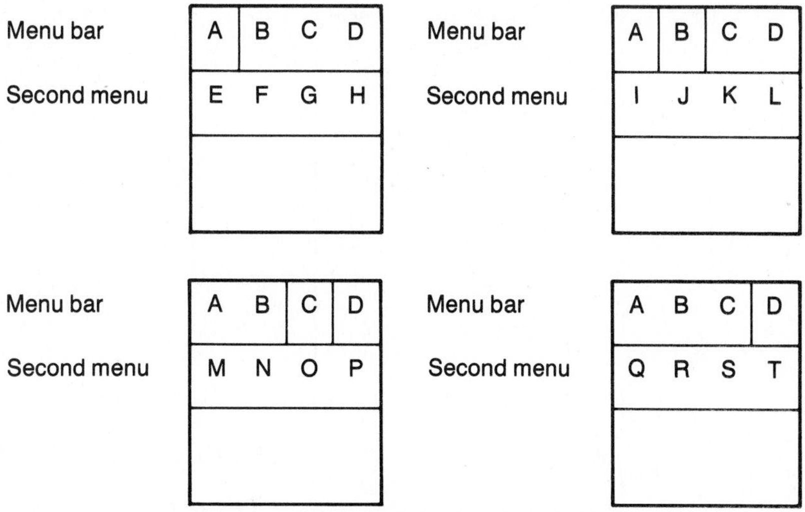

FIGURE 7.6 HIERARCHICAL ARRANGEMENT OF SUBMENUS FOR MENU-DRIVEN SCREEN DESIGN

Pull-Down (Pop-Up). The **pull-down (pop-up)** submenu format is shown in Figure 7.7. It has the same logical concept as the hierarchial arrangement except that the submenu choices are arranged in a vertical format. Only one submenu from the menu bar is visible at a time. This menu interface style (pull-down menu) is incorporated in dBASE III PLUS, a popular database microcomputer software package. Both of these menu formats, hierarchical and pull-down, have the advantage of requiring less area on the screen, but both require considerably more screen programming tools and expertise. However, both formats are familiar to millions of office workers and professionals who are already using them on a daily basis.

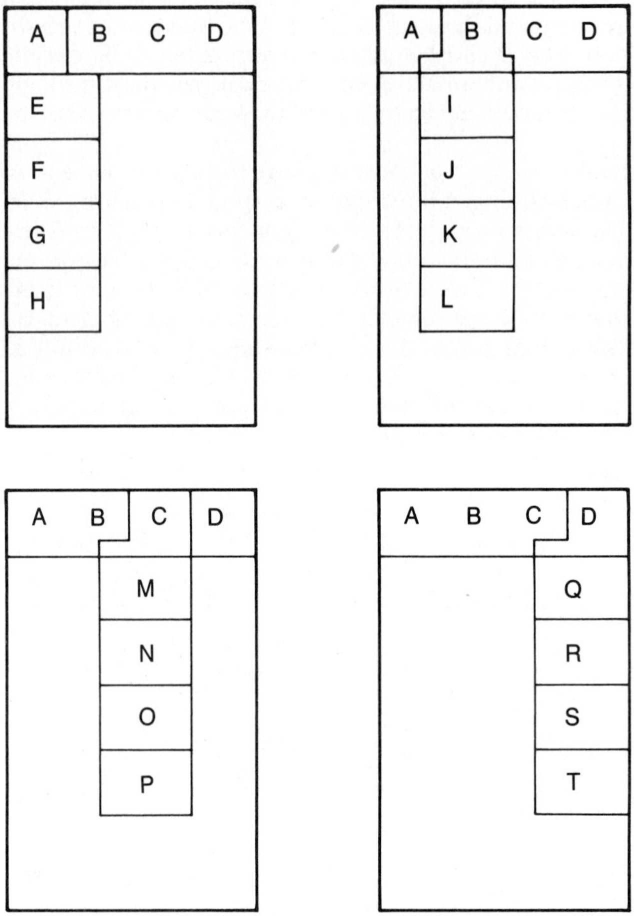

FIGURE 7.7 PULL-DOWN MENU SCREEN DESIGN

Icon. Another popular type of interface is the **icon** environment. In this style of interface, icons (symbols) represent the choices on a menu instead of words. Users select a noun symbol such as a letter, report, or drawing as shown in Figure 7.8 and then select an action to be performed on the noun. Possible verb icons from Figure 7.8 are writing to disk, sending to the printer, or deleting (throwing in the trash can). A noun icon may be dragged and placed on top of a verb icon to tell the computer to perform that action on the selected noun. The icon environment relies heavily on visual and graphical communications. This icon environment is used extensively in Macintosh software products. The icon environment is not restricted to graphical symbols, but uses text along with symbols to facilitate the user interface.

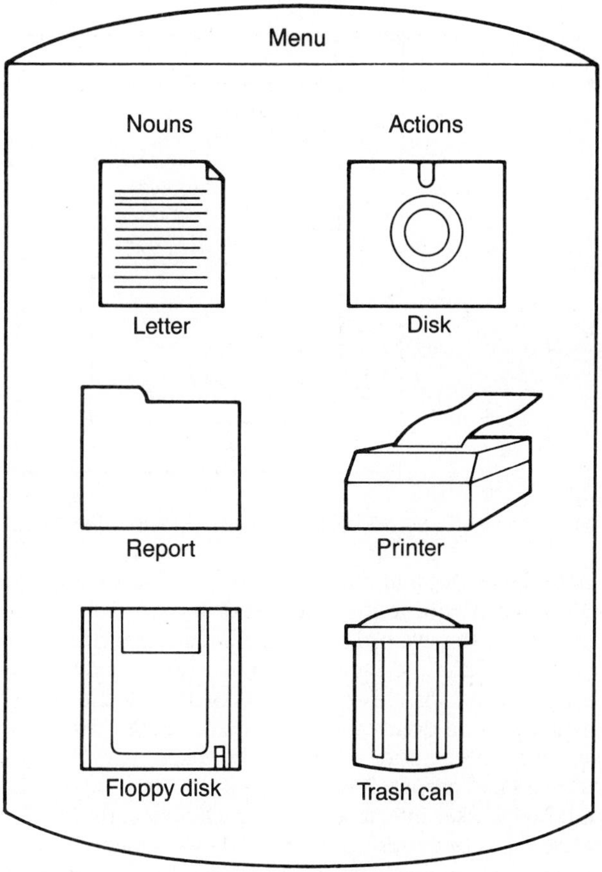

FIGURE 7.8 ICON SCREEN DESIGN

Windows. The last generic type of screen design is called the **windowing environment** that is illustrated in Figure 7.9. Windows are rectangles or frames of information that appear on the computer screen. Users can view, edit, rearrange, enlarge, and perform similar manipulations on windows and their contents. Windows may overlap each other. One window may contain the text of a memo and another window might contain a business graph. The user has considerable control over the windows and their appearance on the screen. Special windows, called *dialog boxes*, are windows where users actually enter information about a task to be performed. Another special window, called an *alert box*, may appear when the system wants to alert the user to unusual situations (no printer paper, disk is full, no file available, and so on). The advantage of this interface is multiple-information boxes (windows) are available simultaneously; the disadvantages are that extensive tools and expertise are needed to create the windows on the video system of the computer.

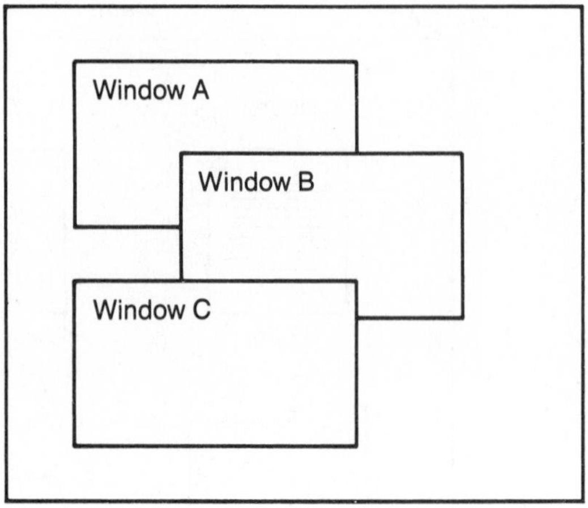

FIGURE 7.9 THE WINDOWING INTERFACE

These screen configurations, question and answer, standard menu, hierarchical menu, pull-down menu, icons, and windows, can be mixed together. The Macintosh environment, for example, uses a standard interface of pull-down menus, icons, and windows. This interface is known to the user as *desktop* because of its symbolic representations of the common tasks done at the desk. Each style has its own special advantages and disadvantages. Users, however, are getting more sophisticated in their use and expectations of user interfaces. An interesting psychological factor, the "homesick syndrome," is evolving from users of computer information systems. When asked what user interface design participants prefer, many prefer the interface design of the first computer application they learned. Very few users in the business environment are exposed to all interfaces in their daily routine.

Input Devices

Each of the interface configuration types that we have discussed can facilitate a variety of physical input devices for the user. The user can input through these various screen formats by using the keyboard, mouse, light pen, touch-sensitive screen, or voice.

Keyboard. The most common physical input method is the **keyboard**. The user types characters as answers to questions or moves a cursor to a menu and makes a selection by pressing the Enter key. The most commonly used keyboard layout, the QWERTY, was patented as part of the first mechanical typewriter by Sholes, Glidden, and Soule in 1864. The keyboard was deliberately designed to reduce the speed of skilled typists in order to reduce the probability of jamming the keys. Despite its awkward and inefficient key layout, the QWERTY keyboard, shown in Figure 7.10, is still the most commonly used keyboard in business offices.

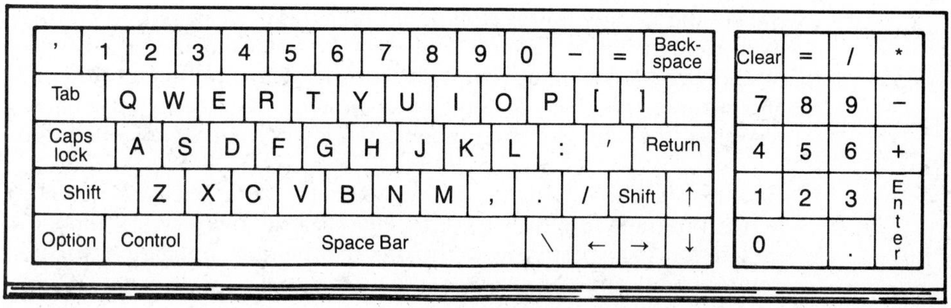

FIGURE 7.10 THE QWERTY KEYBOARD

An added de facto standard, the cursor keys have been superimposed on the numeric keypad on the IBM-PC series of keyboards. The cursor keys enable a user to move the cursor on the screen (in steps) to the right, left, up, or down. The user then can position the cursor over a menu selection, and, by pressing the Enter key, the selection is transferred from the display screen to the computer program. Thus, through cursor keys and software, the keyboard can be used as a pointing device for menu selection.

Mouse. The second most common input device is the **mouse**. It is also termed a **pointer** or **locating device**. The mouse is a small instrument about the size of a deck of playing cards that is attached to the computer by a thin cable. The mouse has one, two, or three buttons for user control. As a user moves the mouse around on a desktop pad or other surface, the cursor on the display is moved accordingly. Through the use of the buttons, the user can convey actions to the computer. For example, by pressing the mouse button while the cursor is on an icon, the user can activate the task indicated by the selected symbol. The mouse is standard equipment with some computer systems (Macintosh), and many claim that is is very easy to use. Studies show that the mouse is particularly useful for people who use computer systems over a long, continuous work session. The mouse allows considerable freedom in moving both the hand and the entire body, but also requires additional desk space.

Touch-Sensitive Screen. Another common input device is the **touch-sensitive screen**. This device is a special screen which allows the user to touch a portion of the screen (icon, menu choice, and so on) and communicate the selection through software to the computer program. These screens are often used in general public information systems for the average user in banks, malls, Disneyland, and so on. This type of screen is also common to educational applications. Touch-sensitive screens are best used for applications requiring infrequent use and where coarse pointing is adequate. They have the disadvantage of accidental activating and potential dirty screens.

Light Pen. A fourth input device is the **light pen**. The light pen is a small wand that is attached to the computer by a cord. The user positions the pen on a portion of the screen. A small photocell in the pen emits light. This increase in brightness on an area of the screen generates a signal to the computer.

Voice. A new input device, **voice**, exists in varying stages of development. The user speaks and the computer equipment uses the voice signals to control the computer. Even though this is a simple concept, the extensive use of voice-driven systems is not yet here. Voice input is best and most effective in systems where the user's hands and eye are not free. Because voice systems require step-by-step confirmation of response, they are not recommended for noisy or stressful environments.

How do we know which input device is the best? Each of the devices adds an expense, programming overhead, mechanical and/or electrical functionality, and user preferences. The best input is the one that fits the application, the user, the working environment, and the budget.

Input devices and screen interfaces can be combined. For example, any type of screen layout could be matched with most any input device. For example, in today's business and office, many computer applications have a WIMP interface: a combination of screen design and input device. A WIMP environment is a user interface composed of windows, icons, menus, and pointer device. This kind of interface is common to the Macintosh and IBM-PC microcomputer world. The possible combinations of screen layout and input device(s) are only limited by the designer's imagination, the firm's budget, the user requirements, and the programmer's development tools (for controlling the video or computer screen).

Integration Interface. One of the most current trends in user interface design for expert systems is the **integration** of the expert system with a spreadsheet or database format. Businesses and management professionals are already acquainted with the tabular format used in spreadsheet and database applications, as shown in Figure 7.11.

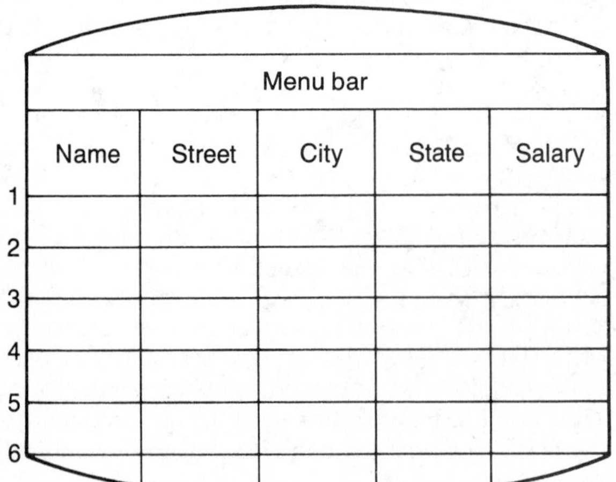

FIGURE 7.11 TABLE FORMAT FOR SPREADSHEET/DATABASE INTERFACE

Since expert systems contain large amounts of information and facts, it is a natural link connecting existing spreadsheet/database-like formats to the contents of an expert system. This is particularly true in the information systems world of both mainframe and microcomputer-based applications. Many users now view the spreadsheet/database format of a table as the front end to an expert system. In some systems, the user can fill in a table and the expert system software will convert the table format to production rules, as illustrated in Figure 7.12.

Table from the user

	Condition	Condition	Action	Action
Record 1	A	B	C	
Record 2	A	D	F	B
Record 3	B		G	H
Record 4	G	D	H	

Rules generated by the expert system

Rule 1:
IF A
AND B
THEN C

Rule 2:
IF A
AND D
THEN F AND B

Rule 3:
IF B
THEN G AND H

Rule 4:
IF G
AND D
THEN H

FIGURE 7.12 TABLE INTERFACE FOR PRODUCTION-RULE GENERATION IN EXPERT SYSTEMS

The expert system software converts the information in each record (row) of spreadsheet/database information to a production rule. For example, record one of ABC blank, is converted to

IF A AND B THEN C

The first two parts (fields) of each row are interpreted as antecedents (IFs), and the last two fields are considered as actions (THENs). Thus, business expert systems are being constructed on top of the familiar and functional interfaces already common in the business world.

Effective User Interface Guidelines for Expert Systems

This section will summarize some basic guidelines for the development of effective user interfaces. There is no set of ten magical rules that will automatically guarantee that the user interface will be optimal in design, content, or format. There are, however, basic guidelines that should be considered when designing an expert system. Whether the user is a domain-specific expert (lawyer, accountant, surgeon, aircraft mechanic, and so on), or a more general user (public citizen, consumer, and so on), the basic communications between the expert system and the intended user determine the functionality and efficacy of the system. Good screen design and user interaction for a well-designed expert system will enhance the performance of the system.

We will take a look at guidelines for the two facets of the user interface: screen display and user interaction via some input device. These two components comprise the user interface. First, let's take a look at the design and organization of the screen display.

Screen Display Guidelines

Some general guidelines or directions for effective **screen display** in expert systems are described as follows.

1. **Use uncluttered, well-spaced screens.**
   The user screens should be uncluttered with appropriate spacing between fields, lines, and text. Experts advise that only 15 to 20 percent of the screen space should be utilized. Unnecessary items are distracting to the task at hand.
2. **Avoid paragraphs of text at the screen.**
   Paragraphs of text should rarely be used on the screen. Reading from a display terminal is not the same as reading from or browsing through a book, so organize information into vertical lists instead of paragraphs. If paragraphs are necessary, however, display part of the text, then allow the user to press a key to continue with the next part. A mixture of upper-case and lower-case text is more readable than using all capitals.
3. **In general, left-justify text and right-justify numbers.**
   Text and number lists should be distinctly formatted. Lists of text should be left justified; that is, the leftmost letter of each word in the list should be aligned vertically to the left. In contrast, numbers should be right justified, aligned vertically to the right. When using decimal values with varying decimal places, the list of numbers should be decimal aligned. These examples are shown below:

Left Justify	Right Justify	Decimal Align
Investments	4,300	34.78
Stocks	543	123.6
Bonds	678,413	6.789

   This arrangement of lists is easiest to read.
4. **Limit the number of menu selections from five to seven.**
   In general, a user can retain information from about seven items at a time. Therefore, the number of selections from a single menu or pull-down submenu should be limited to between five and seven items. Each one should be numbered

(1,2,3,4). Use letters only with a short menu list of three or four selections identified by codes (i.e., D for delete, U for update, and A for add). The items can be listed by time, function, number, importance, or other criteria. A general rule of thumb, however, is to list the menu options by frequency of use, with the most frequently used at the top of the menu screen (breadth) and by the *highest* level of menu (depth).

5. **Be consistent in wording and location of prompts.**
The wording and location of prompts, fields, and and other identifiers should be consistent throughout the screens. Use uniform wording of phrases. For example, do not use change the record on one screen and *update* the record on another. With date entry fields, maintain the same formats for name, social security number, date, and so on throughout all screens. The screen formats should match the formats used in printed reports. The prompts to the user should always appear in a corresponding location. If the lower-left hand corner of the screen is used to display the message on how to move to the next screen, retain that relative positioning in all appropriate screens. Keep the language consistent with the expectations of the user of the system. This means to adhere to the vocabulary of the user. If the user is an accountant, then the term debit and credit are fine, but they are not appropriate for the general user referring to money paid in and money paid out.

6. **Use reversed videos or color for data entry fields.**
If a user is filling in the various items on a form-like screen, each data entry field should be highlighted. Reversed video (the opposite of the screen background: black letters on a white background or white letters on black background) is one popular method in many business-oriented information systems. Color is another way to draw attention to a particular field. Windowing is still another technique used to highlight the fields to be used. The system should not permit the user to alter information or words that are not to be changed on the screen. In other words, the programmer should "protect" these screens when the screen programs are being implemented.

7. **Use color and graphics to add to screen design.**
Color can be a useful asset to screen design if it is available on the video system. It can be used to highlight, to contrast, and to make complex diagrams such as maps appear more readable. Color on diagrams make intricate detail more discernible for the user. Care should be given in selecting the color of the background (blank screen) and the color of the text that appears on the screen. Certain color combinations are hard to read, such as red letters on a blue background, for example. The designer of the system should make sure that if the color screens are displayed on a black and white monitor, that the visual effects of the screen are still discernible and pleasing to the eye.

8. **Let the user select some characteristics of the screen interface.**
For those applications where usage is extensive by the same user, some method of configuring or tailoring the screen environment for the individual should be available. For example, if color is used, then the user should be able to select certain colors for his or her working environment. If a beep or sound is used to identify the end of a field or other warning, then the user should be able to turn the

noise or sound off. Different people have different reactions to color, sound, and so on, and these minor characteristics can be very annoying to those who use the system continually. If the users, on the other hand, vary from day to day, then the screen characteristics should be determined by the designer of the system. Advising systems used by the general public are a type of expert system where each user should not be allowed to change the characteristics of the terminal display.

The preceding rules are to be considered as guidelines for general screen design for expert systems. The more specific and narrow the domain of the expert system, the more these rules may have to be adjusted to fit the functional needs of the specific expert system application.

Guidelines for the Use of Input Devices

In this section we will look at guidelines for implementing interaction through screen displays. Interaction between the user and the system is sometimes called **dialogue**, similar to a conversation between two individuals. Besides considering rules for implementing effective dialogue, we will explore general rules for using different input devices.

1. **Minimize the number of keystrokes.**
   To perform tasks and moves between menus, the number of keystrokes, or other required actions, to complete the functions should be as few as possible. If users are working with codes, they should be short in length. The depth of menus should be taken into consideration at design time.

2. **Use a two-level command or menu selection structure.**
   If the system is driven by commands, or a menu, then the instructions should exist at two levels, one for the beginner and one for the more experienced user. A beginning user does not mind selecting "D" for document, "P" for print, and "Go" to start the process of printing. As the user gains experience, this three step process, is abbreviated to entering DPG (in one step). The same principle applies to menu selection when the user is very familiar with the system. This two-level command or menu selection structure is accommodating to users with different levels of expertise in using a system.

3. **Help the user navigate through the system.**
   Effective dialogue and functionality are fostered when the user understands how to progress through a system. This concept is analogous to reading the symbols on a roadmap. To determine which way to go, the symbols (or prompts) must be understood. Likewise, in a computer or expert system, the user must recognize whether they are in the mode to look at production rules, change a rule, or observe the execution of a set of rules. They also must understand how to move from one mode to another. Proper symbols and understanding of how to navigate through a system are important for the user.

4. **Provide on-line help.**
If the user is unsure of backward chaining, he or she should be able to invoke the help system (press the Help key) and find information about backward chaining. If the user does not remember what information is to be entered, then an on-line help option could review the user. On-line help is supplementary to the formal training and written documentation of the system. These help systems are considered standard features, not only to expert systems, but to any computer information system.

5. **Quick response time should be guaranteed.**
Response time is the amount of time (in seconds or smaller time units) that it takes for the computer system to respond to the user input. Users on mainframe or microcomputer systems are accustomed to a two second response time. No one likes to wait to get the task completed. This is particularly important in multiuser or networked systems. The response time is a function of both the hardware and the software. Response time is important at design time and also after the system is implemented because of continual changes in the system and working environment.

6. **Avoid blank screens during any dialogue session.**
As a response in a dialogue session, the user should see an appropriate response. Many times, there are searching and sorting techniques that, unfortunately, take considerable time (or so it seems). Instead of leaving the display screen blank, some message appropriate to the task should appear to the user. For example, if the expert system is firing the rule base, then a message such as "Searching the rule base" should appear on the screen. Users are likely to be more patient if there is an explanation for the lapse of time. Hence, for the user, appropriate messages are preferred to blank screens.

7. **Implement an undo feature in the commands.**
An undo command is one that reverses a command or action that has just been implemented; but not all actions in a system are reversible or undoable. Users have become accustomed to this helpful system interface, making the implementation of this feature by programmers a useful design enhancement.

8. **Simplify error messages.**
Error messages, warning messages, and other related feedback should be in terms that are understood by the user. They are information to the user, not the programmer. For example, the message, "Check disk drive door to make sure it is closed," is a better feedback to the user than "System failure: abort, retry?" Messages like "syntax error" or "Runtime error 256" are not particularly useful to users. In addition, users should be involved in *approving* the messages that are built into the operation of an expert system, to ensure their understanding of them.

9. **Provide for atypical users.**
Most computer systems are designed for people who have 20/20 vision, are right handed, and have full-color vision. Many people, however, have vision problems, are color-blind, or are left handed. Input devices, such as numeric keypad or trackball, provide for left-handed users. Color display screens, for color-blind

users, should appear readable and discernible on black and white monitors. An expert system that is to be used by a wide variety of users must take into consideration the atypical user.

10. **Minimize the number of changes.**
    If the keyboard system is combined with another device such as a mouse or light pen, minimize the changes from keyboard to device. When another input device is used together with the keyboard, frequent changes between the two styles can be confusing.

These guidelines are to be considered during the design stage of the expert systems life cycle. Incorporating user-friendly procedures is easiest and most effective during the design stage. The best judge of a user interface is not a given set of rules, but an evaluation by the user. Attention to the user interface design will reap countless benefits to the acceptability, functionality, and efficacy of the intended expert system.

Case Study: A User Interface for WPHELP

As more and more people use computers, both in the workplace and in the home, the quality of the user interface is becoming increasingly more important for vendors and users. People want computer software that is user-friendly. Today's user interfaces have improved, but still there is much to be done. Let's consider what, ideally, would be the user interface for WPHELP.

First, our expert system should have the capability of either keyboard or mouse input. The use of a mouse has become very popular in recent years, and it may be available to the user.

We would like the communication between the user and WPHELP to be as English-like as possible, so we need natural language understanding capabilities. Voice input/output is a possibility for future versions of WPHELP, but the technology is not well developed at this point in time.

Communication with the user should incorporate all four methods of screen design discussed in the chapter: question and answer, menus, icons, and windows.

Question and answer screens should be developed in ordinary English. They should allow for the user to respond in an open-ended fashion, as though he or she were conversing verbally with a human expert. Voice would be the ideal medium for question and answer, but the keyboard will have to do for some time to come. These screens will allow the user to express freely his or her word processing needs.

Menu selection and icon screens would be useful for allowing the user to make selections about desired attributes of a potential word processing system. These screens could be easily implemented using a mouse or a keyboard.

The alternate use of different input devices may be bothersome to users who prefer to use only one device. The use of a mouse would not allow the use of the free-expression capability of the question and answer screens, so we will have to decide whether to use only the keyboard or gamble on combining two devices.

Windows would also be very useful. WPHELP might make use of three windows on the screen simultaneously. One window might show the question and answer communication between the user and the expert system (seeking one-half of the screen).

A second window could be used to show keyword summaries of the user responses. As a user, it is easy to forget what responses have been made and, rather than querying WPHELP, the information could be easily retrieved. Perhaps the window size could be one-fourth of the screen.

The third window (also one-fourth of the screen) could be available for help on word processing terminology or on the use of WPHELP. Good help facilities will go a long way towards the achievement of the goal of user-friendliness.

Next, WPHELP should have report-generation capabilities for the printer in a format that can be designed by the user. Different users usually have some quirks about how reports of findings are to be formatted. Depending on the user's desires, the report either could be printed out or stored electronically for later retrieval.

Finally, WPHELP should have a database and a spreadsheet attached to it. The database could store in summary form complete details about the selected word processing package. The spreadsheet would assist the user in making an analysis of the cost impact of the purchase of the selected word processing package for his or her business.

Key Points

- An expert system is composed of three parts: knowledge base (rules, facts), inference engine (reasoning mechanism), and the user interface (communications vehicle between the user and the expert system).
- The user interface is analogous to an atmosphere surrounding a planet. The user interface has physical, perceptive, and psychological components.
- The user interface is important to the overall success of the operation of the expert system.
- Identifying the user's tasks is critical to designing the user interface.
- The user interface is effected by the type of screen design and the method of implementing interaction (dialogue) between the user and the expert system (input device).

- There are four common types of screen design:
  - Question and answer
  - Menu selection
  - Icons
  - Windows
- There are many input devices for effective communication or a dialogue between the user and the expert system. The six most common are:
  - Keyboard-cursor keys
  - Mouse
  - Touch-sensitive screen
  - Light pen
  - Voice
  - Integration interface
- The QWERTY keyboard of 1864 is still the most popular keyboard in offices today.
- A WIMP interface is a term describing a user interface of windows, icons, menus, and pointers (usually a mouse).
- A user interface can be any imaginative combination of screen format and user input device.
- No set of magical rules will ensure an effective user interface, but consideration of good screen design guidelines will enhance the expert system.
- The following are general guidelines for effective screen design:
  - Use uncluttered, well-spaced screens.
  - Avoid paragraphs of text at the screen.
  - In general, left-justify text and right-justify numbers.
  - Limit the number of menu selections from five to seven.
  - Be consistent in wording and location of prompts.
  - Use reversed videos or color for data entry fields.
  - Use color and graphics to add to screen design.
  - Let the user select some characteristics of the screen interface.
- Guidelines for effective user communications or dialogue with input devices are as follows:
  - Minimize the number of keystrokes.
  - Use a two-level command or menu selection structure.
  - Help the user navigate through the system.
  - Provide on-line help.
  - Quick response time should be guaranteed.
  - Avoid blank screens during any dialogue session.
  - Implement an undo feature in the commands.
  - Simplify the error messages.
  - Provide for atypical users.
  - Minimize the number of changes.
- An interface for the general user (consumer, citizen, voter, and so on) must be designed differently than the interface for a domain-specific expert (doctor, lawyer, or mechanic).
- A WIMP interface, or touch-sensitive screen, would be the preferable interface for the case study WPHELP because of the versatility of the users of the system.

Exercises

1. Define user interface.
2. What is the most common screen format? ____________________
3. What is the most common input device for computer systems today?

   ____
4. Given the four pull-down menus in Figure 7.13, identify a heading that would be appropriate to identify each submenu.

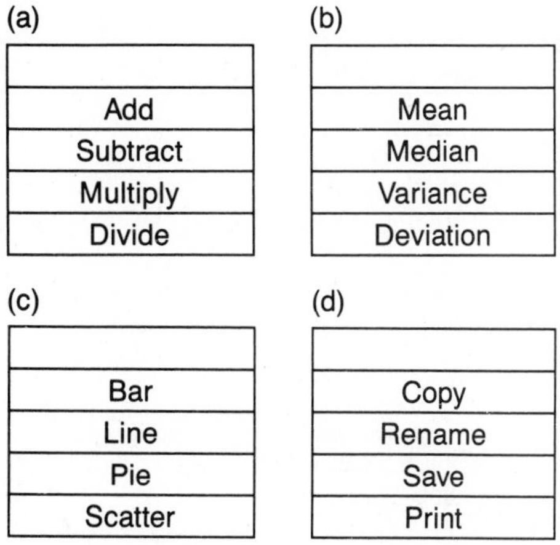

FIGURE 7.13 PULL-DOWN MENUS

5. Place the following topics under the most appropriate pull-down menu in the menu bar in Figure 7.14. Some topics may apply to more than one submenu.

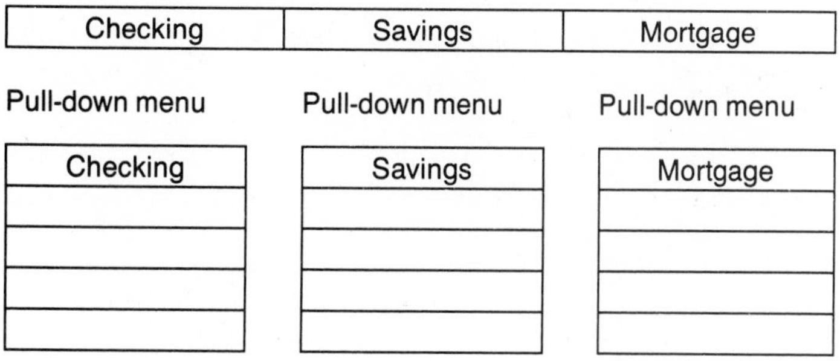

FIGURE 7.14 MENU BAR AND PULL-DOWN MENUS

Escrow	Adjustable rates
Cost of checks	Money market
Monthly service charge	Certificates of deposit
Principal	Closing costs
Points	Insurance
Fixed	Rate of interest

6. Given the hierarchical menu structure in Figure 7.15, translate the command structure into a tree structure of menu screens.

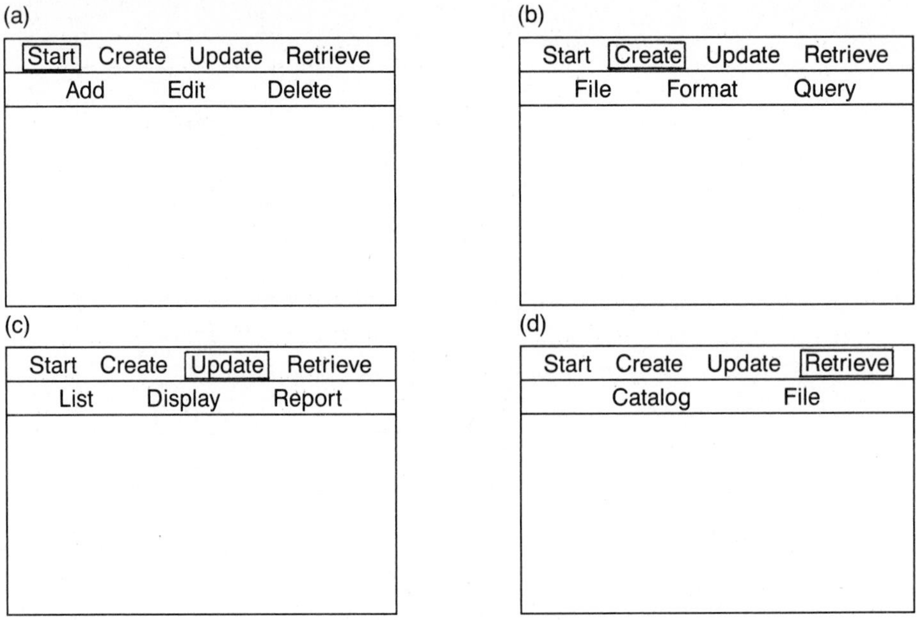

FIGURE 7.15 HIERARCHICAL MENU STRUCTURE

7. Given the tree structures in Figure 7.16 translate the information into a menubar with pull down submenus.

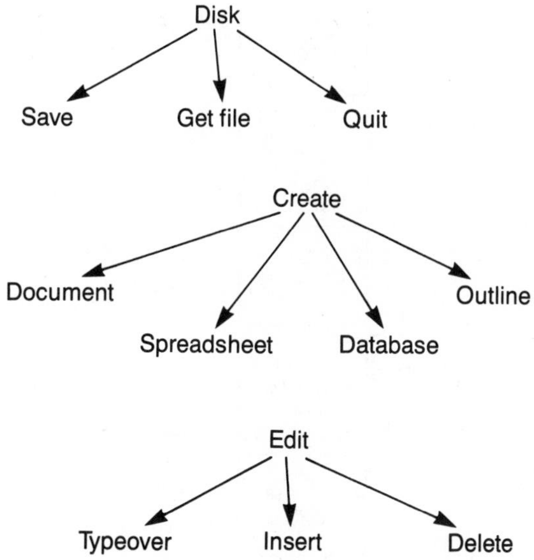

FIGURE 7.16 TREE STRUCTURES FOR MENU INTERFACE

8. Using Figure 7.17, match the word meaning on the left to the icon on the right for the Career Advisement Expert System.

1. ____ a. Lawyer
2. ____ b. Pharmacist
3. ____ c. Doctor
4. ____ d. Teacher
5. ____ e. Accountant
6. ____ f. Dentist
7. ____ g. Veterinarian

FIGURE 7.17 MATCHING MEANINGS TO ICONS

9. Each of the six screens in Figure 7.18 violates at least one user interface guideline. Identify the violations.

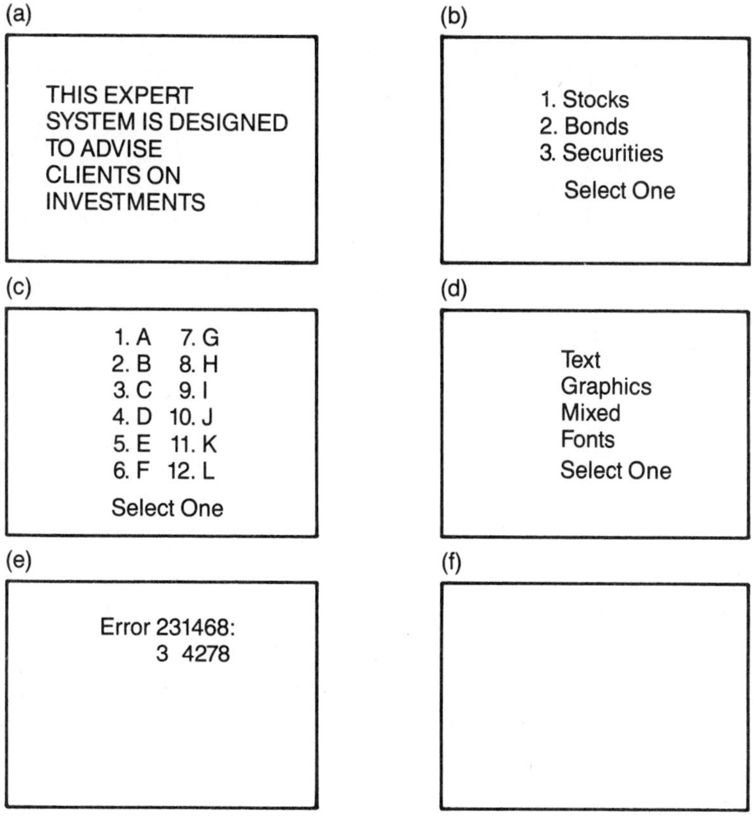

FIGURE 7.18 VIOLATIONS OF USER INTERFACE GUIDELINES

Assignments

1. Design icons for a campus information expert system for a nearby community or four-year college. By each icon, write the noun or verb appropriate for the symbol.
2. Expand the list of guidelines for effective interfaces by consulting the book *Human-Computer Interface Design Guidelines* by G. Martin Brown, Ablex Publishing Co., 355 Chestnut Dr., Norwood, NJ, 07648. Chapter 14 is a summary list of the guidelines presented and explained throughout the book.
3. Write a written report featuring the desktop interface of the Mcintosh microcomputer. A good reference is *Human Interface Guidelines: The Apple Desktop Interface*, by Apple, Addison-Wesley Publishing Co., New York.
4. For detailed information about existing interfaces for expert systems, read *Expert Systems: The User Interface* (a collection of works on expert system interfaces) edited by James Hendler, Ablex Publishing Corporation, 1988.

5. At the end of this chapter, before the Case Study, we mentioned that there were several references on user interface concepts that could be useful for further study. The list of references includes:

    Shneidermann, B., *Human Interface Guidelines: The Apple Desktop Interface*, Menlo Park, CA, Addison-Wesley, 1987.

    Brown, G.M., *Human-Computer Interface Guidelines*, Norwood, NJ, Abley Publishing, 1988.

    Carroll, J., Ed. *Interfacing Thought*, Boston, MIT Press, 1987.

    Hendler, J., Ed. *Expert Systems: The User Interface*, Norwood, NJ, Abley Publishing, 1988.

    Rubin, T., *User Interface Design for Computer Systems*, NY, Halsted Press (Division of John Wiley), 1988.

8

SOFTWARE ENGINEERING AND EXPERT SYSTEMS DEVELOPMENT/ INTEGRATION

In the last three chapters, we have examined what is involved in creating the three component parts of an expert system. We are now ready to put these pieces together to make our expert system a reality.

In this chapter, we will examine the relationship between software engineering and expert systems including a discussion of the software life cycle, the expert system life cycle and appropriate software engineering techniques that should be used in expert system development. We will then discuss the various phases of expert system development. Potential difficulties that may be encountered will be examined. Finally, we will discuss the issues involved in integrating the expert system into the organization.

Software Engineering and Expert Systems

An expert system is a piece of software. In some ways, an expert system is like conventional software, and in other ways it is quite different. In this section, we will discuss the life cycles for both conventional software and expert systems and how software engineering techniques can be used in the development of expert systems.

The Software Life Cycle

To understand the importance of software engineering, it is helpful to understand the **software life cycle**, which is concerned with what happens to a piece of software from the time the idea is born until the time it is discarded. The software life cycle is illustrated in Figure 8.1.

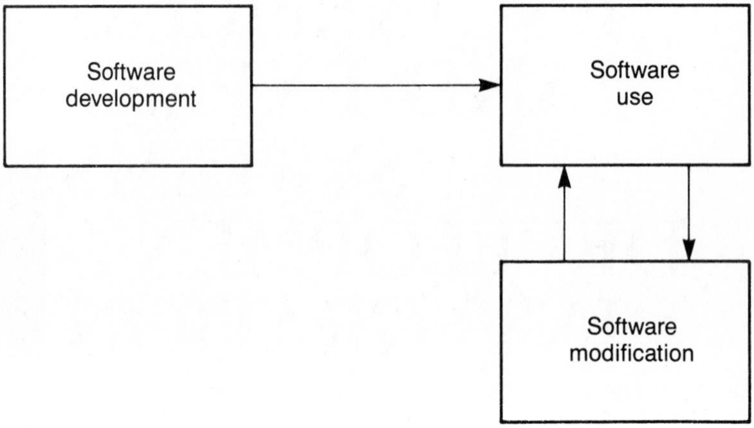

FIGURE 8.1 THE SOFTWARE LIFE CYCLE

The figure shows that once the software has been developed, it enters a *looping pattern* between use and modification. The software stays in this loop until it is time to be discarded. Such a looping pattern is common for any product that is manufactured. The product cycles between use and repair/maintenance until it eventually wears out and is replaced.

Software does not wear out. After its development, it moves into the use phase where it is likely that someone determines there are errors in the software or that changes are required. The software then loops through this pattern because, once errors are corrected or changes are made, new problems may arise during the next use phase. A potential difficulty with making changes to software is the risk of causing new problems. For example, changes in an accounting procedure will cause changes to be made in a program that handles accounts payable or accounts receivable. It is often the case that these changes may cause problems that will not be discovered until some later time.

It is useful to examine at this point the relationship between the development and modification phases of the software life cycle. The amount of time and effort spent in the modification phase is likely to be inversely proportional to the time and effort spent in the development phase. That is, more time and effort spent in the development phase may cause less time and effort to be required in the modification phase. If care is taken early-on to ensure proper system design and implementation, then the resulting system is more likely to meet most of the user's needs. Also, it is likely that there will be fewer errors to correct in the modification phase.

It is clear that a great deal of importance must be placed on the development phase. This is true in any software development situation, but is especially true with large software systems where many people are involved. A methodical approach using software engineering techniques is needed.

In a systematic approach, there are several required steps. Our discussion here will be brief; therefore, if you want further detail, you may wish to consult books such as *Software Engineering: A Practical Approach* by O. Pressman [McGraw-Hill, 1982] or *Introduction to Systems Analysis and Design* by J. Kendall [Allyn and Bacon, 1987].

The first step in the development phase is to **formalize** the problem specifications. It is at this point when the decision is made that software will be appropriate for the given application. The requirements are then isolated and production begins. These requirements are refined and become the specifications of the application. For example, the application might require that data be accessed only by authorized personnel.

The set of specifications thus form the basis for the software. This process of formalization is analogous to the use of a blueprint to build a building or the use of CAD/CAM (computer-aided design/computer-aided manufacturing) to manufacture a product.

The formalization process should maximize the understanding of the objective of the application by both the user(s) and the software developer. If the process does not work in this way, then additional time and effort that can be avoided will be needed later in development to make changes.

Formalization is probably the most difficult part of the development phase. It requires the software developer (who may or may not do the actual programming) to be a skilled communicator to ensure clearly stated requirements. Often, users are not good at articulating their application needs. Sometimes a manager will provide limited input to indicate the parameters of the application. Except a short time constraint for completion, there may be little direction. The software developer is then responsible for most of the formalization and presenting the specifications to management for review.

The second step involves the design of the software system structure. At this point, the application must be divided into a series of tasks or modules. At the same time, techniques for interfacing the modules must be considered to minimize the time spent in future system maintenance. The software developer must ensure that all of the specifications have been accounted for in the design of the software system.

Implementation of the software system is the third step. This involves the actual creation of the software program. As in the design step, implementation is accomplished on a modular basis using the modules defined in the design process. As modules are completed, their interface to other modules in the software system must be thoroughly tested. This testing is tedious and at times is considered to be of little importantance by system developers. Slighting the testing process in this step, however, usually leads to the creation of larger and more difficult problems when the entire system is put together, which otherwise may have been avoided.

The fourth step involves the testing and debugging of the entire software system. Do all the modules interact properly with each other? What bugs remain that were not found in the design step? Also at this time the overall software system is assessed. Does the software have satisfactory performance for the user, and have all original specifications been met? These questions must be resolved now.

When this step of the software system development phase is completed, the system should require a minimal time in the modification phase, except for changes requested after the original formalization stage.

The final step in the development phase is the preparation of documentation for the software system. This step is very important since poorly documented software will often become unusable. Poorly written documentation greatly complicates the efforts of people assigned to the modification phase and also makes it very difficult for the user. The worst case could result in the software system being seldom or never used. If the latter occurs, then a lot of time, effort, and money will have been wasted.

Just like good help, good documentation is hard to find. For a variety of reasons, documentation on most software systems rates mediocre at best. Providing well-written system documentation takes time and effort and is usually the area that falls short of user expectations. Good documentation makes good software better; poor documentation can make good software unusable.

The Expert System Life Cycle

Because an expert system is a software system, there are a number of similarities between the software life cycle and the expert system life cycle. There are, however, some differences that will become clear in our discussion. The **expert system life cycle** is illustrated in Figure 8.2.

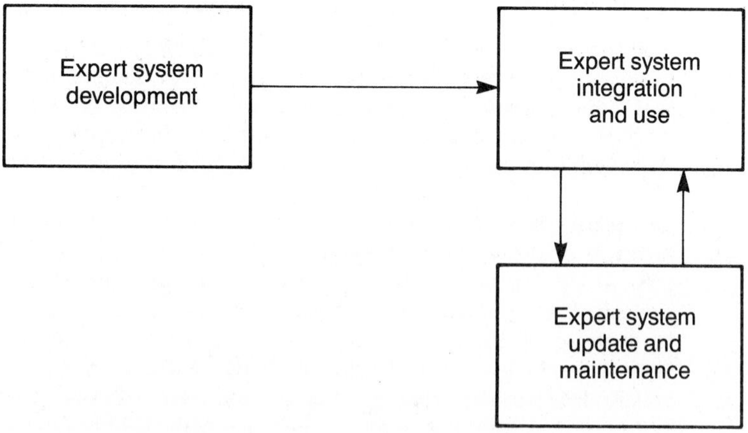

FIGURE 8.2 THE EXPERT SYSTEM LIFE CYCLE

In the development phase of the expert system life cycle, the expert system is actually created. This is analogous to the development phase in the software life cycle. The same basic steps are used in the development of the expert system except for some unique differences.

First, a conventional software system is designed to deal with a single application or problem. Its specifications are developed in conjunction with the user who has a task to be accomplished.

On the other hand, an expert system is intended to solve a range of applications or problems in a narrow domain of knowledge. Knowledge, usually from a human expert, must be captured and put into a form that can be understood by the expert system. While formal specifications are not developed as with a conventional software system, the domain of the knowledge must be clearly defined. The knowledge engineer who develops the expert system works with the human expert to acquire the knowledge but does not, generally, work with the user. The exception to this is when there are particular needs of the user in interacting with the expert system, such as vocabulary used in system/user interaction.

The use and modification phases of the expert system life cycle are analogous to the corresponding phases in the software life cycle. In the use phase, the expert system is put into the role of solving problems related to the domain area just as the conventional software system is used to deal with the desired application. The modification phase is where the knowledge base is updated or modified and errors are corrected. As with conventional software, the expert system loops between its use and modification phases.

In comparing the differences in the two life cycles, we can best summarize them in this way. Conventional software, by its nature, is usually designed to accommodate changing user needs. It is expected from the beginning that there will be modifications. Because conventional software development is a very competitive business, there is a great deal of pressure to get the software to the market place as soon as possible. Often, less than adequate testing results in a high rate of errors present in the software as it enters the use phase. Consequently, more time and effort is needed in the modification phase to customize needs and to correct errors. This description of conventional software will be disputed by some software developers, but, sadly, it is reality.

On the other hand, an expert system must be of high quality before it is released for use; it must be considered high performance software. In general, it is not in a competitive marketing situation so that it is not faced with the "hurry up" dilemma of conventional software.

This discussion can be summarized in Figure 8.3 which shows a comparison of the time spent during the life of development and modification/maintenance phases for conventional software systems and expert systems. As the figure shows, there is a wide variance in the time spent on the different phases during the life cycle.

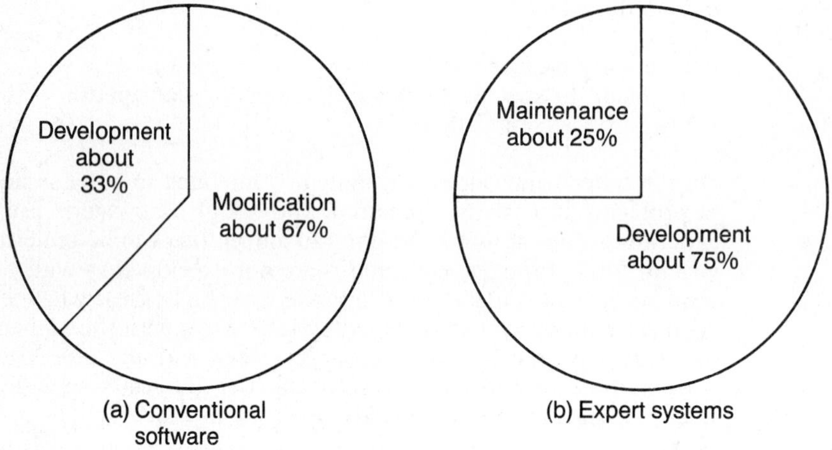

FIGURE 8.3 COMPARISON OF TIME SPENT IN THE LIFE CYCLES

The development phase of the expert system life cycle contains several stages, which include:

1. Problem analysis
2. Problem formalization
3. Knowledge acquisition
4. Knowledge representation
5. Prototype development
6. Full system development
7. System evaluation and documentation

We can briefly summarize the objectives of each step as shown in Figure 8.4.

Details of the first four steps were discussed in Chapter 5. We will now discuss details of the last three steps.

STEP	PURPOSE
1. Problem analysis	— Determine if the problem is appropriate for expert system development.
2. Problem formalization	— Design the basic structure of the expert system.
3. Knowledge acquisition	— Locate an expert and acquire knowledge from the expert.
4. Knowledge representation	— Determine how the knowledge should be represented and choose a development tool.
5. Prototype development	— Initially test the system design, knowledge representation, and development tool choices.
6. Full system development	— Construct the full expert system.
7. System evaluation and documentation	— Finalize system evaluation and documentaion before system goes into use.

FIGURE 8.4 STEPS IN EXPERT SYSTEM DEVELOPMENT AND THEIR PURPOSES

The Software Engineering Methodology

The role of software engineering is to provide some level of law and order in the chaotic software development process. This role can be summarized in Figure 8.5.

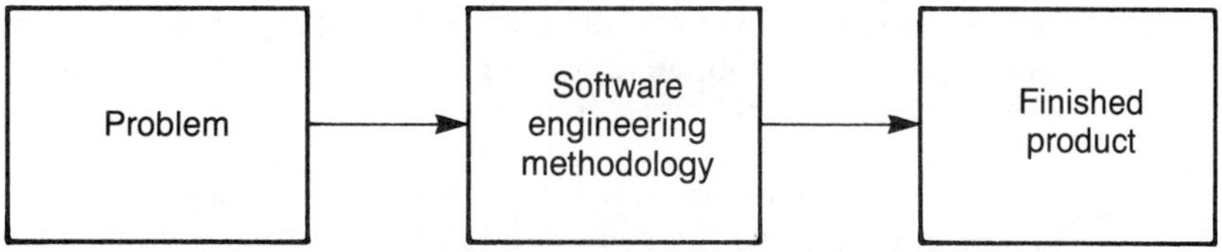

FIGURE 8.5 THE EFFECT OF SOFTWARE ENGINEERING ON SOFTWARE DEVELOPMENT

When a project emerges as a candidate for software development, several conditions are certainly true. First, there is a wide variation of the form of the project, such as its definition and scope. It is assumed that there will be a relatively high cost for the development process.

The software developer must take this dynamic situation and fit the project into a framework for development of the desired software. This is best accomplished by using techniques of software engineering.

Software engineering techniques should produce plans for the development process including timetables and structured design for the software. It will also use the software life cycle as a model for the development of the software.

The result of the application of software engineering techniques is a product that should have certain characteristics. Included among these characteristics are:

— Fully documented

— Verified, validated and tested

— Cost effective

— On-time completion

— Easily manipulatable and enhancible

These characteristics are certainly reasonable and appropriate. The attainment of these characteristics must be the goal of every software development project whether the product is conventional software or an expert system.

Putting the Expert System Together

Prototype Development

The fifth step in the development of the expert system involves the development of a **prototype** of the expected final version of the expert system. The prototype represents a piece or chunk of the final system and has a number of purposes which we will examine.

Before we discuss the purposes of prototyping, we need to note that the process of knowledge acquisition should be performed in parallel with the prototyping process. We will not elaborate further on the knowledge acquisition process as this was discussed in detail in Chapter 5.

Prototyping has several purposes. First, it is an opportunity for the knowledge engineer to *validate* the choice and definition of the problem to be solved. Is there any misunderstanding about the nature and/or scope of the problem by the knowledge engineer?

A second purpose of prototyping is to make an initial determination of the *appropriateness* of the chosen development tool. Of course, not all possible difficulties in the use of the tool would surface at this point; but, if a gross mistake in the tool choice has been made, it is now likely to become evident. It would be very frustrating nearing the end of the full development process to discover that the chosen development tool did not, in fact, work as expected, thus forcing a change to a new tool.

A third purpose of prototyping is to provide the opportunity for the knowledge engineer to *assess* the initial completeness of the knowledge acquisition process. In consultation with the human expert(s) the opportunity to validate the initial results of the creation of the knowledge base is assessed. There is a side benefit to this interaction with the human expert(s). Active involvement between the human expert(s) and the expert system is likely to sustain the interest of the human expert(s). This is important in the development of expert systems since the interest may wane over time. It also fosters communication between the knowledge engineer and the human expert(s).

A fourth purpose of prototyping is to give the knowledge engineer an opportunity to initially *evaluate* the design of the expert system. If design flaws are encountered, they are more readily corrected at the prototyping stage.

The prototype can also serve as an initial test of the reactions of a group of potential users to its output. Involving potential users in this process can assist in correcting any problems with the user interface, for one. Suppose, for example, that the language used in the user interface is inappropriate for the end user; it could be corrected at this time.

A final purpose of prototyping is that it gives an opportunity for *management* in the development process. Viewing initial development results helps keep management informed and may go a long way in determining potential assistance if additional resources are needed by the knowledge engineer.

The statement of these six purposes obviously indicates a number of measures that will and should occur in the actual prototyping process.

The knowledge engineer should have a clear picture of what the final expert system should do and look like. This clear picture, however, must exist not only in the engineer's mind, but in the minds of all concerned. Tools, such as flowcharts of the sequence of events and story boards (scripts), may be very useful; every attempt should be made to make the system design available in a visual form whether on paper or on a computer. This visual information will be helpful to others (human experts, management, and so on) who are involved in the development process.

The knowledge engineer also must analyze the knowledge that has been gathered. What is known? What is not known? What relationships among portions of knowledge need to be explored?

Finally, the development of the prototyping should be accomplished as soon as possible. This is desirable for all concerned and will expedite the inclusion of changes that may need to be made. As the knowledge engineer gains experience in developing expert systems, the prototyping process will likely become easier to implement.

It should be clear that prototyping is an important part of the expert system development process. Time and effort taken at this point will be rewarded as the process moves to completion. We cannot overstate the importance of the prototyping stage.

Full System Development and Evaluation

The sixth step of expert system development involves the **extension** of the prototype into the full expert system. At this stage, initial problems discovered in the prototyping stage should be solved. It is now a matter of putting the components together.

The knowledge engineer continues to expand the knowledge base towards its final form as indicated by the initial problem identification and expert system specifications. Continuous interaction between the knowledge engineer and the human expert(s) is needed for validation of the acquired knowledge. This validation often is performed successfully by presenting new problem situations to both the expert system and the human expert that are still within the specified knowledge domain and comparing the results for consistency.

As new knowledge and rules are being added to the knowledge base, the effects of these additions must be assessed relative to the inference engine. Is there a degradation of performance of the system after the addition of more knowledge and rules? Lower performance levels may be evidenced by, for example, more time needed to solve a given problem, inconsistent or unexpected results, or incorrect results. These situations may be caused by searching techniques used on the knowledge base or conflicting rules. If one or more such problems occur, they should be addressed immediately because they will likely compound themselves if ignored.

There may also be a problem in the original design of the knowledge base or in the choice of the expert system development tool. The choice of knowledge representation could also be a problem. While the prototyping stage should have identified these issues, problems sometimes "fall through the cracks." This situation is more likely to happen with an inexperienced knowledge engineer but can also occur even with the most experienced knowledge engineer.

The user interface must be continuously evaluated through contact with potential end users. As we mentioned in Chapter 7, the user interface is typically the most neglected component of the expert system, especially if time becomes a major constraint.

Appropriate management personnel should be given periodic progress reports and demonstrations of the expert systems as it is being developed. This progress update should provide information only. The knowledge engineer should not allow management to say "well, that looks fine. . . but I would like the system also to do. . .". There may never be an end to this scenario with noncompletion of the expert system as the result.

When the system has been completed, there must be a final testing and evaluation period. This testing and evaluation is often fulfilled by a person or group of people who did not actively participate in the construction of the expert system because they will give a more realistic evaluation of the expert system. However, potential end users of the expert system should also participate in this final testing and evaluation process.

We do not mean to suggest that the knowledge engineer and the human expert should be totally left out of the final testing and evaluation process. Clearly, these two people must be included. Rather, it means that a community of people will be needed for the most successful evaluation.

Plans for maintenance must also be formulated and executed during the full system construction process. Documentation on updating the system, ongoing maintenance of the system, and the use of the system, must be provided. Development of this documentation should be a continual process which begins at the start of prototyping and endures through the final phases of construction of the full system.

Difficulties in Expert Systems Development

Companies wishing to apply expert systems technology to solve their problems encounter several types of difficulties. These difficulties include such things as scarce resources, time for development of the expert system, errors in the expert system itself, and its inherent limitations. In this section, we will examine these difficulties and the impact they have on development.

Scarce Resources

Within a company or organization, there is tremendous competition for **resources**. There is rarely sufficient time, personnel, or money to accomplish management's goals. The overall objective of every organization is to increase productivity at the same or lower cost.

It is thus very difficult to free resources for expert systems development. There are basically two reasons for this. First, expert systems, like its parent field AI, is a new technology. It has not yet established a track record of success and is relatively unfamiliar to many computer specialists and managers. No one doubts its potential, but many have adopted a "wait and see" attitude. The decision makers in the organization must be convinced that the use of expert systems technology will, in fact, increase productivity at a justifiable cost.

The second problem is that a number of companies and organizations are attempting to enter the arena of expert systems development. Because the technology is new, there is a shortage of experienced knowledge engineers and other trained personnel able to meet the demand. Owing to this scarcity, hiring a consultant to do expert systems work becomes more expensive than may be justifiable. To overcome this problem, a number of companies are training in-house personnel to fill the void. This solution presents some difficulties during the learning period when employees are not available to perform their assigned job responsibilities. Consequently, the slack must be taken up elsewhere in the organization.

Development Time

Development of expert systems cannot be hurried. Depending on the application, it will take months or possibly even years to complete the development process. This is especially true when the knowledge engineer is inexperienced.

One of the major obstacles of development is the time for knowledge acquisition process. Executed properly, the process of extracting the knowledge from the human expert, in order to create a complete knowledge base, cannot be rushed. It takes maximum effort on the parts of both the knowledge engineer and the human expert to complete the knowledge acquisition process successfully.

Many expert system development projects are team efforts. A team effort always seems to take extra time simply because of its inherent nature.

From another angle, time constraints can also pose a problem. Often, a time limit is placed on the completion of the expert systems development project. This is unfortunate but understandable. When this limitation is enforced, there may be a tendency to believe that increasing the team size will decrease development time. More than one organization has fallen into this trap. But a study of group dynamics indicates that there is an optimum team size, and exceeding this size usually turns out to be counterproductive.

Sources of Errors

In the development process and in the expert system itself, there are a number of sources where errors can occur. These **sources of errors** are summarized in Figure 8.6.

SOURCE	ERROR
Human expert	Incorrect or incomplete knowledge
Knowledge engineer	Semantic errors in communication with the expert, knowledge gaps
Knowledge base	Syntax errors in format, errors caused by incorrect or incomplete knowledge and uncertainty
Inference engine	Bugs in the inference engine and/or development tool, incorrect rule priorities or rule location in the knowledge base
User interface	Incorrect content of communication between the expert system and the end user

FIGURE 8.6 SOURCES OF POSSIBLE ERRORS IN THE EXPERT SYSTEM

The basis of knowledge for the expert system is the human expert's knowledge. If this knowledge is *incorrect* or *incomplete*, then these same errors will be present in the knowledge base.

It may be desirable to have another expert or a panel of experts to certify the human expert's knowledge. This would be important if the expert system were concerned with human life situations such as in a medical diagnosis expert system.

Semantic errors can occur in the interaction phase between the human expert and the knowledge engineer. The message may become lost in the translation; this is more likely to happen with inexperienced knowledge engineers or engineers who have not become as familiar with the domain area as could be expected. An error can also be caused by gaps in the knowledge stream.

Syntax errors in the knowledge base can be caused by using an incorrect form of a rule or a fact. These errors should be flagged by the development tool but may not be.

Errors may occur in the inference engine due to *bugs* in either the structure of the engine or in the development tool. *Rules* may have incorrect priorities or may be inserted incorrectly (in the wrong place) in the knowledge base.

Finally, *content* errors can occur in the user interface. Users may be given incorrect or incomplete instructions causing a breakdown in the system effectiveness and use.

Most, if not all, of these errors should be corrected during final system evaluation before it is released to users. In reality, the total elimination of errors is very difficult and increases in difficulty as system size and complexity grows.

Inherent Limitations

For all the things it does well, the current state of the expert system technology has some **inherent limitations**. As long as these limitations are recognized and accounted for, they are less likely to cause severe problems.

At the present time, expert systems are not capable of acquiring knowledge directly. The acquisition process must utilize a knowledge engineer who then translates the knowledge into a form that is understandable by the expert system. Researchers are working on the development of automated acquisition software, but this software is some years away from commercial use.

At the present time, expert systems are not capable of dealing with knowledge that has a mixed representation. For example, an expert system can not deal, in the same application, with knowledge consisting in part in the form of rules and also in the form of semantic nets. Such mixing capability might be appropriate for applications that merge several representations.

Current expert systems are not capable of refining their own knowledge bases. Such refinements might include combination of rules with the same conclusion or elimination of redundant or contradictory rules. These actions must be performed externally.

A final limitation is that an expert system cannot learn from experience. This would be a desirable characteristic because learning from experience is an integral part of a human expert's capability. The ability to learn from experience is being avidly pursued by researchers but is still several years away from the commercial world.

Integration of the Expert System into the Organization

The final stage of the expert system development process is its **integration** into the organizational structure. This stage actually puts the final expert system *into production*.

The integration process, however, does not start after the completion of the expert system, as might be implied. It starts with the initial idea of building an expert system.

One key to the successful integration of the expert system is the early involvement of management and other personnel whose work will be affected by the presence of the system. As we suggested earlier, involvement of these people in the planning stages and the effect of their input during the development process is likely to improve chances for acceptance of the expert system. The system must be seen for its potential improvements in productivity and its preservation of job security. Successful integration of the expert system depends upon how well these two views (increased productivity and job security) of the expert system are espoused. This task is the job of the project leader (who may or may not be the knowledge engineer).

From the perspective of the organization, the arrival of the expert system cannot be a disruptive process. The organization must be able to continue to function in an efficient manner with as little interruption as possible.

From the expert system development perspective, the expert system must be seen as making a contribution to the attainment of the goals of the organization. The development team, including the human expert and the knowledge engineer, must feel that there is a well-defined and accepted place in the organization for the expert system.

Finally, from the management perspective, inclusion of the expert system must increase productivity. It must also preserve a stable employee morale.

A Final Remark

It is clear from our discussion in this chapter that the development process for an expert system is a complex one. The successful completion of an expert system depends on the cooperative efforts of a number of people from beginning to end. Well done, the expert system development process can be a major asset to an organization's future; poorly done, the process can cost the organization a great deal of time, money, and effort.

Case Study: WPHELP

So far, we have attempted to use our sample expert system, WPHELP, to illustrate the theory of expert systems. Some of the illustrations have been actual examples, while others have been postulated. We will continue using WPHELP to illustrate our purpose in the modules.

While WPHELP is a hypothetical system, its development throughout the chapters illustrates the principles of software engineering discussed in this chapter. In its present form, WPHELP can be described as being in the prototype stage of development. As more rules are added, it has the potentiality of becoming a marketable expert system for the selection of a word processing package for a small business.

Key Points

- An expert system is a piece of software and so its development process can use principles of software engineering.
- The software life cycle contains three phases: development, use, and modification.
- In the software life cycle, approximately 67% of the time and effort is spent in the modification phase, and approximately 33% of the time and effort is spent in the development phase.
- The steps in the development phase of the software life cycle include:
  - Formalization of the software specifications
  - Design of the software system structure
  - Construction of the software system
  - Testing of the software system
  - Documentation of the software system
- The expert system life cycle includes the following phases: development, use/integration, and updating/maintenance.
- In the expert system life cycle, approximately 75% of the time and effort is spent in the development phase, and approximately 25% of the time and effort is spent in the updating/maintenance phase.
- The development phase of the expert system life cycle includes the following steps:
  - Analysis of the problem
  - Formalization of the problem
  - Knowledge acquisition
  - Knowledge representation
  - Prototype development
  - Full system development
  - System evaluation and documentation
- The role of software engineering is to bring law and order to the chaos of software development.
- The software product that results from the software engineering process should have the following characteristics:
  - Fully documented

  - Verified, validated, and tested
  - Cost effective
  - Completed on time
  - Easily manipulatable and enhancible
- Knowledge acquisition should be performed in parallel with the prototyping process.
- Prototype development has several purposes:
  - Validate the choice and definition of the problem to be solved.
  - Make initial determination of the appropriateness of the chosen development tool.
  - Assess the initial completeness of the knowledge acquisition process.
  - Initially evaluate the design of the expert system.
  - Provide an initial test of the reactions of potential users.
  - Allow management to see initial results of the expert system development process.
- Full system development is an extension of the prototype, but problems may occur during the extension process.
- The final system evaluation must be complete and thorough and include outside evaluations and potential users.
- Difficulties in the development of an expert system include scarce resources, development time, sources of errors, and inherent limitations of expert systems.
- To successfully integrate the expert system into the organizational structure,
  - The integration process must begin at the beginning of the expert system development phase.
  - Early involvement of management and other personnel whose work will be affected by the presence of the expert system is important.
  - The arrival of the expert system cannot be a disruptive process to the organization.
  - The expert system must be seen by all concerned as making a contribution to the organization.
  - The presence of the expert system must increase productivity.

Exercises

1. What is the relationship between expert systems and software engineering?
2. Describe the software life cycle.
3. Describe the expert system life cycle.
4. Describe the software engineering methodology.
5. Compare and contrast the development phases of the software and expert system life cycles.
6. Name the seven steps in the development of an expert system. What is the purpose of each step?
7. What are the purposes of developing a prototype?
8. Describe the processes of full system development and final system evaluation.
9. Discuss the four major areas of difficulties in the development of expert systems.

10. What strategies should be used to integrate the expert system into the organizational structure?

Assignments

1. The final evaluation of an expert system is the final phase of the development. In Chapter 5 (Assignment 5) and Chapter 6 (Assignment 3) you developed a rule-based knowledge base for each of a series of problems. For each knowledge base, outline a plan for final evaluation of the knowledge base. Your plan should include the following:

   a. How the rules will be verified.
   b. How the inference chain(s) will be validated. (Include a complete set of test data).
2. Read and summarize the two articles that deal with the application of software engineering techniques. Discuss how the content of these articles might apply to the development of expert systems. Good sources of articles may be found in *BYTE, AI Expert,* and *PC AI*; however, there are other sources as well.

9

THE FUTURE OF EXPERT SYSTEMS

Expert systems technology is gaining widespread acceptance in the commercial world. Companies are talking about their successes with the technology. Other companies are experimenting with the technology, and new applications continue to surface. The interest has created a demand for new and better expert systems development tools that can be used by less experienced knowledge engineers. Improvements in computer hardware/software technology and a desire by vendors to produce quality development tools have led to a greater use of expert systems technology as it proceeds towards maturity.

In the future, we will see improvements in several areas of expert systems technology including knowledge representation, knowledge acquisition, development tools, expert systems design and the programming of expert systems. In this chapter, we will briefly examine these areas. We will also discuss the future availability and cost of expert systems and the concept of intelligent systems. Our final case study scenario will outline a future word processor.

Knowledge Representation

As we pointed out in Chapter 3, the choice of a **knowledge representation scheme** is a key to effective expert systems development. Current models of knowledge representation will be improved and extended. For example, the rules model might be extended to include the direct use of *inheritance* which is characteristic of semantic networks.

There is likely to be an integration of different representation schemes in the same expert system. This would allow an expert system to receive and use knowledge from more than one model. That is, knowledge represented as rules could be combined with knowledge represented as a semantic net or in the form of predicate calculus. The advantage would be that expert systems technology could be applied to applications where the knowledge is represented in more than one way.

Finally, there will be new knowledge representation schemes developed that will be easier and more powerful to use; for example, research on a **model-based knowledge representation** scheme which uses a model structure. The knowledge is given to the representation model, and the model converts the knowledge into the scheme. The knowledge is entered through a dialog between the model and the knowledge engineer, thus freeing the engineer from actually converting the knowledge into the representation scheme. Elements of this technique are already being seen in some expert system shells.

Other new knowledge representation schemes will allow the use of a single time dimension. The **script knowledge representation scheme**, currently under development, allows the use of specifications such as done-before and done-after.

Automated Knowledge Acquisition and System Development

The use of **automation** in the future development of expert systems is very feasible and appealing. Its use is of special interest for knowledge acquisition and on the development of self-learning systems. In this section, we will examine its use in separate but closely related areas.

As discussed in Chapter 5, the task of knowledge acquisition is a complex one. It requires the full cooperation of both the human expert(s) and the knowledge engineer. A problem in the use of manual methods of knowledge acquisition, such as the interview and the analysis of verbal conversations between the human expert and the knowledge engineer, is that there is potentially a loss of valuable time by both people. A second potential problem is that of inaccuracy and/or knowledge gaps. Even when the knowledge engineer is skilled and experienced in the knowledge acquisition process, there is still a loss of productive time that might be spent elsewhere by the human expert. In addition, the human expert may not be able to explicitly give the full details of his or her reasoning in obtaining the solution to the problem. These problems must be addressed for the knowledge base development process to be successful.

These problems and uncertainties surrounding the manual methods of knowledge acquisition have paved the way for the development of **automated knowledge-acquisition tools** [Parsaye and Chignel 1988]. These tools provide a structure that can be filled through the use of a computer program. Their use diminishes the role of the knowledge engineer as the facilitator of the knowledge-acquisition process.

Another major problem with the manual methods of knowledge acquisition is, as the reader can imagine, the cost involved. Automated knowledge-acquisition tools can decrease costs of acquiring knowledge in several ways. Martin and Oxman [1988] listed some of these ways.

1. Decrease the amount of time required to acquire the knowledge.
2. Decrease the skill level required of the person acquiring the knowledge.
3. Automate some aspects of the knowledge acquisition process.
4. Enable users and human experts to add to the knowledge.

It seems reasonable that these steps would decrease costs. It is usually the case that the human expert and a skilled knowledge engineer are both high-priced personnel. Reducing the time required of the human expert in the knowledge-acquisition areas means that more time can be spent doing what he or she does best, being an expert. The knowledge engineer can be freed up from some of the mundane tasks of knowledge acquisition such as collecting statistical data. Also, the knowledge engineer need not be called back to the site to update or modify the expert system if someone else such as a user can make modifications to the expert system's knowledge base.

The cost of knowledge acquisition can also be decreased if the needed skill level of the knowledge engineer can be decreased. Knowledge engineers can be very expensive. It is possible to train a person who, given guidance by the knowledge engineer, can use automated tools for knowledge acquisition or perform acquisition tasks that do not require as high a skill level. This would be analogous to the use of paramedics and paralegals. Also, the increasing quality of the knowledge-acquisition capabilities of expert system shells means that a less skilled person perhaps can perform as well as an experienced knowledge engineer. But, a word of caution is appropriate: investigate the alternatives before implementing this method of decreasing cost.

Automating some aspects of the knowledge-acquisition process can help decrease costs. The use of information will also allow other people, both users and human experts, to add to the knowledge base. There will, however, likely be some areas of the knowledge acquisition process which cannot be automated, such as the determination and closing of "gaps" in the knowledge base. Automated knowledge-acquisition tools are not yet capable of this function.

Research and development work dealing with future automated knowledge-acquisition tools is being done in the industrial world and at universities. Activities have centered in the areas of automated tool development, automated consistency-check tools and self-learning systems [Martin and Oxman 1988].

The development of automated knowledge-acquisition tools allows more people to serve as knowledge engineers at a lower skill level than ordinarily needed, as we mentioned before. The expanded pool of available people allows more expert systems to be built with the result that expert systems technology will become more useful to more applications. It should be feasible to develop cost-effective automated tools to deal with the tasks of knowledge-acquisition.

Automated consistency-check tools would be used to refine the knowledge base so that duplicate or contradictory rules would be eliminated. For example, if two rules had the same conclusion but with different premises, the knowledge engineer would be notified so that appropriate changes could be made. As another example, two rules might have the same premise but have contradictory conclusions. Suppose these two rules were present in the knowledge base:

Rule 1: IF there is a fire,
THEN throw water on it.

Rule 2: IF there is a fire,
THEN don't throw water on it.

The tool would indicate to the knowledge engineer that Rules 1 and 2 were contradictory and, as before, changes could be made. Automated consistency-check tools also appear to be feasible, but much more work needs to be done.

Most researchers in expert systems believe that **self-learning systems** will be the future model for expert systems. These systems would make use of automated knowledge-acquisition tools but would also make use of automated techniques for refining and updating the knowledge base. These systems would have the capability of using *inductive* techniques and have the ability to learn from experience. Automation would be very much a part of a self-learning system.

The development of self-learning systems would enable expert systems to more closely resemble the activities of a human expert. Most experts increase their expertise through experience. They use inductive reasoning by hypothesizing on a set of examples. Through experience, the set of examples increases or is modified with the possible result that hypotheses are modified. An inductive, self-learning system would emulate the expert's behavior.

There are a number of applications for *automated induction systems*. Such systems could search large databases and look for relationships that might exist. For example, marketing strategies for merchandise items such as clothing or children's toys could be formulated with an induction system. Over time, these strategies could be re-examined as new data became available.

It is also hoped that self-learning systems will be able to take knowledge from different forms (representations) and combine it into a single knowledge base. For example, a self-learning system might combine knowledge from a textbook or manual with knowledge from experience to create and update a knowledge base. Diagnostic, control, repair, and educational/training systems would benefit from this induction capability.

System Development Tools

Initially, expert systems were built with the use of high-level languages. While the use of these languages had some merit, they were usually general-purpose languages and did not lend themselves particularly well to the inclusion of intelligence as an integral part of the expert system. Informing schemes had to be built from scratch. Although the high-level languages had limitations, they were the only tools available.

The appearance of expert system shells caused a change in the way that expert systems are developed. Unfortunately, the first shells were, in general, not very powerful because the shell technology was not well developed. Newer versions of the shells will have much more powerful utilities, such as graphics and more natural-language interfaces, that will be well within the grasp of the shell user. The future shells will have an appearance of CAD-like capability.

Martin and Oxman [1988] note that intelligent design tools will assist the knowledge engineer in a number of ways. Included among these are:

1. Determining problem domain characteristics
2. Ensuring that all important problem attributes are considered
3. Determining which knowledge representation(s) and inferencing mechanism(s) are used
4. Assessing system user capabilities and selecting appropriate user interface design schemes
5. Helping to select appropriate shells for given applications and determining if other software tools are needed

The effect of these advances in expert systems tools technologies will result in a higher quality expert system that will be able to deal more effectively with an enlarged number of applications.

User Interfaces

A definite trend in recent years is to improve the design and effectiveness of the **user interfaces** for expert systems. These improvements have been made in both the content of the communication and the physical means of communication between the user and the expert system. The majority of the improvements have come, however, in the content phase.

The term "user friendly" is familiar to many users and software developers. It has had a rather ill-defined meaning as it has been applied, but most people who use the term have at least an intuitive, if not formal, understanding of what it means.

The term has had a significant impact on expert systems development. Historically, communication between an expert and a non-expert on the expert's domain of knowledge has not been easy. The expert usually has communicated in what might be called the "domains," which is not always known by the user. The vocabulary of computers is an excellent example of "domainese."

The vocabulary content and level of the expert must be translated to the user by the expert system. The trend is towards the use of natural language and help facilities so that the expert system is as easy to use as possible for the user.

The use of natural-language interfaces is the attempt to make the human/machine interaction as natural as possible. There is a great deal of research going on in the area of natural-language processing. However, significant breakthroughs have been constrained by the complexity of the problem.

The techniques of **key-word analysis** and **syntactic/semantic analysis** have been the usual techniques used in natural language processing work. Because of the nature of the English language with many words having multiple meanings, key-word analysis has had limited popularity. Syntactic/semantic analysis appears to have a much brighter future.

The physical aspects of the user interface will likely undergo dramatic changes in the future. Traditionally, the physical interface situation has the user sitting in front of a terminal with a keyboard and the screen as the communication media. Communication is of the form "I speak, you listen and then you speak, I listen" where "speak" means putting messages on the screen via the keyboard or the computer's character generator and "listen" means seeing a message on the screen or entering a message into the computer's memory. It is rather an inhuman way of communicating.

Expert systems of the future will have a new meaning for "speak" and "listen." The user will actually talk to the expert system and the expert system will talk to the user. This communication will be achieved with the use of *speech recognition* and *synthesis* (speech production) technologies housed in the computer. And, the communication will be in ordinary English.

Research in speech recognition and synthesis technologies has progressed somewhat slowly so far. Success has been limited as the same constraints faced by natural language, memory limitations, and computing speed are also faced by researchers in speech recognition and synthesis.

In the future, expert systems will have user interfaces that will facilitate communication. The interfaces will be verbal and user friendly with maximum attention paid by expert systems developers to the quality of the user interface.

Availability and Cost

The increasing popularity of expert systems and the extended number of possible applications has been evident in recent years. At the present time, expert systems technology is available in some form to almost any business that has a need for it. The increased number of knowledge engineers and availability of affordable development tools have created a healthy environment for expert systems technology; this availability of people and tools will continue to grow in the future.

We must warn, however, that just because the technology is available, expert systems technology is not for every business nor for the solution of every problem. A careful apriori-needs analysis must be performed by any business or individual seeking to implement expert systems technology. As we have previously pointed out, expert systems technology is not a panacea.

Currently, the technology has significant inherent limitations. Keeping these limitations in perspective, as well as performing a careful, initial-needs analysis, will assist a business in making a proper decision about whether to implement expert systems technology. A major factor in this decision is the cost. The costs to develop expert systems must be justified.

While it is true that the price of computer hardware has decreased dramatically over the years, the same cannot be said for computer software. Software development requires people and the cost of people has tended to increase; the trend is likely to continue, even with the advent of automated development tools, some of which were described earlier in this chapter. Consequently, the cost of developing an expert system is likely to increase. However, it is quite possible that the expense of expert system development can be justified. In addition to the initial outlay for development, there is the cost of updating and maintaining the expert system after its development. Again, people are involved and so costs are not likely to decrease.

The development of automated tools will help bring down the costs of expert systems. There will be a high initial cost for the tools, but this will be offset by a likely reduction in the number of people needed. It will be interesting to see what happens.

Intelligent Systems

As we consider what is next for expert systems, we will find that they will be integrated with other systems, such as computer or manufacturing systems, to form **intelligent systems**. Prior to this point, we have considered expert systems in only a stand-alone mode.

The integration of expert systems with other systems affords the opportunity for more efficient and effective operation of the system. An expert system can be used to monitor or control the system, diagnose problems, or a number of other tasks. For example, suppose we have a robot with an expert system embedded in it. If the robot develops a malfunction, the expert system could diagnose the problem and report its findings to a human who could then repair the robot. The diagnostic function performed by the expert system could save hours of troubleshooting time for the human. In another situation, the robot may be programmed to perform a particular task. If the conditions of the environment in which the task was to be performed changed (such as weather or object mislocation), the expert system could reprogram the robot to meet the changed environmental conditions, thus, probably saving time and money.

From this brief discussion, it is clear that expert systems can be very useful when integrated with other systems. In the future, many more applications will make use of expert systems, enabling each application to be performed in an intelligent manner.

Case Study: The Future Word Processor

In our case study for Chapter 9, we thought it might be interesting to consider the future word processor. It is likely that it will be an intelligent word processor with some very useful features. Consider this scenario.

Mary Jones, claims adjuster for the Federated Insurance Company, arrives at her office on Monday morning to face a very heavy day. Severe thunderstorms and a tornado had hit the community on Saturday and Sunday, causing a great deal of paper work to settle the claims. There are also a number of reports to file with the district office.

Mary sits down at her desk with a cup of coffee and switches on her word processor. She can communicate verbally with the word processor, using a header, which also is directly linked to the district office so that electronic mail can be used.

Mary begins by filing a report to her boss in the district office recounting her weekend activities dealing with the storm damage. It was a hard weekend on Mary and she decides to let her word processor write the report. She gives her essential information to the word processor which then composes the report. After a few seconds of work, the system asks Mary if she would like to review the report to determine if any important details were omitted. The review of the document can be done either auditorily, visually on the screen, or from hard copy. Mary elects the auditory method and as she listens, she recalls some missing details. At the end of the review, Mary indicates the details to be added. The system constructs appropriate sentences and integrates them into the report. After a review of the changes, the report is sent electronically to the district office and a copy is filed on Mary's hard disk.

Next, Mary must deal with the various claims forms. She verbally enters the necessary information about each claim (name, address, description of loss, and so on). Reports on each claim are then generated using the appropriate template and sent electronically to the district office.

Altogether, it has taken Mary less than an hour to perform a set of tasks that might have taken her and a secretary, without a word processor, well over a day to complete. Since Mary is also an insurance agent, she now has time to do what she enjoys best: leave the office to work with her clients.

The scenario we have just presented is not far from reality. It is easy to see that intelligent systems, such as the word processor in our example, will be more productive in the future.

Key Points

- Expert systems technology is gaining widespread acceptance in the commercial world.
- Expert systems technology will be improved in the areas of knowledge representation, knowledge acquisition, system tools, and user interfaces.
- Expert systems of the future will likely be able to deal with more than one knowledge representation scheme at the same time.
- New knowledge representation schemes will be developed to be more powerful and easier to use, and allow the use of single-time dimension.
- Two problems of manual knowledge-acquisition methods (such as interviews and analysis of verbal conversations) are the loss of valuable time and potential problems with inaccuracy and/or gaps in the knowledge.
- The problems and uncertainties of time loss and potential knowledge inaccuracies/gaps have paved the way for the development of automated knowledge-acquisition tools.
- Another major problem with the manual methods of knowledge acquisition is the cost.
- There are several ways to decrease the cost of knowledge acquisition.
  - Decrease the amount of time required to acquire the knowledge
  - Decrease the skill level required of the person acquiring the knowledge
  - Automate some aspects of the knowledge-acquisition process
  - Enable users and human experts to add to the knowledge
- There is a trend to sell the packaged knowledge for purposes other than use in an expert system.
- Research and development work dealing with automated knowledge-acquisition tools is being done in both the industrial world and universities.
- Automated knowledge-acquisition tools will allow more people to serve as knowledge engineers at a lower skill level, and it should be feasible for these tools to be cost-effective.
- Automated consistency-check tools would be used to locate duplicate or contradictory rules in the knowledge base.
- Self-learning systems are the hope of the future for expert systems.
- Most experts increase their expertise through experience.
- It is hoped that self-learning systems can take knowledge in different representations and combine it together into a single knowledge base.
- Expert systems were initially developed using general-purpose, high-level languages.
- Expert system shells will become more powerful and easier to use.
- Intelligent design tools will aid the knowledge engineer in a number of ways including:
  - Determining problem domain characteristics
  - Ensuring that all important problem attributes are considered
  - Determining which knowledge representation(s) and inferencing mechanism(s) are used
  - Assessing system user capabilities and selecting appropriate user interface design schemes
  - Helping select appropriate shells for given applications

- A definite trend in recent years has been to improve the design and effectiveness of user interfaces in expert systems.
- The user interface is concerned with the content of the communications and the physical aspects of the communication.
- The term "user friendly" has meant many things to many people in the past but will take on new meaning in the future for expert systems.
- There has always been a problem in the communication between an expert and a nonexpert in the expert's domain of knowledge.
- The use of natural-language interfaces is the attempt to make the human/machine interaction as human-like as possible.
- Key-word analysis and syntactic/semantic analysis are the techniques used in natural-language processing.
- Natural-language processing is constrained by computer memory limitations and computing speed.
- Physical communication between the user and the expert system has traditionally been through the keyboard and the terminal screen.
- Speech recognition and synthesis technologies are good possibilities for the physical interface but suffer from the same constraints is natural-language processing.
- User interfaces in expert systems of the future will be verbal and user friendly with increased attention paid by expert systems developers to the quality of the interface.
- Presently, expert systems technology is available, in some form, to almost any business that has a need.
- A careful apriori-needs analysis must be performed by any business or individual seeking to implement expert systems technology.
- Cost is a major factor in the decision about implementing expert systems technology.
- While computer hardware costs have decreased, software development costs have tended to rise.
- Automated tools, although costly, initially, will bring the cost of expert systems down.
- Expert systems can be integrated with other systems such as computer or manufacturing. The result of the integration of an expert system with another system has come to be called an intelligent system.
- Intelligent systems, such as the intelligent word processor, will increase productivity in many future applications.

Exercises

1. What are the improvements will be made in knowledge representation schemes?
2. What are the problems of manual methods of knowledge acquisition?
3. How can the cost of knowledge acquisition be decreased?
4. What are the characteristics of automated knowledge-acquisition tools?
5. What is the purpose of automated consistency-check tools?
6. What are the characteristics of self-learning systems?
7. What improvements will be made in system development tools?

8. Discuss the two major aspects of the user interface.
9. What is the effect of natural-language processing on the user interface? What is the current status of this technology?
10. What is the effect of speech recognition and synthesis on the user interface? What is the current status of these technologies?
11. Describe the user interface of the future expert systems.
12. What factors will affect the availability of expert systems in the future?
13. How will cost impact the future of expert systems?
14. Describe the concept of an intelligent system.

Assignments

1. Locate recent (last two years) articles that deal with each of the major sections (excluding the Case Study) of the chapter. Read and summarize one article for each section. ***The Readers Guide to Periodical Literature*** in the library might be a good place to start.
2. You are familiar with the concepts of database and spreadsheet. Design an intelligent system that could be integrated with each. What characteristics would your designed systems have? How would productivity be increased?
3. Design your expert system of the future. What characteristics would it have?
4. The Japanese have undertaken the development of a model for the future of AI and expert systems, called the Fifth-Generation Project. The project has a ten year duration that began in 1984 and is a cooperative effort between Japan's public and private sectors. The project is described in a book by E. Feigenbaum and P. McCorduck entitled ***The Fifth Generation*** (Addison-Wesley, 1983). With the help of your reference librarian, locate a copy of this book. What are the implications for business as a result of the assumed successful completion of the project?

Part II

THE APPLICATIONS

Module 1

EXPERT SYSTEMS AND VP-EXPERT

There is an increasing interest and emphasis in today's business world concerning the topic of expert systems. Expert systems, computer programs that mimic the knowledge of a human expert, are already being used efficiently and profitably in business, manufacturing, training, government, and other areas. In this module we will explore expert systems in general, show overview examples, explain the purpose of using VP-Expert (a tool to develop expert systems), and guide the reader through the preliminary tasks of making backup disks, formatting disks, and making data disks.

Introduction to Expert Systems

Expert systems are a part of a technology called artificial intelligence. Artificial intelligence (AI) seeks to create intelligent systems through hardware and software to perform certain tasks or solve problems. Other fields of artificial intelligence in addition to expert systems are robotics, machine vision, natural-language processing, and general problem solving. We will concentrate on understanding expert systems for the business world.

Expert systems are designed to behave like an expert in a particular field or domain of knowledge. Like a human expert, an expert system draws information from a user and then by using its own ''internal experience and resources'' gives advice, makes suggestions, delivers an answer, predicts an outcome, or some similar behavior. The purpose of having an expert system is to manage and run a business (or other activity) more economically and efficiently. Expert systems are also useful because they can be more permanent than a human expert. Human experts change companies, go on vacation, retire, and so on. With proper maintenance of hardware and software, expert systems can remain on the job permanently.

Creating expert systems involves several steps. First, some problem domain must be identified, such as diagnosing a medical disease, repairing computer networks, writing mortgage loans, determining credit approvals, and so on. Once the problem area is determined, then a team of knowledge engineers, domain experts, and users can work to create an expert system that will help solve the problem. The expert is needed to provide the knowledge about the problem. The knowledge engineer is the one who identifies the needed knowledge and translates it into structures that computers use; and the user of the proposed system is needed to give advice and suggestions about the usability of the system in the normal workday environment. If proper teamwork is present, then there is a greater chance of producing a usable expert system.

The expert system is actually a software program that runs on some computer (supercomputer, mainframe, minicomputer, or microcomputer). It may be written in a language (PASCAL, C, BASIC, and so on) or with a special tool (shell). To use a shell, you do not have to be a programmer. We will confine our attention to producing expert systems for business with a tool (shell) called **VP-Expert**.

Expert system software has three conceptual parts: the knowledge base, the inference engineer, and the user interface. The knowledge base is often a set of rules (or other representation) and facts about the problem area. The inference engine is the mechanism that reasons or infers conclusions after examining the knowledge base. The user interface is the communication between the user and the actual software. A typical interface is the way that users communicate through a video display terminal. These three logical components are pictured in Figure M1.1.

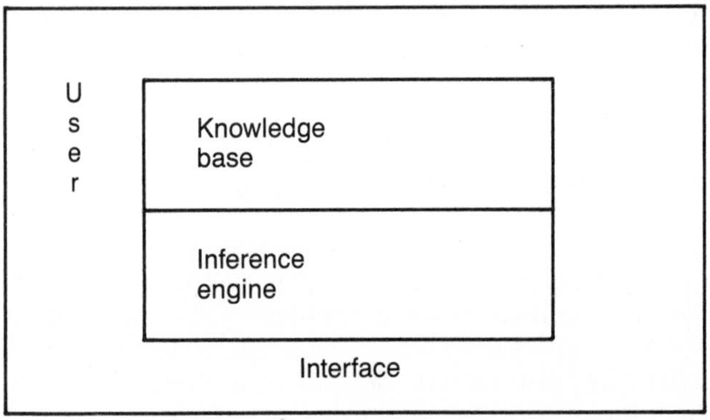

FIGURE M1.1 THE THREE LOGICAL PARTS OF AN EXPERT SYSTEM

Examples of Expert Systems

Expert systems can help in various applications. They can assist in the functions of controlling, debugging, designing, diagnosing, instructing, simulating, interpreting, planning, predicting, and repairing. An expert system can give advice on investments, determine the acceptability of a credit application, predict backorders, control inventory, design investment portfolios, or give advice on the purchase of a car. Managers could use an expert system to simulate personnel situations. A traditional computer program can determine a mortgage balance, but it can not give advice to a client on whether or not to buy, or what mortgage plan to follow. A traditional computer system may ticket a passenger for a vacation, but the system cannot advise the client on the best vacation for the least money. Expert systems can help in these areas.

Expert systems are also used in other application areas. An expert system may advise a mechanic on repair procedures. Car-trouble analysis, microcomputer troubleshooting, or airplane maintenance can be improved with the use of expert systems. In the field of medicine, special expert systems can diagnose ailments and suggest possible treatments. In the field of manufacturing, an expert system can control a production process. In the field of education, expert systems can be used as effective tutors. Clearly, we have a wide range of potential expert systems across many areas of application.

Emphasis of the Modules: VP-Expert

In this wide range of applications, you will learn how to create a expert system. The purpose of the modules of this book is to give you step-by-step instructions in creating an expert system with the tool or shell, VP-Expert. This particular tool combines economy, ease of use, and the ability to use spreadsheet and database files already known to business. The step-by-step procedures to be used are detailed in the modules. The theory and underlying principles of expert system technology are given in Chapters 1 through 9. The reader may choose first to do the hands-on activities (Modules 1 through 8), or to read the conceptual information (Chapters 1 through 9), or combine one theory and one practice (Chapter 1, Module 1, Chapter 2, Module 2, and so on). The purpose of the modular sections is to give you a simple, sequential "recipe" for using and creating expert systems with VP-Expert. The modules, exercises, and assignments are designed to give you hands-on experience with VP-Expert. The exercises are designed as a guided review of material in the modules, whereas the assignments are *extended* hands-on exercises from the module. The expert systems used in the applications section are chosen for educational use rather than performance. Small expert systems are used at first so you can get a clear overview of an entire expert system.

VP-Expert is a software tool or shell from Paperback Software International in Berkeley, CA. The software that comes with this book is an educational version, 2.1. The major differences between the education version and the regular version are capability and cost. The educational version which comes with this book has three limitations:

1. The size of each knowledge base is limited to 16K (16,384 bytes).
2. Only three separate knowledge bases may be chained together.
3. The maximum number of database records which can be used to create an expert system is 150.

Given that the objective is to learn how to create expert systems with VP-Expert, these limitations are not serious.

Getting Started with VP-Expert

Before you can use VP-Expert there are some preliminary but important tasks to be performed. The VP-Expert shell must be backed up, the Sample Files Disk must be backed up, a new Data Disk must be created, and the system requirements must be checked. In particular, you will need three double-sided disks in order to do the following:

1. Make a backup copy of VP-Expert and label it as a backup.
2. Make a copy of the Sample Files Disk and label it as a backup.
3. Create a Data Disk.

In order to run VP-Expert, you will need the following:

1. IBM-compatible microcomputer.
2. 384K or more RAM (640K total needed to use all of VP-Expert's features).
3. Two double-sided disk drives (a hard disk drive is recommended).
4. DOS version 2.xx or higher.

To use the graphics features, you will need a graphics card such as CGA, EGA, or VGA, Hercules monochrome, or other compatible video card.

Start by first creating the backups and Data Disks (explained in the next section). Details on using a hard disk are presented in the Appendices. Upon successful completion of these tasks, we will be able to us VP-Expert in Module 2.

Creating Backups and Data Disks

Data Disks are used to store the expert system files that you create — separate from the Sample Files Disk of the modules. Hence, we need to provide for backup and recovery before we use the new tools. In any computer application, we must protect ourselves against the accidental loss of data and damage to programs. Thus, the first thing to do is to back up the software that comes with this book. The conceptual steps to do this are listed as follows:

1. Produce new labels for the backups to be made.
2. Place write-protect tabs (tape) on the notch on the disks to be copied (original disks).

3. Give the computer the DISKCOPY command from DOS (operating system) to copy all files from A drive to B drive and then press ENTER.
4. Place the new labels on the new disks (backups).
5. Format a Data Disk or work disk.
6. Store the original disks in a safe dry place.

The first procedure in diskette backup is to create the labels for the disks. Using a pen or felt-tip pen, fill out three labels according to the information given in Figure M1.2. Careful attention to this simple task may save you time and effort in the long run.

```
Label for VP-Expert backup
          VP-Expert Ed. Ver. 2.1 backup
          Your name
          Date
Label for Sample Files Disk
          Sample Files Disk backup
          VP-Expert Ed. Ver. 2.1
          Your name
          Date
Label for Data Disk
          Data Disk
          VP-Expert Ed. Ver. 2.1 files backup
          Your name
          Date
```

FIGURE M1.2 LABELS FOR BACKUPS AND DATA DISKS

The version number is necessary due to problems created by the use of different software versions. Your name is needed in case you lose the disk, and the other information is needed because the number of disks grows exponentially; you will soon forget. Have the labels ready before you make the backups.

With the labels written, you are ready to create the physical backups. In order to guard against *accidents* in losing data, place a write-protect tab on each of the two original disks to be copied. A **write-protect tab** is a piece of tape that you fold over the notch that appears on the right side of your diskettes as shown in Figure M1.3.

A disk with a write-protect tab can be accessed (read) but cannot be changed (written to). If you do not have the usual silver or black tabs, use a piece of masking tape, but be sure that the tape is firmly on the diskette and does not get caught in the disk drive.

To create the backups of VP-Expert and the Sample Files Disk, you may use the DISKCOPY command. At the `A>` prompt and with VP-Expert in the A drive and a disk in the B drive, enter:

```
A>DISKCOPY A: B:
```

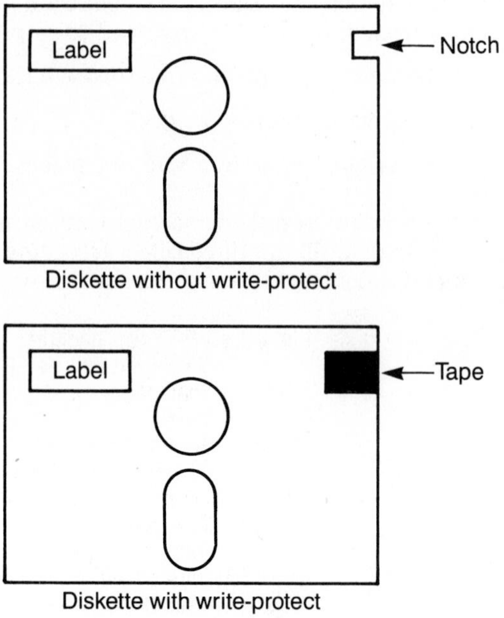

FIGURE M1.3 WRITE PROTECTION FOR A DISKETTE

to create your backup copy on the disk in the B drive. Place the appropriate label on the new disk. Repeat the same procedure for making a backup of the Sample Files Disk.

To create a Data Disk for future use, format your third disk. With a DOS disk in the A drive and a disk in the B drive, enter:

```
A>FORMAT b:/s/v
```

When the system asks you for a volume name, enter:

Data Disk

To implement certain features of VP-Expert you will need to copy certain files from the original two disks to your new Data Disk. With the VP-Expert Disk in the A drive and your new Data Disk in the B drive, enter:

```
COPY vpxi.exe b:
```

Replace the VP-Expert Disk in the A drive with the Sample Files Disk and enter:

```
COPY vpxhelp.exe b:
COPY vpxhelp.chp b:
```

When you are finished, check to make sure that your Data Disk is correct by entering:

```
A>b:
B>dir
```

The VP-Expert files on your Data Disk should match those shown in Figure M1.4. Now, put the original VP-Expert and Sample Files Disk away in a safe place. Then we are ready to start VP-Expert.

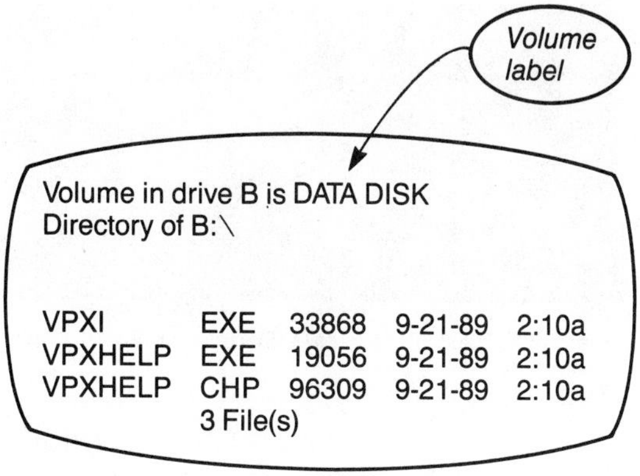

FIGURE M1.4 DIRECTORY OF THE NEW DATA DISK

Starting VP-Expert

Let's start up VP-Expert to make sure that we have everything ready in order to use VP-Expert in subsequent modules. In your computer environment go to the `A>` prompt and follow these instructions:

1. Place VP-Expert (backup) in the A drive.
2. Place the Sample Files Disk (backup) in the B drive.
3. At the `A>` Prompt, enter:
   `vpx`
   and press the ENTER key. You should now see the screen that is shown in Figure M1.5.
4. Move the light bar from 4Consult to 8Quit by pressing the Right Arrow key (found on the far right of your keyboard) and then press the ENTER key. You should now be back at the `A>` prompt.

   If all went well, you have accessed VP-Expert and exited the software. This is represented visually in Figure M1.6 which tells us that to enter VP-Expert we use vpx and to exit, we use 8Quit.

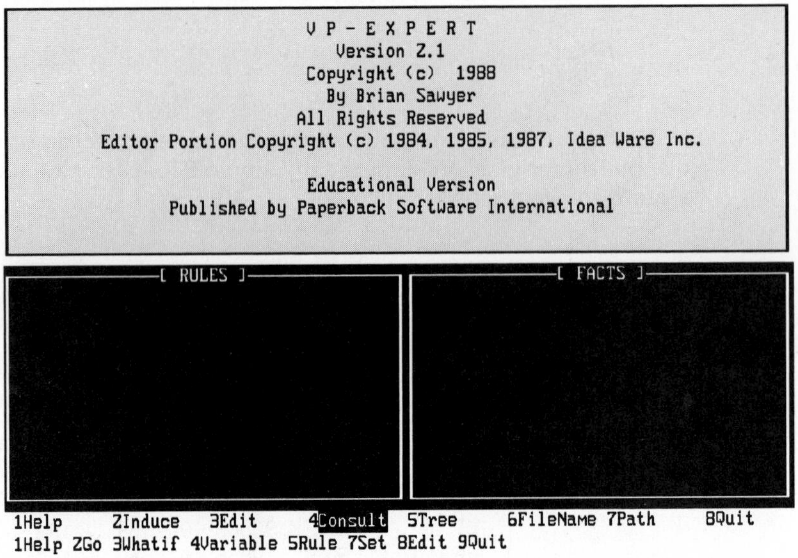

FIGURE M1.5 STARTING VP-EXPERT

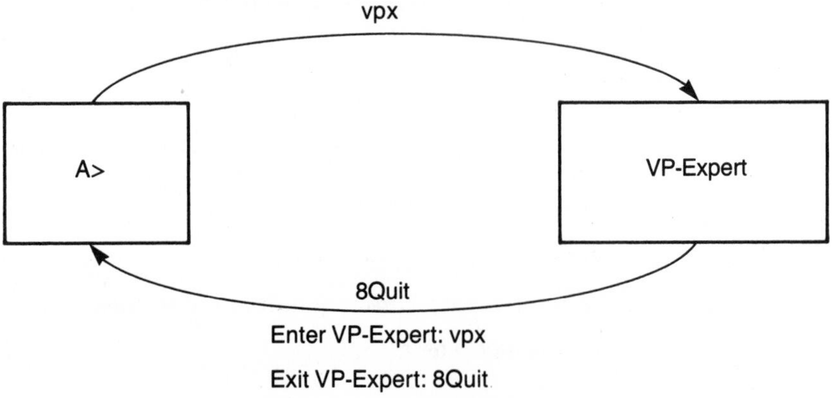

FIGURE M1.6 USING VP-EXPERT

Getting "in, out, and around software" (navigating) is important for productive sessions with the computer. If you have any problems, check to make sure that VP-Expert is in the A drive. Other problems may be associated with the system requirements; a user has no way of looking at a computer and knowing its memory size. To check the version number of DOS or the operating system, enter ver at the **A>** prompt. In any computer environment, it is useful to have the system hardware (memory size, graphics board, and so on) listed on an index card that is attached to the front or side of the computer. This will save endless hours of frustration in trying to run new microcomputer software. It might be a good idea to ask the person in charge of your computer environment to provide this information.

Now with the original software put aside, our backups made, and our completion of a short test of VP-Expert, we are ready to begin work with VP-Expert.

Key Points

- Expert systems are part of a technology called artificial intelligence or AI.
- Expert systems are software programs that emulate the intelligence and knowledge of a human expert.
- An expert system can be used in business, manufacturing, government, and education to control, debug, design, diagnose, instruct, simulate, interpret, plan, predict, or repair.
- Expert systems in business can perform specific tasks like controlling inventory, managing an investment portfolio, advising on mortgage loans, planning a new building, predicting interest rates, and so on.
- Programmers can implement an expert system with a programming language. Non-programmers can produce expert systems without programming by using a tool called a shell.
- The emphasis of the modules is to present easy, step-by-step instructions on how to create and use expert systems with a microcomputer expert system shell called VP-Expert.
- You may read all the modules first (applications), the theory (chapters), or combine them in pairs as you go.
- In order to use VP-Expert (or any other microcomputer software), you should write-protect the original disks, create backups of each original disk, create data disks to store your files, label the new backups properly, and store the originals in a safe place.
- To use VP-Expert you will need a backup copy of VP-Expert, a backup of the Sample Files Disk and a Data Disk. The Sample Files Disk will be used to run and modify examples, and the Data Disk will be used when you create your own expert systems.
- The DISKCOPY command of DOS is used to create the backups. The syntax to copy all files on the A drive to a disk on the B drive is: DISKCOPY a: b:.
- The system requirements for running VP-Expert are an IBM-compatible microcomputer, DOS 2.xx or higher, 384K of memory (640K to run all the features of VP-Expert), and two double-sided disk drives (or a hard disk system).
- To start VP-Expert enter vpx and press ENTER. To exit VP-Expert, select 8Quit and press ENTER.

Exercises

1. a. Name the three parts of an expert system.
   b. Name five business applications using expert systems.
2. Why do you place write-protect tabs on diskettes?
3. What is the purpose of a backup disk?
4. Each of the following DISKCOPY commands has a syntax or "spelling" error(s). Identify the error.
   a. DISKCOPY A : B :
   b. DISKCOPY A:B:
   c. DISKCOPY A B
   d. DISKCOPY A A
   e. DISKCOPY A;B
5. Match the command on the left to the task on the right.

____ 1. DISKCOPY	a. Formats and copies
____ 2. VER	b. Makes a duplicate
____ 3. FORMAT	c. Makes a disk usable
____ 4. COPY	d. Reveals the version number of the operating system

6. Mark the following statements T (true) or F (false). VP-Expert:
   a. ____ is a programming language like COBOL or PASCAL.
   b. ____ comes from Paperback Software International of Berkeley, CA.
   c. ____ requires 200K of memory.
   d. ____ runs under any DOS.
   e. ____ is a microcomputer software development tool.
7. To run VP-Expert, enter ____ .
   a. go
   b. vp
   c. vpe
   d. vpx
   e. vpxt

Assignments

1. From your computer system, fill in the information below

   Type of computer ____________________

   Version of DOS ____________________

   Memory size ____________________

   Graphics adapter ____________________

   Mouse ____________________

2. a. Check the contents of your VP-Expert backup. Do this by placing the disk in the A drive and entering dir. The names of your files should appear on the screen.
   b. To obtain a printout of what appears on the screen press the SHIFT key and the PRTSC key at the same time. Use printscreen to obtain a list (directory) of the files on your backup disks.
   c. How many files are on the disk?

3. Repeat Assignment 2 using your Data Disk.

4. The Sample Files Disk has so many files that the screens scroll faster than you can read. To remedy, this enter:

   ```
   A>DIR/W
   ```

   Columns of file names appear but dates and file sizes are missing. To send the complete directory to the printer and screen, enter:

   ```
   CTRL PRTSC
   DIR
   CTRL PRTSC
   ```

   The CTRL PRTSC command is a toggle to send screen output to the printer. The command is given again to turn off the printing.
   a. Obtain a printout of the directory of the Sample Files Disk.
   b. How many files are on the disk?
   c. How many free bytes are left on the disk?

5. When you enter vpx to start VP-Expert, you are executing a file called vpx.exe. Using the printout in Assignment 2 or the command

   ```
   DIR vpx.exe
   ```

   find out how large the file is.

6. If a file has an extension of .kbs it is an expert system file. Place the Sample Files Disk in the A drive and enter:

   ```
   A>DIR *.kbs
   ```

   to display all files that end with .kbs.
   a. How many .kbs files are on the Sample Files Disk?
   b. Obtain a printout by using the CTRL PRTSC before and after the DIR *.kbs command.

7. Most disks have a text file that gives information about the disk.
   a. Use the DIR command to see if a Readme or similar file is on the Sample Files Disk.
   b. If there is, display the contents of the file with the command

      ```
      A>TYPE file.ext
      ```

   c. To obtain a printout of the file, enter:

      ```
      COPY file.ext<PRN
      ```

      or

      ```
      COPY file.ext LPT1
      ```

      You must type the exact name of the file name. When you have typed in the instruction, press the ENTER key.

8. Repeat Assignment 7 for a file called Files.lst on the VP-Expert backup disk.

9. DOS has two types of commands: internal and external. DISKCOPY is an external command, whereas FORMAT and COPY are internal commands.
   a. Look up the difference between internal and external commands in the DOS manual.
   b. How does this explain the problem and or frustration that users have with the error message "file not found"?

10. Obtain a printout of the opening screen of VP-Expert by:
    a. Getting into VP-Expert.
    b. Using printscreen (see Assignment 2).
    c. Exiting VP-Expert.

Module 2

EXAMPLES OF EXPERT SYSTEMS

We want to run our first expert system to select a word processor. To do this we must learn to use the Main Menu to set the path, select the file, and then run the expert system with the Consult Menu. We will then run another version of the same expert system that will show us the parts of the system and examine the software that produced the interactive expert system. After using the system, we'll explore the help facilities within the VP-Expert system environment.

Using VP-Expert

We will use VP-Expert to run our first expert system or consultation. The expert system will advise us on selecting a word processor for IBM-compatible microcomputers used in a small business. Our first example will be small and somewhat limited in its advice, but a small system rather than a large one is easier to conceptualize at first.

The Main Menu

To get started, boot the system and proceed until you get to the A prompt (`A>`). Place the VP-Expert system software in the A drive and the Sample Files Disk (backup) in the B drive. (Hard disk users will use the C drive. See Appendices for hard disk usage.) Type vpx and press the ENTER key. Your screen should look like Figure M2.1.

Another name for this screen is the **Main** Menu. The information on the screen identifies the software (VP-Expert), the version (Educational 2.1), and the publisher (Paperback Software International). The bottom of the screen shows the Main Menu choices consisting of eight items. The menu or menu bar is arranged in horizontal format. The menu bar shows the eight choices, which are:

```
1Help 2Induce 3Edit 4Consult 5Tree 6FileName 7Path 8Quit
```

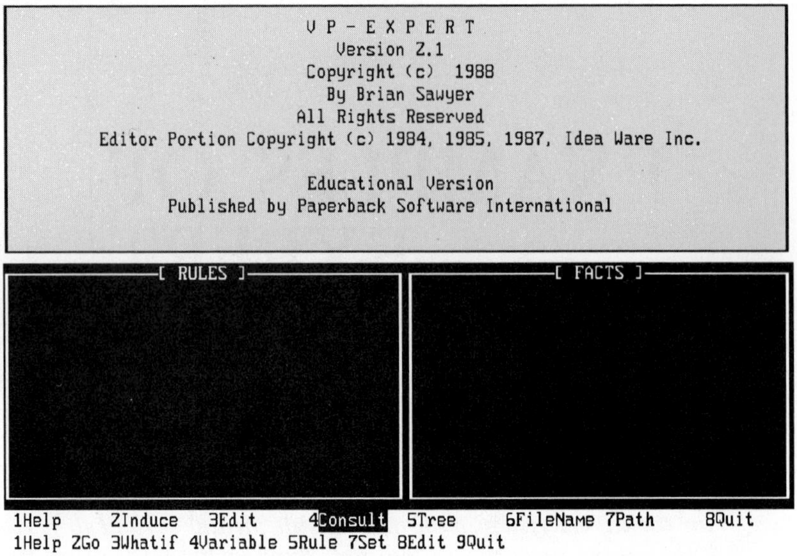

FIGURE M2.1 VP-EXPERT OPENING SCREEN OR MAIN MENU

The words underneath the menu bar identify or explain one of the options. For example, the opening screen in Figure M2.1 identifies the menu choice 4Consult. The message underneath 4Consult is a submenu of 8 choices as shown in Figure M2.1. If you press the Right or Left Arrow key, the light bar (lighted box) moves right or left and the message line changes.

Our purpose is to run a sample expert system. VP-Expert calls this a **consultation** or **consult** for short. In order to run a consultation with an expert system, we must first do two things: (1) tell the computer where to find the file, and (2) what the name of the file is. Hence, we will use the following three Main Menu choices in this order:

Step 1. Identify where the files are using 7Path.
Step 2. Select the file name by using 6FileName.
Step 3. Run the chosen expert system file by using 4Consult.

It is a good idea to always start with Step 1. Tell the computer where to find files (path) whenever we get into VP-Expert, regardless of the task.

Let's select the B drive as our path, wp1 as our expert system, and run or consult with this file name. Follow these steps:

Step 1. Press the Right Arrow key until the light bar is on 7Path. Press the ENTER key. The phrase "What is the new pathname?" will appear in a box on the screen. Type b: and press the ENTER key. (Hard disk users will use the C drive). Use the BACKSPACE key to correct any typing errors before pressing ENTER.

Step 2. Using the Right Arrow key, move the light bar to 6FileName and press ENTER. The message "Choose a File:" will appear on the screen. A list of file names will appear underneath the message. This list may extend beyond what you see. Using the Arrow keys, move the light bar to wp1. When the light is on the bottom row, file names will scroll up when the Down Arrow key is pressed. When the light bar is on wp1, press the ENTER key. If you already know the file name, you may type the file name, wp1, and then press ENTER. (If no file names appear or if you can't find the right files, then you have the wrong disk in the B drive or you didn't set the path correctly.)

Step 3. With the path identified as the B drive, the file as wp1, and the light bar on 4Consult, press the ENTER key to enter the Consult Menu.

The opening screen for the Consult Menu is shown in Figure M2.2.

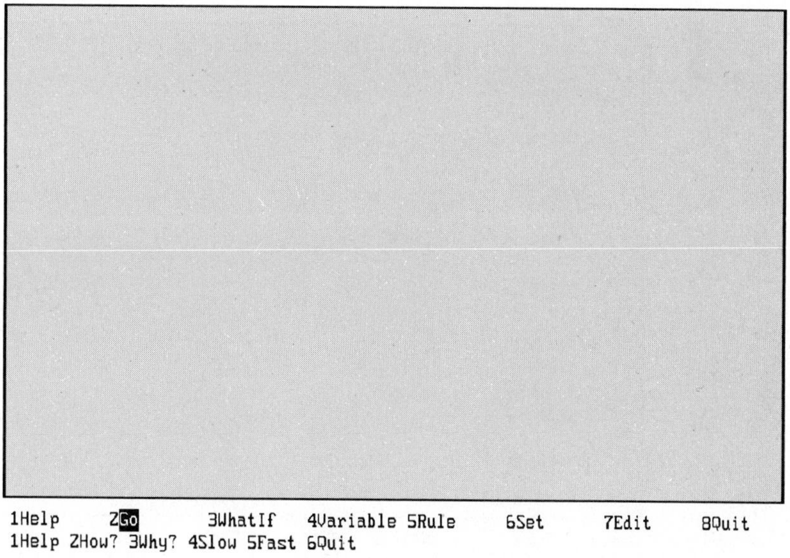

FIGURE M2.2 THE OPENING SCREEN FOR THE CONSULT MENU

If you do not see this screen, then retry the steps. If the message "File not found" appears, you may not have the proper path. If the message "Not enough memory" appears, then VP-Expert does not have enough internal memory (RAM or random access memory) to load the file. Correct this either by trying a lower version of DOS or using a machine with 640K of RAM. Hopefully these errors did not occur.

Consultation Sessions

The only identification for our Consult Menu of Figure M2.2 is on a blank screen with a menu at the bottom, with 2Go highlighted. The menu bar at the bottom of the screen tells us that we have eight options for consulting with the expert system that is now loaded in memory. Notice that the menu bar is on option 2Go, which has a submenu of six choices. When the 2Go option is selected, control will pass to the loaded expert system or .kbs file. You will then follow the instructions from the expert system software until the end of the consultation. For example, press the ENTER key when the light bar is on 2Go. You should see Figure M2.3 which is the start of the sample expert system wp1.kbs.

Follow the instructions on the screen and press the SPACEBAR to start the advising example. The screen will be cleared and a question will appear on the display.

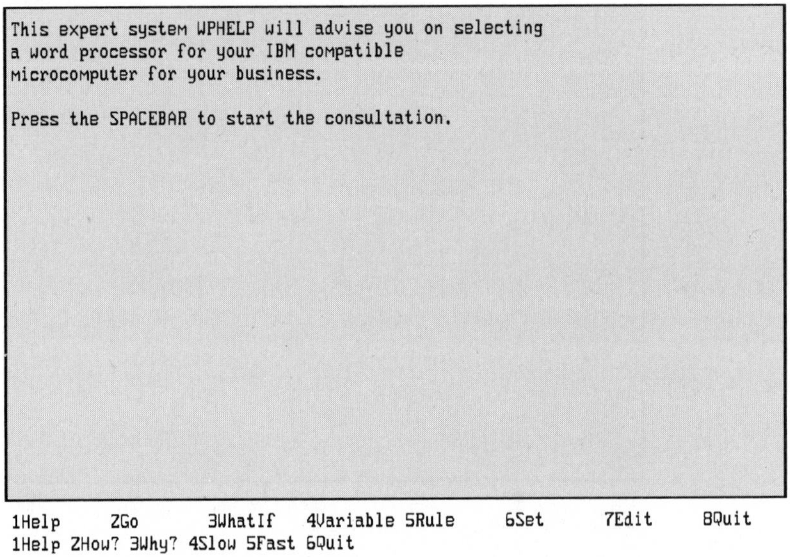

FIGURE M2.3 OPENING SCREEN FOR RUNNING A CONSULTATION WITH wp1.kbs

You are asked to identify the type of documents, simple or complex, that you plan to produce.

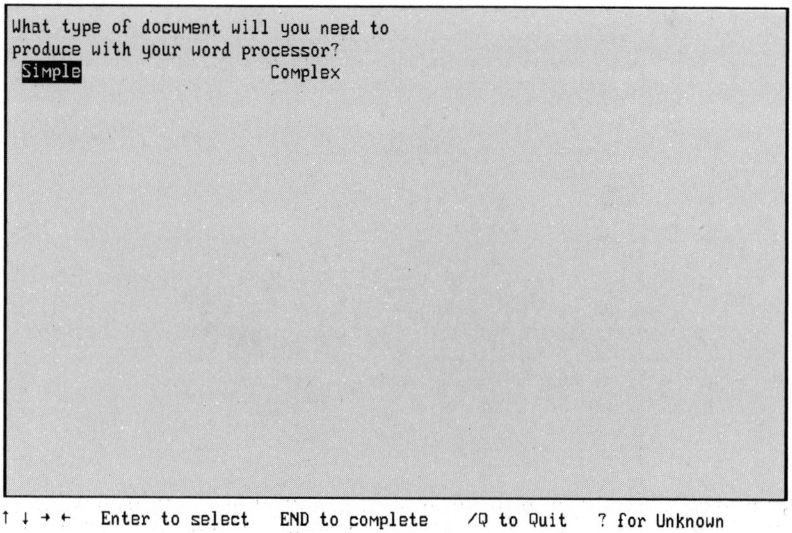

FIGURE M2.4 SELECTING THE TYPE OF DOCUMENT IN wpl.kbs

You may answer a question by following these steps:

Step 1. Move the light bar to your selection. (Simple)

Step 2. Press the ENTER key. A triangle will appear on the screen to mark your choice.

Step 3. Press the END key (on the right of your keyboard). This completes the selection for a given question.

Notice that these instructions are also listed on the bottom of the screen shown in Figure M2.4.

Make "Simple" your selection by pressing ENTER and then the END key. Your display should look like Figure M2.5 which now has a second question concerning available money.

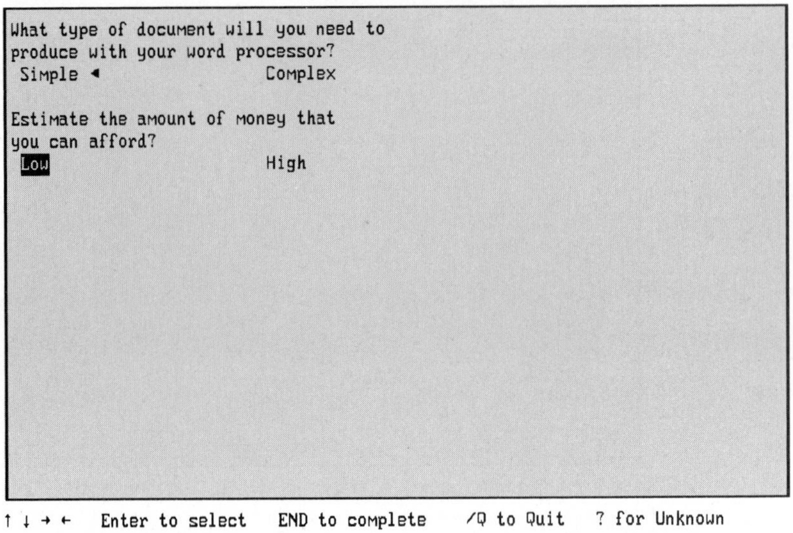

FIGURE M2.5 SELECTING THE COST IN wpl.kbs

Select "Low" as the answer to this second question by pressing ENTER and then the END key. Your screen should now look like Figure M2.6 where the expert system replies "WPHELP advises Product A."

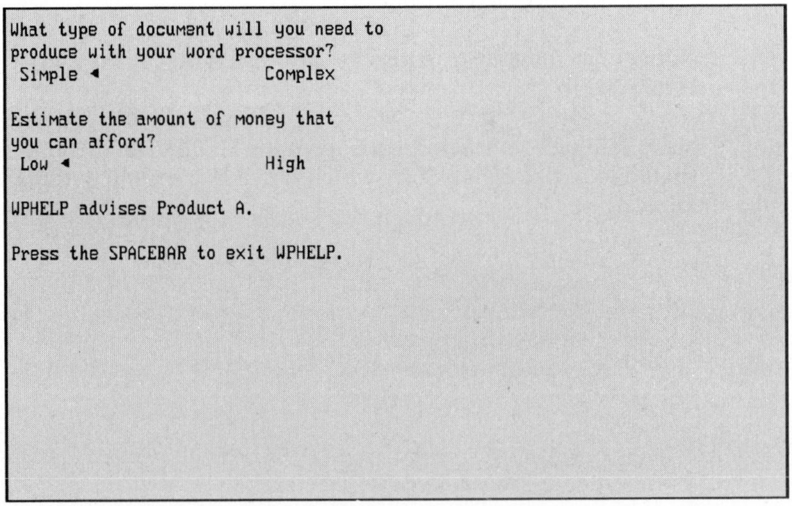

FIGURE M2.6 THE ADVICE FROM WPHELP IN FILE wpl.kbs

In other words, the expert system advises you that Product A is a word processor for simple documents at a low cost. The message "Press the SPACEBAR to exit WPHELP" directs you on how to exit the consultation and return to the Consult Menu. What would the WPHELP system advise you if you had given different choices? Rerun the expert system (by selecting 2Go), and verify that the expert system gives the advice shown in Figure M2.7. To start the system select 2Go from the menu bar and make selections by using the arrow keys, ENTER, and END.

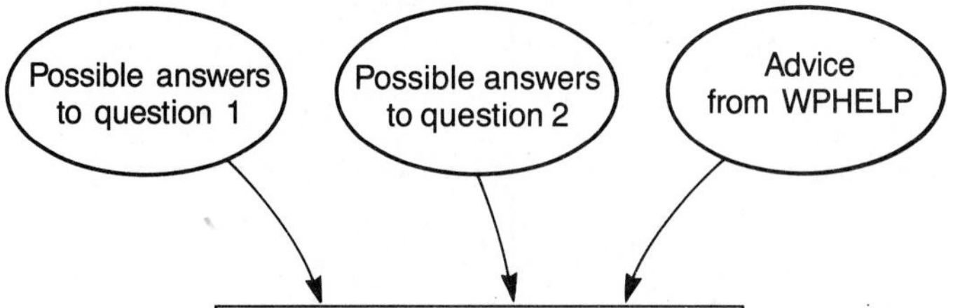

Functionality	Cost	Advice
Simple	Low	Product A
Simple	High	Product A
Complex	Low	None
Complex	High	Product B

FIGURE M2.7 SELECTIONS AND ADVICE FROM WPHELP (wpl.kbs)

Notice that the expert system is called WPHELP, but the file name is wpl. You now have completed your first consultation session with a small expert system. When you have finished, select the 8Quit option and return to the Main Menu.

Alternate Methods for Menu Selection

VP-Expert allows you to enter commands in other ways. There are four ways to make menu choices in VP-Expert. The first way that we have used is moving the light bar with the arrow keys and pressing the ENTER key. Alternate ways are as follows:

1. Type the number corresponding to the command.
2. Press the function key corresponding to the number by the desired option.
3. Type the first letter of the command.

Thus, in the Main Menu, to select the consult option (4Consult) we can simply type a 4 to get to the Consult Menu. Another way would be to press the F4 function key which is to the left or top of your keyboard. Still another way is to type an upper-case or lower-case c. All these different methods will achieve the same objective: to select the 4Consult option from the Main Menu. Even though you are free to use any method you like, we will use the light bar method and names to make the words meaningful in "navigating" through VP-Expert.

Identifying the Three Parts of an Expert System

We stated that an expert system was composed of three logical parts: the knowledge base (facts and rules), inference engine (reasoning mechanism), and user interface (communications). This is shown in Figure M2.8.

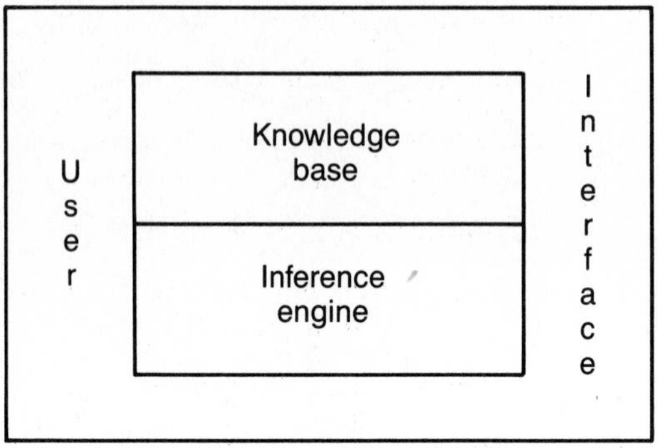

FIGURE M2.8 LOGICAL COMPONENTS OF AN EXPERT SYSTEM

Where are these three parts in the example WPHELP system? We will run a slightly different version of our example so that these parts appear for you.

Viewing the Component Parts

To expose the three components of an expert system, run the file named wp2.kbs. Assuming that the path is still the B drive, follow these steps at the Main Menu:

Step 1. Move the light bar to 6FileName and press ENTER. Select wp2 by typing the words or use the arrow keys to move the light bar to wp2. Press ENTER.

Step 2. With the light bar on 4Consult, press ENTER.

Your display should now look like Figure M2.9.

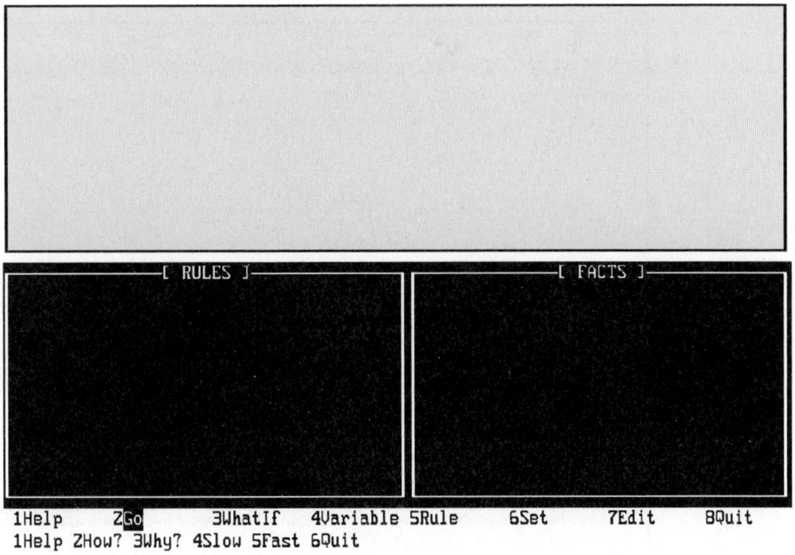

FIGURE M2.9 OPENING SCREEN FOR LOADING wp2.kbs

Your screen should now be divided into three parts or **windows**. When we start the consultation, we shall see the purpose of these windows on the screen when we run the knowledge base or expert system file.

Select the option 2Go to start the consultation with wp2.kbs. Now follow the message on the screen and press the SPACEBAR to start the session with WPHELP. When the first question appears on the screen, your display should appear like Figure M2.10 with messages within the lower left-hand window called the Rules Window. This window is telling us what the inference engine is doing.

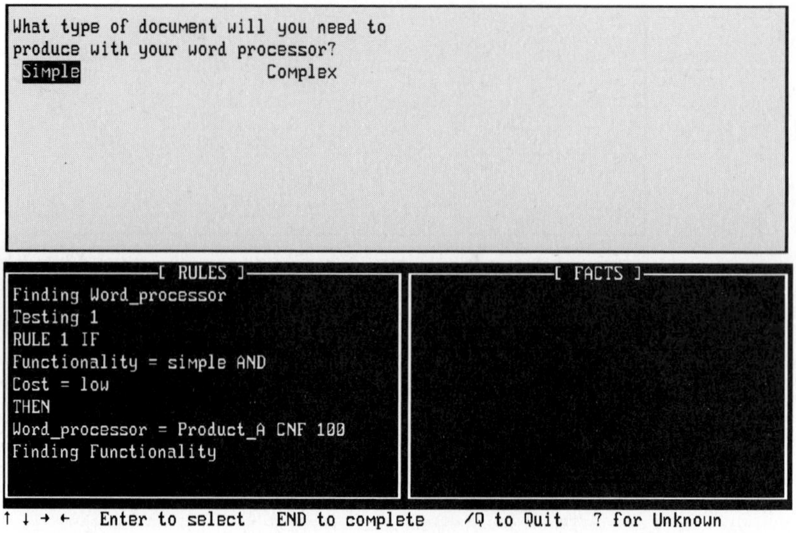

FIGURE M2.10 FIRST QUESTION FROM wp2.kbs BEFORE SELECTION

The comment "Finding Word_processor" tells us that the inference engine is seeking to find a value of an unknown variable that a programmer has called Word_processor. The inference engine goes to the first rule that has that variable in it. In our case it is Rule 1. This is what "Testing 1" means. Rule 1 is also displayed for you. The rule is in terms of variables called Functionality and Cost. The last comment "Finding Functionality" means that the inference engine wants to know the functionality or type of document to be produced. This window is called the Rules Window where the inference engine is showing you what rules it is testing and what facts it is trying to find from the user.

Now make a selection of "Simple" (by pressing ENTER and END), and your display should now contain the information shown in Figure M2.11.

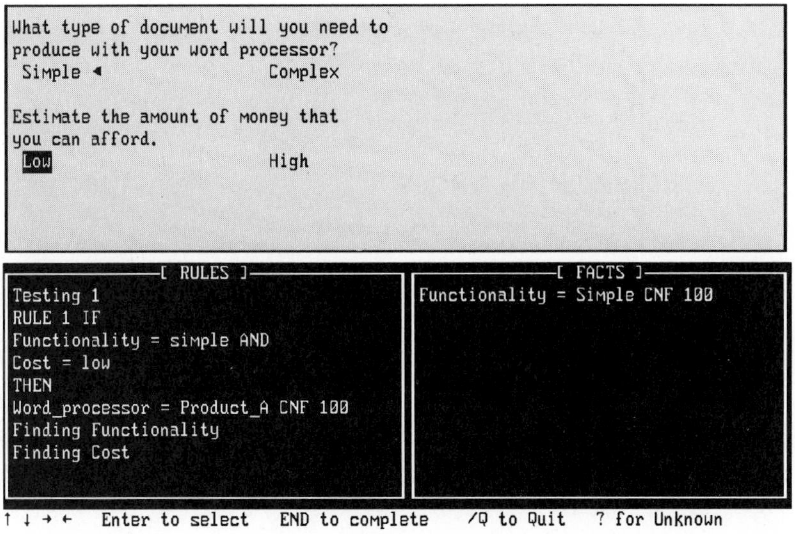

FIGURE M2.11 THE CONSULTATION SCREEN AFTER ANSWERING THE FIRST QUESTION IN wp2.kbs

The window in the lower right-hand corner tells you that the value of Functionality (variable) is Simple. The inference engine knows this because you made the selection. You told the expert system this fact. The Rules Window on the left now adds the information that the inference engine is trying to find the Cost. Notice that Cost and Functionality are in the IF part of Rule 1, which is displayed. If Functionality had a value of Simple and Cost were Low, then the Word_processor (variable) would be assigned a value of Product A. In other words, Rule 1 from the knowledge base would be "fired." Make this happen by selecting Low with the ENTER and END keys. Now the system identifies Product A as our selection in Figure M2.12.

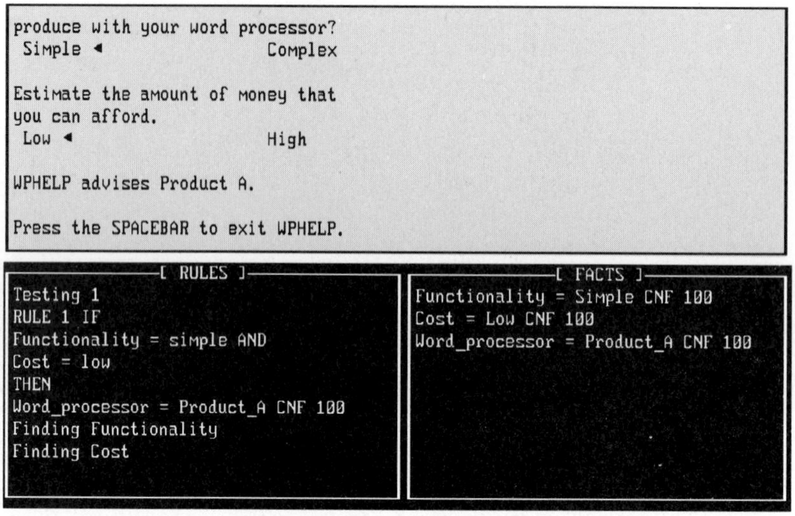

FIGURE M2.12 THE CONSULTATION SCREEN AFTER ANSWERING THE SECOND QUESTION IN wp2.kbs

The message Word_processor = Product A is in the lower right-hand window or Facts Window.

In Figure M2.13 we can summarize our screen configuration by saying that the top window is the Consultation Window where the user interacts or communicates with the expert system.

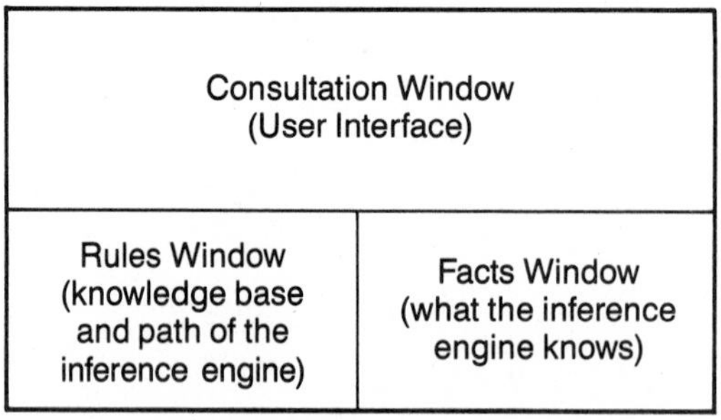

FIGURE M2.13 STRUCTURE OF THE CONSULTATION SCREEN

Another name for the Consultation Window is the user interface. The window on the bottom left is the Rules Window where the inference engine displays what variable it is trying to find and what rule from the knowledge base it is testing. The bottom right-hand window is the Facts Window where the inference engine displays the values of the variables that it knows. Hence, we are close to viewing the three parts of an expert system: the user interface, the knowledge base, and the inference engine. (What caused the windows to appear or disappear depended on the absence or presence of a special command, RUNTIME, in the software. Generally speaking, a user doesn't want the Rules and Facts Windows to appear, but for learning about expert systems, we want the windows to appear.)

Press the SPACEBAR to end the consultation and return to the 2Go option of the Consult Menu. Note that the Consultation Window is cleared, but the Rules and Facts Windows still have messages.

Interaction with a Consultation

When you are viewing and using an expert system, VP-Expert allows you to exercise control over the characteristics of the session. The 2Go option has a menu of six options as shown in in Figure M2.14. These options are available during the running of a consultation. To use these options press the slash key (/).

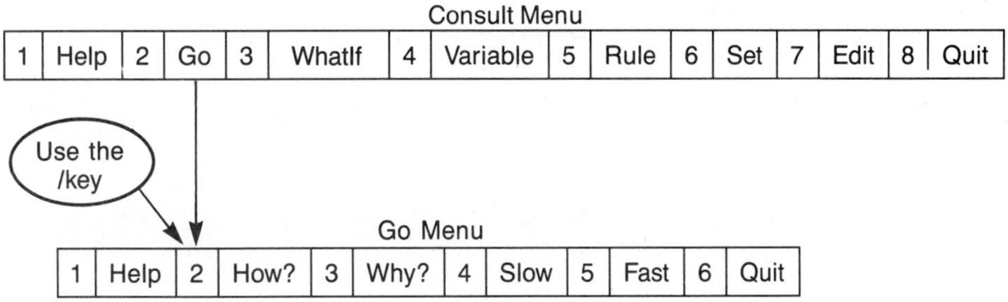

FIGURE M2.14 THE CONSULT MENU WITH THE GO MENU

This temporarily suspends the consultation. Then you can move the light bar with the arrow keys to the option you want and press ENTER. The first option is 1Help; the second choice, 2How?, will display the reason for the assignment of a value to a variable. The 3Why? option shows why a question is being asked. The 4Slow option will slow down the scrolling of the rules and variables in the windows. This will allow you to easily read the text in the windows. The more often the 4Slow option is selected, the slower the consultation operates. The 5Fast option is the reverse of 4Slow and returns the speed of the consultation to the faster speed when selected. The 6Quit option returns you to the Consult Menu. This allows you to exit a consultation at any time. The important idea is that you can use these options anytime during the running of a consultation by pressing the Slash key and making a choice with the light bar and the ENTER key.

Rerun the file wp2.kbs using the same selections as identified in Figure M2.7. Interrupt the session with the Slash key and experiment with the options. Verify also that the advice is the same as given in wp1.kbs as shown in Figure M2.7.

There are still other ways to interact with the consultation. You may use the 3Whatif, 4Variable, or 5Rule options from the Consult Menu. After you have run a consultation, you may ask what the advice would be if one variable response was changed. Instead of rerunning the system, move the light bar to the 3Whatif option and press ENTER. A window will appear which contains a list of all the variables used in the consultation.

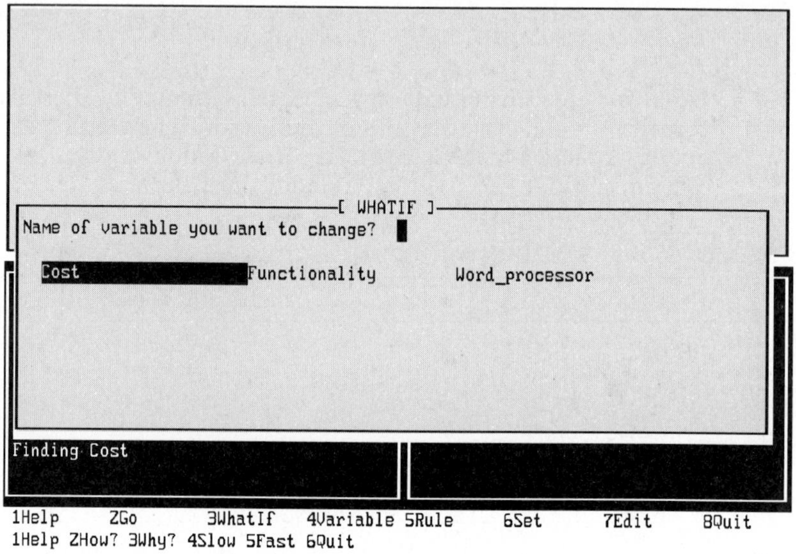

FIGURE M2.15 WHATIF OPTION OF THE CONSULT MENU

See Figure M2.15. Use the arrow keys to select the variable that you want to change. (Note the PgUp and PgDn keys are used if there are more variables than will fit in the window.) Press ENTER and make the change by using the arrow keys and pressing ENTER and END. To find out the value of a particular variable select the 4Variable option on the Consult Menu.

As shown in Figure M2.16, the variable option will ask you to select the variable that you want to see. Select Word_processor and press ENTER. The value of the variable Word_processor from the consultation will be displayed in the Consultation Window.

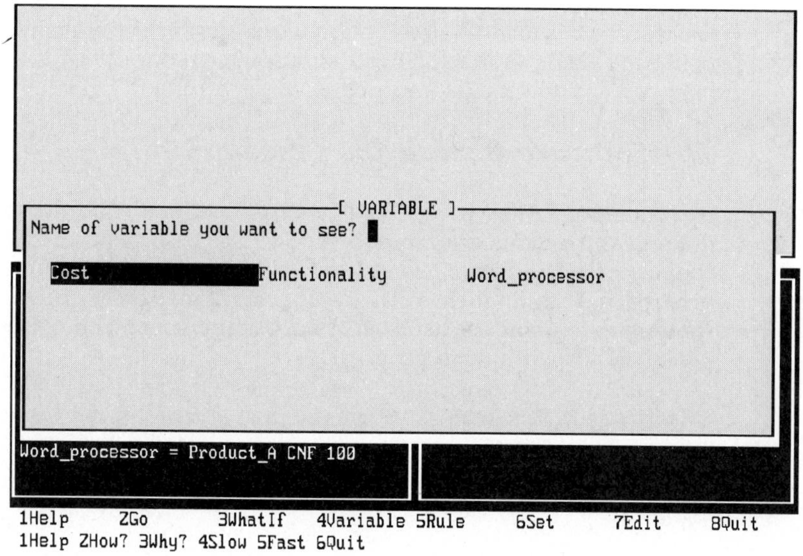

FIGURE M2.16 VARIABLE OPTION OF THE CONSULT MENU

To look at a given rule, select the 5Rule option. Again a window of information will appear as in Figure M2.17. Use the arrow keys to select the number of the rule you want displayed and then press ENTER.

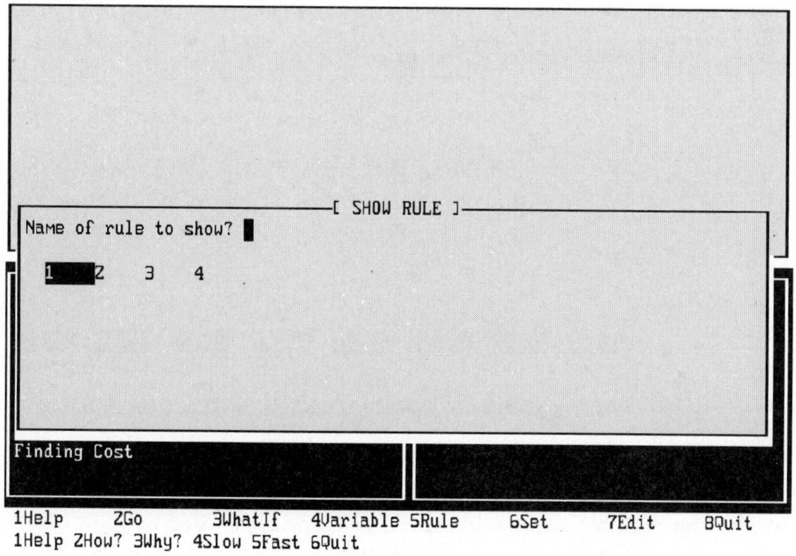

FIGURE M2.17 RULE OPTION OF THE CONSULT MENU

The difference between the "slash menu options" and the three options that we have just discussed is that the slash option works during a consultation and the three new options (3Whatif, 4Variable, 5Rule) are used after a consultation is run. These commands help you to find specific information about a rule or variable in the expert system.

The Software Behind the Consultation

By running WPHELP in wp2.kbs we obtained three windows that helped us to see not only the user interface, but the knowledge base and the activity of the inference engine (reasoning mechanism). Now let's take a look at the software behind the expert system to again identify the three parts of an expert system. In order to do this we want to examine the actual **software** at the screen and obtain a hard copy printout of the expert system program.

Obtaining a Printout. We assume that you are in the Consult Menu after running wp2.kbs. We will use the editor's screen facility and printer facility to obtain a printout. Select the 7Edit option from the Consult Menu. After pressing the shift key, you should see the screen shown in Figure M2.18.

```
                                             Editing: Old File b:\wp2.kbs

!The file wp2.kbs shows the three parts◂
!          of an expert system through windows.◂
◂
ACTIONS◂
       DISPLAY "This expert system WPHELP will advise you on selecting ◂
a word processor for your IBM compatible micro-◂
computer in your business.◂
◂
Press the SPACEBAR to start the consultation.~"◂
        CLS◂
        FIND Word_processor◂
        DISPLAY "WPHELP advises {word_processor}.◂
"◂
        DISPLAY "Press the SPACEBAR to exit WPHELP.~◂
"◂
        CLS; ◂
◂
RULE 1 ◂

+
Insert On    Document Off                         Boldface Off Underline Off
 1       2       3Srch↓  4       5Rplc↓  6       7GbRpc↓ 8       9Rept↓  10
```

FIGURE M2.18 SCREEN DISPLAY WHEN THE EDITOR LOADS wp2.kbs

All the text on the screen is the software program for wp2.kbs. Notice that the file name the editor is displaying is shown in the upper right-hand corner. Note also that the path name is included with the file so that the complete name is b:\wp2.kbs. The b: tells us that the file is stored on the B drive, the wp2 is the first part of the file name, and .kbs is the second part of the file name (extension).

Certain editor conditions such as insert on, document (mode) off, boldface off, and underline off are indicated at the bottom of Figure M2.18. The next line is another menu bar of function keys. The 10Print option means to use the F10 or function key ten to print the entire document (even though you may only see part of it on the screen). You can see the rest of the document on the screen by using the page down (PgDn) and page up (PgUp) keys on the right side of your keyboard. The task at hand is to obtain a printout so follow these steps:

Step 1. Make sure your printer is on and has paper.

Step 2. Press the F10 key.

Step 3. When a printer options screen comes up, leave the settings alone; simply press the END key.

The computer screen will display a message that it is printing and then return you to the editor mode. Since all we wanted to do now is print a file, we can exit the editor now.

There are many ways to exit the editor, depending on what changes we want to make to the file. When you press the ALT key, the menu bar at the bottom changes options. The ALT key in combination with the function keys gives us different options. We will use ALT-F8 to abandon the editor without making changes to the program. Therefore, to exit the editor, hold down the ALT key and press the F8 key. The editor will ask you (at the bottom of the screen) if you really want to do this. Type lowercase y and VP-Expert should take you back to the Consult Menu. Since we want to discuss the printout, move the light bar to the 8Quit command and press ENTER to exit the Consult Menu; press 8Quit again to exit the Main Menu. You should be back at the A> prompt. (You may be prompted to insert a DOS diskette with COMMAND.COM in order to proceed.)

Examining the Printout. A copy of the file wp2.kbs is given in Figure M2.19. We have divided our VP-Expert program into three parts called Actions, Rules, and Statements.

The Actions block contains the strategic reasoning mechanism of the inference engine. It tells the inference engine what to look for. From Comment 1 or C1 on Figure M2.19, we observe that a DISPLAY command sends an opening message to the user. Whatever variable is listed after the FIND clause (C2 on Figure M2.19) is what the inference engine is trying to find or conclude. In our case, the inference engine is looking for the value of the variable Word_processor.

The Rules section contains the knowledge base or expertise of the system. In our case we have four rules, expressed in the IF-THEN format. The THEN parts are determined by the values of the variables, Functionality and Cost, in the IF parts. The Statements block at the end of the program helps control the user interface so that the user can select values for the type of document (Functionality) and values for Cost.

The ASK statement (C3 and C4) is followed by a variable and then words in quotes. The words in quotes appear on the display screen. The CHOICES statement after

```
!The file wp2.kbs shows the three parts
!          of an expert system through windows.
```

Actions

```
ACTIONS
          DISPLAY "this expert system WPHELP will advise you on selecting
a word processor for your IBM compatible micro-
computer in your business.

Press the SPACEBAR to start the consultation.~"                  C1
          CLS
C2 -->    FIND Word_processor
          {DISPLAY "WPHELP advises {word_processor}.
"
          {DISPLAY "Press the SPACEBAR to exit WPHELP.~        } --> C5
"
          CLS;
```

Rules

```
RULE 1
IF        Functionality=simple AND
          Cost=low
THEN      Word_processor=Product_A;

RULE 2
IF        Functionality=simple AND
          Cost=high
THEN      Word_processor=Product_A;

RULE 3
IF        Functionality=complex AND
          Cost=low
THEN      Word_processor=none;

RULE 4
IF        Functionality=complex AND
          Cost=high
THEN      Word_processor=Product_B;
```

Statements

```
ASK Functionality : "What type of document will you need to
produce with your word processor?";                    <-- C3

CHOICES Functionality : Simple, Complex;

ASK Cost : "Estimate the amount of money that         <-- C4
you can afford.";

CHOICES Cost : Low, High;
```

FIGURE M2.19 THREE PARTS OF A VP-EXPERT PROGRAM

the ASK statement sends the possible values for a specific variable to the screen. After the inference engine has completed its search, it displays the value of the Word_processor and an exit message for you. See C5.

What the user sees at the screen comes from the three DISPLAY commands in the Actions block (C1 and C5) and from the ASK statements (C3 and C4) in the Statements block. This is shown as two partial screens in Figure M2.20. The comment numbers from the code of Figure M2.19 are matched to the resulting comments on the screen display of Figure M2.20.

```
This expert system WPHELP will advise you on selecting
a word processor for your IBM compatible micro-
computer in your business.

Press the SPACEBAR to start the consultation.
```

C1

```
produce with your word processor?
 Simple ◄                    Complex

Estimate the amount of money that
you can afford.
 Low ◄                       High

WPHELP advises Product A.

Press the SPACEBAR to exit WPHELP.
```

C3

C4

C5

FIGURE M2.20 USER INTERFACE SCREENS FOR CONSULTATION WITH WPHELP (FROM wp2.kbs)

Notice that the first statements on the screen come from the first DISPLAY statement in the Actions block, (C1 from Figure M2.19). The next two questions with choices (C3 and C4) come from the Statements block, but the last sentences on the screen come from the last two DISPLAY statements in the Actions block (C5). The command DISPLAY "WPHELP advises {word-processor}" is used to tell you what the value of the Word_processor is after the inference engine has examined the rules and obtained facts from you. We will discuss the syntax (spelling and special rules) that relate to programs in later modules.

Obtaining Help

Besides learning how to run a consultation and how to obtain a printout of the software, you should know how to obtain any **help** that VP-Expert might provide. In order to do this, perform the following steps:

Step 1. At the A> prompt, type vpx and press ENTER.

Step 2. The Main Menu will appear. Move the light bar to 7Path and enter b:. Press ENTER. Move the light bar to 1HELP. Press ENTER.

Step 3. You will be instructed to insert the Sample File Disk. Since you already did this, just press ENTER.

VP-Expert went to the Sample Files Disk and loaded some help files. The Main Menu Help screen should look like Figure M2.21. This screen is a summary of the options of the Main Menu. Notice that we have used all of them except Induce, Edit, and Tree. The Edit of the Main Menu is the same as 7Edit from the Consult Menu.

```
                              MAIN MENU
Related: CONSULT MENU  GO MENU  INDUCE MENU  SET MENU  TREE MENU         »

 Help          Calls the help system.

 Induce        Creates a working knowledge base from an induction
               table contained in text, database, or worksheet file.

 Edit          Invokes the Editor and loads the current knowledge base.

 Consult       Loads the current knowledge base into memory and displays
               the Consult Menu.

 Tree          Displays a menu of options for viewing the results
               of a consultation trace.

 FileName      Lets you change the currently active knowledge base.

 Path          Sets the directory path used to access knowledge base files.

 Quit          Returns to system prompt.

↑/↓-Scroll  PgUp/PgDn-Page  Home-Top  End-Bottom  Esc-Topics  P-Print  F1-Keys
```

FIGURE M2.21 THE MAIN MENU HELP SCREEN

There are additional facilities available which are found on the instruction bar at the bottom of the menu. Press the ESCAPE key (ESC), and your screen should be identical to Figure M2.22. A list of alphabetical topics appear on the left, and instructions are on the right. The instructions tell you to use a single letter and the arrow keys to locate your desired topic.

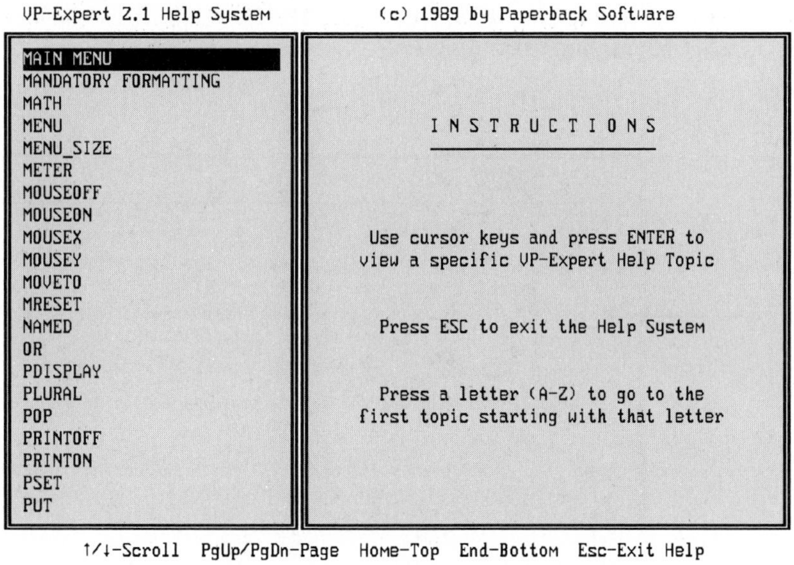

FIGURE M2.22 THE OPENING SCREEN FOR THE VP-EXPERT HELP SYSTEM

Let's find the Help screens for the Consult Menu and get a printout. Follow these steps:

Step 1. Type lowercase c.

Step 2. Using the Down Arrow key, move the light bar until it is on CONSULT MENU. Press the ENTER key.

Step 3. Press P to obtain a printout.

The VP-Help facility has a reference feature. Look at the long strip at the top of the screen in Figure M2.23. Topics related to the Consult Menu are listed across the top. You can use the arrow keys to find information on a related menu. (The reference list may go off the screen). To utilize these options, a summary of the keystrokes is displayed by pressing the F1 Key. Press the ENTER key while the light bar is on SET MENU. The Set Menu Help screen will appear. Obtain a copy by typing P for print. Now we will press ESC to return to the alphabetical topics list. Press ESC to exit the Help System and return to the Main Menu.

Our work with VP-Expert for this module is now complete. Choose 8Quit and press ENTER to return the system to the **A>** prompt.

We have concluded our use of the microcomputer for Module 2, but let's discuss the printout of the Consult Menu Help screen shown in Figure M2.23. We have used all of these options except the Set option. The Go starts a consultation, and WhatIf, Variable, and Rule options helped us to find information about the system after a consultation. What the Help screen does not show us, however, is that the Go Menu can be accessed by the Slash key. Those options could be activated while a consultation is running. At the top of Figure M2.23 we see that related topics are Go Menu, Set Menu, and Main Menu.

```
                              CONSULT MENU

Related: GO MENU  SET MENU  MAIN MENU

 Help             Calls the help screen.

 Go               Starts a consultation.

 WhatIf           Lets you find out how the outcome of a consultation
                  would change if you assigned a variable a different
                  value.

 Variable         Shows you the values assigned to one or all variables
                  in the last consultation.

 Rule             Displays one or all rules of the current knowledge base.

 Set              Displays an additional menu of options, including
                  the Trace, Slow, and Fast commands.

 Quit             Returns to Main Menu.

↑/↓-Scroll  PgUp/PgDn-Page  Home-Top  End-Bottom  Esc-Topics  P-Print  F1-Keys
```

FIGURE M2.23   CONSULT MENU HELP SCREEN

One point should be clarified about the Edit option. You will find Edit as an option on both the Main Menu and the Consult Menu (Figures M2.1 and M2.2), even though this option was left out of the Help screen by the VP-Expert software authors. You can get to the editor mode from either menu. Many times it is more convenient to use the Go and Edit features from the same Consult Menu. If you experience any unusual "out of memory errors" when using the 7Edit option from the Consult Menu, use the 3Edit option from the Main Menu.

In summary, we have conducted consultations with a simple expert system, identified the three parts of an expert system, obtained a printout of the expert system program (wp2.kbs), discussed the program, and examined the help facilities in VP-Expert. In the next module we will look at the knowledge base (production rules or simply rules) in more detail.

Key Points

- VP-Expert is accessed by typing vpx at the A> prompt.
- The opening screen or Main Menu has eight options.
- Menu options may be selected in any of four ways:
  - Move the light bar to your choice and press ENTER.
  - Enter the number by the menu choice.
  - Press the function key with the same number.
  - Type the first letter of the menu choice.
- The extension name for VP-Expert files is .kbs (for knowledge base).
- 4Consult on the Main Menu is the choice for running an expert system or knowledge base file (.kbs). Then 2Go is selected from the Consult Menu.
- Before running an expert system, use the 7Path option to indicate where the file is located (b: or B drive) and the 6FileName option to select the file.
- When running an expert system (consultation), make choices by pressing the ENTER key followed by the END key.
- The file wp1.kbs is the program for advice on selecting a word processor while the file wp2.kbs is the same expert system except that the user can view the Rules Window and the Facts Window as the expert system runs.
- When using wp2.kbs, you can "see" the three parts of an expert system:
  - The user interface is at the top.
  - The inference engine communicates its actions, rules, and values of variables via the two bottom windows, the Rules and Facts Windows.
- When running an expert system, you may press the Slash key to bring up the Go Menu of 1Help, 2How?, 3Why?, 4Slow, 5Fast, and 6Quit. These options will help you understand how the inference engine is working during a consultation.
- After running an expert system, you can select the options, 3WhatIf?, 4Variable, and 5Rule from the Consult Menu to find information about the variables and the rules.
- To obtain a printout of an expert system program (.kbs), or file, select the B drive on 7Path, the desired file in 6FileName, and then 3Edit from the Main Menu. Once inside the editor, press the F10 key followed by the END key. Exit the editor by pressing the ALT and F8 keys at the same time. (ALT-F6 will save the file and exit at the same time). You may also use the 7Edit option from the Consult Menu.
- A VP-Expert program is composed of three parts
  - Actions (Strategy or plan of the inference engine)
  - Rules (IF-THEN rules)
  - Statements (Commands to obtain choices, or information from the user)
- The FIND command in the Actions block of a program identifies the work to be done by the inference engine. What the inference engine is trying to find or conclude is identified by the variable after the FIND command.
- The text within quotes in a DISPLAY command will be directed to the screen as information for the user.
- To obtain help from VP-Expert, select the 1Help option from the Main Menu or other menus. Follow the instructions on the screen to look up a term for more information.

Exercises

1. Check the options that are on the Main Menu.

    ____ Exit

    ____ Quit

    ____ Go

    ____ Stop

    ____ Edit

    ____ Directory

    ____ Path

    ____ Help

2. Name the command from the Main Menu to

    get out of the menu. ______________________________

    select a knowledge base program. ______________________________

    tell the computer where files are located. ______________________________

    actually run a program. ______________________________

3. Check which options are on the Consult Menu.

    ____ Run

    ____ Go

    ____ Variable

    ____ Rule

    ____ Edit

    ____ Print

    ____ Stop

    ____ Help

4. List the four different ways to select 4Consult from the Main Menu.

    1) ______________________________

    2) ______________________________

    3) ______________________________

    4) ______________________________

5. Select the two successive commands needed to run an expert system.

   a. Consult, Run

   b. Consult, Go

   c. Run, Consult

   d. Go, Consult

6. Write the other three sets of commands that you could use to run an expert system. Assume you start at the Main Menu.

   1) ____

   2) ____

   3) ____

7. Check the following options that are part of the Go Menu.

   _____ Help

   _____ Go

   _____ How?

   _____ Why?

   _____ Slow

   _____ Fast

   _____ Print

   _____ Quit

8. Write the name of the options from the Consult Menu to

   a. find a rule in the knowledge base. ______________________

   b. see what advice the system gives if one variable is changed.__________

   c. run a knowledge based program. ______________________

   d. display the value of a variable. ______________________

9. Which option from the Main Menu do you use to print a copy of a .kbs file?
   a. 1Help
   b. 2Induce
   c. 3Edit
   d. 4Consult
   e. none of these

10. How can you access the Edit option?

Assignments

1. Run wp2.kbs again. During the consultation, use the Slash key to select the 3Why? option. Obtain a copy of the answer that appears on the screen by pressing the Shift (Up Arrow) and print screen (PRTSC) keys at the same time.
2. Using wp1.kbs or wp2.kbs, do the following:
   a. Identify the variable names.
   b. Tell how many rules are in the knowledge base.
   c. Identify Rule 3.
3. The only difference in the programs wp1.kbs and wp2.kbs is that wp1.kbs has the RUNTIME command and wp2.kbs does not. Verify this by obtaining a printout of wp1.kbs. Remember to
   a. set the 7Path (b:).
   b. select 6FileName (wp1.kbs).
   c. select 3Edit (to use the F10 print option).
4. Using the 1Help option of the Main Menu, obtain a printout of the information about these topics.
   a. Edit commands
   b. Cursor command
   c. Delete commands
   d. Function Keys
   e. Go Menu
   f. Runtime
   g. Shift Function keys
   h. ALT Function keys
5. Using the file Taxguide.kbs from your Sample File Disk, run the expert system.
   a. What is the purpose of the Taxguide system?
   b. How many rules are in the Taxguide system?
   c. Obtain a printout of Taxguide.kbs.
   d. On the printout, draw a box around each of the Actions, Rules and Statement blocks. Label each.
6. Use VP-Expert to display files. Set the 7Path to b: and the 6FileName to wp2. Now load wp2.kbs with 3Edit. Within the editor, you can display files on a specified drive. Follow these steps.
   1) Press ALT-F7.
   2) In reply to the message "Which files do you want to list?", type
      b: *.kbs
   3) Press ENTER.
   4) Press Shift and PRTSC simultaneously to obtain a printout. (F10 and END do not work here.)
   5) Press ESC.
   6) Press ALT-F8 to exit without saving changes. Answer Y to the message.

7. An alternate way to display files is from DOS. At the A> prompt, place the Sample Files Disk into the A drive. Type
   DIR *.kbs
   to display all the knowledge base files. Press Shift PRTSC simultaneously to obtain a printout.
8. As we use the Sample Files Disk, the modules will instruct us to create certain files. To make sure that the Sample Files Disk has enough room, find out how much space in bytes is free on the disk. Follow these steps.
   1) Place the Sample Files Disk in the A drive.
   2) Type dir/w or dir.
   After the file names are listed, DOS will tell you the number of files and the number of bytes free. Record this information.
   a) Number of files: ______________________
   b) Number of bytes free: ______________________
9. The file vpx.exe on the VP-Expert Disk executes when you type VPX. Find out how large the file is by typing DIR VPX.EXE at the A> prompt.

   ____

Module 3

THE KNOWLEDGE BASE: PRODUCTION RULES IN VP-EXPERT

The knowledge base is a key part of an expert system. We will concentrate on understanding how VP-Expert structures its knowledge base. We will take a detailed look at production rules (IF-THEN), variables in production rules, optional parts of rules called ELSE and BECAUSE, and rules with compound parts (AND, OR). The concept of a PLURAL variable will be discussed. Using the INDUCE command, we will use a table file to generate a "bare bones" knowledge base without programming. We will conclude with ways to modify our induced knowledge base program to improve the user interface.

Forming Rules

VP-Expert can give us a format to write rules, but it cannot guarantee that the rule represents knowledge. Three terms—data, information, and knowledge—are sometimes confused. *Data* is simple facts or measurements. *Information* is organizing data so that it is useful to a user. *Knowledge* is the refinement of information so that productive and efficient problem solving can occur. Assuming that you have the knowledge, VP-Expert has a certain format that you must place it in.

Use of IF-THEN Rules

The model that VP-Expert uses to represent or structure knowledge is the most common model, production rules. VP-Expert does not use semantic nets, frames, or the predicate calculus models. *Production rules* are IF-THEN sentences where the IF part is the condition (premise) with the THEN part called the conclusion. For example, in the rule

If the document is complex, then use Product B.

The condition (premise) is "If the document is complex", and the conclusion is "use Product B." The condition and conclusion are both assertions and each may be either a true assertion or a false assertion. When using IF-THEN rules, we are allowed to say that the conclusion is true only when the condition is true. If the premise is false, then we can't conclude the truth value of the conclusion. We sometimes say that a rule **fires**; by this we mean that we know that the condition is true, so that we can conclude that the conclusion is true (**fires**). If a condition is false, then the rule does not **fire**.

Optional Parts of IF-THEN Rules: ELSE and BECAUSE

VP-Expert allows two optional parts to a rule: ELSE and BECAUSE. The format of the rule is as follows:

```
IF condition
        THEN conclusion1
        ELSE conclusion2
        BECAUSE "          "
```

A rule in VP-Expert will always have a condition and a conclusion1. The ELSE conclusion and BECAUSE may or may not be there. An IF-THEN rule may or may not fire; but in an IF-THEN-ELSE form, the rule always fires. If the condition is true, then condition1 is true. If the condition is false, then condition2 is true. Both conditions (separated by an ELSE) can not fire in the same rule at the same time.

The BECAUSE option only adds information and has nothing to do with the firing of the rule. The BECAUSE option is followed by a sentence or words enclosed in quotes. The words following a BECAUSE are displayed to the user when the 2HOW? or 3WHY? options are selected when a consultation is run. It is up to the designer of the system to make sure the BECAUSE statement is clear and readable. For example,

```
IF the document is complex
        THEN select Product B
        ELSE select Product A
        BECAUSE "Product B will process more complicated documents
        than Product A."
```

If the condition (document is complex) is true, then conclusion1 (select Product B) is true. If the condition is false, then conclusion2 (select Product A) is true. In either case, the rule is fired because of the ELSE option. If the rule did not have the ELSE option, then the rule would fire only if the condition were true, and the rule would not fire if the condition were false. Moreover, the text "Product B will process more complex documents than Product A" would appear to the user if the 2How? or 3Why? options of the Go Menu were selected. If a rule does not have a BECAUSE part, then the rule itself is displayed for the 2How? or 3Why? options. The BECAUSE option adds only to the understanding of the rule and does not affect the firing of the rule.

Variable and Relational Operations for Rules

Any condition and conclusion must be in a particular format for VP-Expert to understand. The sentences are usually composed of relationships between variables and constants (or other variables). In order for VP-Expert to understand this last IF-THEN rule, we would have to reword it in terms of variables and constants, and relationships between them. In the rewording, we have:

RULE 7

IF Functionality = complex

THEN Word_processor = Product_B

ELSE Word_processor = Product_A

BECAUSE "Product B can process more complicated documents than Product A.";

The RULE, IF, THEN, ELSE, and BECAUSE are called *key words* or *reserved words*, and the 7 is called a rule name or label. The variables are Functionality and Word_processor. The values or constants are complex, Product_B, Product_A, and the text in quotes after BECAUSE. The first equals sign is a relational operator. This indicates the relation, the same as, to us in the rule. This is shown in Figure M3.1. VP-Expert has its own rules for forming or spelling variable names.

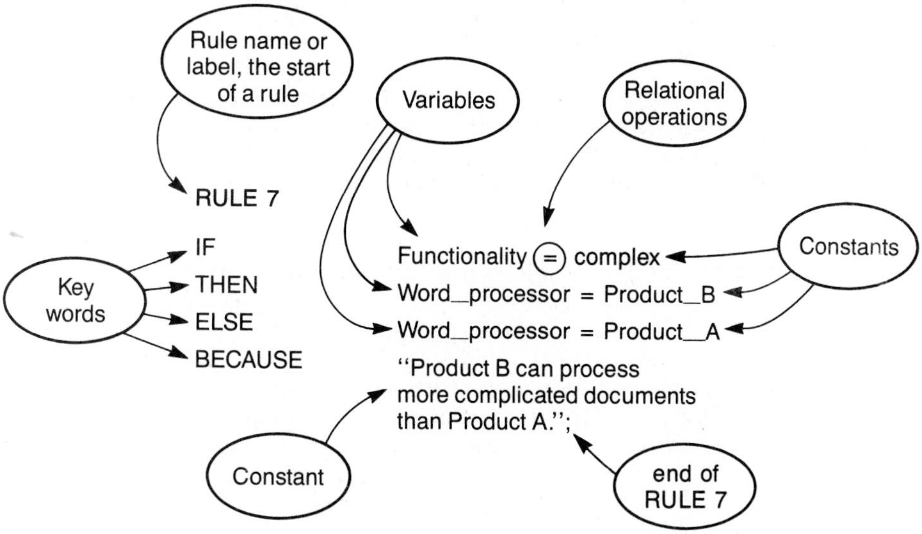

FIGURE M3.1 PARTS OF AN IF-THEN-ELSE-BECAUSE RULE

Other relational operators are allowed in the premise, but only the equals sign, used as an assignment, is allowed in the conclusion. The start of a rule is marked by the word RULE and the end of the rule by a semicolon(;).

Let's discuss the variables used in the condition and conclusion of our rule. A VP-Expert variable can have up to 40 characters. Symbols that can be used include letters of the alphabet (uppercase, lowercase, or mixed), numbers, and the special characters _ $ %^ |. Spaces are not allowed so the underscore symbol is used. This is why the variable, **give advice**, is illegal in VP-Expert; so instead, we use give_advice for readability. Moreover, each rule must start with the key word RULE, then a space, and then a label name. Label names and variable names follow the same requirements. We will use capitals for key words and certain commands, but this is only a matter of choice. Besides the relational operator =, we can use other comparisons between variables and constants in conditions. They are:

- = equals
- < is less than
- <= is less than or equal to
- > is greater than
- >= is greater than or equal to
- <> is not equal to

If we want to compare the value of a variable to the value of another variable, we have to put the second variable in parentheses. For example, to compare Balance and Savings, we could write

IF Balance=(Savings), THEN Advice=save_more;

VP-Expert requires the variable on the right of the equals sign to be in parentheses. It directs the system to find the variable Savings and compare the value of Savings to the value of Balance. Each of our rules in the knowledge base must adhere to all of these rules of spelling and formatting (syntax).

Rules with Compound Conditions (AND, OR)

The *condition* of a rule may contain compound parts, that is, they may be joined by two connectives (AND,OR). VP-Expert allows up to twenty different conditions to be connected. When you have two or more parts connected by an AND or OR, you need to find the truth value of the entire compound condition. The compound part is considered true for an AND statement, only when all of the parts are true; however, the truth value of an OR statement is false only when all parts are false. This is summarized in Figure M3.2 for compound AND and OR statements.

The inference engine fires a rule only when it knows the truth value of the combined condition to be true. If there is a compound condition (AND, OR), then the inference engine has to ascertain the value of each part of the compound condition to determine if the rule fires. Note that if the compound condition is false, then we can't conclude the truth value of the conclusion. The rule does not fire, and the truth value of the conclusion is unknown.

True only when all parts are true

AND Rules

Condition 1	Condition 2	Compound Condition	Conclusion
T	T	T	T
T	F	F	?
F	T	F	?
F	F	F	?

IF condition1 and condition2
THEN conclusion

OR Rules

Condition 1	Condition 2	Compound Condition	Conclusion
T	T	T	T
T	F	T	T
F	T	T	T
F	F	F	?

IF condition1 or condition2
THEN conclusion

False only when all parts are false

FIGURE M3.2 COMPOUND CONDITIONS IN RULES

You might wonder if VP-Expert allows compound conclusions as it does compound conditions. The answer is that VP-Expert does not allow the OR connective between conclusions but allows implied AND conclusions. For example, the following rule is invalid:

```
RULE 4
        IF condition 1
                THEN conclusion 2
                        OR conclusion 3;
```

VP-Expert does not allow OR between conclusions. The following rule, however, is valid:

RULE 4

IF condition 4

THEN conclusion 5

conclusion 6;

The AND connective is not between conclusion 5 and conclusion 6, but it is implied. If condition 4 is true, then both conclusion 5 and conclusion 6 will be true. The implied compound conclusions can also be found after an ELSE.

Let's run an example of each compound rule.

In wp3.kbs there is a small expert system of one compound AND rule. The rule is:

RULE 1

IF Afford=Yes	Condition 1
AND Help=Yes	Condition 2
AND Time=Yes	Condition 3
AND Need=Yes	Condition 4
THEN Advice=proceed	Conclusion 5
ELSE Advice=wait;	Conclusion 6

There are four conditions to this rule (Afford=yes, Help=yes, Time=yes, and Need=yes). Conclusion 5 is Advice=proceed and conclusion 6 is Advice=wait. If all four conditions are true, then the rule fires and Advice=proceed.

To verify this, get to the A> prompt with VP-Expert in the A drive and your Sample Files Disk in the B drive. At the Main Menu, follow these steps after entering vpx:

Step 1. Set the 7Path to b:.

Step 2. Set the 6FileName to wp3.

Step 3. Select the 4Consult option.

Step 4. Select the 2Go option.

Try running wp3.kbs with the values in rows 1, 4, 10, and 16 from the following table to verify some of the 16 possible results. You probably noticed something interesting when you tried to verify row 4. The search by the inference engine ended (you were asked no more questions) when the first no reason was entered. This happened because, as soon as one condition in an AND rule is false, VP-Expert ceases to do anything more with the rule.

Run	Condition 1 Afford	Condition 2 Help	Condition 3 Time	Condition 4 Need	Conclusion Advice
1	Yes	Yes	Yes	Yes	Proceed
2	Yes	Yes	Yes	No	Wait
3	Yes	Yes	No	Yes	Wait
4	Yes	Yes	No	No	Wait
5	Yes	No	Yes	Yes	Wait
6	Yes	No	Yes	No	Wait
7	Yes	No	No	Yes	Wait
8	Yes	No	No	No	Wait
9	No	Yes	Yes	Yes	Wait
10	No	Yes	Yes	No	Wait
11	No	Yes	No	Yes	Wait
12	No	Yes	No	No	Wait
13	No	No	Yes	Yes	Wait
14	No	No	Yes	No	Wait
15	No	No	No	Yes	Wait
16	No	No	No	No	Wait

Now let's try an OR rule with an ELSE option. If all parts of a compound OR condition are false, then the condition (after the ELSE) is fired. If one or more conditions in the IF part are true, the rule will fire and the conclusion before the ELSE will be true. The file wp4.kbs is a small system advising you if you need or don't need a word processor. The single compound OR-IF-THEN-ELSE rule in wp4.kbs is:

```
IF Letter=Yes                       (Condition 1)
    OR Resume=Yes                   (Condition 2)
    OR Notice=Yes                   (Condition 3)
    OR Paper=Yes                    (Condition 4)
THEN Advice=need                    (Conclusion 5)
ELSE Advise=do_not_need;            (Conclusion 6)
```

When one or more of the conditions is true, then Conclusion 5 is true. When all four conditions are false; then the ELSE part (Conclusion 6) is fired. The possible results are as follows:

Run	Condition 1 Letter	Condition 2 Resume	Condition 3 Notice	Condition 4 Paper	Conclusion Advice
1	Yes	Yes	Yes	Yes	need
2	Yes	Yes	Yes	No	need
3	Yes	Yes	No	Yes	need
4	Yes	Yes	No	No	need
5	Yes	No	Yes	Yes	need
6	Yes	No	Yes	No	need
7	Yes	No	No	Yes	need
8	Yes	No	No	No	need
9	No	Yes	Yes	Yes	need
10	No	Yes	Yes	No	need
11	No	Yes	No	Yes	need
12	No	Yes	No	No	need
13	No	No	Yes	Yes	need
14	No	No	Yes	No	need
15	No	No	No	Yes	need
16	No	No	No	No	do_not_need

Note again that there are 16 possible selections for the four variables. To access wp4.kbs, follow these steps:

Step 1. Exit the Consult Menu with 8Quit.

Step 2. Select 6FileName and enter wp4.

Step 3. Select 4Consult.

Step 4. Select 2Go.

Verify the results (advice) for runs 1, 5, 15, and 16 from the above table.

What happens, moreover, if an AND and OR appear in the same rule? This rule

```
RULE 1
        IF condition 1
        AND condition 2
        OR condition 3
THEN conclusion;
```

contains both AND and OR between three conditions. Which connective is evaluated first, AND or OR? A possible problem is shown in Figure M3.3.

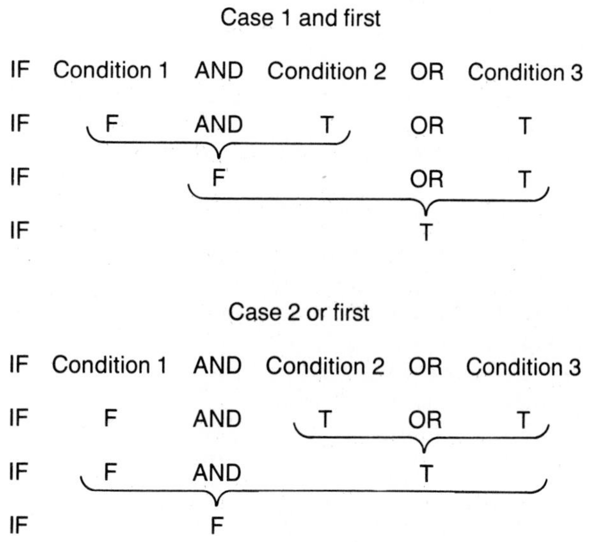

FIGURE M3.3 PROBLEM IN THE ORDER OF EVALUATING COMPOUND CONDITIONS

Let's assume that condition 1 is false, condition 2 is true, and condition 3 is true. If we evaluate AND first, followed by OR (Case 1) the final result is a true (compound) condition. But if we evaluate OR before AND as in Case 2, then the final result is a false (compound) condition.

To fix this possible problem, VP-Expert assumes Case 2: that is, OR is evaluated first even though it doesn't appear first. VP-Expert does not allow you to change the order by inserting parentheses. Parentheses are allowed only for numerical evaluation not logical evaluations.

Mathematical Calculations in Rules

VP-Expert has built-in mathematical operators and functions for use in expert systems programs. The four basic arithmetic operators are implemented with the following symbols:

Operation	Symbol
Addition	+
Subtraction	−
Multiplication	*
Division	/

Special mathematical and trigonometric functions are also implemented. In the list below, X stands for a numeric value or a variable with a known numerical value. The functions are:

Mathematical functions

@ABS(X) Returns the absolute value of X
@EXP(X) Returns the value of the exponential function
@LOG(X) Returns the natural logarithm of X
@SQRT (X) Returns the square root of X

Trigonometric functions

@COS(X) Returns the cosine of angle X
@SIN(X) Returns the sine of angle X
@TAN(X) Returns the tangent of angle X
@ACOS(X) Returns the arccosine of angle X
@ASIN(X) Returns the arcsine of angle X
@ATAN(X) Returns the arctangent of angle X

For trigonometric functions, the X represents radian values rather than degree values.

There is a difference in the syntax of arithmetic operators and mathematical functions. The basic arithmetic operators simply use the symbol between two numeric values or variables. The mathematical and trig functions must start with the @ symbol and involve only one number (parameter). All numeric calculations, however, must be contained in parentheses. This signals VP-Expert to suspend the work of the inference engine and perform the calculation. Moreover, when the calculation is assigned to a variable, the calculation must be to the right of the equals sign, and the variable must be on the left side of the equals sign. In other words, variable = (6 * price) is a legal statement, but (6*price) =variable is not a legal statement. In order for the calculation to be made, however, we must first know the value of price.

Calculations can be performed in both the condition and conclusion parts of rules, but in both cases, the calculations must be on the right side of any **equals** or **assignment** statement. We will explain assignment statement by analyzing the following three statements.

```
Statement 1     IF A=6
Statement 2     IF A=(B-6)
Statement 3     IF A=3
                     THEN B=(A*4)
```

In Statement 1, the value of the variable A is being compared to six to determine if the relationship is true or false. Six is not being assigned to A. Moreover, no math calculation is performed. In the second statement, the subtraction of six from the value of B is being compared to A to determine if the two numbers are equal. In Statement 3, the IF part is still a comparison, but the THEN part involves an assignment. The value of A will be multiplied by 4. The result is then assigned to the variable B. In other words, the equals in the IF part is a comparison, but the equals sign in the THEN part is an assignment. Here is an example where the same symbol, =, has two different meanings in our rule construction. We can summarize the use of mathematical calculations by the following points:

1. Place the calculations inside parentheses.
2. Special functions must start with @.
3. The value of variables must be known before the calculating process.
4. Assignment statements must have calculations only on the right side of the =.

We will find many uses for our arithmetic operators and math functions, such as computing ratios, percents, averages, and standard deviations, which are just a few examples of needed statistics in the business world.

Plural Variables with Rules

VP-Expert allows a special type of variable with rules called PLURAL. This means that the value of the variable may take on more than one value during the consultation. When the inference engine encounters a PLURAL variable as part of a condition or conclusion, it will check for more than one value of that variable. If a variable is not known as PLURAL, then the inference engine will stop its work after finding one value for that variable. One practical reason for using a PLURAL variable is that the user can make more than one selection from a question. For example, in wp4.kbs, we had to ask four questions to get the information we needed about the kinds of documents. If we change the program and create a variable called Activity, and declare it PLURAL, then we need only to ask one question, which can have more than one answer. This makes the consultation shorter for the user. At this point, exit wp4.kbs by using 8Quit from the Consult Menu. The next file we will use is wp5.kbs, so let's load that file from the Main Menu using 6FileName.

The file on the Sample Files Disk, wp5.kbs, is a change of wp4.kbs and has a new rule with a PLURAL variable called Activity. A copy of wp5.kbs is shown in Figure M3.4.

The OR rule now contains one variable called Activity as part of the four conditions. The ASK statement has been changed to direct the user to make more than one selection if it applies. The instructions for accomplishing this are included in the message on the screen. The CHOICES command lists all the possible documents along with NONE_OF_THESE. At the very end of the program there is a command PLURAL: Activity. This tells us that the one variable Activity can have more than one value. VP-Expert will allow up to ten PLURAL variables in a program.

When you run wp5.kbs, notice the method to select more than one answer to a question. Move the light bar to the choice and press ENTER. A mark will appear by your selection. Move the light bar to another choice and press ENTER. Another mark will appear. When you have made all of your selections for the question, signal VP-Expert that your choices are all made by pressing the END key.

Run a consultation with wp5.kbs by selecting 4Consult and 2Go. Try the 5Rule option after the consultation is over to see the knowledge base. Now, rerun wp4.kbs for purposes of comparison.

```
!The file wp5.kbs uses a PLURAL variable,
!         Activity, in a compound OR IF-THEN-ELSE-BECAUSE.
!
!ACTION BLOCK

ACTIONS
                    Display "WPHELP will advise you on whether you need a word pro-
cessor or not.

Press the SPACEBAR to start the consultation. ~"
          CLS
          FIND advice
          DISPLAY "You {advice} a word processor at this time.

         Press the SPACEBAR to exit WPHELP. ~"
         CLS;

!RULES BLOCK

RULE 1
IF        Activity=Letters
          OR Activity=Resumes
          OR Activity=Notices
          OR Activity=Papers
THEN      Advice=need
ELSE      Advice=do_not_need
BECAUSE"If you generate frequent letters, resumes, notices, or papers, then you need a
          word processor.";

!STATEMENTS BLOCK

ASK Acitivity: "Which of the following documents do you need
to write for your business? Select your answers by pressing
the ENTER key. After you have made all your selections, press
the END key. If you don't need to write any of these documents,
select NONE-OF-THESE (with ENTER, END).";

CHOICES Activity : Letters, Resumes, Notices, Papers, None_of_These;

Plural : Activity;
```

One question, many answers

Plural variable

FIGURE M3.4 A PROGRAM WITH A PLURAL VARIABLE (wp5.kbs)

It is interesting to compare wp4.kbs and wp5.kbs. They both give the same advice on whether or not you need a word processor. The knowledge base in each consists of one rule, but the number of variables in the rule differs. The second program, wp5.kbs, is probably easier to use because there is just one question to answer, but with multiple selections. This is the use of the PLURAL variable. As you have seen from all the examples, the same knowledge base can be expressed in different ways, depending on the construction of the IF-THEN rules and the dialogue needed with the user. Now return to the Main Menu with 8Quit.

So far we have discussed the format of IF-THEN rules, relational operators, compound rules, mathematical calculations, and the PLURAL variable. All of these have been parts of pre-existing programs. Now we will explore a way to create a knowledge base from a simple table, without writing the program.

Creating an Expert System from a Table

At this point, we have presented example expert systems displaying the format of the rules in the knowledge base. There is another way to create or **induce** not only a knowledge base, but an expert system, from a table. Even though an expert system can be created from a database (table), or a spreadsheet (table), we will now concentrate on creating an expert system from a table of text.

Logic Behind Table Files

In a VP-Expert system there is a conversion format from the rows and columns of a table to the rules. Consider the table in Figure M3.5 which shows the logical placement of condition headings, conclusion headings, and values of the headings.

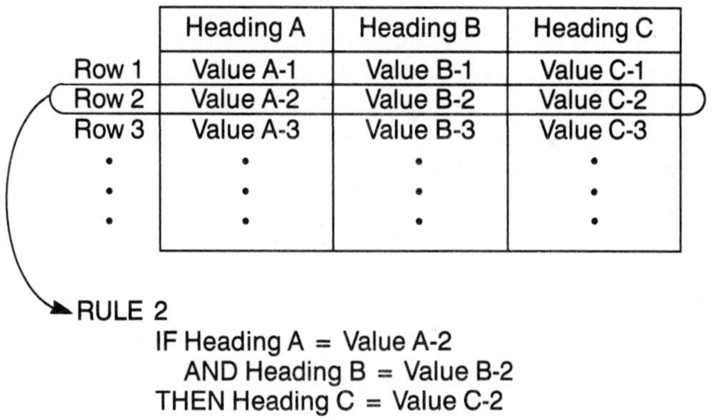

FIGURE M3.5 LOGICAL TRANSLATION FROM ROWS TO RULES

The table is divided into rows and columns. Each row of the table (except the headings) will become a rule in the knowledge base. The contents of the first two columns will become the conditions of the IF part, and the last column will become the conclusion of the rule. For example, row 2 would give the rule "IF HeadingA=ValueA-2 AND HeadingB=ValueB-2, THEN HeadingC=ValueC-2.

Let's take our word processing example. Consider the table file shown in Figure M3.6.

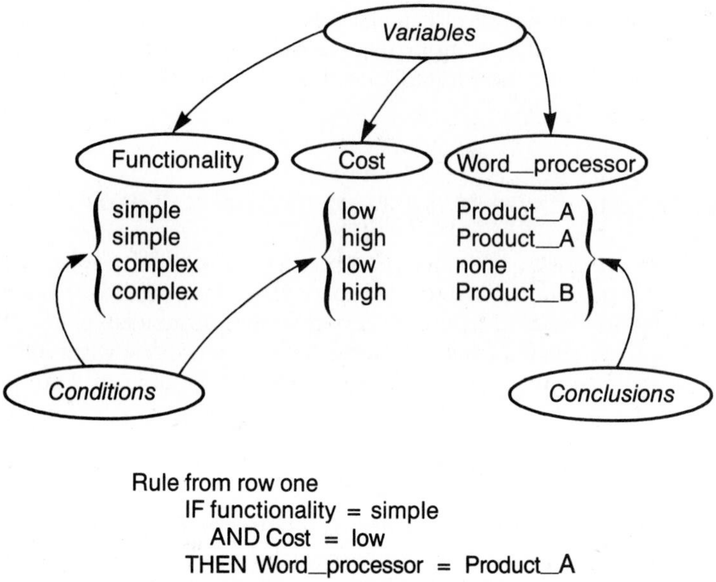

FIGURE M3.6 TABLE FILE (wp1.tbl)

We will assume that the first row identifies the variables. That is, the variables are Functionality, Cost, and Word_processor. Since the table has four rows under these headings, there will be four rules in the expert system to be created from this table. From the first row underneath the headings of Functionality, Cost, and Word_processor, the following rule will be created:

RULE 1

IF Functionality = Simple

AND Cost = Low

THEN Word_processor = Product_A;

The data in the fourth row under the headings would give us:

RULE 4

IF Functionality = complex

AND Cost = high

THEN Word_processor = Product_B;

Moreover, notice that an AND is inserted between the first two column values, and the third column value is the conclusion. The nice part of this method is that the resulting expert system will run in a fixed format without any programming. Let's take an example of a table and from it, **induce** or create an expert system.

Translation of a Table File to a Knowledge Base File

Select the 2Induce option from the Main Menu. You will see the Induce Menu as shown in Figure M3.7.

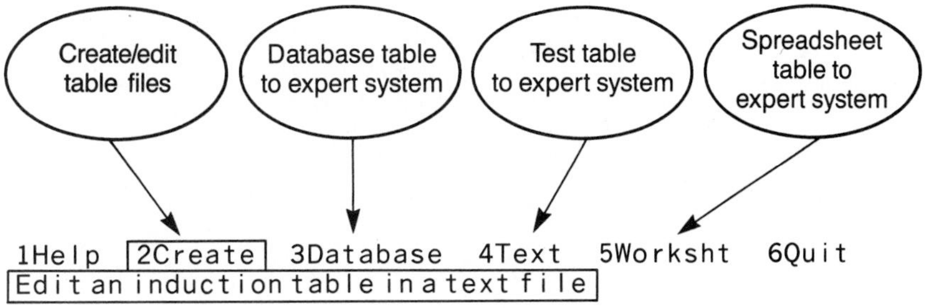

FIGURE M3.7 MENU FOR THE 2INDUCE OPTION

An expert system can be induced from an existing database table, (3Database), a worksheet (5Worksht), or a text-table (4Text). The 2Create option will allow us to create or change an existing table of text. The 2Create will invoke the regular text editor (word processor).

VP-Expert must have a file name with an extension of .tbl for a text table in order to create an expert system with a .kbs extension. We already have a table called wp1.tbl on the Sample Files Disk. Let's take a look at this file by following these steps:

Step 1. Select 2Create from the Induce Menu. The message "Choose a text file." will appear along with a list of files. The file names that appear are only files with a .tbl extension.

Step 2. Select wp1 by entering either wp1 or moving the light bar to this choice and pressing ENTER. You are now in the editor for text tables and your screen should look like Figure M3.8.

Note that the message, "editing old file b:\wp1.tbl", is displayed in the upper right-hand corner. The table file is in the middle of the screen, and the menu bar is across the bottom. The only difference between this editor (2Create) and the editor from the Main Menu is that this editor loads only table files (.tbl). The first row of the table identifies the variables, and the remainder of the rows represent potential rules. The format is that the last column is the conclusion and the conditions connected by AND come from the first two columns.

The reason for loading the file wp1.tbl with the 2Create option is simply to see the file. If we wished, we could change the table or create a new text table for a new expert system. For now, just obtain a printout of the table by pressing F10 followed by the END key. (This is identical to the printing option in the Main Menu editor.) To exit the table editor, press ALT-F8. Answer y to the question. You should now be back to the Induce Menu of Figure M3.7. We will use the table file wp1.tbl to induce an expert system or knowledge base file. We are now ready to generate, or induce, a new expert system program using our table file. (If you do not have 640K of memory, the induced file will not be created.) Select the 4Text option from the Induce Menu. The following screens, shown in Figure M3.9, will appear.

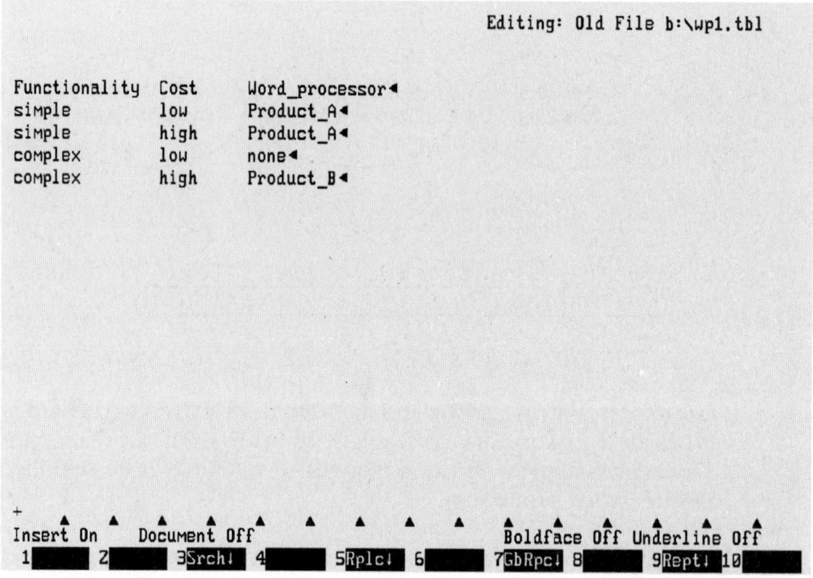

FIGURE M3.8 THE TABLE FILE (wp1.tbl) IN THE INDUCE EDITOR (2CREATE)

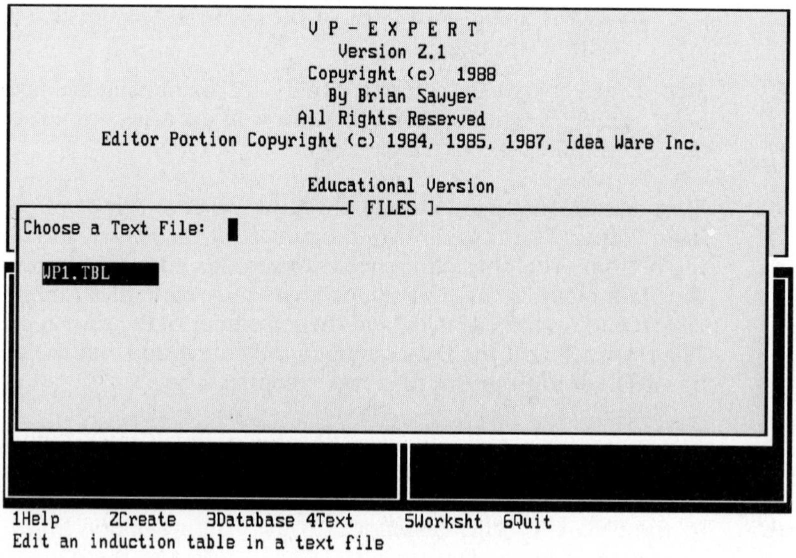

FIGURE M3.9 IDENTIFICATION OF THE TABLE FILE

The first message asks for the table file (.tbl) that we want to use. Again select wp1. The next screen message asks for the name of the file (.kbs) to be induced (formed or created) from the selected table file. Since we already have a knowledge base called wp1.kbs, we will enter a different file name. Enter inwp1, which stands for "inducing from wp1.tbl," and press ENTER. VP-Expert will now create a file called inwp1.kbs, which is a minimal expert system.

With the existence of a table (.tbl) file, the system will generate a knowledge base. The new file will be saved as inwpl.kbs on the B drive. When the light bar returns to the 2Create option, select the 6Quit option of the Induce Menu and return to the Main Menu. To run the induced expert system, inwp1.kbs, we follow these steps to run a regular consultation:

Step 1. Select the 6FileName option and then enter inwp1..

Step 2. Select 4Consult to get to the Consult Menu. The familiar message that the file is being loaded will be displayed.

Step 3. Select the 2Go option.

You are now in the regular Consultation mode. In response to the questions at the screen, select "simple" and then "high". The consultation should respond with "The value of word processor is Product_A." At the end of the consultation your screen should appear as Figure M3.10.

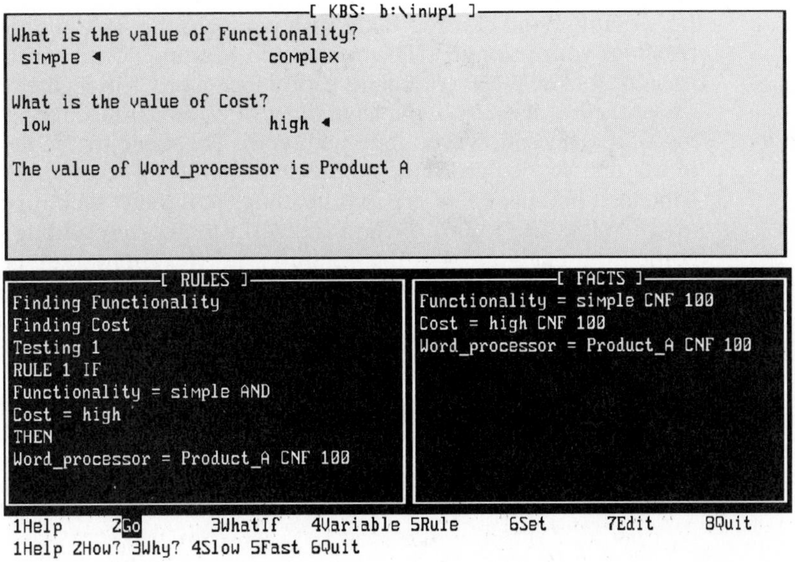

FIGURE M3.10 CONSULTATION SCREEN FOR INDUCED EXPERT SYSTEM (inwp1.kbs)

This consultation was generated from a table and no programming was required.

There are some differences, however, in the first wp1.kbs program and the one induced from a table in inwpl.kbs. The induced version has a rigid format. The questions to the user are phrased as "What is the value of ___________". Also there are no introductory comments to tell the user what the system is about or instructions to start or exit the consultation. Yet, the expert system is usable and was created without any knowledge of programming.

Let's take a look at the software for the induced expert system. To obtain a printout of the file inwp1.kbs, we follow the usual steps. Assuming that inwpl.kbs has already been selected under the 6FileName option, follow these steps to obtain a printout of the induced file (or any kbs file):

Step 1. Select the 7Edit option of the Consult Menu.

Step 2. In the editor, press the F10 key followed by the END key.

Step 3. Exit to the Consult Menu by pressing ALT and F8 and typing y.

Step 4. Return to the Main Menu with 8Quit.

The printout of inwp1.kbs along with the table file is shown in Figure M3.11. This is the code that was generated when you selected 4Text (from the Induce Menu). If you didn't create the induced file because of memory limitations, use the backup copy called inwp1b.kbs on your Sample Files Disk.

Let's examine the **canned** code, and compare the table file to the knowledge base file from your printouts. The conclusion heading (Word_processor) is taken as the variable for the FIND command (Comment 1 or C1 in Figure M3.11). The four rows under the headings from the table file give us the knowledge base (C2). The numbering of the rules, however, start with zero. The value of the heading and the values in the first two columns are connected by AND. The two ASK (C3) statements are generated because there are two headings (columns) that appear in the conditions of the rules. The values of the variable in the corresponding CHOICES command come from reading down the column with the appropriate heading. For example, reading down the Cost column, there are two distinct values, low and high; consequently these values are placed in the CHOICES command after the ASK command for that variable, Cost. Since there are two headings for conditions, there are two ASK commands with the corresponding CHOICES commands. The DISPLAY command (C4) prints to the screen the value (Product_A) found by the inference engine. The original wp1.kbs file, moreover, had a RUNTIME statement which did not allow the display of the Rules or Facts windows. An induced knowledge base, however, has the windows so that the activity of the inference engine is revealed.

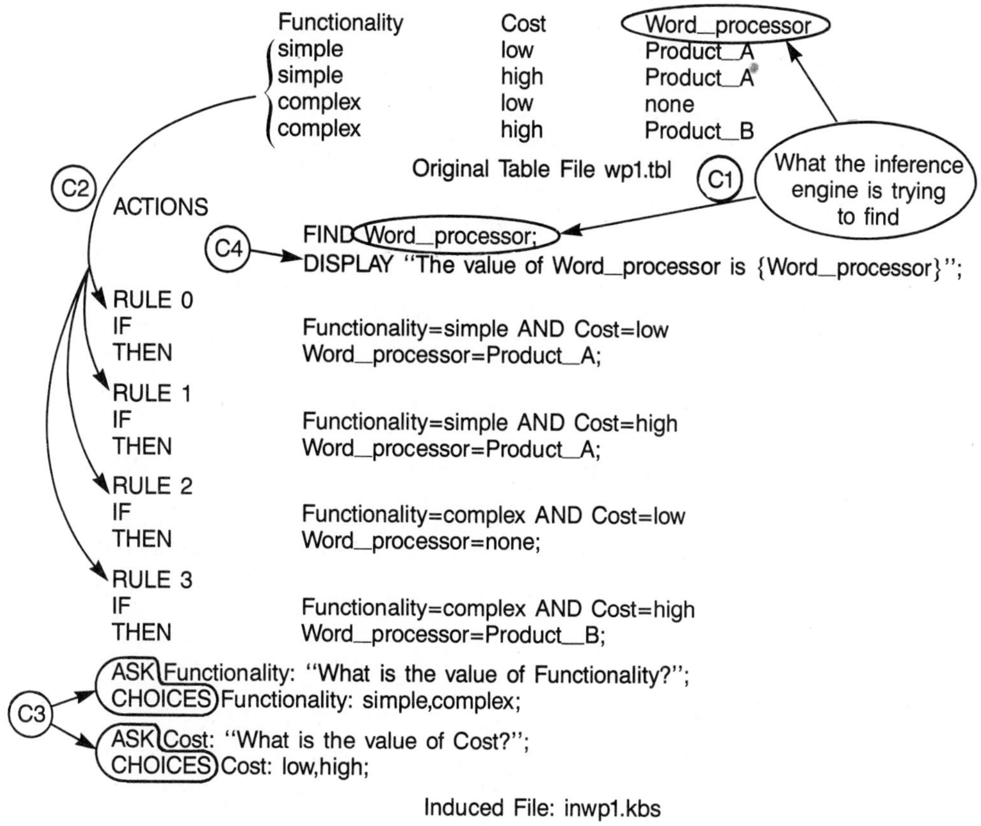

FIGURE M3.11 COMPARISON OF A TABLE FILE (wp1.tbl) AND THE INDUCED EXPERT SYSTEM FILE (inwp1.kbs)

What is the real power of the 2Induce option? Obviously, it creates a **form**, or **canned**, expert system without programming. Another advantage of using the 2Induce option is to generate the basics of our program, and then make a few changes to meet our specific needs. This can save a lot of time in keying in and debugging a program.

There are limitations, however, to using this option. You must be sure that the rules of the intended knowledge base are accurately represented in a table. All conditions must be included in order for the 2Induce option to create a valid expert system. The old adage, GIGO—Garbage In, Garbage Out, is very appropriate here. As we proceed through the modules, we will let you as the user decide on the value of the 2Induce option of VP-Expert.

Let's summarize the logical concepts behind the use of the 2Induce option before proceeding. The 2Induce option (Induce Menu) allows you to create a knowledge based system from a text, database, or spreadsheet table. For now we will use a text table. You can create your own table by using the 2Create option of the Induce Menu.

This option automatically produces a text file with a .tbl extension. An existing table file can also be modified or changed with this same option. Assuming the existence of a table file, you select the 4Text option from the same Induce Menu and indicate the table file you want and the intended name of the induced .kbs file. Once the induced file is created under the 4Text option (in the Induce Menu), the induced file can be run in a regular consultation session by selecting the 6FileName (.kbs) from the Main Menu and then by selecting 4Consult and 2Go. Note that table files, moreover, are created and changed in the Induce Menu, but .kbs files are manipulated within the 3Edit and 4Consult options of the Main Menu. The commands within the 2Create of the Induce Menu and 3Edit of the Main Menu, however, are the same editing or word processing commands.

The Complete Induction Cycle: Table to an Expert System

We will now turn our attention to the mechanics of creating a table file to induce an expert system and then using the Main Menu editor to change and modify the induced program. The editor (2Create) of the Induce Menu will work only on text or table files, whereas the editor of the Main Menu will utilize only program (.kbs) files

Creation of Table Files. Place your Data Disk in the B drive. During file creation, we generally will not use the Sample Files Disk (to avoid unnecessarily damaging files by accident). We will use the 2Create option of the Induce Menu to create the following table.

The information in this table is designed to tell you

Tutorial	Telephone_help	Buy_product_X
yes	yes	yes
yes	no	maybe
no	yes	maybe
no	no	no

whether you should purchase a particular product called X. The logic is to buy a particular Product X if both a tutorial and telephone help are yes (available). If only one source of help is available, then the advice to buy is maybe. If neither type of assistance is available, our expert system will advise you not to buy Product X.

To create this table file, follow these steps:

Step 1. Insert your Data Disk in the B drive.

Step 2. Set the 7Path to B:.

Step 3. Select the 2Induce option from the Main Menu.

Step 4. Select the 2Create option from the Induce Menu.

Step 5. In reply to the message, "Choose a text File." enter buy. (Note that this file does not yet exist.)

Step 6. When you see a blank screen, except for the message "Editing new file b: buy.tbl" in the upper right-hand corner and a menu bar at the bottom, you are in the text editor for tables. Now the task is to enter the rows and columns of text that are given in the table. To move from one column to another, you may use the TAB key (which may have two arrows pointing in opposite directions) or the SPACEBAR (for blanks). When you come to the end of a row, be sure to press the ENTER key. You will see the familiar wedge mark when you do. If you make a mistake, type over it and use the DEL key to delete unwanted letters. Use the arrow keys to move around on the screen. When you enter the underscore as part of the variables (telephone_help and buy_product_x), you will have to use the SHIFT key. Once you have the table entered as described in the steps, press the ALT and F5 keys to save the file but remain in the editor. To obtain a printout of the table, press the F10 key. When the screen appears, press the END key. When the printing is complete, exit the table editor with the ALT and F6 keys, and answer y to the question.

The Induced Knowledge Base File. Now that the buy.tbl text table has been created and stored on our Data Disk in the B drive, we are ready to *induce* a knowledge base from this file. Select the 4Text option from the Induce Menu. In response to the question "Choose a file" enter buy (without an extension) and press ENTER. In response to the next question "Choose a file" for the induced .kbs file, type inbuy without an extension and press ENTER. The red light on the B drive will come on and then the light bar will return to 2Create when the induced file has been created. We are now finished with the options of the Induce Menu. Select the 6Quit option and return to the Main Menu.

Now in the Main Menu, we need to run the consultation. Follow these familiar steps:

Step 1. Select 6FileName and enter inbuy.

Step 2. Select 4Consult from the Main Menu.

Step 3. Select 2Go from the Consult Menu.

When the consultation screen appears, select no to the first question and yes to the second. Remember, to make selections, press the ENTER key followed by the END key. When the consultation is over, the system advises maybe for Product_X. Your screen should look like Figure M3.12 after the consultation is over.

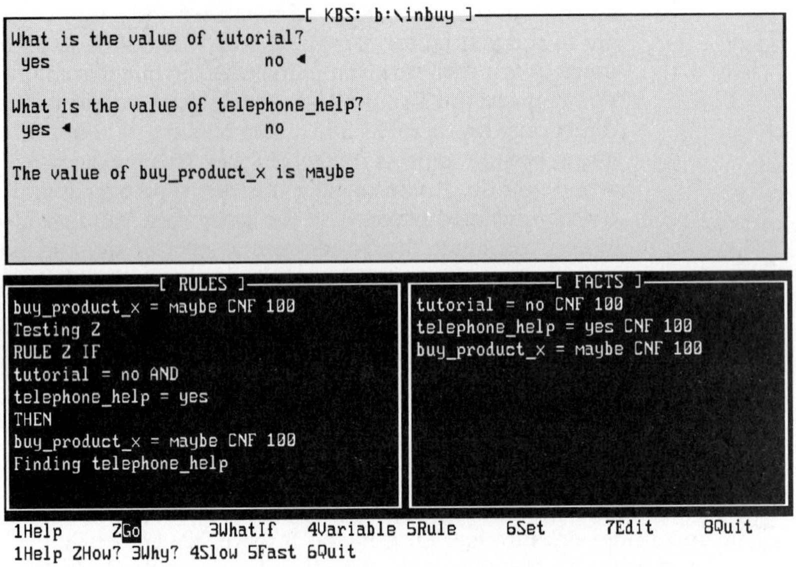

FIGURE M3.12 CONSULTATION SCREEN FOR THE SECOND INDUCED KNOWLEDGE BASE PROGRAM

Even though the messages to the user could be improved, the induced file runs just like a program that was written by a programmer. Rerun the consultation three more times to verify that the advice is the same as given in the original table file.

Now the task is to obtain a printout of the program file, inbuy.kbs, which was induced from the table file (buy.tbl) that we created. The familiar steps are as follows:

Step 1. Select the 7Edit option from the Consult Menu. (The selected file name is still inbuy.kbs.)

Step 2. When you are in the editor with the file loaded, press the F10 key and then the END key to obtain a printout. If you wanted to read the program file from the display screen, use the page up (PGUP) and/or page down (PGDN) keys.

The program file in your printout should be identical to the program file in Figure M3.13. You should be congratulated; you have just generated your first expert system program! In the next section, we will do a few modifications on the induced file (inbuy.kbs) so that **it runs better for the user**. Press ALT-F8 and enter y to go to the Consult Menu. Return to the Main Menu with 8Quit.

```
                    Table File (buy.tbl)
tutorial         telephone_help        buy_product_x
yes              yes                   yes
yes              no                    maybe
no               yes                   maybe
no               no                    no

ACTIONS
          FIND buy_product_x
          DISPLAY "The value of buy_product_x is {buy_product_x}";

RULE 0
IF        tutorial=yes AND telephone_help=yes
THEN      buy_product_x=yes;

RULE 1
IF        tutorial=yes AND telephone_help=no
THEN      buy_product_x=maybe;

RULE 2
IF        tutorial=no AND telephone_help=yes
THEN      buy_product_x=maybe;

RULE 3
IF        tutorial=no AND telephone_help=no
THEN      buy_product_x=no;

ASK tutorial: "What is the value of tutorial?";
CHOICES tutorial: yes,no;

ASK telephone_help: "What is the value of telephone_help?";
CHOICES telephone_help: yes,no;
```

FIGURE M3.13 INDUCED KNOWLEDGE BASE FILE (inbuy.kbs)

Changes in the Induced Knowledge Base File. Now we know how to generate an expert system program without programming, but to make it usable in the business environment, the program should be adjusted to make it more understandable during a consultation run. Hence, we will make changes to the .kbs file with the editor in VP-Expert just like we would make changes to a letter or other document with a word processor. Even though the emphasis in this module is on the knowledge base, it is appropriate here to make the knowledge base **usable**. Therefore, in this last section, we will briefly take you through the mechanics of basic changes to a program file. The complete set of commands for using the VP-Expert editor is available from the VP-Expert Help Facility.

Before we start, we offer this advice to experienced users of word processors. If you already know a word processor, we recommend that you may want to use it to change program files (.kbs) or to create table files (.tbl). There are only two points to consider. First, your word processor must let you translate a document file to a nondocument (ASCII) file. This means that the file will not have hidden and special control characters and symbols which can cause errors if the file is read by different software. The second consideration is the fact that table files must have a .tbl extension and programs must have a .kbs extension. If your word processor creates a different extension automatically, you can change the file extension with the DOS command, RENAME. To change the name of a file at the `A>` prompt, enter:

RENAME oldfile.name newfile.ext

This assumes that the old file is on a disk in the A drive. Hence, if you can translate document files to nondocument files with the proper extension on a word processor that you already know, then we recommend that you use it instead of learning and using the VP-Expert editor for extensive changes. We leave that decision to you. We will, however, give you the basics for using the editor from VP-Expert.

The task at hand is to take the program file inbuy.kbs, and make changes in the file. The changes that we will make are illustrated in Figure M3.14. We will make six changes to the program file and we will discuss the logic of the changes before the mechanics of effecting each change.

```
(C1) ACTIONS
               (C2) FIND buy_product_x
               (C3) DISPLAY "the value of buy_product_x is {buy_product_x}";

(C4)
RULE 0
IF             tutorial=yes AND telephone_help=yes
THEN           buy_product_x=yes;

RULE 1
IF             tutotiral=yes and telephone_help=no
THEN           buy_product_x=maybe;

RULE 2
IF             tutorial=no AND telephone_help=yes
THEN           buy_product_x=maybe;

RULE 3
IF             tutorial=no AND telephone_help=no
THEN           buy_product_x=no;

ASK tutorial: "What is the value of tutorial?"; (C5)
CHOICES tutorial: yes,no;

ASK telephone_help: "What is the value of telephone_help?"; (C6)
CHOICES telephone_help: yes,no;
```

C1	Insert comments and blank line
C2	Insert DISPLAY message
C3	Insert DISPLAY message
C4	Rename rule labels
C5	Change question
C6	Change question

FIGURE M3.14 PROPOSED CHANGES TO INDUCED KNOWLEDGE BASE FILE (inbuy.kbs)

As indicated in Figure M3.14, the changes are represented by circles. Change 1 is to add three new lines—a comment line, a blank line, and the RUNTIME command. The RUNTIME command will turn the Rules and Facts windows off during a consultation run. Change 2 will insert a DISPLAY command that gives an introductory message to the user. When we do this we will have to delete the semicolon from the DISPLAY command. Change 3 will modify the DISPLAY statement so that the user knows the advice from the expert system at the end of the consultation and will insert an ending message.

For Change 4, we will modify the Rule labels from 0, 1, 2, and 3 to One, Two, Three, and Four. The last two, Changes 5 and 6, will reword the phrasing of the questions to the user. When we finish these program alterations, our induced file (inbuy.kbs) will be like the updated program in Figure M3.15. Once these changes have been made, either with your own word processor or with the VP-Expert editor, we must test the program file to make sure it runs correctly.

```
!The file is inbuy.kbs.                                  (C1)
                RUNTIME;

ACTIONS
                DISPLAY "Welcome to WPHELP."             (C2)
                DISPLAY " "
                FIND buy_product_x                       (C3)
                DISPLAY "Concerning the purchase of product x,
                we say {buy_product_x}."
                DISPLAY " "
                DISPLAY "       End of consultation.";
RULE ONE                                                 (C4)
IF              tutorial=yes AND telephone_help=yes
THEN            buy_product_x=yes;
RULE TWO
IF              tutorial=yes AND telephone_help=no
THEN            buy_product_x=maybe;
RULE THREE
IF              tutorial=no AND telephone_help=yes
THEN            buy_product_x=maybe;
RULE FOUR
IF              tutorial=no AND telephone_help=no
THEN            buy_product_x=no;
ASK tutorial: "Is a tutorial available for product X";   (C5)
CHOICES tutorial: yes,no;
ASK telephone_help: "Is telephone help available from    (C6)
the company that sells product X?";
CHOICES telephone_help: yes,no;
```

FIGURE M3.15 UPDATED VERSION OF INDUCED KNOWLEDGE BASE FILE (inbuy.kbs)

We will now perform the changes using the VP-Expert editor. The basic instructions are as follows:

1. To move around the screen: use the arrow keys.
2. To insert a letter or word: use typeover.
3. To delete a letter or word: use the DEL key.
4. To add a blank line above: use the CTRL and ENTER keys.
5. To delete a line: use the CTRL and y.

Even though there are many more useful commands, this minimal set will let us make the desired changes.

To get started, we assume that we have VP-Expert in the A drive and our Data Disk in the B drive. We are in the Main Menu with the 7Path as b:. Select 6FileName and identify the needed file as inbuy by typing or selection. Select 3Edit. We are now ready to make change 1 as indicated in both Figure M3.14 and Figure M3.15. Follow these steps:

Step 1. Move the light bar to the first line, first column (on top of the A in Actions).

Step 2. Press the CTRL and ENTER keys simultaneously to insert a blank line above the cursor. Press the same keys two more times.

Step 3. Move the light bar to the first row, first column and enter "!The file is inbuy.kbs." as a comment line. (The wedge mark on the screen indicates that the ENTER key has been pressed.) The exclamation point (!) is used to indicate a comment line.

Step 4. Move the cursor to the first column below the comment line. After pressing the SPACEBAR eight times, enter RUNTIME; before pressing ENTER.

To effect the changes for C2 and C3 follow these steps:

Step 1. Move the light bar to the first position of the line with the FIND command. Create two blank lines with the CTRL and ENTER keys.

Step 2. Move the light bar to the first position of the blank line below Actions. Press the SPACEBAR eight times and then enter DISPLAY "Welcome to WPHELP."

Step 3. Move the light bar to the first position of the next blank line. Press the SPACEBAR eight times and enter DISPLAY "   " (so that a blank line will appear on the user's screen).

Step 4. Move the light bar to the line that has the DISPLAY instructions underneath FIND. Delete this line by pressing CTRL and y. Press CTRL and ENTER four times to create four blank lines.

Step 5. Enter the three DISPLAY instructions (four lines) from Change 3 (C3) of Figure M3.15.

Be sure to include the semicolon after the "End of Consultation" phrase. This signals the end of the Actions block to VP-Expert. Your program file should now look like the changes indicated in C2 and C3 in Figure M3.15.

Continuing, we will make the changes to the Rule labels. It is not really necessary to change Rule labels, but we think zero is an awkward way to label rules—and we want to make the point that Rule labels can be words, not merely numbers.

To make the changes for C4, follow the steps:

Step 1. Move the light bar to the 0 of RULE 0. Press the DEL key and then enter ONE.

Step 2. Repeat this same procedure changing 1 to TWO, 2 to THREE, and 3 to FOUR in the appropriate rule.

(Notice that we did not change the meaning of the IF-THEN rules at all.)

To complete the fifth change (C5) follow these steps.

Step 1. Move the light bar to the W of the question "What is the value of tutorial?" Press the DEL key until all the text is deleted except the two quotes.

Step 2. Enter the new question: Is a tutorial available for product X?.

To complete the last change (C6), use these steps:

Step 1. Move the light bar to the W from "What is the value of telephone_help?" Press the DEL key until only one quote and the wedge mark are left.

Step 2. Enter the following partial new question: Is telephone help available from. A wedge mark will indicate that an ENTER key is still at the end of this line.

Step 3. In order to put the rest of the question on the next line, move the light bar to the first C on the last CHOICES command. Put a blank line above this line by pressing CTRL and then ENTER.

Step 4. Move the light bar to the first position of this blank line. Type the words: the company that sells product X?";. Don't forget to include a semicolon after X?". Now compare your program changes to the updated file of Figure M3.15. The placement of semicolons (;) at the end of certain commands is important. There is only one semicolon in the Actions block, but there is a semicolon at the end of each rule and at the end of each ASK and CHOICES command, and the capital RUNTIME command.

Now that we think we have all the correct changes, to be sure, we need to save the program and run it. To save and exit the editor, press the ALT and F6 keys and reply y to the question.

Now in the Main Menu, select the 4Consult option for a test run. Each time a program file is loaded from the 4Consult option the file is checked for spelling and syntax errors. This is one reason for the lengthy delay in loading. If there are no typing errors, then you should see a screen indicating that the file has been loaded. Select the 2Go option. In response to the two questions, select no and then yes. Your Consultation screen should be the same as the screen in Figure M3.16.

The communication messages on the screen make the expert system easier to use. In Figure M3.16, Change 1 does not appear at the Consultation screen because it is a comment line used for information only. The RUNTIME instruction closes the Rules and Facts windows. Change 2 is a welcome statement to the user. Changes 5 and 6 are the rephrasing of the induced questions. The result or advise from the system resulted from Change 3.

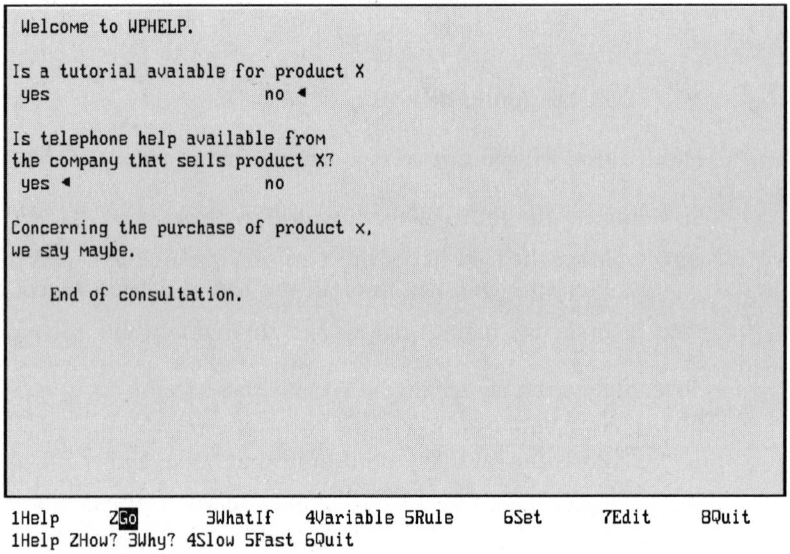

FIGURE M3.16 CONSULTATION SCREEN FOR UPDATED FILE (inbuy.kbs)

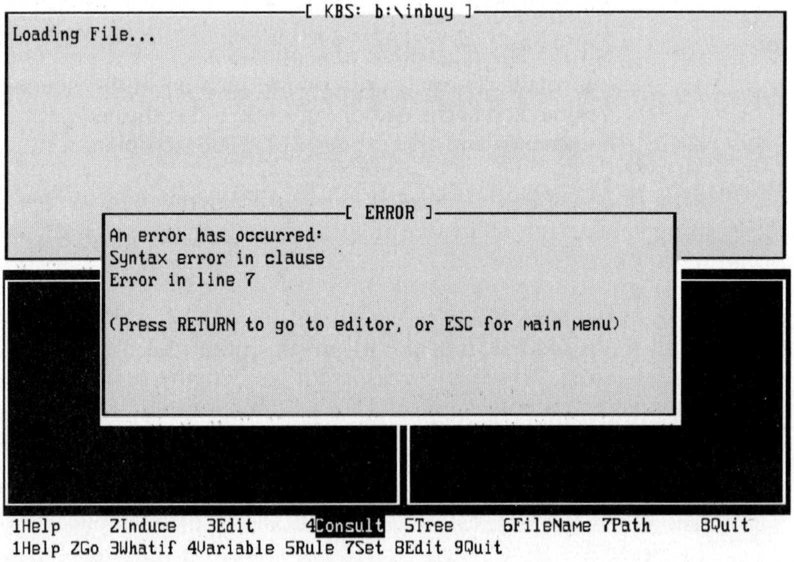

FIGURE M3.17 POSSIBLE ERROR MESSAGE FROM VP-EXPERT FOR UPDATED FILE (inbuy.kbs)

You may not have obtained the message that the file had been loaded. Instead you may have received a message that looks like the one displayed in Figure M3.17. This message tells us that there is something wrong with line 7; hence, the consultation cannot be run.

Press the RETURN key (ENTER to us), which returns you to the editor where you will correct the mistake. Actually, the error may be above line 7, on line 6, or even on line 5. Identifying the error is now the challenge. Compare your program to the one in Figure M3.15 to try to find your mistake. If you are a good typist, you probably didn't make a mistake. If you can't get your program to run, you will find a copy of the original and induced files under the file names buy2.tbl, inbuy2.kbs, and inbuy3.kbs on the Sample Files Disk.

We have completed our task of changing an induced program so that it is more usable. The larger the knowledge base, the more time the 2Induce option will save you. We do recommend, however, that you modify the program to make the knowledge base more usable. In this section, we concentrated on the knowledge base—how to form rules, to create table files, to induce a knowledge base, and to update induced program files. In the next module, we will discuss the inference engine and how it works.

Our final task for this module is to power down our system and deactivate the printer. If you are not at the `A>` prompt, choose 8Quit from the Main Menu and exit to DOS.

Key Points

- The method for structuring the knowledge base for VP-Expert is production rules—not semantic nets, frames, or predicate calculus.
- The production rules take the form of IF-THEN with ELSE and BECAUSE as optional parts.
- The IF part of a rule can include one or more conditions. The THEN part contains the conclusion(s). The optional ELSE part also contains alternative conclusions if the condition is false. The BECAUSE option does not affect the logic of a rule, but adds an explanation if the user uses the 2How? or 3Why? options during a consultation run.
- The IF part of a rule may be a simple condition or a compound condition using AND or OR. Up to twenty conditions are allowed in the IF part of a rule.
- The IF part of an IF-THEN rule is evaluated to be either true or false. When the IF part is true, the conclusion fires or is true. When the IF part is false, the rule does not fire in an IF-THEN structure.
- IF-THEN-ELSE rules always fire. When the IF statement is true, the condition(s) between the THEN and ELSE will be true. When the IF statement is false, the condition(s) after the ELSE are true.
- When the IF part contains a compound statement connected by ANDs, the conclusion is then true only if all parts of the compound statement are true.

- When the IF part is composed of compound statements connected by ORs, the condition is then false only when all parts of the compound conditions are false.
- If the condition of an IF-THEN rule contains both AND and OR, the OR will be evaluated first regardless of its placement in the condition.
- The IF part of a rule is composed of a variable, a relational operator, and a constant, number, or other variable. If an additional variable is used, it is enclosed in parentheses.
- The relational operators for the IF part of a rule are:
  - = equals
  - < is less than
  - <= is less than or equal to
  - > is greater than
  - >= is greater than or equal to
  - <> not equal to
- The OR connective is not allowed in conclusions, but compound conclusions equivalent to ANDs are implied.
- Arithmetic calculations can be a part of a condition or a conclusion. The four arithmetic operations are:
  - + Addition
  - − Subtraction
  - * Multiplication
  - / Division
- Special mathematical functions, @ABS(X), @EXP(X), @LOG(X), and @SQRT(X) can be used in VP-Expert programs.
- Trigonometric functions are also available.
- When using mathematical calculations, they must always be to the right of the relational operator and also inside parentheses.
- An assignment statement means that the value on the right side of the equals sign (=) is moved to the variable on the left side of the equals sign. Assignment statements are found in conclusions.
- In order for a variable to have more than one value during a consultation run, the variable must be declared as PLURAL. A program can have more than one PLURAL variable.
- A canned expert system program can be generated from a database, spreadsheet, or text table.
- The 2Induce option from the Main Menu contains the Induce Menu for creating/editing text tables (2Create) and generating (4Text) a knowledge based file (.kbs).
- The Induce Menu is as follows:

```
1Help   2Create   3Database   4Text   5Worksht   6Quit
```

- To induce an expert system from a table file, first create the table (2Create) and generate the knowledge based file with 4Text of the Induce Menu.
- The 3Edit option of the Main Menu may be used to make changes or modifications to any induced .kbs file.
- Induced files need modifications so they are more usable to the business community.
- The mechanics of using the VP-Expert editor are given in the VP-Expert's Help Facility.
- If you already know a word processor, you may use it to create and/or change table or knowledge based files. Be sure that the word processor will translate your files to nondocument files and that the extension name is .tbl for table- and .kbs for knowledge-based files (for use with VP-Expert).

Exercises

1. Indicate which of the following variables are valid (V) or invalid (I).
   a. COST ____
   b. cost ____
   c. cOSt ____
   d. COST/____
   e. $COST ____
   f. 7COST ____
   g. COST7 ____
   h. COST_7 ____
   i. COST-7 ____

2. Which of the following statements are valid (allowed) in VP-Expert? Mark V (Valid) or I (Invalid) by each.
   a. x=3 ______
   b. x?3 ______
   c. x=(y−3) ______
   d. x=abs(y) ______
   e. x=@abs(y) ______
   f. x=(@abs(y)) ______
   g. x−3=y ______
   h. x−3* ______
   i. (y−3)=x ______
   j. abs(y)=x ______
   k. @abs(y)=x ______
   l. (@abs(y))=x ______

3. Write a BECAUSE statement appropriate for each of the rules shown in Figure M3.13.

4. Consider the following rule:
   IF Savings > 5000 OR
   Gross_pay_per_month > 3000
   THEN qualify = yes.
   a. Indicate (Y or N) whether the rule will "fire" for the following values of savings and gross_pay_per_month.

Savings	Gross pay	Qualify?	Rule fires?
2000	40000		
2500	2500		
6000	4000		
7000	2700		

   b. Change OR to AND in the rule. Does the rule fire for the same pairs of values?

5. Obtain a printout of wp3.kbs.
   a. Circle all variables (on the paper).
   b. Draw a box around all relational operators.
   c. Underline all words that the user sees at the screen.
   d. What is condition 2 and conclusion 2 in Rule 1?
   e. What is the advice given if all questions are answered No?
6. Repeat Exercise 5 with wp4.kbs, wp5.kbs, and inbuy.kbs.
7. Using the following table to induce an expert system, answer the listed questions.

Name	Type	Model	Advice
A	B	C	D
E	F	G	H
I	J	K	L

   a. How many conditions would be in each rule?
   b. What column represents the conclusion?
   c. How many rules would be induced?
   d. How many ASK statements would be induced?
   e. What is the last rule?
8. Using Exercise 7,
   a. What ASK statements would be induced?
   b. What CHOICE statements would be induced?
9. Given the rules below, write out the table file that could induce it.

```
RULE 0
   IF Cost=400 and Warranty=Yes
   THEN Advice=OK;
RULE 1
   IF Cost=400 and Warranty=No
   THEN Advice=No;
RULE 2
   IF Cost=800 and Warranty=Yes
   THEN Advice=Maybe;
RULE 3
   IF Cost=800 and Warranty=No
   Then Advice=No;
```

10. Use the VP-Expert Help Facility to obtain a printout for each of the following topics
    a. IF THEN
    b. AND
    c. OR
    d. RULE
    e. ELSE
    f. BECAUSE
    g. INDUCE MENU
    h. CURSOR COMMANDS
    i. ALTERNATE KEYS
    j. FUNCTION KEYS
    k. EDITOR COMMANDS

Assignments

1. Run the expert system investl.kbs which is on your Sample Files Disk. Answer the following:
   a. What is the purpose of the expert system?
   b. How many rules are in the knowledge base? What kind of rule(s)?
   c. How many variables are in the program (.kbs) file?
   d. Write out a text table that could be used to induce investl.kbs before modifications.
2. Run the expert system invest2.kbs from your Sample Files Disk.
   a. What is the purpose of the expert system?
   b. How many rules are in the knowledge base? What kind of rule(s)?
   c. Compare the rules from investl.kbs to those of invest2.kbs.
   d. Could a text file induce this knowledge base?
3. Run the expert system taxhelpl.kbs from your Sample Files Disk. Answer the following:
   a. What is the purpose of the system?
   b. How many rules are in the knowledge base? What kind of rule(s)?
   c. How many variables are in the program file?
   d. On a run of the program answer No to all questions. What happens?
4. Run taxhelp2.kbs from the Sample Files Disk. Answer the following:
   a. What is the purpose of the expert system?
   b. How many rules are in the knowledge base? What kind of rule(s)?
   c. How many variables are in the program?
   d. Answer no to all the questions. Is the advice valid?
   e. Why is a PLURAL needed in the program?
5. Run Taxhelp3.kbs from your Sample Files Disk. Answer the following:
   a. What is the purpose of the program?
   b. How many rules are in the knowledge base? What kind of rules?
   c. How many variables are there in the program?
   d. Compare Taxhelp2.kbs and Taxhelp3.kbs.
6. Using the 2Create option of the Induce Menu and your Data Disk,
   a. Create a table file from the table in Exercise 7. Call in Example.tbl.
   b. Use the 4Text option of the Induce Menu to induce Example.kbs.
   c. Run a consultation with Example.kbs.
   d. Obtain a printout of Example.kbs.
   e. Divide the printout into the three parts of a VP-Expert program, Actions, Rules, and Statements.

7. Using the table below and your Data Disk, perform the following.

Backups	Spell_Checker	Advice
Yes	Yes	Buy
Yes	No	No
No	Yes	No
No	No	No

   a. Create a table file called Example2.tbl using the 2Create option of the Induce Menu.
   b. Induce Example2.kbs from Example2.tbl by using 4Text of the Induce Menu.
   c. Run a consultation with Example2.kbs.
   d. Obtain a printout.
   e. Divide the printout into 3 parts, Actions, Rules, and Statements.

8. Assume that Assignment 7 (Example2.kbs) is advising you not to buy a particular word processor unless the package creates automatic file backups and comes with a spelling checker.
   a. On the printout, write out new questions and messages to the user.
   b. Using your Data Disk and the 3Edit option of the Main Menu, implement your changes to improve Example2.kbs.
   c. Obtain a printout.
   d. Run a consultation with the changed version of Example2.kbs.

9. Using the results of Assignment 8,
   a. Convert the rules of Example2.kbs to one IF-THEN-ELSE rule.
   b. Using the 3Edit of the Main Menu, delete the four rules (using CTRL-Y) and replace with one IF-THEN-ELSE rule.
   c. Run a consultation with your new Example2.kbs.
   d. Does the consultation offer the same advice as in Assignment 8?

10. Find an article that compares the features of word processing packages. Try the report on "Advanced Word Processors—Familiar New Features" from *PC World,* (Special Issue, Third Annual Software Review), July, 1989, pp. 96-115.
    a. Using the summary evaluation tables, select a subset of information to induce a potential expert system.
    b. Create this table with 2Create of the Induce Menu and call it Features.tbl.
    c. Induce an expert system Features.kbs using 4Text from the Induce Menu.
    d. Run a consultation with Features.kbs.
    e. Obtain a printout of Features.tbl and Features.kbs.
    f. Does your expert system need a PLURAL variable in order to give accurate and complete advise from the table?

11. In using the Induce Menu, we created new files on the Sample Files Disk. At the `A>` prompt, place the Sample Files Disk in the A drive.
    a. How many free bytes are left on the disk?________________
    b. The 2Create option uses VPXI.EXE. How large is this file? __________
    c. How large is wp1.tbl? ______________________
    d. How large is inwp1.kbs?____________________

Module 4

THE VP-EXPERT INFERENCE ENGINE

In this module we will examine how the inference engine works to solve a problem. The inference engine is trying to move from an initial state to a goal state. Two ways for achieving this solution are backward chaining and forward chaining. We will use 2Trace of the Set Menu and 5Tree from the Main Menu to trace the behavior of the inference engine. These results can be viewed as a Text tree or a Graphics tree. VP-Expert uses backward chaining techniques, but forward chaining can be implemented with the WHENEVER command. We will look also at the placement of goals and rules within the structure of a program or .kbs file. This module will end with a discussion of how the inference engine deals with certainty and uncertainty.

Inference Engine Logic

The purpose of problem solving is to move from an initial state to a goal state. In order to do this we may have to go through intermediate states. In an expert system, the inference engine has to search though the rules trying to find the goal state or reach a conclusion. VP-Expert uses **deductive logic** for the operation of its inference engine, not induction or abduction (see Chapter 4). This means we assume that the rules in the knowledge base are valid; hence the rules fire when the conditions are true.

Backward Chaining

The two ways that the inference engine operates or reasons with rules are called forward and backward chaining. VP-Expert uses **backward chaining**. This means that the goal state, or conclusion, is assumed and the conditions are checked to see if that assumed goal is correct. Consider the rules given in Figure M4.1.

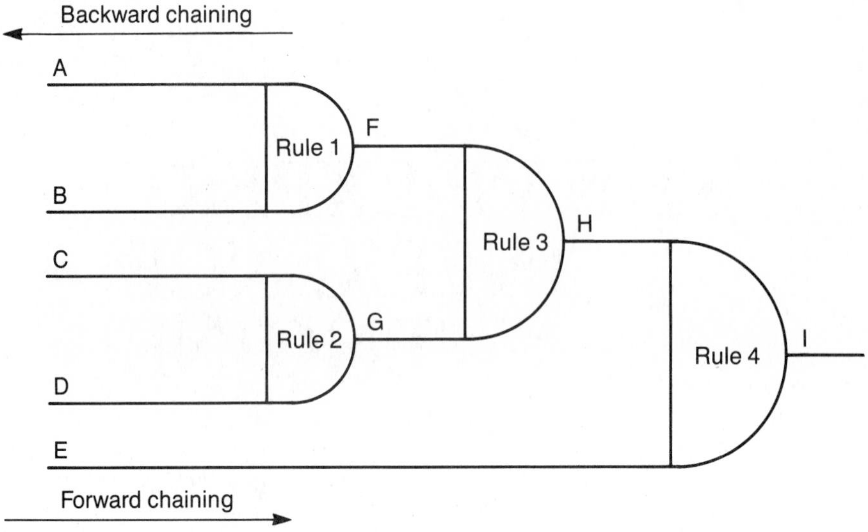

FIGURE M4.1 FORWARD AND BACKWARD CHAINING

Here the goal state is named I. This would be stated as FIND I in a VP-Expert program file. If the goal state I is not known, then FIND I turns control over to the inference engine. The inference engine would work backward and look at the conditions of rules where the conclusion was I, the goal state. The only rule with I as the conclusion is Rule 4. The inference engine would examine Rule 4 and try to find the truth value of the conditions, H and E. If the truth values are known, the search stops and a conclusion is reached if both H and E are true. If H is unknown, the inference engine will look for rules where H is the conclusion and try to determine its value. If its value is not known, then VP-Expert will ask or query the user. This process continues until VP-Expert finds the truth values of the initial states, A,B,C,D, and E, and makes a determination on a value for the goal state I.

Forward Chaining

Forward chaining, on the other hand, would start at the conditions (initial states) and work toward the conclusions (goal states). You may hit many conclusions, none of which you may want. VP-Expert has a WHENEVER command that is placed in front of a rule. Whenever the value of a variable in the condition changes value, the rule is tested. This partially implements forward chaining.

Confidence Factors (CNF)

Before we proceed to examples of backward and forward chaining concepts in VP-Expert, we should consider **confidence (certainty) factors** or **CNF**. Confidence factors are whole numbers ranging from 1 to 100. If a rule has a CNF 100, then we are 100% sure that we are correct. A CNF 0 indicates that we are absolutely sure that the conclusion is false (invalid). Numbers closer to 100 indicate higher degrees of confidence. In general, the larger the CNF value the better. If a rule has a CNF 75, then we are 75% confident that the rule is true. Both the IF and the THEN parts of a rule may have individual confidence factors. We will discuss how these values are assigned in detail in Module 6, but here we will encounter CNFs as we trace the behavior of the inference engine.

Trace of the Inference Engine: Backward Chaining

Let's turn our attention to **tracing** the activity of the inference engine when an expert system is active. Assuming that the 7Path (b:), 6FileName, and 4Consult have been selected, we use the 6Set option from the Consult Menu to specify that we want to trace the activity of the inference engine. The Trace must be set before you run a consultation (2Go) with the knowledge base file. After the consultation is over, the results can be seen by exiting the Consult Menu and using the 5Tree option of the Main Menu. The Tree Menu will let us view both a *textual trace* and a *graphical trace* of the consultation activity. Once you exit the Consult Menu, the Trace is no longer active. The next time you enter the Consult Menu, you have to reset the Trace option. The logic of this procedure is shown in M4.2. The Trace is set from the Consult Menu but viewed from the 5Tree option of the Main Menu.

We will use the file wp2.kbs as our example. The knowledge base consists of the following four Rules:

```
RULE 1
IF          Functionality=Simple AND
            Cost=Low
THEN        Word_processor=Product_A;
RULE 2
IF          Functionality=Simple AND
            Cost=High
THEN        Word_processor=Product_A;
RULE 3
IF          Functionality=Complex AND
            Cost=Low
THEN        Word_processor=none;
RULE 4
IF          Functionality=Complex AND
            Cost=High
THEN        Word processor=Product_B;
```

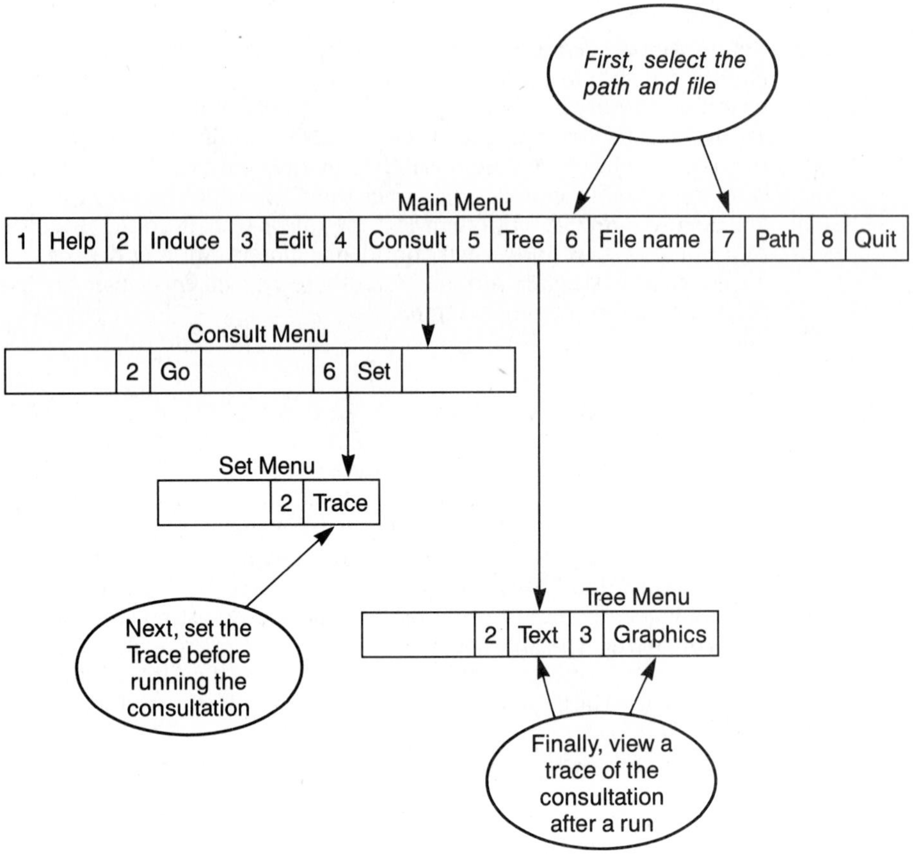

FIGURE M4.2 PROCEDURE FOR USING THE TRACE OPTION

All of these rules have Word_processor as a conclusion. This is our goal state since the command "FIND Word_processor" appears in the .kbs file and the value of the variable Word_processor is not known.

Using the Trace Command

We will now set the Trace command and slow down the scrollings of the messages in the Rules and Facts windows by following these steps.

Step 1. At the familiar **A>** prompt, get into VP-Expert with VP-Expert in the A drive and the Sample Files Disk in the B drive.

Step 2. Type vpx. When the Main Menu appears, select 7Path and enter b:. Then select 6FileName and select wp2.kbs.

Step 3. Select 4Consult.

Step 4. At the Consult Menu, choose 6Set. The Set Menu will have six choices.

Step 5. Now select 2Trace. This command will tell VP-Expert to save the messages from the Rules and Facts windows as a consultation runs. The saved messages will be put in both a text and graphics tree for you to view after the consultation.

Step 6. In order to view the messages better, slow down the scrolling in the windows by selecting the 3Slow option from the same menu. When the light bar returns to 2Trace, move the cursor and select 3Slow again. Repeat this four more times so that you can read all the messages on the screen.

Step 7. Exit the Set Menu by choosing 6Quit.

You are now ready to run the consultation with the Trace mode active. The following table shows the possible values that we could enter for the four possible runs of wp2.kbs.

Run	Functionality	Cost	Word_processor
Run1	Simple	Low	Product_A
Run2	Simple	High	Product_A
Run3	Complex	Low	none
Run4	Complex	High	Product_B

The values for the conditions are in the Functionality and Cost columns. The advise is the value of the variable Word_processor in the last column. Select 2Go and let's trace Run1 by selecting Simple and Low. As you run the consultation, the messages in the Rules window and the Facts window will be similar to these:

```
Finding Word_processor
Testing (Rule) 1
Finding Functionality
Functionality=Simple CNF 100
Finding Cost
Cost=Low CNF 100
Word processor=Product_A CNF 100
```

This is the activity of the inference engine as it searches for a value for Word_processor. The CNF is the confidence factor which has defaulted to 100. As the inference engine tests a rule, the entire rule is displayed in the Rules Window.

Viewing a Text Tree

After we have completed the consultation with Run1, we can view the trace. This will take us back to the Main Menu to the 5Tree option. Follow these steps:

Step 1. Exit the Consult Menu with 8Quit.

Step 2. Choose the 5Tree option from the Main Menu. You should see a menu of 1Help 2Text 3Graphics 4Quit.

Step 3. Select the 2Text for a text trace of our consultation with wp2.kbs.

A text file should appear on your screen, as shown in Figure M4.3.

```
                                              Editing: Old File b:\wp2.trc
Line
  1   Testing b:\wp2.kbs◂
  2   (= yes CNF 0 )◂
  3   !   Word_processor◂
  4   !   !   Testing 1◂
  5   !   !   !   Functionality◂
  6   !   !   !   !   (= Simple CNF 100 )◂
  7   !   !   !   Cost◂
  8   !   !   !   !   (= Low CNF 100 )◂
  9   !   !   (= Product_A CNF 100 )◂

Insert On   Document Off                        Boldface Off Underline Off
1      2      3Srch↓ 4      5Rplc↓ 6      7GbRpc↓ 8      9Rept↓ 10
```

FIGURE M4.3 TEXT TREE FOR Run1 OF wp2.kbs

The familiar menu bar of the editor appears at the bottom. (Text under the Tree menu is different from Text under the Induce menu.) The message "Editing Old file b:\wp2.trc" appears in the upper right-hand corner. The file with extension .trc was created during our consultation run when the Trace mode is active.

Let's interpret this text file. There are three different messages that could appear in the lines of the **Text tree**. If the line containing "Testing" is followed by a Rule label, then this is the rule being tested. If the line contains the name of a variable (Word_processor, Functionality, Cost), then the inference engine is trying to find a value for that variable. If the line contains a parenthesis, this means that the value inside has been assigned (found) for the indicated variable. The value can be matched to the variable by reading up the column of exclamation marks located to the left of the value.

Let's discuss the Text tree (trace) shown in Figure M4.3. Line 1 tells us that we are tracing file b:\wp2.kbs. Unfortunately, line 2 is useless information so we will ignore it. Line 3 indicates that the goal is to find a value for the variable Word_processor. Line 4 tells us that the first rule in the knowledge base that contains Word_processor as a conclusion is Rule 1. Hence, the inference engine is examining the conditions in Rule 1. Line 5 tells us that Functionality is a variable in the condition of Rule 1. Line 6 identifies that Simple is a value for the variable Functionality. (This fact came from the user input.) Line 7 indicates that Rule 1 has another variable called Cost as part of the conditions. Then line 8 tells us that Cost has been assigned a value of Low. The last line of the trace, line 9, indicates that the value of Product_A has been assigned to the variable Word_processor. Again, this was part of Rule 1. We match the variable to the value by moving left on the value line and up until we hit a variable name (not a rule name).

To obtain a printout of the text tree, use the familiar editor commands of F10 followed by End. To exit the editor without changes to the file contents or name, press ALT and F8 and reply Y to not saving the file. Obtain a printout and then exit the editor (text trace). You will be at the Tree Menu. If you have a graphics card on your system, then you can view the graphics tree of our past run. If you don't have a graphics card, then exit to the Main Menu with 4Quit.

Viewing a Graphics Tree

To view a **graphical tree structure** of the trace, select 3Graphics from the Tree Menu. Your screen should appear similar to Figure M4.4.

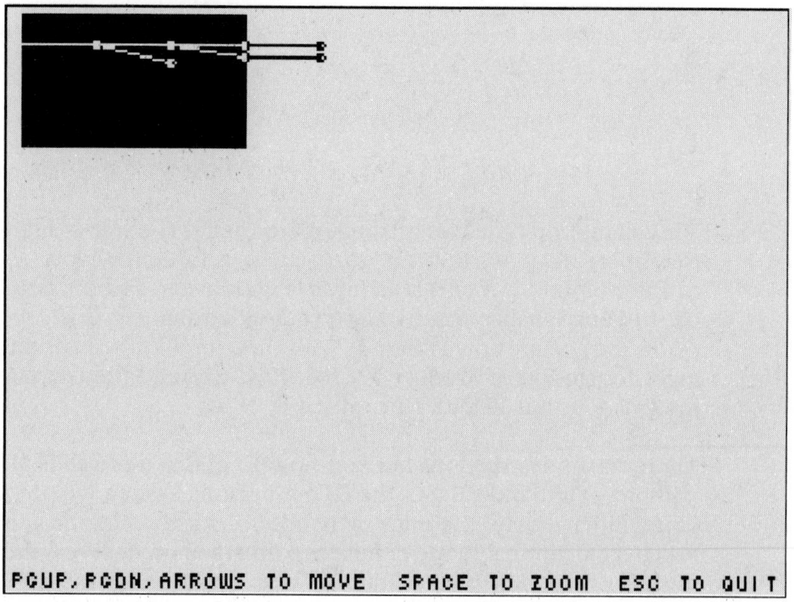

FIGURE M4.4 OPENING SCREEN FOR DISPLAYING A GRAPHICS TREE

A highlighted box appears in the upper left-hand corner of the display. Pressing the Right Arrow key moves the lighted box to another part of the Graphics tree. If you press the SPACEBAR, the contents of the lighted box will be enlarged. This movable lighted box and the zoom (enlarge) features are necessary to examine a large Graphics tree. Press the Right Arrow key and then the SPACEBAR. Your graphics tree should now resemble Figure M4.5. The enlargement shows text and arrows on the tree.

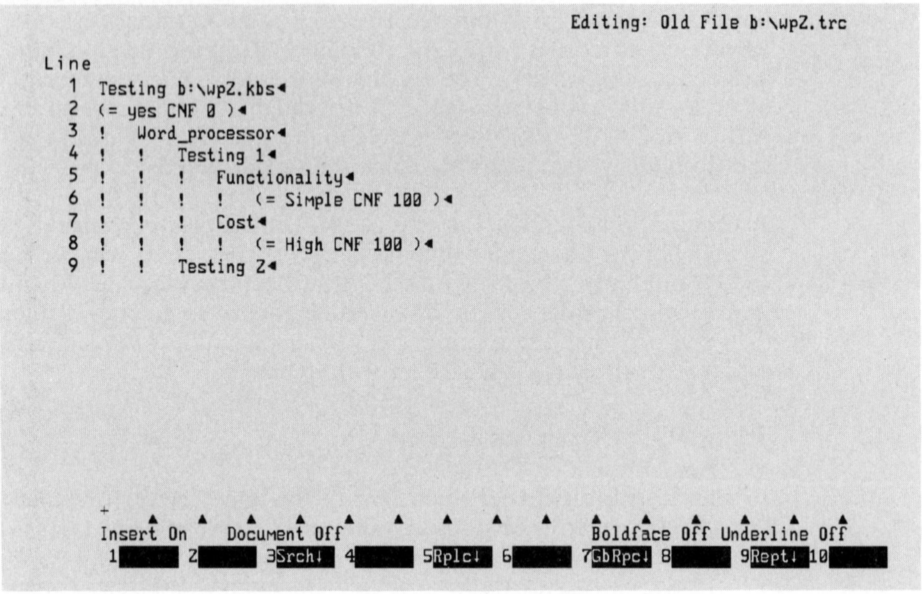

```
                                        Editing: Old File b:\wp2.trc
Line
  1  Testing b:\wp2.kbs◂
  2  (= yes CNF 0 )◂
  3  !   Word_processor◂
  4  !   !   Testing 1◂
  5  !   !   !   Functionality◂
  6  !   !   !   !   (= Simple CNF 100 )◂
  7  !   !   !   Cost◂
  8  !   !   !   !   (= High CNF 100 )◂
  9  !   !   Testing 2◂

     Insert On   Document Off                  Boldface Off Underline Off
     1      2      3Srch↓  4      5Rplc↓  6      7GbRpc↓ 8      9Rept↓ 10
```

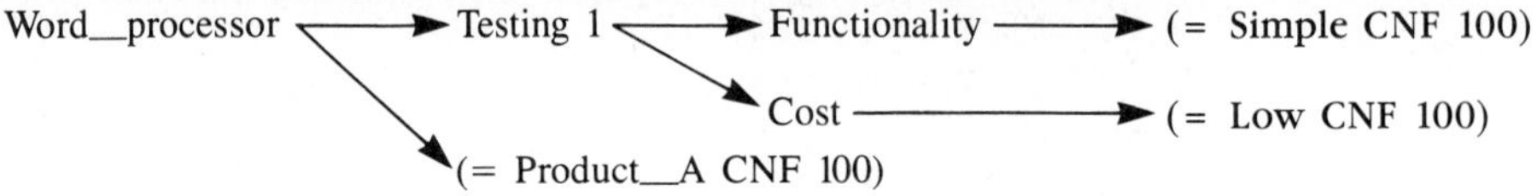

FIGURE M4.5 GRAPHICS TREE FOR Run1 OF wp2.kbs

We will interpret the tree reading left to right. (The tree is sideways.) The top of the tree (root) identifies that the goal state is a value for Word_processor. This leads to a test of Rule 1, then a search for Functionality, and finally an assignment of Simple to Functionality. Rule 1 also requires a value for Cost; so a search for Cost is made and a value Low is found. With these two known conditions, Rule 1 fires giving a conclusion of Product_A. The Text tree and the Graphics tree give the same information, but in different formats.

There are no instructions here on how to obtain a printout of the Graphics tree. If you press Shift and PRTSC, the DOS operating system will print out the words, but you will have draw the lines by hand. To exit the Graphics tree section, you have to return to Normal mode rather than Enlarged mode. Press the SPACEBAR to return to the normal view of the Graphics tree. Press ESC to exit the Graphics tree. When you return to the Trace Menu, exit to the Main Menu with 4Quit. We will now obtain traces of the other runs of wp2.kbs.

Tracing Additional Consultations

The first run (Run1) of wp2.kbs was simple because it involved only the first rule in the knowledge base. We will now run wp2.kbs but with different values. In each case, set the trace before each different run of the consultation. Then exit to the Main Menu and enter the Tree Menu to view the Text and Graphics trees. Obtain printouts of each tree.

To start this off, select 6FileName (wp2.kbs), 4Consult, 6Set, 2Trace, and 6Quit. At the Consult Menu run wp2.kbs (2Go), but enter the values Simple and High (Run2). Your Text trace and Graphics tree resemble Figure M4.6.

```
                                                Editing: Old File b:\wp2.trc
Line
  1  Testing b:\wp2.kbs◄
  2  (= yes CNF 0 )◄
  3  !   Word_processor◄
  4  !   !   Testing 1◄
  5  !   !   !   Functionality◄
  6  !   !   !   !   (= Simple CNF 100 )◄
  7  !   !   !   Cost◄
  8  !   !   !   !   (= High CNF 100 )◄
  9  !   !   Testing 2◄
 10  !   !   (= Product_A CNF 100 )◄

Insert On     Document Off                       Boldface Off Underline Off
1       2       3Srch↓  4       5Rplc↓  6       7GbRpc↓ 8       9Rept↓  10
```

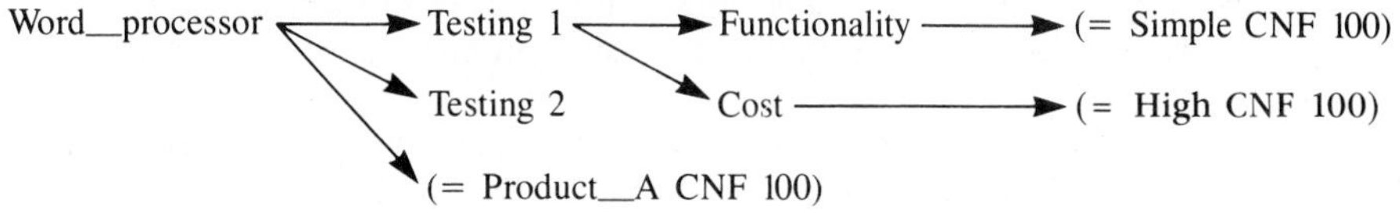

FIGURE M4.6   TEXT AND GRAPHICS TREES FOR Run2 of wp2.kbs

Notice on line 8 of the Text trace that Rule 1 did not fire; hence, the inference engine went to the next rule that contained Word_processor, in our case Rule 2. The same information is displayed with the Graphics tree.

Run wp2.kbs again with values Complex and Low (Run3). The resulting traces are given in Figure M4.7.

```
                                          Editing: Old File b:\wp2.trc
Line
  1  Testing b:\wp2.kbs◂
  2  (= yes CNF 0 )◂
  3  !   Word_processor◂
  4  !   !   Testing 1◂
  5  !   !   !   Functionality◂
  6  !   !   !   !   (= Complex CNF 100 )◂
  7  !   !   Testing 2◂
  8  !   !   Testing 3◂
  9  !   !   !   Cost◂
 10  !   !   !   !   (= Low CNF 100 )◂
 11  !   !   (= none CNF 100 )◂

     Insert On    Document Off                Boldface Off Underline Off
     1      2      3Srch↓  4      5Rplc↓  6      7GbRpc↓ 8      9Rept↓ 10
```

Graphics tree

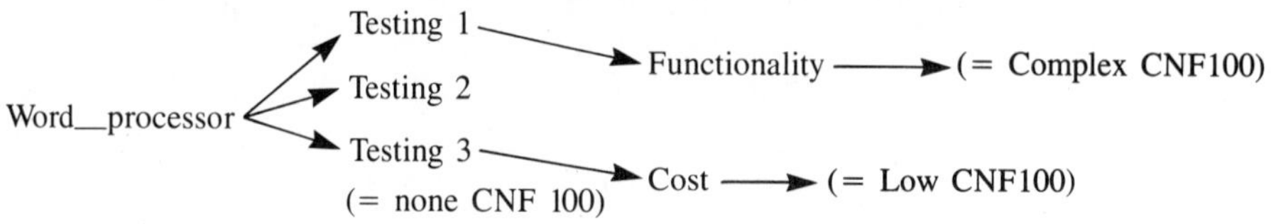

FIGURE M4.7 TEXT AND GRAPHICS TREE FOR Run3 OF wp2.kbs

Observe line 6 where Functionality=Complex made the compound condition false so that the rule does not fire; hence the inference engine went to the next rule Rule 2. Since Rule 2 also has a false compound condition, it too will not fire. The search is now on Rule 3 where the inference engine is now hunting a value for Cost (line 9).

Again activate a consultation with wp2.kbs, but enter values of Complex and High (Run4). As you can observe in Figure M4.8, the inference engine has to test all four rules (lines 4, 7, 8, and 11) before it can reach a conclusion. Since the inference engine does a sequential (top to bottom) search, the placement of the rules can affect the length of the search, but not the final results. Let's move on to another example with the trace option.

```
                                          Editing: Old File b:\wp2.trc
Testing b:\wp2.kbs◄
(= yes CNF 0 )◄
!    Word_processor◄
!    !    Testing 1◄
!    !    !    Functionality◄
!    !    !    !    (= Complex CNF 100 )◄
!    !    Testing 2◄
!    !    Testing 3◄
!    !    !    Cost◄
!    !    !    !    (= High CNF 100 )◄
!    !    Testing 4◄
!    !    (= Product_B CNF 100 )◄

Insert On   Document Off                    Boldface Off Underline Off
1       2       3Srch↓  4       5Rplc↓  6       7GbRpc↓ 8       9Rept↓  10
```

Graphics Tree

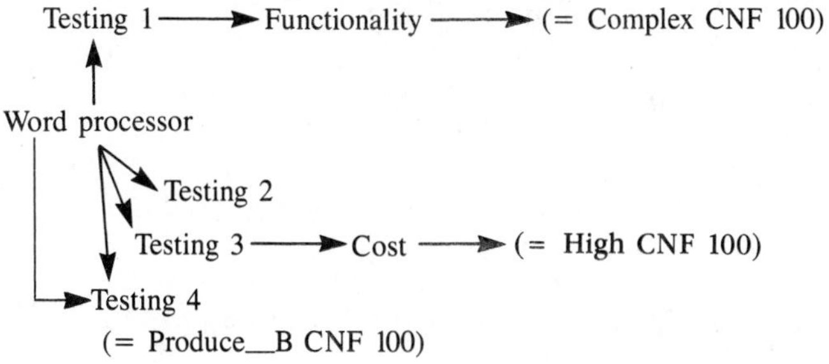

FIGURE M4.8 TEXT AND GRAPHICS TREE FOR Run 4 OF wp2.kbs.

Tracing a More Complex Example

Each of the rules in our example wp2.kbs had the goal variable Word__processor as the conclusion. What does the inference engine do if the rules are not as simple? Let's consider an example where the conclusion in some rules is the condition in other rules. We will modify our knowledge base so that complex or simple "Functionality" is somewhat more precise. Eliminating *fuzzy logic* is desirable (see Chapter 4).

We will assume that our different types of documents can be classified according to their degree of complexity. Writing a short memo is quite different than generating a two-column newsletter with graphics. If we know the kind of document, then we can classify it as one of four types, called type1, type2, type3, or type4. The higher the type number, the more complex word processor will be required. If we know the type of document, then we can classify the functionality as simple or complex. In other words, functionality is the conclusion in one rule, but the condition in other rules. Our new program, wp6.kbs, is given in Figure M4.9.

```
!The file wp6.kbs has six rules. Conclusion of some rules are conditions in other rules.
ACTIONS
          DISPLAY "This expert system WPHELP will advise you on selecting a word
          processor for your IBM compatible micro-computer in your business.
Press the spacebar to start the consultation."
          CLS
          FIND Word_processor
          DISPLAY "WPHELP advises {word_processor}."
          DISPLAY " "
          DISPLAY "     Press the SPACEBAR to exit WPHELP.~"
          CLS;
RULE 1
IF        Functionality=Simple AND Cost=Low
THEN      Word_processor=Product_A;
RULE 2
IF        Functionality=Simple AND Cost=High
THEN      Word_processor=Product_A;
RULE 3
IF        Functionality=Complex AND Cost=Low
THEN      Word_processor=None;
RULE 4
IF        Functionality=Complex AND Cost=High
THEN      Word_processor=Product_B;
RULE 5
IF        Document=type1 OR Document=type2
THEN      Functionality=Simple;
RULE 6
IF        Document=type3 OR Document=type4
THEN      Functionality=Complex;
ASK Document : "Select the column of of the most complex documents that you need to
produce in your business.
     Type1          Type2          Type3          Type4
     Letter         Report         Resume         Newsletter
     Memo           Term Paper     Form Letter    Brochure
";
CHOICES Document : Type1, Type2, Type3, Type4;
ASK Cost : "Estimate the amount of money that you can afford?";
CHOICES Cost : Low, High;
```

FIGURE M4.9 PROGRAM CODE FOR wp6.kbs

Note that Functionality is part of the conditions in Rules 1,2,3 and 4, but Functionality is a conclusion in Rules 5 and 6. Also there is a new ASK command to identify the document type for the variable Document. The ASK command for the Functionality variable has been eliminated.

We will now create a Text tree and Graphic tree trace of wp6.kbs. Assuming that we are now in the Main Menu with the B drive as the default drive, follow these abbreviated steps to run the trace:

6FileName (wp6)
4Consult
    6Set
        2Trace
        3Slow (five times)
        6Quit
    2Go (Select Type3 and High)
    8Quit
5Tree
    2Text (Get a printout)
    3Graphics (Get a printout)
    4Quit
(Back to Main Menu)

The indentation of a command in the above list indicates the menu depth of the command. All commands in a column under a heading belong to the same menu.

After you have completed the listed steps, your Text trace should be the same as shown in Figure M4.10.

```
                                              Editing: Old File b:\wp6.trc

Line
   1  Testing b:\wp6.kbs◂
   2  (= yes CNF 0 )◂
   3  !   Word_processor◂
   4  !   !   Testing 1◂
   5  !   !   !   Functionality◂
   6  !   !   !   !   Testing 5◂
   7  !   !   !   !   !   Document◂
   8  !   !   !   !   !   !   (= Type3 CNF 100 )◂
   9  !   !   !   !   Testing 6◂
  10  !   !   !   !   (= complex CNF 100 )◂
  11  !   !   Testing 2◂
  12  !   !   Testing 3◂
  13  !   !   !   Cost◂
  14  !   !   !   !   (= High CNF 100 )◂
  15  !   !   Testing 4◂
  16  !   !   (= Product_B CNF 100 )◂


      Insert On    Document Off                 Boldface Off Underline Off
      1      2      3Srch↓ 4      5Rplc↓ 6      7GbRpc↓ 8      9Rept↓ 10
```

FIGURE M4.10 TEXT TREE FOR wp6.kbs

The inference engine tests RULE 1 because it is the first rule which contains Word_processor as a conclusion. Hence, the inference engine is now trying to find Functionality (the first condition in the compound IF part). The first rule to contain Functionality as a conclusion is RULE 5. But RULE 5 will only fire if the variable Document is known. In line 8 the inference engine finds the value of Document,

Type3, from the user input. In line 10, RULE 6 is tested and fired to conclude that Functionality=Complex. The inference engine now searches for rules (after RULE 1) with Functionality=Complex as the condition; hence RULE 2 and RULE 3 are tested. On line 13, after finding Functionality=Complex as part of the compound condition, the inference engine now tries to find a value for Cost. From the user, the Cost is High. Since RULE 3 does not fire, RULE 4 is tested next. This rule fires and the conclusion is Word_processor=Product_B. Again note the sequential search by the inference engine down the list of rules which have Word_processor as the conclusion. If RULE 4 had been placed as the first rule in the list, then the search would have been shorter, but the same conclusion would have been reached. The graphics tree of wp6.kbs is given in Figure M4.11.

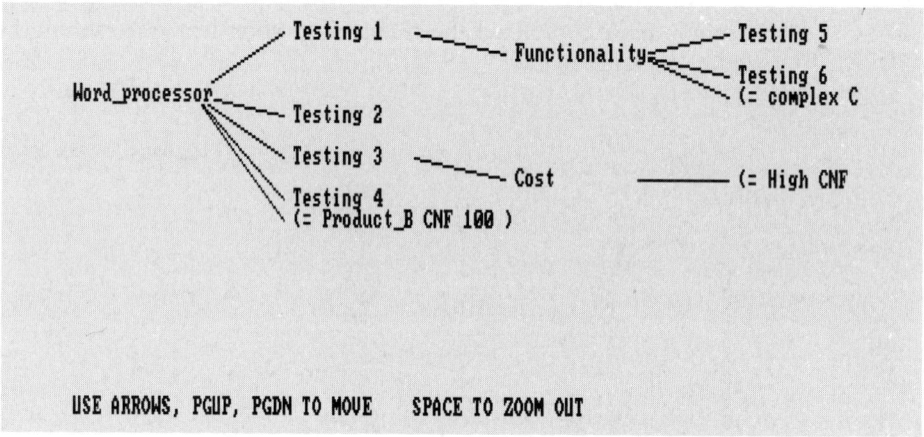

FIGURE M4.11 GRAPHICS TREE FOR wp6.kbs

In fact this figure combines two enlarged sections of the graphics tree. The same trace information is given, but in a left-to-right and down orientation. For now exit VP-Expert and return to the **A>** prompt.

All of the examples with tracing wp2.kbs and wp6.kbs show the backward chaining activity of the inference engine. The search starts from conclusions and goes back to conditions. In the next section we will discuss the opposite control strategy, forward chaining, the moving from condition to conclusion.

Use of WHENEVER: Forward Chaining

Even though backward chaining is the control strategy used by VP-Expert, **forward chaining** can be achieved. The use of the WHENEVER command (as the beginning of a rule) causes the rule to be tested whenever the value of a variable contained in the condition changes value. When a WHENEVER rule is found to have a true conclusion, the THEN part is executed. In other words, when there is a change in the variable in the condition, the rule is automatically checked for firing, regardless of the strategy of the VP-Expert inference engine.

Consider the following example:

```
WHENEVER    Cost_too_high
IF          Cost > =500
THEN        DISPLAY"Consider volume discounts.";
```

Keywords are WHENEVER, IF, THEN, and DISPLAY. The phrase Cost_too_high, serves as a Rule label and abides by Rule label restrictions. The rest of the syntax is identical to IF-THEN rules. If the value of the variable Cost changes in value, the WHENEVER clause checks the rule for firing. The WHENEVER format does not have an ELSE or BECAUSE part. If more than one WHENEVER rule names the same changed variable (Cost), then the WHENEVER rules are checked in the order that they occur in the knowledge base. The WHENEVER rule is known in AI programming as a "deamon" because it watches the variables referenced by the IF condition, and executes each time the condition is true.

FIND as the Goal Variable

It is appropriate to discuss the placement of the goal variable, the **FIND command**, in a program. Since this command turns control over to the inference engine, it is important to understand any rules regarding its placement and relation to the rest of an expert system program (kbs).

Instruction Types and Order

VP-Expert has two types of commands: statements and clauses. **Statements** may be used (almost) anywhere in the program, but **clauses** can be used only in the Actions Block and in the conclusion of rules. Of the commands that we have discussed, here are their classifications as to instruction (command type):

Statements	Clauses
ACTIONS	CLS
ASK	DISPLAY
CHOICES	FIND
PLURAL	
RULE	

As you can observe, the FIND instruction is a clause and not a statement. It may be more meaningful to say that FIND is a word that starts a clause. The VP-Expert Help Facility will always tell you the instruction type (statement or clause) in its explanation of the command.

The three parts of a VP-Expert program, Actions, Rules, and Statements, behave in different ways. The commands listed in the Actions block are executed in the order they appear. When a FIND command is encountered, the inference engine takes over. When the inference engine is finished, control passes back to the next line in the Actions block. The inference engine searches the Rules block in the order that we have discussed and uses statements (ASK, CHOICES) from the Statements block as needed. The order of the statements in the Statements block has no effect on the inference engine. (CHOICES statements should come after the appropriate ASK statements, of course.) We can summarize this information concerning instruction type, parts of a program, and effect of order in a table. This formation is summarized below:

ORDER	PART	CONTAINS
Order dependent	Actions	Statements, clauses
Partially order dependent	Rules	Statements, clauses in conclusions only
Not order dependent	Statements	Statements

The Actions block contains statements and clauses which are executed in the order they are listed. The Rules block is composed of statements and clauses in the conclusions of rules. These rules are partially "order dependent" if they contain the goal variable. The Statements block contains only statements and is not order dependent. When the inference engine needs to know the value of a variable (which it cannot find in the rules), then the appropriate ASK statement will be invoked, regardless of its order in the last part of the program. No action, however, is taken by the inference engine if a FIND variable has a known value.

Placement of the FIND Clause

Since the **FIND clause** identifies the goal variable, it is restricted to the Actions Block and the conclusion of rules. We have already seen many examples of the FIND command in this position.

The FIND clause can be part of the conclusion of a rule, but not the condition. For example, the rule below is correct in VP-Expert:

```
RULE    Networking
IF      Environment=Networked
THEN    Network=Yes
        FIND Networked_word_processor;
```

In this rule, if our environment has networked computers, then two (AND) conclusions are reached. The variable Network is assigned the value Yes and the FIND instruction turns control over to the inference engine to find a value for Networked_word_processor. If this rule fired when the inference engine was using another FIND instruction, then work would cease on that FIND until a value of Networked_word_processor was found. In this example, it would be incorrect to place a FIND command in the IF part.

Since the WHENEVER clause indicates a rule, you might conclude that the FIND command could be in the corresponding conclusion. Unfortunately, VP-Expert does not allow this. The FIND command cannot be placed in the conclusion of a WHENEVER rule. In other words, the following example is incorrect:

```
WHENEVER Networking
IF       Environment=Networked
THEN     Network=Yes
         FIND Networked_word_processor;
```

The FIND command must be left out of WHENEVER rules.

Can the FIND command occur more than one time in the Statements block or in appropriate rule conclusions? The answer is yes. If multiple FIND instructions occur, then the inference engine completes its search for the first FIND command before it starts a search for the second. Hence, it is possible to have multiple goal variables (or states) in VP-Expert applications.

Uncertainty and the Inference Engine

The inference engine not only has to search through the rules for values, but has to deal with certainty, or confidence, levels of the results. We will explore how the inference engine handles various confidence factors (CNF) for rules. We will also take a look at how the inference engine handles "I don't know" or "?" as input from the user during a consultation.

Confidence Factors

So far, the **confidence factors** or **CNF** that we have seen in the Rules window, the Facts window, or Tree traces have been CNF 100. If no confidence factors are programmed into the rules, then the value defaults to 100, complete certainty. Obviously, not all decisions are black and white, but somewhere in between. A well-developed expert system will have confidence factors that come from the *experts* in the domain field.

Confidence factors in VP-Expert are whole numbers between 0 and 100. Complete uncertainty is indicated by CNF 0 and complete confidence by CNF 100. If the CNF is 50, then we are only 50% sure of our premise, conclusion, or rule. In general, an expert system is more reliable as the CNF value assigned to the final conclusion or goal variable increases.

Even though it is possible to program CNF into the rules, there is another way to explore how CNF values are handled and calculated by the inference engine. When a user is running a consultation, he or she can enter a confidence factor before making a selection. These are the logical steps:

Step 1. When a question with various selections appears on the consultation screen, move the cursor to your selection.

Step 2. Press the HOME key and a small box will appear by your selection.

Step 3. Enter a number between 0 and 100. The number will appear by your selection. Press ENTER followed by END to make your regular selection.

As the consultation runs, the CNF numbers will appear by the appropriate rules and variables in the bottom windows. When you view a trace, either Text tree or Graphics tree, these CNF numbers will be listed. If you make a mistake trying to enter a number during a consultation, there are two ways to correct it. One way is to press HOME again and enter the correct number. If you made an incorrect selection, press the DEL key to erase the selection and the CNF number.

We will set the Trace function, run a consultation, enter CNF numbers, and then observe the results from the Rules and Facts windows and the Text tree of the trace.

We will use wp6.kbs, the knowledge base with the six rules. During the consultation we will enter 90 for the CNF for Type3 (Document) and 80 for the CNF of Cost. Return to the VP-Expert Menu with your Sample Files Disk in the B: drive, follow these abbreviated steps:

```
7Path (b:)
6FileName (wp6)
4Consult
        6Set
                2Trace
                6Quit
        2Go
        For Type, move the cursor to Type3, press the HOME key, enter
        90, make the selection with the ENTER and END keys.
        For Cost, position the cursor on High, press the HOME key,
        enter 80, make the selection with the ENTER and END keys.
        8Quit
5Tree
        2Text
        4Quit
(End at Main Menu)
```

If everything went smoothly, then your last Consultation screen with wp6.kbs should look like Figure M4.12.

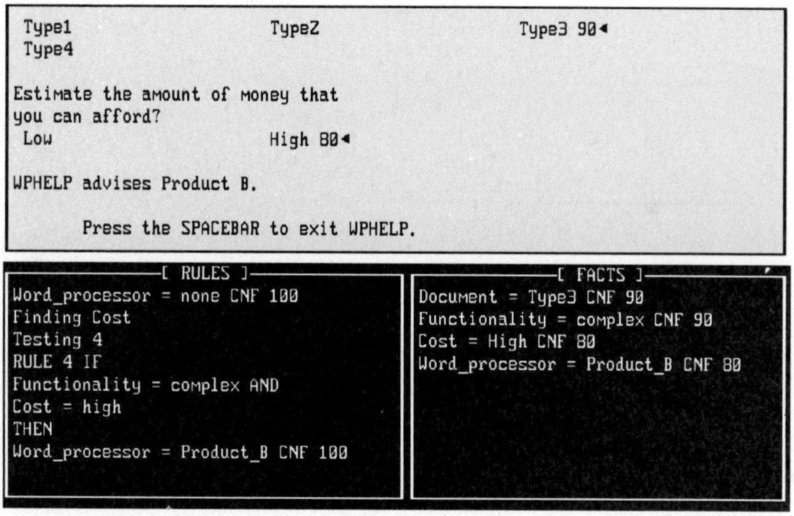

FIGURE M4.12 LAST CONSULTATION SCREEN WITH CNF NUMBERS FOR wp6.kbs

Notice that the entered CNF value of 80 shows on the Consultation window. The default values of 100 in the Rules window, and the input values (CNF 90 for Type3 and CNF 80 for Cost), appear in the Facts window. The inference engine reports that the ***intermediate variable*** Functionality has been assigned CNF 90 and that the goal state, Word_processor = Product_B, has CNF 90. These calculations are from the inference engine. The same information is given with the Text tree (trace) of wp6.kbs in Figure M4.13.

```
                                          Editing: Old File b:\wp6.trc


Testing b:\wp6.kbs◄
(= yes CNF 0 )◄
!   Word_processor◄
!   !   Testing 1◄
!   !   !   Functionality◄
!   !   !   !   Testing 5◄
!   !   !   !   !   Document◄
!   !   !   !   !   !   (= Type3 CNF 90 )◄
!   !   !   !   Testing 6◄
!   !   !   !   (= complex CNF 90 )◄
!   !   Testing 2◄
!   !   Testing 3◄
!   !   !   Cost◄
!   !   !   !   (= High CNF 80 )◄
!   !   Testing 4◄
!   !   (= Product_B CNF 80 )◄



+
Insert On    Document Off                        Boldface Off Underline Off
 1      2      3Srch↓  4      5Rplc↓  6      7GbRpc↓ 8      9Rept↓ 10
```

FIGURE M4.13 TEXT TREE WITH CNF NUMBERS FOR wp6.kbs

Let's see how VP-Expert handles CNF for compound rules. Select wp3.kbs. This is the version that helps a user decide whether to buy now or wait. The rule base of wp3.kbs is one compound AND Rule. When you run the consultation, enter the following values:

First question, (Afford), 90, Yes
Second question, (Help), 80, Yes
Third question, (Time), 70, Yes
Fourth question, (Need), 60, Yes

Use the same instructions given for running wp6.kbs, but change the file name and input during the consultation.

After running your Consultation, your last Consultation screen should resemble Figure M4.14 and your Text tree should look like Figure M4.15.

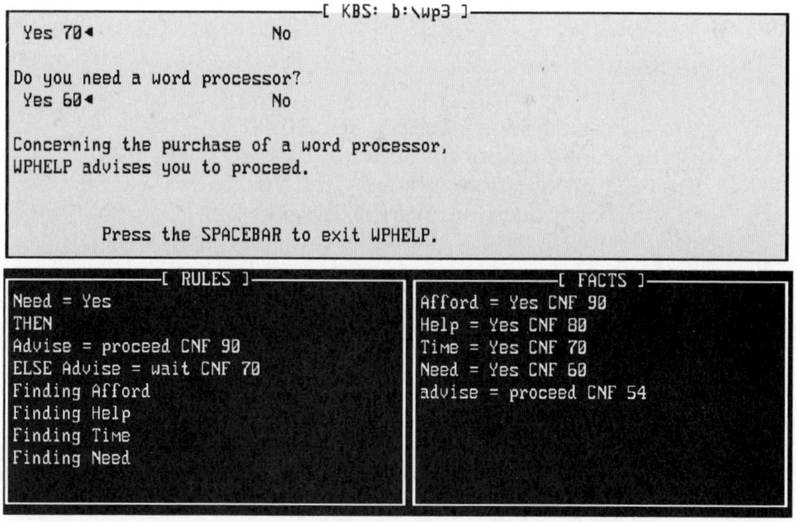

FIGURE M4.14 LAST CONSULTATION SCREEN WITH CNF NUMBERS FOR wp3.kbs

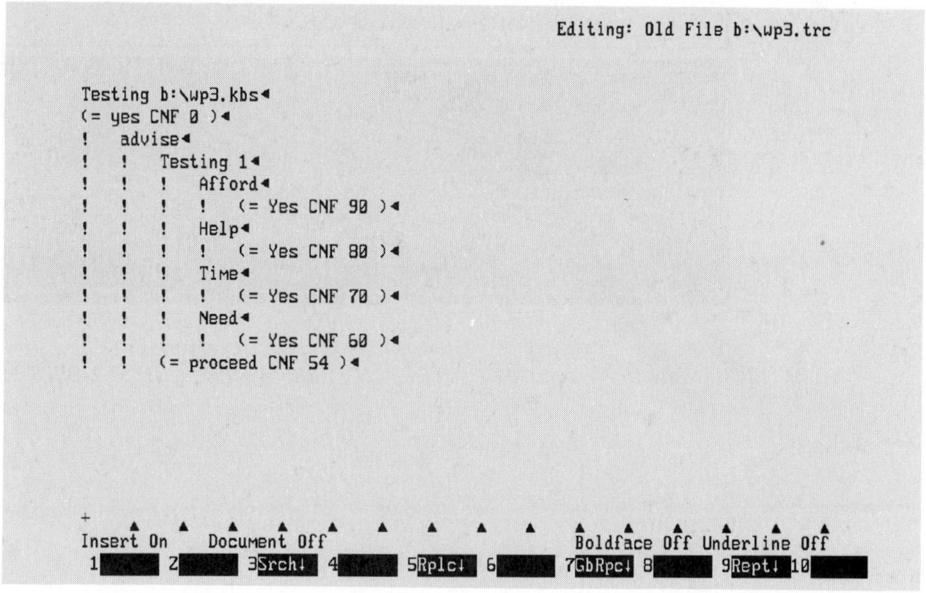

FIGURE M4.15 TEXT TREE WITH CNF NUMBERS FOR wp3.kbs

Observe that when the CNF values were 90, 80, 70, and 60 for the four AND conditions, the conclusion was given a CNF value of 54 by the inference engine.

Let's try an OR rule. Use wp4.kbs and enter the following values for the indicated selections:

> First question, (Letter), Yes, 90
> Second question, (Resume), Yes, 80
> Third question, (Notice), Yes, 70
> Fourth question, (Paper), Yes, 60

Use the same instructions for wp6.kbs but change the file name and the user inputs. Your last Consultation screen and Text tree (trace) should appear as shown in Figures M4.16 and M4.17, respectively.

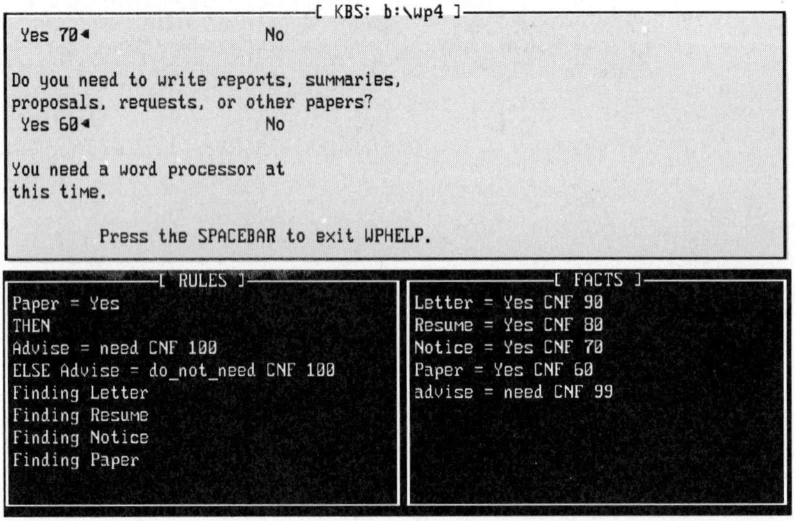

FIGURE M4.16 LAST CONSULTATION SCREEN WITH CNF NUMBERS FOR wp4.kbs

```
                                        Editing: Old File b:\wp4.trc

Testing b:\wp4.kbs◄
(= yes CNF 0 )◄
!   advise◄
!   !   Testing 1◄
!   !   !   Letter◄
!   !   !   !   (= Yes CNF 90 )◄
!   !   !   Resume◄
!   !   !   !   (= Yes CNF 80 )◄
!   !   !   Notice◄
!   !   !   !   (= Yes CNF 70 )◄
!   !   !   Paper◄
!   !   !   !   (= Yes CNF 60 )◄
!   !   (= need CNF 99 )◄

+
Insert On   Document Off                 Boldface Off Underline Off
 1      2      3Srch↓  4      5Rplc↓  6      7GbRpc↓ 8      9Rept↓ 10
```

FIGURE M4.17   TEXT TREE WITH CNF NUMBERS FOR wp4.kbs

Interestingly enough, the inference engine assigned a CNF value of 99 when the user entered 90,80,70, and 60 as the CNF values for the four OR conditions. The calculated CNF is higher than the input values.

Unknown Values

There is another aspect of uncertainty, unknown values, that the inference engine must deal with. What happens if the user does not know or understand a question during the consultation? VP-Expert allows the user to enter the question mark (?). The ? as a reply indicates ***I don't know.*** The inference engine can handle this entry if the designer or programmer included rules dealing with the appropriate variable and a key word, UNKNOWN. When the user inputs a ? at the screen, the inference engine searches for a rule with variable = UNKNOWN. Including rules to handle direct user input of ? can help to make an expert system more usable. (If the question mark (?) is given as an option to select from a list, then the inference engine does not translate to the key word UNKNOWN.)

Let's consider an example using UNKNOWN as part of the condition in rules. We have added two rules to wp6.kbs and changed the user input to direct screen entry. Our new file is wp7.kbs. The two new rules are:

RULE 7	
IF	Document = UNKNOWN
THEN	Word_processor = wait_for_now
	DISPLAY"Examine your business functions for word processing before buying.";
RULE 8	
IF	Cost = UNKNOWN
THEN	Word_processor = none_for_now
	DISPLAY " Consult your manager or boss to determine your budget.";

Each Consultation has two parts, an assignment statement and a message to the user. If the user enters a ? for type of document, we will advise him or her to review the business functions before buying. If a ? is entered for Cost, then your manager or boss should be consulted to determine your budget.

From the Main Menu select wp7 as your file. Then set the Trace option. When running the consultation, enter ? as your reply to type of document. The last Consultation screen for this run with wp7.kbs is shown in Figure M4.18 and the Text tree in Figure M4.19.

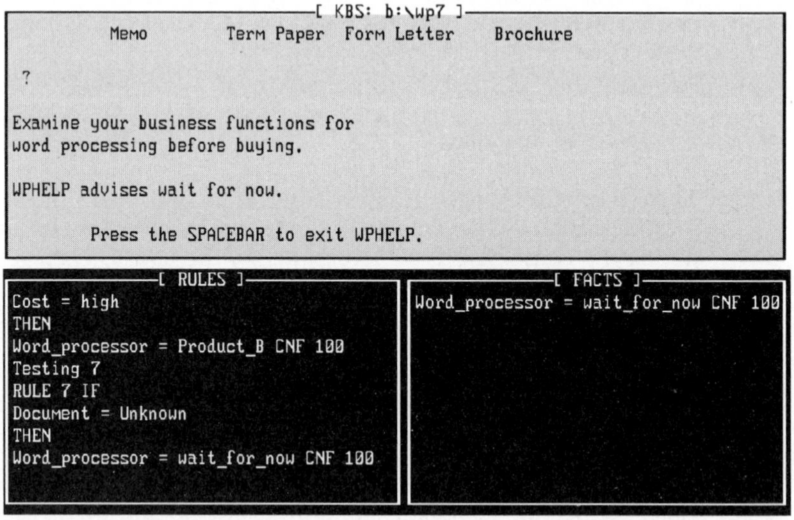

FIGURE M4.18 LAST CONSULTATION SCREEN WITH DOCUMENT UNKNOWN FOR wp7.kbs

```
                                        Editing: Old File b:\wp7.trc

Testing b:\wp7.kbs◄
(= yes CNF 0 )◄
!   Word_processor◄
!   !   Testing 1◄
!   !   !   Functionality◄
!   !   !   !   Testing 5◄
!   !   !   !   !   Document◄
!   !   !   !   Testing 6◄
!   !   Testing 2◄
!   !   Testing 3◄
!   !   Testing 4◄
!   !   Testing 7◄
!   !   (= wait_for_now CNF 100 )◄

Insert On    Document Off                       Boldface Off Underline Off
 1       2       3Srch↓   4       5Rplc↓   6       7GbRpc↓  8       9Rept↓  10
```

FIGURE M4.19 TEXT TREE WITH DOCUMENT UNKNOWN FOR wp7.kbs

In both figures note that Rule 7 was tested for Document=UNKNOWN.

After completing this Consultation, rerun wp7.kbs, but this time type in Type3 as the answer to the documents question, and a ? for Cost. The last Consultation screen and Text tree for this run appear in Figures M4.20 and M4.21, respectively.

```
Estimate the amount of money that
you can afford?  Enter low, high, or ?.
 ?

Consult your manager or boss to
determine your budget.

WPHELP advises None for now.

        Press the SPACEBAR to exit WPHELP.

[ RULES ]
Document = Unknown
THEN
Word_processor = wait_for_now CNF 100
Testing 8
RULE 8 IF
Cost = Unknown
THEN
Word_processor = None_for_now CNF 100

[ FACTS ]
Document = Type3 CNF 100
Functionality = complex CNF 100
Word_processor = None_for_now CNF 100

1Help 2How? 3Why? 4Slow 5Fast 6Quit
```

FIGURE M4.20 LAST CONSULTATION SCREEN WITH COST UNKNOWN FOR wp7.kbs

```
                                   Editing: Old File b:\wp7.trc

Testing b:\wp7.kbs◄
(= yes CNF 0 )◄
!   Word_processor◄
!   !   Testing 1◄
!   !   !   Functionality◄
!   !   !   !   Testing 5◄
!   !   !   !   !   Document◄
!   !   !   !   !   !   (= Type3 CNF 100)◄
!   !   !   !   Testing 6◄
!   !   !   !   (= complex CNF 100 )◄
!   !   Testing 2◄
!   !   Testing 3◄
!   !   !   Cost◄
!   !   Testing 4◄
!   !   Testing 7◄
!   !   Testing 8◄
!   !   (= None_for_now CNF 100 )◄

Insert On   Document Off                Boldface Off Underline Off
1      2      3Srch↓  4      5Rplc↓  6      7GbRpc↓ 8      9Rept↓ 10
```

FIGURE M4.21 TEXT TREE WITH COST UNKNOWN FOR wp7.kbs

In both figures you can see that Rule 8 was fired for the condition Cost = UNKNOWN. Remember that the question mark (?) is used only for typing replies, not for selecting from lists. In our examples, the CNF numbers defaulted to 100 because we did not program them into our knowledge base (rules).

After you have finished your consultations with wp7.kbs, exit VP-Expert and return to the `A>` prompt to end your session with VP-Expert for Module 4.

In this section we have explored how the inference engine searches through a rule base (backward chaining), how to create a Text or Graphics tree of a Consultation, how to identify the different instruction types, how to place the FIND command, how to enter CNF or confidence factors, and how to use the ? as input. In the next module we will continue with more information about developing the knowledge base.

Key Points

- The inference engine is the reasoning mechanism of an expert system.
- VP-Expert uses deductive logic, not induction, or abduction.
- The two types of control strategies for inference engines are backward chaining and forward chaining. Backward chaining moves from the conclusion to condition, while forward chaining moves from condition to conclusion.
- VP-Expert uses backward chaining. Forward chaining can be implemented with WHENEVER rules.
- The goal state is the value of the variable named by the FIND command.
- The behavior of the inference engine can be traced with a Text tree or a Graphics tree. The Trace option must be selected before the consultation is run. The steps are as follows:

```
7Path (b:)
6FileName
4Consult
        6Set
                2Trace
                6Quit
        2Go
        8Quit
5Tree
        2Text
        3Graphics
        4Quit
```

- The text tree is displayed as text from the editor using a .trc file. Use F10 and END to get a printout. Exit with ALT and F8.
- The Graphics tree appears as a sideways tree. Individual sections can be enlarged with the zoom feature. To obtain a partial printout, use the Shift and PRTSC and draw the arrows (lines). To exit, get out of Zoom (SPACEBAR) and then ESC.

- There are two types of commands or instruction types for VP-Expert programs. They are statements and clauses. Statements can occur almost anywhere, but clauses are restricted to the Actions block and the conclusions of rules.
- FIND is a clause. There can be multiple FIND in the Actions block or in conclusions. The FIND command, however, cannot appear in WHENEVER rules.
- CNF numbers are whole numbers between 0 and 100 and represent the degree of certainty or confidence in a condition, conclusion, or rule. Zero is complete uncertainty, and 100 is complete confidence.
- Users can input CNF values during a consultation with direct data entry. When the cursor is on the appropriate key, press the HOME key and enter the number. Then make the selection.
- The question mark (?) can be allowed as user input during direct entry in a consultation if there are rules containing the appropriate variable and the key word UNKNOWN.

Exercises

1. Which of the following options belong to the Set Menu?
   a. Trace
   b. Track
   c. View
   d. Fast
   e. Go
2. Which of the following options belong to the Tree Menu?
   a. View
   b. Trace
   c. Text
   d. Graphics
   e. Go
3. Order the following options into a logical sequence to produce a Text tree of a consultation.
   a. Go
   b. Consult
   c. Trace
   d. Path
   e. FileName
   f. Set
   g. Text
   h. Tree

4. Assume that theses rules are in order from 1 to 6 and backward chaining is used:
   a. RULE 1
      IF A
      THEN F
   b. RULE 2
      IF B
      THEN G
   c. RULE 3
      IF F
      THEN G
   d. RULE 4
      IF D
      THEN G
   e. RULE 5
      IF E
      THEN F
   f. RULE 6
      IF F AND G
      THEN H

   a. Which rule will the inference engine test first for FIND F?
   b. Which rule will the inference engine test first for FIND G?
   c. Which rule will the inference engine test first for FIND H when H has a known value?

5. Given the trace in Figure M4.22, match the variables to the values.

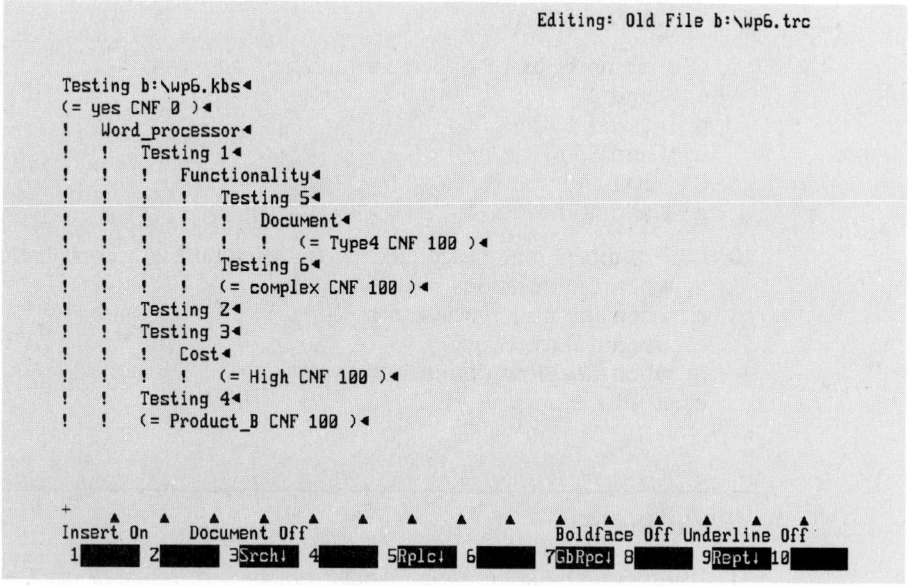

```
                                        Editing: Old File b:\wp6.trc

Testing b:\wp6.kbs◄
(= yes CNF 0 )◄
!   Word_processor◄
!   !   Testing 1◄
!   !   !   Functionality◄
!   !   !   !   Testing 5◄
!   !   !   !   !   Document◄
!   !   !   !   !   !   (= Type4 CNF 100 )◄
!   !   !   !   Testing 6◄
!   !   !   !   (= complex CNF 100 )◄
!   !   Testing 2◄
!   !   Testing 3◄
!   !   !   Cost◄
!   !   !   !   (= High CNF 100 )◄
!   !   Testing 4◄
!   !   (= Product_B CNF 100 )◄

Insert On    Document Off                      Boldface Off Underline Off
1       2       3Srch↓  4       5Rplc↓  6       7GbRpc↓ 8       9Rept↓  10
```

FIGURE M4.22 TEXT TREE

6. Tell whether order is important or not important for each of the following:
   a. Two ASK instructions
   b. Two FIND instructions
   c. Two DISPLAY instructions
   d. Two RULES

7. Circle the following instructions with C for clause or S for statement:

a. RUNTIME	C	S
b. ASK	C	S
c. CHOICES	C	S
d. FIND	C	S
e. DISPLAY	C	S

8. Mark each of the following instructions as valid (V) or invalid (I).
   a. FIND X
      FIND Y
   b. IF FIND X = FIND Y
      THEN Z=M;
   c. IF X=Y
      THEN FIND Z;
   d. WHENEVER Low
      IF X=Y
      THEN FIND Z;
   e. IF X=Unknown
      THEN FIND Y;

9. CNF numbers in VP-Expert are numbers between
   a. 0 and 1
   b. −1 and 1
   c. 0 and 100
   d. −100 and 100
   e. 1 and 100

10. CNF numbers may be entered by the user during a consultation
    a. when the questions have selections.
    b. when the user types in a reply.
    c. when a trace is on.
    d. when the Slow option is active.
    e. all of the above.

Assignments

1. Using the VP-Expert Help Facility, obtain a printout of each of the following topics:
   SET MENU
   TREE MENU
   CLAUSE
   STATEMENT
   CNF
   WHENEVER
   FIND
   BACKWARD CHAINING
   FORWARD CHAINING

2. With the trace on, rerun file wp3.kbs from your Sample Files Disk. During the consultation enter No to the first question and Yes to the rest. Obtain both a Text tree and a Graphics tree of the resulting consultation.

3. With the Trace option on, run program wp4.kbs from your Sample Files Disk. Answer No to the first question. Obtain both a Text tree and a Graphics tree of the resulting consultation.

4. With the Trace on, run the file Taxguide.kbs from the Sample Files Disk. During the consultation, enter confidence factors (CNF) above 50 and make any selections you like. Obtain both a Text tree and Graphics tree of the resulting consultation.

5. Let's change the order in which rules are listed and compare the path of the inference engine. Do the following:
   a. Copy wp6.kbs from your Sample Files Disk to your Data Disk.
   b. Get into VP-Expert and use the editor to change the knowledge base so that the rules appear as:
      RULE 4
      RULE 5
      RULE 1
      RULE 2
      RULE 3
      Be sure to save these changes.
   c. Obtain a Text tree trace of a consultation with the changed wp6.kbs.
   d. Compare your Text tree to Figure M4.22.
   e. Can the order of rules affect the work of the inference engine?

6. Let's trace the activity of the inference engine when the FIND variable has a value.
   a. Copy wp2.kbs from the Sample Files Disk to your Data Disk.
   b. Using the VP-Expert editor insert the statement
      Word_processor = Product_X
      above the FIND instruction. Be sure to save this change.
   c. Obtain a Text tree trace of a consultation with the changed wp2.kbs.
   d. Explain the results of the consultation and Text tree trace of the changed version of wp2.kbs.

7. For a challenge, take the knowledge base (rules) on investing from Assignment 2 in Chapter 2 and do the following:
   a. Write out the necessary commands and rules to create a .kbs file.
   b. Using the editor from the Main Menu enter your code.
   c. Save the file INVEST and store it on your Data Disk.
   d. Run the expert system entering different CNF numbers.
   e. Obtain a Text tree and a Graphics tree of one consultation.

8. When you run a consultation with the 2Trace option active, VP-Expert creates a file with a .trc extension. With your Sample Files Disk in the A drive and at the A> prompt:
   a. Type DIR *.trc
      How many trace files were created when you used Module 4? __________
   b. Delete the trace files with A>ERASE *.trc
   c. How many free bytes are left on the Sample Files Disk? __________

Module 5

USING DATABASES AND SPREADSHEETS WITH THE KNOWLEDGE BASE

The business world over the past decade has stored tremendous amounts of information in computer-based database files and worksheet files. These files may be on mainframes or microcomputers. Acquiring the knowledge and expertise for an expert system, however, is a difficult process. Specialists, called knowledge engineers, are responsible for extracting such information from experts and then translating the information into usable expert systems. One of the exclusive features of VP-Expert is its interface to selected database and spreadsheet (or worksheet) files. This information is the backbone of most businesses, and its incorporation into expert systems could save both the knowledge engineer and the company time and money.

VP-Expert lets you interface to data in existing database files that were created with dBASE II, dBASE III PLUS or VP-Info. Worksheet linkage is to spreadsheets created with Lotus 1-2-3 (Versions 1A, 2.0, and 2.01) or VP-Planner. Hence, if your business has any applications using these tools, then the existing files can be the front end for an expert systems application. This is a tremendous time saver for the knowledge engineer. Another advantage is that the data has been around and has used repeatedly; hence, the data is (probably) valid and the procedures have been verified.

We start in this module dealing with database access and finish with worksheet access.

Using a Database

We are now looking at how to retrieve records from a database file by using a **loop structure** called WHILEKNOWN-END. We will use the MENU command to help us generate a list of choices for a user to select. We will explore ways to search for specific records and a method to restrict our records before searching. A procedure for letting the user repeat the searching process will also be explained.

Displaying a Record

Let's tackle the problem of **displaying** a database record through VP-Expert. A dBASE III PLUS file of five records is shown in Figure M5.1.

```
Set Up  Create  Update  Position  Retrieve  Organize Modify Tools  03:49:38 pm

Record#  WORD_PROCE        NETWORKED SUPPORT  COST
      1  A                 no        fair      200
      2  B                 no        good      200
      3  C                 no        good      200
      4  D                 yes       fair      200
      5  E                 yes       good      500
      6
ASSIST              |<B:>|WPDB                  |Rec: 1/6     |    |
                  Press any key to continue work in ASSIST.

                       BF Module 5 Figure M5.01
```

FIGURE M5.1 DATABASE FILE (wpdb.dbt) CREATED WITH dBASE III PLUS

The database file or table has four columns that are entitled Word_proce, Networked, Support, and Cost. (Record number is not a column in the database, but is generated by the dBASE print facility.) These column headings are called field names or attributes. The field name of Word_proce uniquely identifies each record or row in the database. Each row or record is information about a word processor. For example, record 4 tells us that word processor D has a network version, support is rated as fair, and the price for one licensed copy is $200. From the nature of the data, you would conclude that all columns are character data except the Cost column. This column would be numeric.

In order to read or access this information, you must know the name of the database file, the exact name of the database fields, and the meaning of the information in the table. Our table is called wpdb.dbf. All accessible database files must have an extension of .dbf. The field names as shown in Figure M5.1 are not case sensitive; they may be uppercase or lowercase.

We will now run a consultation that will use this database file with VP-Expert. Our example will ask us what kind of support is required for our word processing. From the database file in Figure M5.1, there are two values for Support, Good or Fair. If the user needs fair (or modest) support, then word processor A or D could be used.

If good support is required, then word processors B, C, or E are possibilities. We will now use the database file and search for the needed information.

The database file from Figure M5.1 is wpdb.dbf and is also on your Sample Files Disk. The example expert system that reads this file is wp8.kbs and is on the Sample Files Disk. The database file and the expert system file must be on the same disk (or in the same directory) when you are running a consultation. Turn on your system and get to the A> prompt. Place VP-Expert in the A drive and the Sample Files Disk in the B drive. Follow these abbreviated steps to search the database file for word processors with ***good*** support:

Type vpx
7Path b:
6FileName (wp8)
4Consult
    2Go (select Good)

The first question from the consultation asks you to select your level of required support. This screen should look like Figure M5.2.

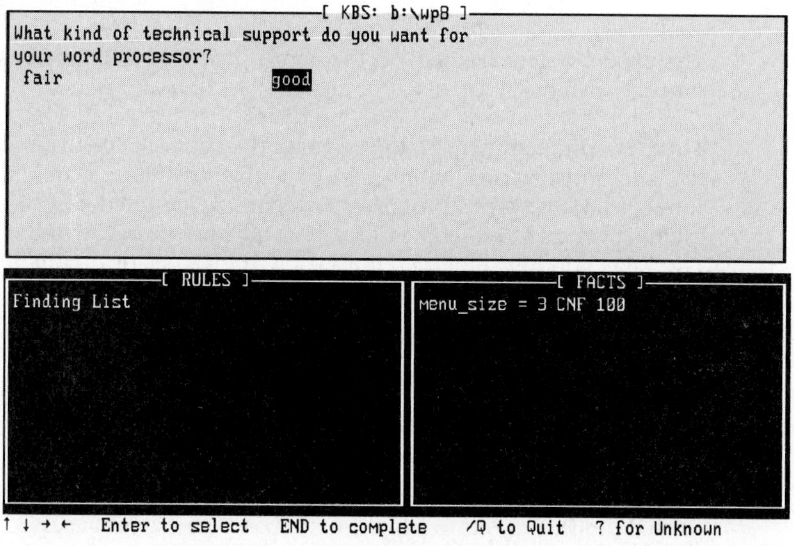

FIGURE M5.2 FIRST QUESTION FROM wp8.kbs

Somehow the expert system knows the possible values of Support (Good, Fair) that were listed in the database file. At the end of the consultation, your screen should be like Figure M5.3.

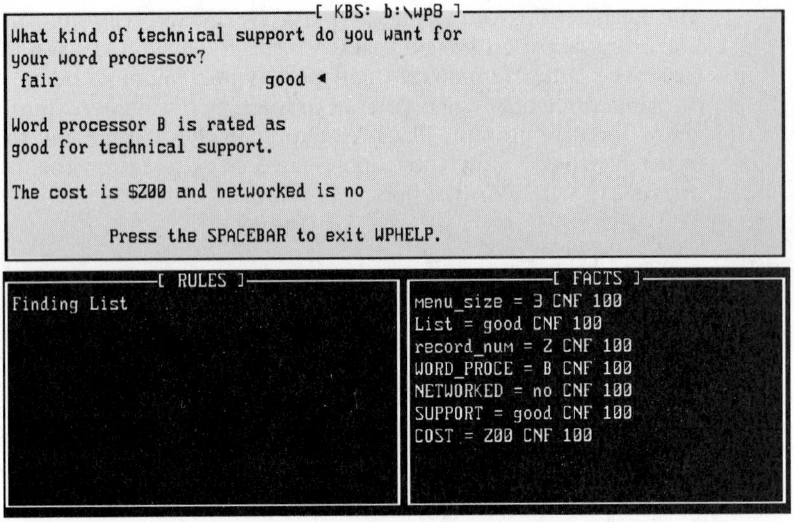

FIGURE M5.3 LAST CONSULTATION SCREEN FOR wp8.kbs

The expert system has replied that word processor B is rated as good for technical support, that the cost is $200, and that Networked is no.

There is a problem here. If you examine the database file from Figure M5.1, there are two additional records, number 3 and 5, that satisfy the search. Both word processor C (record 3) and word processor E (record 5) are rated as good for support. If you examine Figure M5.3, you will see that the Rules window did not display any rules. The Facts window, however, does show the values of the field names for record 2:

record_num = 2
WORD_PROCE = B
NETWORKED = No
SUPPORT= Good
COST= 200

We will now examine the program file, wp8.kbs, to determine how the expert system created the first question from the database values and accessed one correct record. We will then have to correct that program to make it give all the answers available from the database file.

The immediate task is to obtain a printout of the program code. Make sure the printer is on and follow these steps for printing:

```
7Edit
        ALT-F10, END (To obtain a printout)
        ALT-F8, (To exit without saving)
8Quit (Return to the Main Menu)
```

Your printout should be the same as Figure M5.4.

```
!The file wp8.kbs will access a record
!                    from a database file called wpdb.dbf.
!                    The field names in the database file are:
!                    Word_proce, Networked, Support, Cost

ACTIONS
                    DISPLAY "This expert system WPHELP will display information from a
database file.

Press the SPACEBAR to start the consultation.~"
                    CLS
(C1) ------------>  MENU List, ALL, wpdb, Support
                    FIND List
(C2) ------------>  GET List=Support,wpdb,ALL
                    DISPLAY"Word processor {Word_proce} is rated as"
                    DISPLAY"{Support} for technical support."
                    DISPLAY ""
                    DISPLAY"The cost is ${Cost} and networked is {Networked}

                    Press the SPACEBAR to exit WPHELP.~"
                    CLS;

RULE 1
                    IF Support <> UNKNOWN
                    THEN DISPLAY"The technical support for word processor"
                         DISPLAY"{Word_processor} is rated as {Support}."
                    ELSE DISPLAY"We cannot find the information in the"
                         DISPLAY" datbase file.";

ASK List : "What kind of technical support do you want for your word processor?";
```

FIGURE M5.4   PROGRAM CODE FOR wp8.kbs

There are two new clauses, Menu (Comment 1) and Get (Comment 2), that allow us to get to the database records. We will need to understand these in detail. The MENU instruction (along with an ASK) generates the results shown in Figure M5.2. The MENU instruction is a clause that has four distinct parts (parameters) after the keyword MENU. The first parameter identifies a VP-Expert variable, the second parameter tells us that we want to search all the records from the database file (the third parameter without its extension). The fourth or last parameter tells us what database column the menu choices will come from. We can think of Menu in this format:

MENU
VP-Expert variable,
what part of the database is to be searched,
name of the database file,
what database column do we search and place as choices on a menu

In our example, List is the VP-Expert variable, ALL of the database records are to be searched, the name of the database file is wpdb, and the column values under the database field Support are to be made available to a VP-Expert generated ASK question via the variable List. The MENU clause generates the *choices* from the database column. A FIND clause naming the same VP-Expert variable LIST activates a search by the inference engine for a value of the variable. If there are no rules that apply, the inference engine will search for an ASK statement for that variable. In other words, MENU is like *choices* with an ASK statement. The user's choice from the menu is stored by VP-Expert in the variable List.

Let's look at more examples of the MENU clause.

Example 1

The clause MENU Price, ALL, dwpdb, Cost with an ASK statement, would generate a list of two choices, 200 and 500. When the user selects one, its value is stored in the variable called Price. Price is a VP-Expert variable and Cost is a database variable. Don't use the same name for a VP-Expert variable and a database field name (variable). The clause MENU,

MENU Cost, ALL, wpdb, Cost

would cause unpredictable results because the VP-Expert variable and the database variable are the same name. Moreover, the physical name of the database file must be wpdb.dbf, but only the first part, wpdb, is used. The extension must exist, but it is excluded from the clause.

Example 2

The clause, MENU Package, ALL, wpdb, Word_proce, would generate the following choices for the user:

A	B	C
D	E	

When the user makes his selection for a word processor, its value will be stored in the VP-Expert variable Package. Note that the proper spelling of that field name is Word_proce because that is how it is known to the database. Of course, the proper question must be identified with the variable Package in an ASK statement.

Now let's take a look at another new clause, the GET instruction in Figure M5.4. The GET clause searches the database to retrieve the designated records. The clause in wp8.kbs, GET List = Support, wpdb,ALL, tells VP-Expert to find a database record in wpdb.dbf where List = Support and to make all the fields of that record available to VP-Expert. In Figure M5.4 notice that the DISPLAY commands display both VP-Expert values and database values. From the Facts window of Figure M5.3 we know that the search found all values of fields for record 2, but that VP-Expert did not locate all of the proper records.

The reason for this is that the GET clause finds the first record that meets the condition List = Support. We have to force VP-Expert to continue or repeat its search through the database. This is why we will examine a WHILEKNOWN instruction in the next section. This will correct the problem.

Using Loops to Display Records

A repetitive or **loop structure** will solve the problem of retrieving all records *with Support = good* from the database. The GET clause only retrieves the next record in the database that meets the condition. The List = Support parameter does not force it to repeat the search after it has found a record. You can envision a pointer or marker to the top of the database file. When a GET clause is executed the imaginary marker or pointer moves to the next record in the database that meets the condition. The pointer sets at this record until another GET clause is encountered or until the pointer is pointing to the *end of file* or bottom of the file. We need a mechanism to force repetitive use of the GET clause. One answer is the WHILEKNOWN-END structure. Let's run an example that will display all the correct records from the database. Since the Consultation window is small, we have inserted commands in our new example to send DISPLAY statements to the printer as well as the screen. Make sure the printer is on and use wp9.kbs to retrieve and display all the records. Both wp9.kbs and wpdb.dbf are on the Sample Files Disk. At the Main Menu, follow these steps to run our example with printer output (and with the Trace option in effect):

```
6FileName (wp9)
4Consult
        6Set
                2Trace
                6Quit
        2Go (Select good)
(Remain at the Consult Menu)
```

After pressing the SPACEBAR to start the consultation, select Good as the level of needed support. Your final Consultation screen is shown in Figure M5.5. The Consultation window scrolled through these responses even though now only two show on the screen.

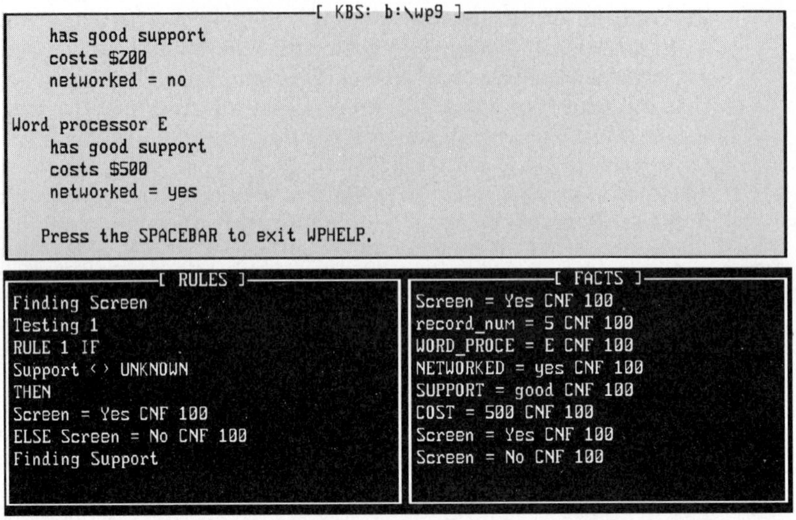

FIGURE M5.5 LAST CONSULTATION SCREEN FOR wp9.kbs (with Support=Good)

The Rules window reveals that it was searching for Screen and testing Rule 1. The Facts window scrolled through many messages. The ending messages reveal that record_num = 5 and the values of the fields for record 5. The last message reveals that Screen = No.

The results of the consultation are better surveyed from the printout than from the consultation itself, as shown in Figure M5.6.

```
Word processor B
    has good support
    costs $200
    networked = no

Word processor C
    has good support
    costs $200
    networked = no

Word processor E
    has good support
    costs $500
    networked = yes
```

FIGURE M5.6 PRINTER OUTPUT FROM wp9.kbs (with Support=Good)

Three word processors, B, C, and E, have good support ratings. If you scan the database file in Figure M5.1, you will conclude that the output is correct. Record numbers 2, 3, and 5 represent the correct search. Before we examine the Text tree, let's check the value of the variables after the consultation with wp9.kbs. At the 2Go of the Consult Menu, select 4Variable. Your screen should now resemble Figure M5.7.

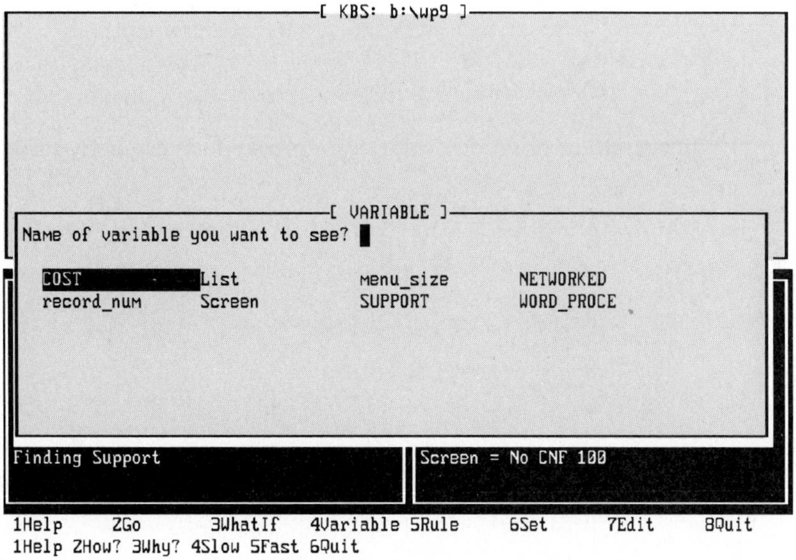

FIGURE M5.7 VARIABLE OPTION AFTER CONSULTATION WITH wp9.kbs (with Support = Good)

Notice that the database variables (field names) are in capital letters and the VP-Expert variables are in lowercase. Check the value of each variable by moving the cursor to the desired variable and pressing ENTER. The value of the selected variable will appear on the screen. To see another variable, you have to select the 4Variable option again.

Your efforts should reveal some interesting characteristics of the values of the variables. You should have found the following:

List = Good	COST = undefined
menu_size = 3	record_num = 5
NETWORKED = undefined	WORD_PROCE = undefined
SUPPORT = undefined	Screen = no

Another word for undefined is UNKNOWN. In other words, there is no known value assigned to this variable at the end of the consultation. List has the value good because we selected that value. Obviously, VP-Expert has an error because the number of menu options (Good, Fair) is 2, not 3. Record num = 5 means that the last record found by the search was number 5. (These values will help us to explain how the

WHILEKNOWN-END loop structure works when we analyze the program code.) Let's examine the Text tree (trace) of the wp9.kbs consultation run with Support=good. Follow these steps to obtain a printout of the associated Text tree file:

8Quit
5Tree
2Text
F10, END (For a printout)
ALT, F6, y (To save and exit)
4Quit
(END at the Main Menu)

The resulting printout of the Text tree should match Figure M5.8.

```
                                                Editing: Old File b:\wp9.trc
Lines
  1      Testing b:\wp9.kbs◂
  2      (= yes CNF 0 )◂
  3      !  List◂
  4      !  !  (= good CNF 100 )◂
  5      !  Screen◂
  6      !  !  Testing 1◂
  7      !  !  (= Yes CNF 100 )◂
  8      !  Screen◂
  9      !  !  Testing 1◂
 10      !  !  (= Yes CNF 100 )◂
 11      !  Screen◂
 12      !  !  Testing 1◂
 13      !  !  (= Yes CNF 100 )◂
 14      !  Screen◂
 15      !  !  Testing 1◂
 16      !  !  !  Support◂
 17      !  !  (= No CNF 100 )◂

         Insert On   Document Off                Boldface Off Underline Off
         1     2     3Srch↓  4     5Rplc↓  6     7GbRpc↓ 8     9Rept↓ 10
```

FIGURE M5.8 TEXT TREE FOR wp9.kbs (with Support=Good)

Note on line 4 of the Text tree that a variable List has value good. Lines 6 to 15 indicate that Rule 1 is being repeatedly tested for a value for Screen. In three tests the value for Screen is found to be Yes. In the last test of RULE 1, Screen has the value no (Line 17). Line 16 reports a variable Support (database field name) and indicates no value (undefined or UNKNOWN).

Let's repeat this exercise but select fair as our level of support. Repeat the abbreviated steps we outlined earlier. If you examine Figure M5.1, you can conclude that the results should be word processors A and D because they are the only records with Support=fair. The last Consultation screen for Support=fair is shown as Figure M5.9. The printer output is the same as the Consultation screen.

```
                        [ KBS: b:\wp9 ]
    has fair support
    costs $200
    networked = no

Word processor D
    has fair support
    costs $200
    networked = yes

   Press the SPACEBAR to exit WPHELP.
```

```
[ RULES ]                          [ FACTS ]
Finding Screen                     Screen = Yes CNF 100
Testing 1                          record_num = 4 CNF 100
RULE 1 IF                          WORD_PROCE = D CNF 100
Support <> UNKNOWN                 NETWORKED = yes CNF 100
THEN                               SUPPORT = fair CNF 100
Screen = Yes CNF 100               COST = 200 CNF 100
ELSE Screen = No CNF 100           Screen = Yes CNF 100
Finding Support                    Screen = No CNF 100
```

FIGURE M5.9 LAST CONSULTATION SCREEN FOR wp9.kbs (with Support=Fair)

When you obtain your printout of the Text tree (trace), it should look like Figure M5.10.

```
                                          Editing: Old File b:\wp9.trc
Lines
  1      Testing b:\wp9.kbs◄
  2      (= yes CNF 0 )◄
  3      !   List◄
  4      !   !   (= fair CNF 100 )◄
  5      !   Screen◄
  6      !   !   Testing 1◄
  7      !   !   (= Yes CNF 100 )◄
  8      !   Screen◄
  9      !   !   Testing 1◄
 10      !   !   (= Yes CNF 100 )◄
 11      !   Screen◄
 12      !   !   Testing 1◄
 13      !   !   !   Support◄
 14      !   !   (= No CNF 100 )◄

         Insert On   Document Off                Boldface Off Underline Off
         1     2     3Srch↓  4     5Rplc↓  6     7GbRpc↓  8     9Rept↓  10
```

FIGURE M5.10 TEXT TREE FOR wp9.kbs (with Support=Fair)

Lines 3 and 4 indicate that the VP-Expert variable List has the value fair. The next lines indicate a search for the variable Screen and subsequent testing of Rule 1. Rule 1 is tested twice concluding that Screen=Yes. The last time the same rule is tested, the result is Screen=No, but the consultation ends. Line 13 lists Support but with no value (undefined or UNKNOWN). We have somehow corrected our problem. The program is reading the database file, and some repetitive process is displaying the correct answers (Product A and D) to condition, Support=fair. Let's examine the program code to find out how this repetitive structure works.

Obtain a printout of the program code for wp9.kbs by following these abbreviated steps starting from the Main Menu with the printer on:

3Edit
F10, END (For a printout)
ALT F8, y (To exit without saving)

Your printout of wp9.kbs is shown in Figure M5.11. Let's take a detailed look at this program.

The printout during the consultation was caused by two commands, PRINTON and PRINTOFF (Comment1 or C1). After the PRINTON command is executed, every DISPLAY statement will be sent to both the screen and the printer. Since the ASK statement is not a DISPLAY statement, the question: "What kind of technical support do you want for your word processor?" was not sent to the printer. Every PRINTON command should be followed (somewhere) by a PRINTOFF.

After you pressed the SPACEBAR to start the consultation, the MENU clause with the ASK statement (Comment2) generated the question with the two choices for Support: fair and good. In other words, the size of the menu is 2. These values came from the database column of Support values. When the user selected a value, VP-Expert stored the value (fair or good) in the variable called List. The GET command then initiated a search by the inference engine to find a database record whose support value is the same as the user's selection.

The looping for the correct records is performed with the WHILEKNOWN-END structure. (Comment 3 on Figure M5.11). Whenever VP-Expert encounters a variable, it is either known or UNKNOWN (undefined). If the variable is known, then it has a value and there is no reason to start a search (FIND) for that variable. If the variable has no value assigned to it, VP-Expert gives it the value UNKNOWN. When you tell the system to FIND a variable with value UNKNOWN, the inference engine takes over to conduct the search. The goal is to change the value of the variable from UNKNOWN to a known value. This concept of *known or unknown* in a WHILEKNOWN-END structure is used to cause a set of instructions to repeat itself. The start of our loop is marked with the key word WHILEKNOWN followed by a variable. In our case WHILEKNOWN is followed by Support, a database field name. The end of the WHILEKNOWN loop is designated by END. All the instructions between the top and bottom may or may not be repeated again. The decision depends on the value of the variable (Support) named after WHILEKNOWN. When the system

```
!The file wp9.kbs will access information
!                from a database file called wpdb.dbf.
!                The field names in the database file are:
!                Word_proce, Networked, Support, Cost
!                A WHILEKNOWN-END loop will be used
!                Print classes will be used.

ACTIONS
                DISPLAY "WPHELP will send information from a database file to the
screen and printer.
Make sure that your printer is on.

Press the SPACEBAR to start the consultation. ~"
         CLS
         PRINTON <--(C1)
(C2)-->  MENU List, ALL, wpdb, Support
         FIND List
       { WHILEKNOWN Support
       {         GET List=Support,wpdb,ALL
 (C3)  {         RESET Screen
       {         FIND Screen
       { END
         PRINTOFF <--(C1)
         DISPLAY " "
         DISPLAY " Press the SPACEBAR to exit WPHELP. ~"
         CLS;

RULE 1
         IF Support <> UNKNOWN
         THEN Screen = Yes
                 DISPLAY " "
                 DISPLAY"Word processor {Word_proce}"
                 DISPLAY"          has {support} support"
                 DISPLAY"          costs ${Cost}"
                 DISPLAY "          networked = {Networked}"
         ELSE Screen = No;

(C2) ASK List: "What kind of technical support do you want for your word processor?";
```

FIGURE M5.11 PROGRM CODE FOR wp9.kbs

encounters a WHILEKNOWN loop it will execute all instructions between the WHILEKNOWN command and the END one time. At that point (the END), VP-Expert will test for the value of the variable that appears after the WHILEKNOWN key word. If that variable has a value, the instructions inside the loop will be executed again. If the value of the variable is UNKNOWN, then VP-Expert will not repeat the instructions, but will continue with the next instruction after the END. If there is no instruction after the END, then the consultation is over. In summary, the loop is executed once regardless of the value of the WHILEKNOWN variable. The loop test is made at the end of the loop to determine if repetition is to occur.

In our case, the test variable is Support. The system executes a GET clause to locate a record in the database wpdb.dbf that has List=Support. List is where the user's MENU choice is stored. The possible values for List are good or fair. Two more instructions are executed before the loop test, in our case, the RESET and FIND clauses. The RESET instruction changes the value of a variable to UNKNOWN, regardless of its earlier status of having or not having an assigned value. When the FIND command encounters a variable name with a value of UNKNOWN, control passes to the inference engine to find the value. At this point, the inference engine searches the Rule base. RULE 1 has a conclusion involving the variable Screen, so that rule is tested.

Let's examine RULE 1. The condition on this rule is expressed as

    IF Support <> UNKNOWN

This reads as "If the database variable Support is not UNKNOWN." This is equivalent to the condition, "If Support is known." Since VP-Expert does not recognize the key word or system value known, the condition must be expressed with *is not UNKNOWN* or <> UNKNOWN. In essence, as long as we can obtain a value for support from the database file, the rule will fire the THEN part and print out the field values. If the Support variable becomes *UNKNOWN,* then the ELSE part of the rule fires and no display to the screen is made. Since the database variable Support has a known value (either fair or good from the database), the rule fires and the subsequent DISPLAY statements transfer the information to the screen. Control passes back to the loop and the END clause.

The test to loop or not to loop is now made. The system looks at the value for Support. Since this value is known from the database, the test of WHILEKNOWN Support is true, so the GET command moves to the next record in the database. The Screen value is changed to UNKNOWN by the RESET command which tests RULE 1 again. The rule fires and the new record information is sent to the screen. Back in the loop the Support variable is examined. If it has a value (good or fair), then the process is repeated again. At some point, a GET clause moves from the last (specified) record and can't find any more. The GET will not go back to the top of the database file. When the GET is past the last record or at the bottom of the file, the system assigns UNKNOWN to the values of the variables in the database. This is illustrated conceptually in Figure M5.12.

The VP-Expert variable List has the value good and the GET statement moves the pointer to record 2, then record 3, and then record 5. The next GET moves the pointer to the end of file. This is when VP-Expert assigns UNKNOWN to Support. Hence, the loop test fails and no more repetitive actions of the loop are allowed. Note that the value of List has not changed; it is still assigned the value good. In summary, the loop is repeated four times. The first three times causes Rule 1 to fire the THEN part because Support is KNOWN. Hence, the three records are displayed on the screen. The last GET clause goes past the end of the database, and Support is now UNKNOWN; hence the ELSE part of the rule fires and no printing occurs. The RESET command activated the search because the variable Screen was reset to UNKNOWN to activate a rule search.

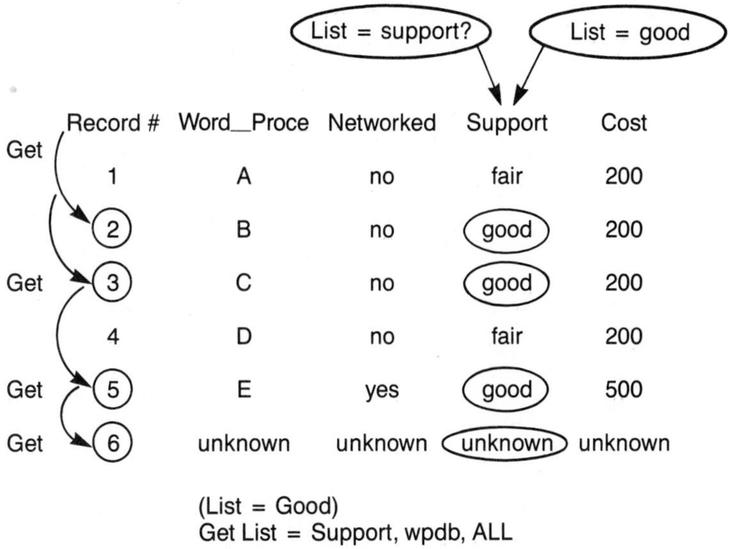

FIGURE M5.12 MOVING THROUGH THE DATABASE WITH GET INSIDE A WHILEKNOWN LOOP (Support = Good)

If the user had selected *fair* from the menu choices shown on the Consultation screen, then the WHILEKNOWN Support loop would have executed three times as illustrated in Figure M5.13.

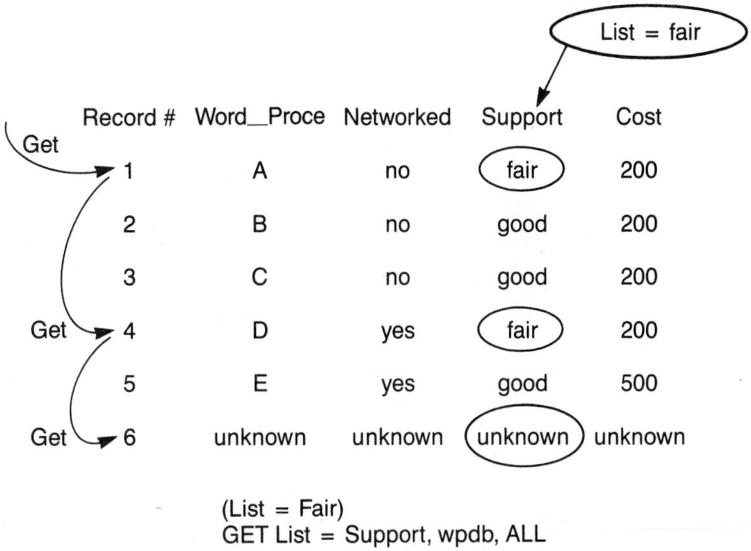

FIGURE M5.13 MOVING THROUGH THE DATABASE WITH GET INSIDE A WHILEKNOWN LOOP (Support = Fair)

Rule 1 would be true the first two times it was tested and would be false the third time. Hence, two records would be printed out, and no record would be printed on the last test.

In summary, we have solved our problem. When the user identifies either good or fair for support, we can get VP-Expert to access the database to display the desired records. In order to do this we have several new instructions:

MENU	Creates a menu of choices from a column of the database
GET	Gets a record from the database that matches what we want
RESET	Changes the value of a variable to UNKNOWN
WHILEKNOWN-END	Loop which tests at the bottom of the loop to determine if the loop is to be repeated.

More examples will help, so let's run another example using databases. The file wp10.kbs will send two questions to the screen with two MENU clauses. The first menu will let you select a rating for Support and the second a value for Cost. Since there are two values for each variable, there are four possible combinations of runs. We will select fair and 200. If you survey Figure M5.1, you can see that there are two records (1 and 4) that meet this condition (Support = fair and Cost = 200). From the Main Menu, load this file, set the trace, run the consultation, and examine the consultation results, text tree, and program code. The abbreviated steps are:

```
6FileName (wp10)
4Consult
        6Set
                2Trace
                6Quit
        2Go (fair, 200)
        7Edit
                F10,END (for a printout)
                ALT-F8, y
        8Quit
5Tree
        2Text
                F10, END (For a printout)
                ALT-F8, y
        4Quit
        (End at the Main Menu)
```

As you run your consultation with wp10, your screen should look like Figure M5.14 when both menus are displayed. (You have selected fair and the second question appears).

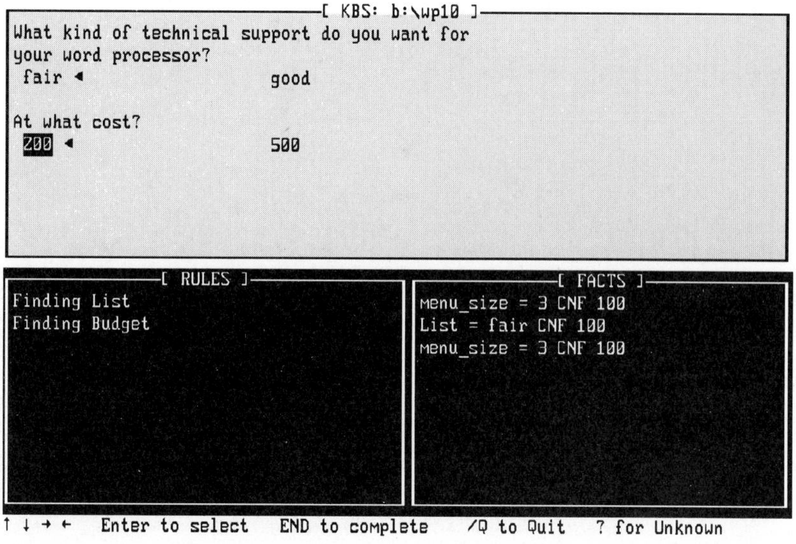

FIGURE M5.14 TWO MENU-GENERATED QUESTIONS FROM CONSULTATION WITH wp10.kbs (with Support=Fair)

Note on this figure that the Rules window is finding List and Budget. In the Facts window, List=Fair. The selection for Budget (200) has not been made yet. Interestingly, the inference engine reports that menu_size = 3 for both questions. Obviously, it is off by one.

Your final consultation screen with wp10 will look like Figure M5.15.

The screen shows that two word processors, A and D, have fair support at a $200 cost. Notice also that record 4 and its values are displayed in the Facts window. The printer output in Figure M5.16 reports the same results. This was activated by setting PRINTON in the program code (and PRINTOFF at the appropriate end of the consultation).

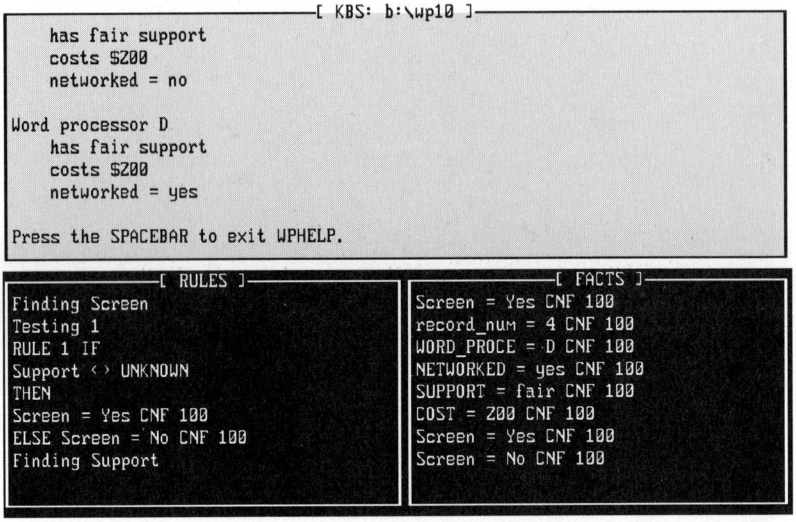

FIGURE M5.15 LAST CONSULTATION SCREEN FOR wp10.kbs (with Support=Fair and Cost=200)

```
Word processor A
     has fair support
     costs $200
     networked = no

Word processor D
     has fair support
     costs $200
     networked = yes
```

FIGURE M5.16 PRINTER OUTPUT FROM wp10.kbs

The Text tree (trace) of the consultation with wp10 in Figure M5.17 reveals the activity of the program code. Lines 3 through 6 indicate that List = fair and Budget = 200. The next lines show a search for the variable Screen. Two times Screen=Yes from Rule 1, but the third time, Screen=No from Rule 1. Support is shown as having no value (UNKNOWN) on Line 15. The program code is given in Figure M5.18.

```
                                          Editing: Old File b:\wp10.trc
Lines
     Testing b:\wp10.kbs◄
     (= yes CNF 0 )◄
     !   List◄
     !   !   (= fair CNF 100 )◄
     !   Budget◄
     !   !   (= 200 CNF 100 )◄
     !   Screen◄
     !   !   Testing 1◄
     !   !   (= Yes CNF 100 )◄
     !   Screen◄
     !   !   Testing 1◄
     !   !   (= Yes CNF 100 )◄
     !   Screen◄
     !   !   Testing 1◄
     !   !   !   Support◄
     !   !   (= No CNF 100 )◄

     +
     Insert On   Document Off              Boldface Off Underline Off
      1     2     3Srch↓  4     5Rplc↓  6     7GbRpc↓ 8     9Rept↓ 10
```

FIGURE M5.17 TEXT TREE FOR wp10.kbs (with List = Fair and Budget = 200)

Let's highlight three points about this code. The two menus were created from the two MENU and two ASK clauses (Comment 1 or C1). Support and Cost are database names, whereas List and Budget are the VP-Expert variables where the values fair and 200 are stored. (Hence, List and Budget are known values). Next examine the GET clause from Comment 2. The two questions imposed the two restrictions, as reflected by the AND statement in the GET command.

List = Support
Budget = Cost

List has the value fair and Budget has the value 200. The variables on the left of the equals sign are VP-Expert names and the ones on the right are database names. A relational operator (=) is between them. This is known as a **database rule** in VP-Expert. Database rules in the GET clause search the database for the next record that meets the database rule. Be careful to observe its format of

VP-Expert_variable   relational operator   field name

```
!The file wp10.kbs will access information
!                    from a database file called wpdb.dbf.
!                    The field names in the database file are:
!                    Word_proce, Networked, Support, Cost
!                    Two menus will be generated.
!                    Print statements are used.

ACTIONS
                    DISPLAY "This expert system WPHELP will display information from a
database file.

Press the SPACEBAR to start the consultation.~"
          CLS
          PRINTON
          MENU List, ALL, wpdb, Support
(C1)      FIND List
          MENU Budget, ALL, wpdb, Cost
          FIND Budget
                                              (C3)
          WHILEKNOWN Support
                    GET List=Support AND Budget=Cost, wpdb,ALL (C2)
                    RESET Screen
                    FIND Screen
          END
          PRINTOFF
          DISPLAY " "
          DISPLAY "Press the SPACEBAR to exit WPHELP.~"
          CLS;
                                              (C3)
RULE 1
          IF Support <> UNKNOWN
          THEN Screen = Yes
                    DISPLAY" "
                    DISPLAY"Word processor {Word_proce}"
                    DISPLAY" has {support} support"
                    DISPLAY" costs ${Cost}"
                    DISPLAY" networked = {Networked}"
          ELSE Screen = No;

     ASK List: "What kind of technical support do you want for your word processor?";
(C1)
     ASK Budget: "At what cost?";
```

FIGURE M5.18 PROGRAM CODE FOR wp10.kbs

Unreliable results may occur if you do not use this format and if you confuse field names and VP-Expert names. Our final comment on wp10 concerns the use of UNKNOWN on Comment 3. The phrases, WHILEKNOWN Support, and IF Support <> UNKNOWN, are both used as control techniques. The first phrase uses Support as the test variable to determine if the loop will be repeated again. The second phrase is used as the condition to RULE 1. Note that the UNKNOWN pertains to a database value, not a VP-Expert variable. Cost would have worked as the control variable as well as Support in this example. In the next section, we will restrict the user's access to a subset of the database. This concept of restricting users to certain data subsets or views is a common and needed procedure in the business world.

Restricting the Database Records

Expert systems deal with specific domains. Many times the domain of expertise may be very specialized. For example, in a medical application, we may have a large database of medical information, but our application is an expert system for cancer treatment and diagnosis. We need a way to restrict the database so that the user of the application sees only information about cancer records. In the business area, we may have a large database of census information, but our expert system application for marketing needs information only on customers under 25 years of age. Restricting the database to a narrower domain is useful in expert systems applications. VP-Expert can achieve this by forcing **conditions**, or **restrictions**, in the MENU and GET clauses of the program code.

Let's modify our WPHELP system again. We will restrict our original database to only those records where the Support rating is good. To our application, the database appears as only three records, B,C, and E, as shown in Figure M5.19. When we search

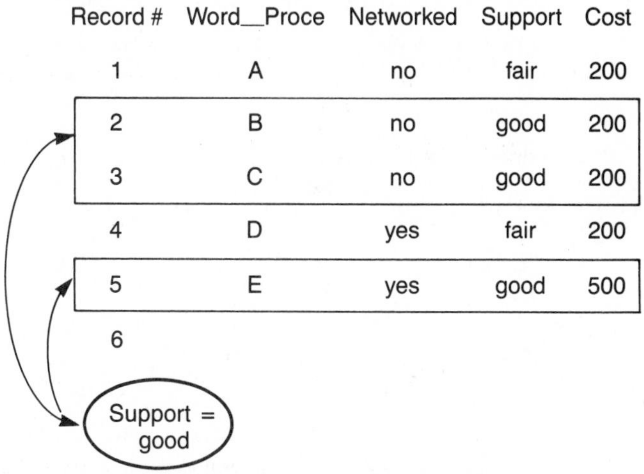

FIGURE M5.19 RESTRICTING THE DATABASE RECORDS

the database by Cost values, records concerning A and D will be excluded. To see the results, run a consultation with wp11.kbs and examine the printer output, a Text tree, and the program code. When the price is to be selected, choose 200. The results should be records B and C because they are the only records in the restricted database that have a cost of $200. If you need the instructions, refer to the previous abbreviated steps. The printer output from wp11.kbs is shown in Figure M5.20. Only two records,

Word processor B
  has good support
  costs $200
  networked = no

Word processor C
  has good support
  costs $200
  networked = no

FIGURE M5.20 PRINTER OUTPUT FROM CONSULTATION WITH wp11.kbs (with Records Restricted to Support=Good)

B and C, have a $200 cost in our restricted database. The Text tree trace shown in Figure M5.21 reveals records restricted to Good (Line 3), that Budget=200 (Lines 4 and 5), and that Screen was evaluated twice as Yes and once as No. The Cost variable has no value (Line 14).

```
                                          Editing: Old File b:\wp11.trc
Lines
  1      Testing b:\wp11.kbs◄
  2      (= yes CNF 0 )◄
  3      (= Good CNF 100 )◄
  4      !   Budget◄
  5      !   !   (= 200 CNF 100 )◄
  6      !   Screen◄
  7      !   !   Testing 1◄
  8      !   !   (= Yes CNF 100 )◄
  9      !   Screen◄
 10      !   !   Testing 1◄
 11      !   !   (= Yes CNF 100 )◄
 12      !   Screen◄
 13      !   !   Testing 1◄
 14      !   !   !   Cost◄
 15      !   !   (= No CNF 100 )◄

         Insert On    Document Off              Boldface Off Underline Off
         1       2       3Srch↓  4       5Rplc↓  6       7GbRpc↓ 8       9Rept↓ 10
```

FIGURE M5.21 TEXT TREE FOR wp11.kbs (with Records Restricted to Support=Good)

The program code for this consultation is given in Figure M5.22. The value Good has been assigned to a VP-Expert variable Kbsupport (Comment 1). In both the MENU (C2) and GET (C3) clause, we use Kbsupport=Support to tell VP-Expert to select the menu choices and to get only those records with Support=good. We have to use this method in order to fit the database rule (variable relational_operator field name) format for the parameter. You would probably call it a trick. But this method does restrict the database records as described. In the WHILEKNOWN-END construct, note

```
!The file wp11.kbs will access and restrict information
!        from a database file called wpdb.dbf.
!        The field names in the database file are:
!        Word__proce, Networked, Support, Cost

ACTIONS
        DISPLAY "This expert system WPHELP will display information from a restricted
database file.
Turn on the printer.

Press the SPACEBAR to start the consultation.~"
          CLS
(C1) ---> Kbsupport = Good
          MENU Budget, Kbsupport=Support, wpdb, Cost <--- (C2)
          FIND Budget
          PRINTON

          WHILEKNOWN Cost
      (C3) --->   GET Budget=Cost AND Kbsupport= Support, wpdb, ALL
                  RESET Screen
                  FIND Screen
          END
          PRINTOFF
          DISPLAY " "
          DISPLAY "Press the SPACEBAR to exit WPHELP.~"
          CLS;

RULE 1
          IF Cost <> UNKNOWN
                  THEN Screen=Yes
                  DISPLAY" "
                  DISPLAY"Word processor {Word__proce}"
                  DISPLAY" has {support} support"
                  DISPLAY" costs ${Cost}"
                  DISPLAY" networked = {Networked}"
          ELSE Screen = No;

ASK Budget: "What cost for a word processor is in your budget?";
```

FIGURE M5.22 PROGRAM CODE for wp11.kbs

that the Cost field name is the control variable. This application, however, has only one ASK because there is only one MENU clause. Our next example will let you browse through all of the database records.

Repeated Displaying of Database Records

Now we will turn our attention to letting the user see any records that he or she wants to see. To do this we need to display a list of the word processors and let the user select the record for display. This time, however, we will restrict the information going to the screen, but we will not restrict the number of records. The length of the search is controlled by the user. Program wp12.kbs will do this. Now run the consultation, and obtain a printout of the Text tree and the program code. When you run the consultation, select C the first time, then A, then E, and then a ? to end the consultation. Refer to the abbreviated steps if needed.

The results of this consultation did not go to the printer. The Text tree in Figure M5.23 shows that the variable Word_processor was signed the value C (Line 4), then the value A (line 8), then E (Line 13), and finally UNKNOWN (Line 17).

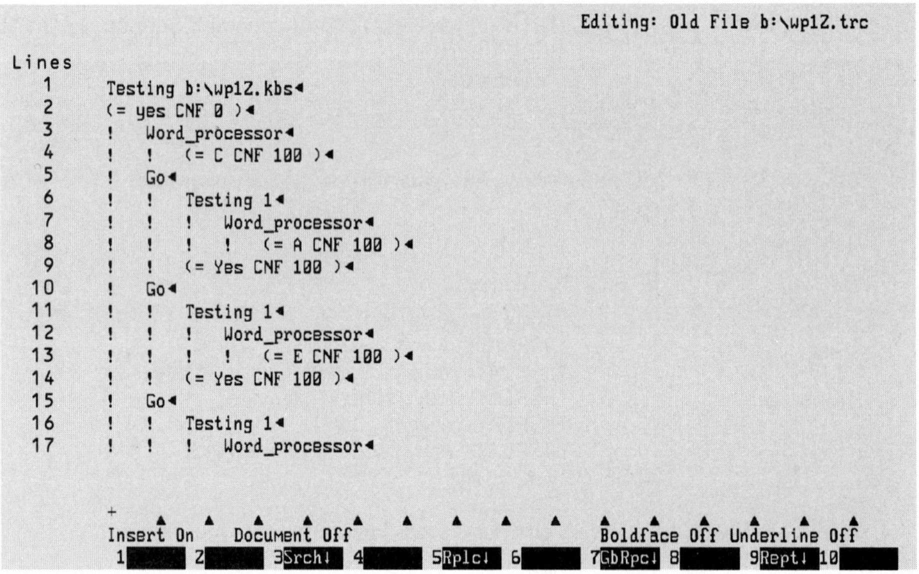

```
                                              Editing: Old File b:\wp12.trc
Lines
  1      Testing b:\wp12.kbs◂
  2      (= yes CNF 0 )◂
  3      !   Word_processor◂
  4      !   !   (= C CNF 100 )◂
  5      !   Go◂
  6      !   !   Testing 1◂
  7      !   !   !   Word_processor◂
  8      !   !   !   !   (= A CNF 100 )◂
  9      !   !   (= Yes CNF 100 )◂
 10      !   Go◂
 11      !   !   Testing 1◂
 12      !   !   !   Word_processor◂
 13      !   !   !   !   (= E CNF 100 )◂
 14      !   !   (= Yes CNF 100 )◂
 15      !   Go◂
 16      !   !   Testing 1◂
 17      !   !   !   Word_processor◂

         Insert On   Document Off                    Boldface Off Underline Off
         1       2       3Srch↓  4       5Rplc↓  6       7GbRpc↓ 8       9Rept↓  10
```

FIGURE M5.23 TEXT TREE FOR wp12.kbs for SELECTING C, A, E, and ?

The program code in Figure M5.24 shows how we achieved this interactive consultation with wp12.kbs.

```
!The file wp12.kbs will access information
!        from a database file called wpdb.dbf.
!        The field names in the database file are:
!        Word_proce, Networked, Support, Cost
!        The user will loop until he/she enters a ?.

ACTIONS
        DISPLAY "This expert system WPHELP will display information from a database
file.

Press the SPACEBAR to start the consultation.~"
C1 →      CLS
          MENU Word_processor, ALL, wpdb, Word_proce
C2 →      WHILEKNOWN Go
                  FIND Word_processor
C3 →              Get Word_processor=Word_proce, wpdb, Support
                  CLOSE wpdb
                  DISPLAY "Word processor {Word_processor} has {Support} sup-
          port."

                  DISPLAY " "
                  DISPLAY "Press any key to continue."
                  CLS
                  RESET Word_processor
C4 →              DISPLAY "Type a question mark ? over a menu choice if you want to
          quit.
                  "
                  MENU Word_processor, ALL, wpdb, Word_proce
                  RESET Go
                  FIND Go
C5 →              MRESET word_processor
          END
          DISPLAY "Press the SPACEBAR to exit WPHELP.~"
          CLS;
RULE 1
          IF Word_processor <> UNKNOWN
                  THEN Go=Yes;

ASK Word_processor: "Select the name of the word processor for which you want sup-
port information.";
```

FIGURE M5.24 CODE FOR wp12.kbs

We have five basic points to consider. The menu of five choices (A, B, C, D, and E) was generated by the MENU clause (Comment 1). We used the ALL parameter for the scope of the choices from the column. The control variable for the WHILEKNOWN loop is Go (Comment 2). Go is a VP-Expert variable, not a field name from the database. Hence, for the loop to stop repeating, its value must become UNKNOWN.

RULE 1, however, has a condition involving another variable, Word_processor and UNKNOWN. The GET clause (Comment 3) shows us that we will retrieve the word processor record identified by the user. The last parameter, Support, indicates that we are only interested in this field, not all fields. After the word processor record is found and displayed, the variable is reset. The DISPLAY statement (Comment 4) tells the user to enter a ? over a menu choice to quit the session. The ? is translated to an UNKNOWN. If the variable were not reset, then only one record would be found in the database.

A new instruction MRESET (Comment 5) is used after a MENU clause to release the internal memory required for the menu choices. If the menu were large, then memory problems could occur, so we release the memory for the menu to avoid this problem.

So far, we have seen how to access records in a database with VP-Expert. We can search for any combination of conditions or we can restrict our search to a subset of the database. New instructions WHILEKNOWN, GET, MENU, RESET, and MRESET help us to accomplish this. Once the database information is accessed, it can be used in the knowledge base.

Changing Records in a Database

Accessing database information is important in an application, but **changing** or **updating** records is vital to the integrity (accuracy) of the database information. VP-Expert allows you to change the contents of a database. Program wp13.kbs will allow you to change the Cost field in the database. This is appropriate in our word processing application because prices change quickly rather than staying constant. We will use a copy of our database file (Figure M5.1) called wpdb1.db1 because our program will change the values in this database through a command called PUT.

From the Main Menu, select wp13.kbs and run the change cost program. Select word processor D and change its cost to 500. As you run the consultation, the update screen will appear like Figure M5.25, showing the old cost of 200 with a new cost of 500.

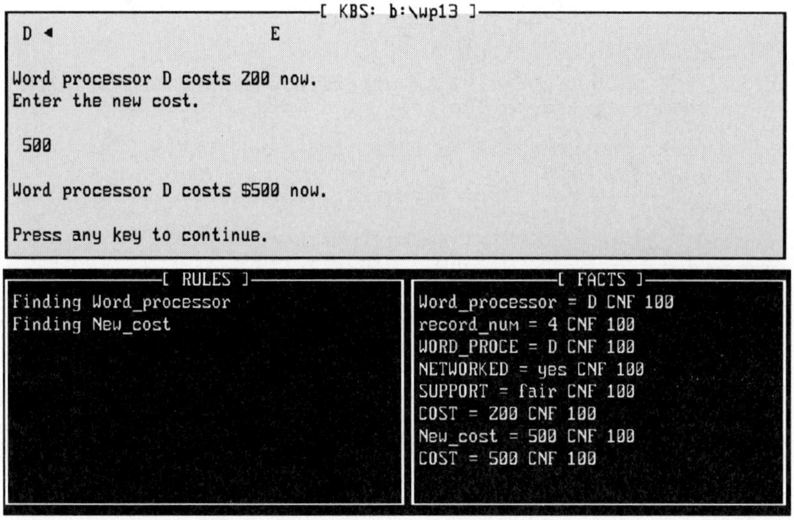

FIGURE M5.25 SAMPLE CONSULTATION SCREEN FOR CHANGING THE COST OF A WORD PROCESSOR (wp13.kbs)

The user supplies the new cost information and the program writes the new cost to the proper record (in our case, word processor D). The user can then choose to change another price of a word processor or exit the consultation. This program code is displayed in Figure M5.26.

```
! The file wp13.kbs will change or update
!         the Cost field in wpdbl.dbf.
!         The field names in the database file are:
!         Word_proce, Networked, Support, Cost
!         The user will loop until he/she enters a ?.

ACTIONS
          DISPLAY "This expert system WPHELP will let you
change or update the cost of a word processor.

Press the SPACEBAR to start the consultation.~"
          CLS
(C1) -->  MENU Word_processor, ALL, wpdbl, Word_proce
          WHILEKNOWN Go
(C2) -->       FIND Word_processor
               GET Word_processor=Word_proce, wpdbl, ALL
               Reset New_cost
               Find New_cost
               Cost=(New_cost)
               DISPLAY "Word processor {Word_proce} costs ${Cost} now."
               DISPLAY " "
(C3) -->       Put wpdbl
               CLOSE wpdbl
               DISPLAY "Press any key to continue.~"
               CLS
               RESET Word_processor
               DISPLAY "Type a question mark ? over a menu choice
if you want to quit.
               "
               MENU Word_processor, ALL, wpdbl, Word_proce
               RESET Go
               FIND Go
               MRESET Word_processor
          END
          DISPLAY "Press the SPACEBAR to exit WPHELP."
          CLS;
RULE 1
          IF Word_processor <> UNKNOWN
                THEN Go=Yes;

ASK Word_processor : "Select the name of the word processor
whose cost has changed.";

Ask New_cost : "Word processor {Word_proce} costs {Cost} now.
Enter the new cost.
";
```

FIGURE M5.26 PROGRAM CODE FOR UPDATE PROGRAM (wp13.kbs)

The first task is to find the correct record, then obtain the new price, and store it in the database. From Comment 1 on Figure M5.26 we use the MENU clause to let the user select the record and then retrieve that record. From Comment 2, the FIND clause causes the ASK New-cost statement to be displayed to the user. The reply is stored in the variable New_cost. In order to transfer the contents of New_cost to the variable Cost, we have to enclose New_cost in parentheses (indirect addressing). If we left the parentheses off, then the Cost would equal the words, New_cost. The command that transfers the new value of Cost to the selected database record is the PUT clause (Comment 3). The format of this instruction is PUT database file. Notice that we had to close the database (Comment 3) so that when we repeat the search for another record, the search would start at the top instead of on the record for word processor D. In the next database section we will add new records to our database.

Adding Records to a Database

New products come out all the time, so we need a mechanism in VP-Expert that allows us to continually add new records to the database. The APPEND command does this. From the Main Menu select file wp14.kbs. When you run a consultation with this example, add a new record with the following information:

Word processor	:	H
Cost	:	599
Support	:	Good
Networked	:	Yes

The database is wpdb1, a copy of wpdb.dbf. The data entry screen will appear as shown in Figure M5.27. It is important to verify the information before it is written to the database. You may also add more records if you like.

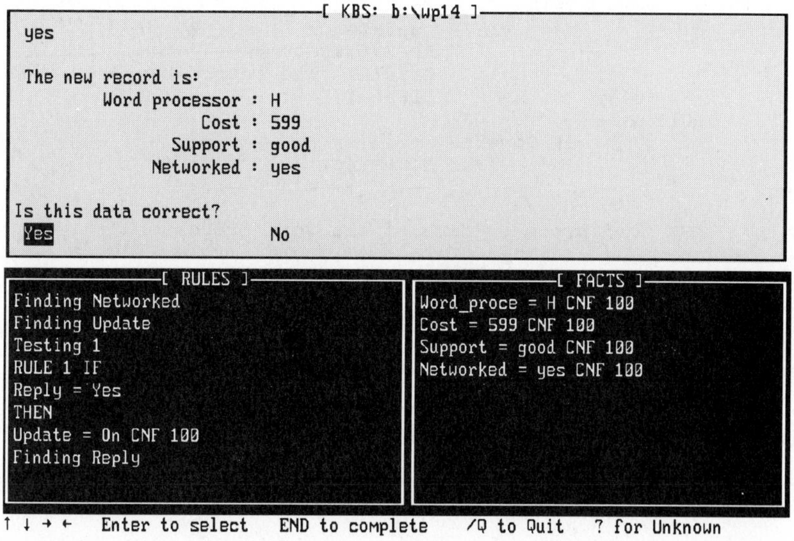

FIGURE M5.27 CONSULTATION SCREEN FOR ADDING A DATABASE RECORD (wp14.kbs)

The program code for this example is illustrated in figure M5.28 In order to accomplish our addition, we had to find the new information from the user, and then **add** or **append** it to the database. Comment 1 on Figure M5.28 shows a series of

```
!The file wp14.kbs will let you add a new
!       word processing record to the database wpdbl.
!       The field names in the database file are:
!       Word_proce, Networked, Support, Cost
!       The user will loop until he/she enters a ?.

ACTIONS
        DISPLAY "This expert system WPHELP will let you add a
new word processing record to the database wpdbl.dbf.

Press the SPACEBAR to start the consultation.~"
        CLS
        WHILEKNOWN More
(C3) ------> RESET ALL
            DISPLAY "Please enter the new record."
            FIND Word_proce )
            Find Cost       }
            Find Support    }  <--(C1)
            Find Networked  )
            DISPLAY " The new record is:
        Word processor : {Word_proce}
                  Cost : {Cost}
               Support : {Support}
             Networked : {Networked}
            "
            FIND Update
            FIND More
        END
        DISPLAY "Press the SPACEBAR to exit WPHELP.~"
        CLS;

RULE 1
        IF Reply = Yes
            THEN  Update=On
                APPEND wpdbl <------------------------------(C2)
                DISPLAY "The record has been added."
                DISPLAY " ";
RULE 2
        IF Go =Yes
            THEN More=yes;


ASK Word_proce : "Name of the word processor?"; <--(C2)

Ask Cost : "Cost ?";

ASK Support : "Support? Enter good or fair.";

ASK Networked : "Networked? Enter yes or no.";

ASK Reply : "Is this data correct?";
CHOICES Reply: Yes, No;

ASK Go : "Do you want to continue?";
CHOICES Go : Yes, No;
```

FIGURE M5.28   PROGRAM CODE FOR ADDING A DATABASE RECORD (wp14.kbs)

FIND clauses which activate the inference engine to send the appropriate questions to the screen. By embedding Update in the conclusion of RULE 1 and More in the condition of RULE 2, the FIND Reply clause will cause us to verify the screen information before firing the rule that APPENDs (C2) the new record information to the database. The RESET ALL command of Comment 3 is needed so that the loop and FIND commands will be reactivated.

The important point here is that database information can be incorporated in an expert system. The database names can be used in the rule base. The results of a consultation can then be written back to the database. For example, as the market grows toward increased networking, we could incorporate budget or maintenance estimates in a rule. For example,

```
If Support = Good and Network = Yes
        THEN Anew_Maintenance = (0.3 * Cost)
```

Networked environments carry a 30% annual overhead for maintenance. The database information can be part of the expert system.

Thus, we have seen how VP-Expert can be the front-end to a database application. We can access information with the MENU and GET commands, repeat our actions with the WHILEKNOWN structure, update records with the PUT clause, and add new records with the APPEND command. Let's now turn our attention to using worksheets (electronic spreadsheets) for the front-end to our expert system.

Using a Spreadsheet

Just as a database can hold large amounts of business information, so do **worksheets**, or **spreadsheets**. This is another existing base of valuable information for potential expert systems. VP-Expert allows you to use existing spreadsheet data as the front-end to an expert system application. Files created with VP-Planner or LOTUS 1-2-3 Version 1A can be used in VP-Expert applications. You can access the data, manipulate it in the knowledge base, and write it back to the spreadsheet. Files created with LOTUS 1-2-3 Version 2.0 or Version 2.01 can be accessed but not written to at this time (except with CCall).

Overview

There are other considerations to be aware of before a spreadsheet is used in a VP-Expert application. First, the spreadsheets can not have blank cells. VP-Expert will skip over blanks and the data will be aligned incorrectly. When data is being written to a spreadsheet, data types must match. If a numeric field is written to a text cell, then the results will be treated as labels. Hence, no calculations can be made. For the reverse situation, writing text to a numeric field will cause the result to be treated as a zero. Structural changes, moreover, cannot be made to the spreadsheet. Only cells that contain data can receive data. In other words, you can not write to new cell locations. If the data to be written is longer than the existing cell length, then the data will be truncated. Despite these limitations, the ability to use certain spreadsheet files as a front-end to an expert system is useful.

Reading from a Spreadsheet

We will use our familiar data on word processing and access it from a spreadsheet. The data shown in Figure M5.29 is stored in a LOTUS 1-2-3 Version 1A file. The cell locations are marked by the usual column/row notation. For example, word processor A is located in cell A2 and the cost of product A is in cell D2. The column headings, WORD_P, NETWORK, SUPPORT, and COST, are in cells A1, B1, C1, and D1 respectively. Spreadsheet labels are not case sensitive, so COST and Cost are not the same headings. We have chosen to capitalize the headings and the product names. All other cells are lowercase. The COST cells are, of course, numeric. The spreadsheet itself is called wpws.wks.

D7: READY

	A	B	C	D	E	F	G	H
1	WORD_P	NETWORK	SUPPORT	COST				
2	A	no	fair	200				
3	B	no	good	200				
4	C	yes	good	200				
5	D	yes	fair	200				
6	E	yes	good	500				
7								
8								
9								
10								
11								
12								
13								
14								
15								
16								
17								
18								
19								
20								

FIGURE M5.29 WORD PROCESSING INFORMATION IN A WORKSHEET (wpws.wks)

As usual, we will use an example from our Sample Files Disk to show how to access worksheets or spreadsheets from within VP-Expert. We will us file wp15.kbs to read the worksheet wpws.wks. Both the program file and spreadsheet file are on the Sample Files Disk. Get to the Main Menu with VP-Expert in the A drive and the Sample Files Disk in the B drive. Then follow the familiar steps to run a consultation with wp15.kbs:

7Path (b:)
6FileName (wp15)
4Consult
  2Go
  (Remain in the Consult Menu)

The consultation will pull the data from the spreadsheet wpws.wks, store it in memory, and display it on the screen. The results of your consultation with wp15.kbs are shown in Figure M5.30.

1	A	no	fair	200
2	B	no	good	200
3	C	yes	good	200
4	D	yes	fair	200
5	E	yes	good	500

FIGURE M5.30 LISTING OF WORKSHEET FILE (wpws.wks) BY PROGRAM wp15.kbs

The four columns of information from the spreadsheet are displayed on the screen along with a numbering of rows (1, 2, 3, 4, and 5). How does VP-Expert accomplish this? The answer is the WKS, or read worksheet clause. This instruction has three parts (parameters) after the key word WKS. The first parameter identifies the VP-Expert variable that will receive the spreadsheet information. The second part tells VP-Expert the location of the desired data in the spreadsheet. The last part identifies the name of the spreadsheet to be accessed. Thus, to read the four columns of data (Figure M5.30), the following four clauses are used:

```
WKS Cword_p, A2..A6, wpws
WKS Cnetwork, B2..B6, wpws
WKS Csupport, C2..C6, wpws
WKS Ccost, D2..D6, wpws
```

The first part of each command is WKS, the second is the VP-Expert variable, the third is the spreadsheet range, and the last is the spreadsheet name without the .wks extension. Note that we have named our VP-Expert variables by inserting an upper-case C in front of the corresponding spreadsheet column name. For readability we chose lower-case for the rest of the variable names. The four variables, Cword_p, Cnetwork, Csupport, and Ccost, must each contain five pieces of data. To identify each part, we place a number (1, 2, 3, 4, or 5) in square brackets after the variable name. For example, after the WKS clauses are executed,

```
Cword_p[1] = A
Cword_p[2] = B
Cword_p[3] = C
Cword_p[4] = D
Cword_p[5] = E
```

We have similar notations for the other variables. The information in row 2 is:

Cword[2] = B
Cnetwork[2] = no
Csupport[2] = good
Ccost[2] = 200

Variables with a name followed by a number in square brackets are known as arrays, dimensioned variables, or subscripted variables. When a variable name appears after the WKS key word, the system assumes that these variables are arrays. We can examine these arrays because they are still in memory after a consultation is run.

You should still be in the Consult Menu where you screen appears similar to Figure M5.30. (If you returned to the Main Menu, run the consultation again.) At the end of the consultation we can examine the value of variables by using the 4Variable option from the Consult menu. We can verify, for example, that

Cword_p[3] = C

Select the 4Variable option. Your screen should appear as Figure M5.31.

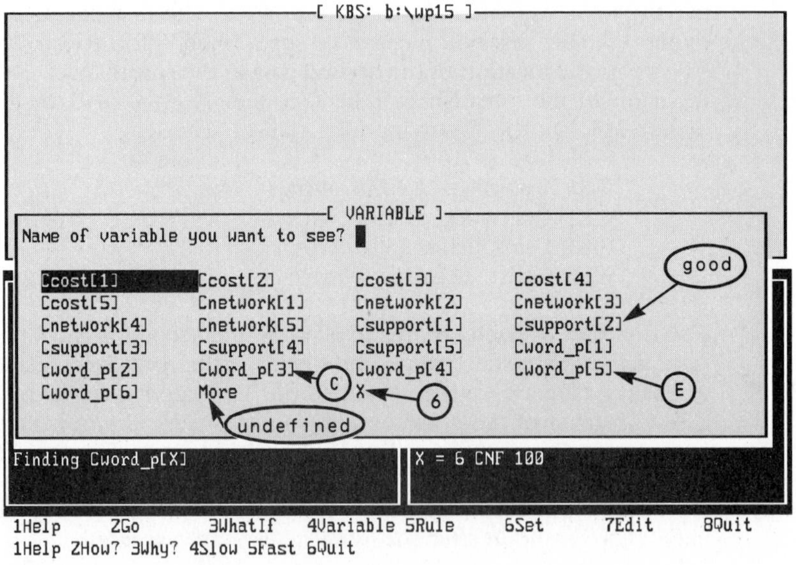

FIGURE M5.31 CHECKING THE VALUE OF VARIABLES AFTER A CONSULTATION WITH wp15.kbs

Select the variable, Cword_p[3], by pressing the arrow keys until the light bar is over this variable. Press the ENTER key to verify that the value of

Cword_p[3] = C

Check the following list of variables by selecting 4Variable, paging down, and selecting the variable:

Cword_p[5] = E
Csupport[2] = good
x = 6
More = Undefined

The VP-Expert system will display these values through the 4Variable option of the Consult Menu.

Now let's read the code for wp15.kbs. Select the 7Edit option of the Consult Menu. Use the F10 and END keys to obtain a printout of wp15.kbs as shown in Figure M5.32.

```
!The file wp15.kbs will access information
!        from a worksheet file called wpws.wks
!        The column headings in the worksheet are:
!        WORD_P, NETWORK, SUPPORT, COST
!        The range is a..1 to d..6

ACTIONS
          DISPLAY "This expert system WPHELP will read all the data
from a worksheet file (wpws.wks) and display it on the
screen and send it to the printer. Turn on the printer.


Press the SPACEBAR to start the consultation.~"
          CLS
          DISPLAY " "
          DISPLAY "Please wait. The worksheet is being loaded.
          "
          PRINTON
          WKS Cword_p, a2..a6, wpws
          WKS Cnetwork, b2..b6, wpws
          WKS Csupport, c2..c6, wpws
C1        WKS Ccost, d2..d6, wpws
          X=1
C2        WHILEKNOWN More
              DISPLAY "{x} {Cword_p[x]} {Cnetwork[x]} {Csupport[x]} {Ccost[x]}
              X=(X+1)
C3            RESET More
              FIND More
          END
          PRINTOFF
          DISPLAY " "
          DISPLAY "     Press the SPACEBAR to exit WPHELP.~"
          CLS;

RULE 1
          IF Cword_p[X] <> UNKNOWN
C4             THEN More=yes;
```

FIGURE M5.32   PROGRAM CODE FOR READING A WORKSHEET FILE WITH wp15.kbs

We have four specific comments to make about this program. From Comment 1 (C1) of Figure M5.32 we see the four WKS clauses that read the columns values into arrays or subscripted variables. The ranges tell the computer where to find the data in the spreadsheet. Note in Comment 2 that the variable X is set to 1 so that we can display the first elements in each of the worksheet rows. After this is displayed, we increase X by 1 (Comment 3). When the More variable is RESET followed by a FIND, then RULE 1 is fired (Comment 4). Since Cword_p[2] = B, the rule is fired and the variable More is assigned the value Yes. Since the END command is next, the system will test the WHILE-KNOWN More condition. This is found to be true, so the loop is executed again. This continues as long as the next word processing record in the spreadsheet exists. When the fifth word processor has been read, the X variable is increased to 6. The value of Cword_p[6], however, is UNKNOWN so the WHILEKNOWN test fails. This is how VP-Expert can display the worksheet data from memory to the screen display.

Let's move to another program example where the data in the spreadsheet is converted to information on the display screen. In addition, this example will allow the user to select an additional, but optional printer output of the spreadsheet values. The program wp16.kbs will use wpws.wks to format the data into information at the screen. Run a consultation with wp16.kbs from your Sample Files Disk to see this display. Be sure that the printer is on before running the consultation with wp16.kbs. Select Yes to the question concerning an additional printout. At the end of the consultation, your screen and printer output should resemble Figure M5.33.

```
WORD PROCESSING INFORMATION
     from Worksheet wpws.wks

Row 1 : Wordprocessor A has
        fair support
        costs $200
        networked is no

Row 2 : Wordprocessor B has
        good support
        costs $200
        networked is no

Row 3 : Wordprocessor C has
        good support
        costs $200
        networked is yes

Row 4 : Wordprocessor D has
        fair support
        costs $200
        networked is yes

Row 5 : Wordprocessor E has
        good support
        costs $500
        networked is yes
```

FIGURE M5.33 OPTIONAL PRINTOUT FROM WORKSHEET (wp16.kbs)

Note that this printout has a title of

WORD PROCESSING INFORMATION
from Worksheet wpws.wks

The reformatting has inserted phrases like "has good support" and "costs $200." This optional printout is a plus to a business application. The converting of data to information is still another asset (even though "networked is no" is an awkward phrase).

Let's analyze the program code for wp16.kbs. Use the 7Edit option of the Consult Menu. Once in the editor, use the F10 and END keys to initiate a printout. Exit the editor with ALT-F8. The printout of wp16.kbs should be identical to Figure M5.34.

We have five comments to make about this code. First, there are four WKS clauses (C1) that read the data from designated ranges into subscripted variables. We see from Comment 2 that a FIND Print clause initiates a search for a value of Reply. This fires the question to the user concerning a printout. If the Reply is Yes, then the PRINTON command is executed and DISPLAY statements in RULE 2 print the title. Within the WHILEKNOWN More loop (C4), DISPLAY statements reformat the variable data into information. The variable X is used to indicate which value of the subscripted variable is to be displayed. When the value of Cw[X] becomes UNKNOWN (X=6), then the loop test fails and the consultation (C5) ends. This completes our discussion of wp16.kbs.

We have seen how the use of WKS clauses with subscripted variables allow access to spreadsheet data. The use of DISPLAY statements with proper formatting allow the transition of spreadsheet data into readable information. In the next section we will discuss the writing of data back to the spreadsheet file.

```
!The file wp16.kbs will access data from a worksheet (wpws.wks).
!        Output of information is to the screen
!        with optional printer output.

ACTIONS
         DISPLAY "This expert system WPHELP will read all the data
from a worksheet file (wpws.wks) and display the rows as
INFORMATION on the screen and allow an optional printout.


Press the SPACEBAR to start the consultation.~"
         CLS
         DISPLAY " "
         DISPLAY "The data will take time to load.
         "
(C2) ->  FIND Print
         WKS Cw, a2..a6, wpws
         WKS Cn, b2..b6, wpws
(C1) ->  WKS Cs, c2..c6, wpws
         WKS Cc, d2..d6, wpws
         X=1
         WHILEKNOWN More
              DISPLAY "            Row {X} : Word processor {Cw[X]} has
                   {Cs[X]} support
                   costs ${Cc[X]}
                   networked is {Cn[X]}
                   "                                          (C4)
              X=(X+1)
              RESET More
              FIND More
         END
         PRINTOFF
         DISPLAY " "
         DISPLAY "       Press the SPACEBAR to exit WPHELP.~"
         CLS;

RULE 1
(C5) ->  IF Cw[X] <> UNKNOWN
               THEN More=yes;
RULE 2
         IF Reply=Yes                                (C3)
              THEN Print=Yes
              PRINTON
              DISPLAY " "
              DISPLAY "             WORD PROCEESING INFORMATION"
              DISPLAY "               from Worksheet wpws.wks"
              DISPLAY " "
       ELSE Print = No;

ASK Reply : "In addition to the screen display,
do you want a printout of the worksheet?";

CHOICES Reply : Yes, No;
```

FIGURE M5.34 PROGRAM CODE FOR wp16.kbs

Writing to a Spreadsheet

Now we will explore how VP-Expert writes new values back to the spreadsheet. We will use the PWKS, or put worksheet clause, to accomplish this task.

Once we have the spreadsheet information in computer memory, we can manipulate it according to any rules we put in the knowledge base. Many times we will need to write changed values back to the spreadsheet. We use the PWKS clause to do this. Run wp17.kbs from your Sample Files Disk. This program allows you to change the values for the Cost column in the wpws1.wks file (a copy of wpws.wks). Run a consultation and change the cost of word processor B from $200 to $300. Enter the same values for the other products.

After running a consultation with wp17.kbs, obtain a printout of the program code. Your program listing should appear as Figure M5.35.

```
!The file wp17.kbs will access data from a worksheet (wpws1.wks).
!        Changes in cost will be written back to
!        the worksheet file.
!

ACTIONS
          DISPLAY "This expert system WPHELP will read all the data
from a worksheet file (wpws1.wks) and write back changes
for the cost of a word processor.

Press the SPACEBAR to start the consultation.~"
          CLS
          DISPLAY " "
          DISPLAY "The data will take time to load.
"
       ( WKS Cw, COLUMN=WORD_P,  wpws1
(C1) --> WKS Cn, COLUMN=NETWIRK, wpws1
       ( WKS Cs, COLUMN=SUPPORT, wpws1
       ( WKS Cc, COLUMN=COST,    wpws1
          X=(1)
          WHILEKNOWN More
               DISPLAY "Word processor {Cw[X]} costs {Cc[X]}.
"
               RESET Current_cost
(C2) -------->  FIND Current_cost
               Cc[X]=(Current_cost)
               X=(X+1)
               RESET More
               FIND More
          END
(C3) -->  PWKS Cc, COLUMN=COST, wpws1
          DISPLAY " "
          DISPLAY "Press the SPACEBAR to exit WPHELP.~"
          CLS;

RULE 1
          IF Cw[X] <> UNKNOWN
               THEN More=yes;

ASK Current_cost : "Enter the displayed cost or a new one.";
```

FIGURE M5.35 PROGRAM CODE FOR wp17.kbs

Let's make three general points about this code. First of all, it was unnoticeable to the user, but the WKS clauses had been changed (C1). Instead of ranges, we used the column headings which appeared in row 1 of the spreadsheet file. The syntax is

COLUMN = column_name.

If we have row names or range labels we could use these with ROW = name and NAMED = range name. In Comment 2, we observe that the user's response to cost is stored in the VP-Expert variable Current_cost. Current_cost is then assigned to Cc[X] in memory. A parenthesis is needed so that the contents of Current_cost is transferred instead of the words "Current_cost." The new information now contained in Cc[X] in memory is transferred to the spreadsheet with the PWKS clause (C3). This clause writes the information in the Cc variable to the Cost column in the spreadsheet wpws1.wks. You can think of PWKS as put to the worksheet.

There is an interesting problem here. If you observed the Facts window of the consultation, you observed new values for the X in Cc. What VP-Expert really does is to append or add the new values to the column of old values. To place the new values where they really belong you have to open the spreadsheet and use spreadsheet commands. This is awkward, but the way it is for now for writing to a spreadsheet. Again, we make the point that once spreadsheet data is available to VP-Expert, it can be utilized in the knowledge base. The resulting information can be written back to the spreadsheet (in an awkward manner). All the subscripted information can be used in rules. For example,

```
If Cs[x] = good AND Cn[x] = yes
        THEN Budget = Cc[x]
                Maintenance = 0.3x (Cc[x]);
```

Networked environments carry larger maintenance overheads. The spreadsheet information can be part of the rule base. The new results, Budget or Maintenance, can be written back to the spreadsheet (if they existed there to start with). It is possible, moreover, to change the format of a spreadsheet cell. The command for achieving this is

WFORMAT clause

Three numeric data types can be specified with this clause, fixed decimal (FIXED), scientific format (SCI), and currency (CURR). Thus, the clause

WFORMAT CURR, 4

would change the Cc (cost) column to four decimals of the currency format. This can be quite useful for formatting reports from the spreadsheet.

Thus, we have seen how the WKS clause reads data from a spreadsheet using arrays or subscripted variables. The PWKS puts changed information back into the spreadsheet. The numeric format of cells can be changed with the WFORMAT clause. We have now seen how VP-Expert can be the front-end to both database and spreadsheet files. In the next module we will take a closer look at confidence factors for expert systems in VP-Expert.

Key Points

- VP-Expert can access information from selected microcomputer database and spreadsheet files.
- Data from database and spreadsheet files can be incorporated into rules in the knowledge base. Results of a consultation can be written back to existing fields or cells in the database or spreadsheet, respectively.
- The large amounts of data in existing database and spreadsheet files foster the development of expert system applications.
- The commands for database usage are MENU, GET, PUT, and RESET.
- The MENU clause generates a list of choices from a column in the database file to accompany a question in an ASK statement. The user's reply from the menu is stored in a variable.
- The GET command is used to transfer data from a database into variables in computer memory.
- The PUT clause is used to transfer data from variables in computer memory to database records.
- The MRESET clause is used to deallocate or release the memory required for the MENU Clause.
- Database field names and VP-Expert variable names should be different.
- The WHILEKNOWN-END loop structure allows the instructions in the loop to be executed once. At the end of the loop, a test is made on the WHILEKNOWN variable. If the variable has a value, the loop is executed again. If the variable has no value (UNKNOWN), then the loop instructions are not repeated.
- The GET clause is placed inside a WHILEKNOWN-END loop in order to read or transfer data from the database record into memory.
- The RESET clause assigns a variable the value of UNKNOWN. When the FIND command comes in from of a variable that is UNKNOWN, the inference engine initiates a search for a known value for the variable.
- For spreadsheets, the commands are WKS, PWKS, and WFORMAT.
- The WKS command sends data from spreadsheet locations to arrays or subscripted variables in computer memory. Data may be transferred by columns, rows, or range names.
- Arrays or subscripted variables will have a numeric value or variable inside square brackets. For example,

  Cost[3]

  is a subscripted variable.
- All designated spreadsheet information is read into computer memory at one time. A WHILEKNOWN-END loop is not needed as with database access.
- A WHILEKNOWN-END loop may be used with a subscripted variable to display or print information.
- Spreadsheet data is transferred from computer memory to spreadsheet locations by the PWKS clause.
- The WFORMAT clause may be used to change the format of an existing spreadsheet cell.
- The PRINTON clauses sends the contents of any DISPLAY statements to the printer. The PRINTOFF cancels any additional printing of DISPLAY statements to the printer.

Exercises

1. Which of the following commands moves data from a database record to computer memory?
   a. PUT
   b. GET
   c. GWKS
   d. PWKS
   e. READ
2. Which of the following commands transfer data from computer memory to a database record?
   a. PUT
   b. GET
   c. GWKS
   d. PWKS
   e. WRITE
3. Using Figure M5.1, write the command to generate the following menus: (Use Reply as the VP-Expert variable.)
   a. A B C
      D E
   b. No Yes
   c. Fair good
   d. 200 500
4. From Figure M5.1, what data is retrieved by the following: (Assume a WHILEKNOWN-END loop.)
   Reply = no
   a. Get Reply = Networked, wpdb, ALL
   b. Get Reply = Networked, wpdb, Cost
   c. Get Reply = Networked, wpdb, Networked
   d. Get Reply = Networked, wpdb, Word_proce
5. What data is retrieved by each of the following commands? (Assume a WHILEKNOWN-END loop and that All means the next record.)
   a. Get All, wpdb, ALL
   b. Get All, wpdb, Word_proce
   c. Get All, wpdb, Support
   d. Get All, wpdb, Cost
   e. Get All, wpdb, Networked
6. What data is retrieved by each of the following commands? (Assume a WHILEKNOWN-END loop.)
   Reply = Yes
   Answer = 200
   a. Get Reply = Networked AND Answer = Cost, wpdb, Word_Proce
   b. Get Reply = Networked OR Answer = Cost, wpdb, Word_proce
   c. Get Reply = Networked AND Answer = Cost, wpdb, Word_Proce
   d. Get Reply = Networked OR Answer = Cost, wpdb, Support.

7. From Figure M5.1, what data is retrieved by the following commands? (Assume a WHILEKNOWN-END loop.)
   a. Reply = 200
      Get Reply = Cost, wpdb, Word_proce
   b. Reply = yes
      Get Reply = Networked wpdb, Word_proce
   c. Reply = fair
      Get Reply = Support, wpdb, Word_proce
   d. Reply = E
   e. Get Reply = Word_proce, wpdb, Word_proce

Assignments

1. We need to clean up the Sample Files Disk after running Text tree traces. Place a DOS disk in the A drive and the Sample Files Disk in the B drive.
   a. To delete the trace files, enter ERASE B:*.TRC
   b. To change to the B drive, enter B:.
   c. To verify that these trace files are gone, enter DIR *.TRC.

2. Using a printout of wp8.kbs
   a. Circle the expert system variables. Draw a rectangle around the database variables.
   b. Repeat (a) for wp10.kbs.
   c. Repeat (a) for wp17.kbs.

3. Copy wp9.kbs to your Data Disk with
   copy wp9.kbs B:my9.kbs
   The new name is my9.kbs. Copy the database file wpdb.dbf to your Data Disk with
   copy wpdb.dbf B:
   The database file has the same name. Get into VP-Expert with your Data Disk in the B drive. In the editor, make these three changes.
   a. On the top line delete the letters my9.kbs and replace with my13.kbs
   b. Delete the instruction CLOSE wpdb1 with CTRL and y.
   c. Run a consultation with my13.kbs. What are the results?

4. Copy wp15.kbs and wpws.dbf to your Data Disk with
   A> Copy wp15.kbs B:my15.kbs
   A> Copy wpws.dbf B:
   Use the editor to change
   X=(X+1) to X=X+1
   a. Will the program still run correctly?
   b. Run a consultation with my15.kbs and record the results.

5. Copy wp11.kbs and wpdb.dbf to your Data Disk with
   A> copy wp11.kbs B:my11.kbs
   A> copy wpdb.dbf B:
   Using the editor, change the condition of RULE 1 to
   IF Support<>UNKNOWN
   a. Will the program still run correctly?
   b. Run a consultation with my11.kbs and record the results.

6. With wp11.kbs on your Data Disk as my11.kbs, use the editor to change the condition of RULE 1 to
   IF Kbsupport<>UNKNOWN
   a. Will the program run correctly?
   b. Run a consultation and record the results.

7. Copy wp10.kbs and wpdb.dbf to your Data Disk with
   A> copy wp10.kbs B:my10.kbs
   A> copy wpdb.dbf B:
   Add rules to the knowledge base that predict the annual maintenance cost to be 30% of the cost of networked word processors. Additional coding will be necessary.

8. Copy wp16.kbs and wpws.wks to your Data Disk with
   A> Copy wp16.kbs B:my16.kbs
   A> Copy wpws.wks B:
   Add rule(s) to the knowledge base that predict the projected annual savings to be the annual cost times
   25% for "good" networked word processors
   15% for "fair" networked word processors
   8% for all others
   Additional coding will be necessary.

9. Use the VP-Expert Help Facility to obtain a printout on each database-related instruction:
   a. WHILEKNOWN
   b. MENU
   c. GET
   d. MRESET
   e. PUT

10. Use the VP-Expert Help facility to obtain a printout on each worksheet related instruction.
    a. Subscripted variables
    b. WKS
    c. PWKS
    d. WFORMAT

Module 6

USING CONFIDENCE FACTORS

Recall that one of the features of an expert system is its ability to deal with uncertainty. From our discussion of the MYCIN expert system in Chapter 6 pages 115 to 123, one of the useful techniques for dealing with uncertainty is the use of certainty factors. Certainty factors are a measure of belief (or disbelief) or confidence in some assertion.

Like many expert system shells, VP-Expert uses certainty factors. VP-Expert uses the term confidence factor (CNF) to refer to certainty factors.

In this module, we will discuss how confidence factors are assigned to both the conditions and the conclusions of a rule. We will also examine confidence factors that are assigned to a rule. Finally, we will discuss how threshold values are used to determine if a rule is to be fixed and how the results of a consultation can be sorted with the use of confidence factors.

Confidence Factors for Rules with AND Conditions

Confidence factors for rule conditions are entered by the user during a consultation with a knowledge base. The CNF is assigned at the time the user chooses a value for a variable; the request of the user by the knowledge base is made by an ASK statement. The selected value of the variable and its assigned confidence factor are then displayed in the Facts window during the consultation.

To review an activity from Module 4 page 278, the user can enter a CNF when making a choice presented by a ASK Statement. This is accomplished by pressing the HOME key before making a selection. After the HOME key is pressed, a highlighted area will appear on the screen; then enter an integer from 0 to 100.

The number that is entered is a measeure of the level (percentage) of confidence that the user has in that selection. A value of 0 for the number indicates absolutely no confidence and a value of 100 for the number indicates complete confidence. If a value less than 40 is entered, VP-Expert assumes a lack of confidence, and this fact is so indicated.

The default value for a CNF is 100. If a selection is made with no CNF entered, then the selection has a CNF of 100.

After the CNF has been entered, pressing the ENTER key binds the indicated CNF to the chosen selection. If an error is made in entering a CNF, the process can be repeated and the new CNF value will replace the incorrect one. If an incorrect selection is made, a change in the selection will cause the old CNF to be disabled. For example, suppose that we have made the selection of "yes" with a CNF of 80 in response to a query from the consultation. We then realize that we should have selected "no." We can change the selection and, in doing so, the CNF of 80 will be deleted from the "yes" selection.

It is often the case in expert systems development that a rule will have more than one condition and that the conditions are connected with the conjunction AND. We have previously discussed this situation in Chapter 6 page 120. When VP-Expert encounters multiple conditions connected with AND, it first checks to see that all of the conditions are satisfied. If so, VP-Expert assigns a CNF to the set of conditions by using the minimum of the set of confidence factors. For example, if we have the following rule:

```
IF condition1 CNF1
AND condition2 CNF2
AND condition3 CNF3
THEN conclusion;
```

the CNF for the set of conditions would be

CNF=minimum (CNF1,CNF2,CNF3)

This technique seems intuitively reasonable since we would expect our confidence level to be no higher than the smallest CNF.

After VP-Expert has determined the CNF for the condition part of the rule, it is then concerned with the CNF of the rule as a whole. To do this, VP-Expert must inspect the CNF of the conclusion. The confidence factor of the conclusion is entered by the expert system developer when the knowledge base is developed. Determining the CNF for the conclusion is the task of either the system developer or the human expert. As with the condition confidence factors, nonspecification of a CNF causes VP-Expert to assign a CNF of 100 to the conclusion.

To calculate the CNF for the entire rule, VP-Expert uses the product of the CNF for the condition and the CNF for the conclusion. That is,

CNF(rule) = CNF(condition)CNF(conclusion)

From this example, suppose that CNF1 = 70, CNF2 = 90, CNF3 = 85, and that the CNF of the conclusion is 95. First, VP-Expert finds the CNF of the AND condition

$$\text{minimum } (70,90,85) = 70$$

Then,

$$\begin{aligned} \text{CNF(rule)} &= (70)(95) \\ &= 6650/100 \\ &= 67 \end{aligned}$$

VP-Expert divided this product by 100 (to obtain a value between 0 and 100) and rounds off, so that a CNF of 67 is assigned to the rule. Again, this seems reasonable. Since our confidence level for the condition is less than 100%, we would expect to have a lower confidence in the rule. If the CNF of the condition is 100, then the CNF of the rule is just the CNF of the conclusion. Likewise, if the CNF of the conclusion is 100, then the CNF of the rule is the same as the CNF of the condition.

Let's illustrate our discussion so far in this section by running a consultation with wp18.kbs. As before, boot up your system, and enter VP-Expert. With your Sample Files Disk in drive B, select the path as b: and the file name as wp18.kbs.

During the consultation, select "yes" for the variable Afford and assign a CNF of 85. Select "yes" for the variable Help and assign a CNF of 75. Finally, select "yes" for both the variable Time and the variable Need, but do not assign a CNF. After you have made your final selection and run the consultation, your terminal screen should look like Figure M6.1.

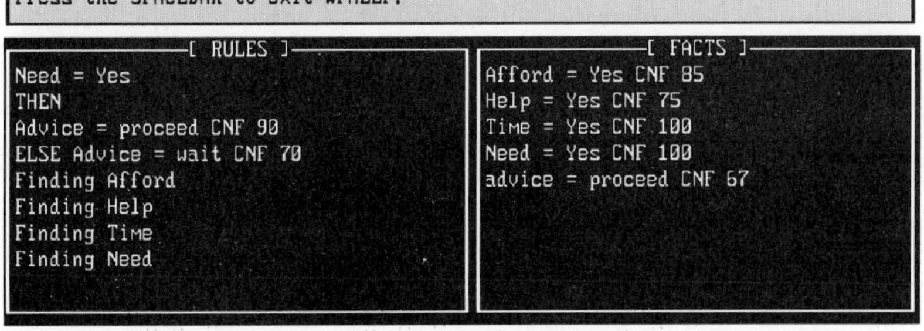

FIGURE M6.1 FINAL CONSULTATION SCREEN FOR wp18.kbs

There are several things that you should note about what you see on the screen. First, in the Consultation window, VP-Expert has advised us to proceed with a CNF of 67. This calculation was made using the CNFs that you entered.

Second, note that the CNF values that you entered for the Afford and Help variables are shown in the Facts window. You did not enter a CNF for either the Time or Need variable, so VP-Expert assigned a CNF of 100 to both of them. The calculated CNF for the rule is 67; you should verify this result by doing the calculations that we just described.

Now, run another consultation of wp18.kbs. This time, make the same selections and assign the same confidence factors for Afford (yes, 85) and Help (yes, 75) variables as in the previous consultation. This time, select "no" for the Time variable but do not assign a CNF. After making the selection for the Time variable, your screen will appear, after the consultation, as shown in Figure M6.2.

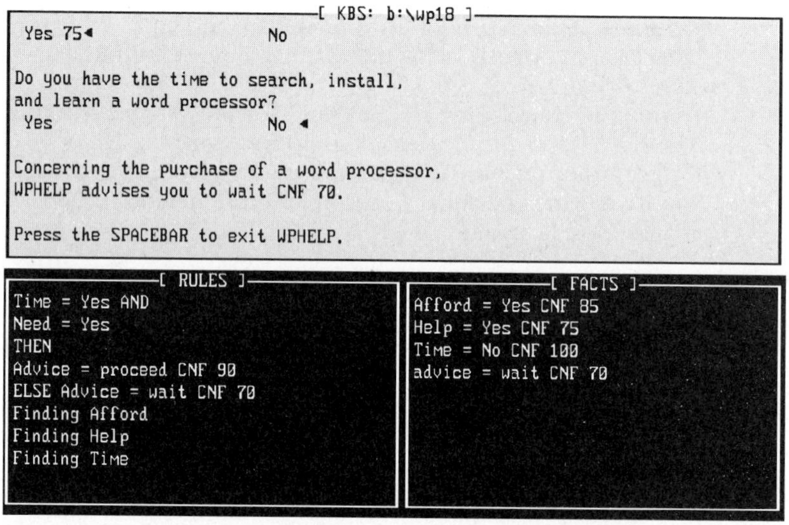

FIGURE M6.2 FINAL CONSULTATION SCREEN FOR wp18.kibs WITH TIME=NO

Several things are different about this screeen and the screen in Figure M6.1. First, VP-Expert did not ask you about the need for a word processor. The consultation ended as soon as you selected "no" for the Time variable. This happened because VP-Expert was working with a rule that had an AND condition. When you entered "no" VP-Expert interpreted the condition of the rule to be false with the result shown as "wait on the selection of the word processor." Inspecting the Rules window, you will note that the rule has an ELSE segment attached to it. Whatever is contained in the ELSE segment is concluded if the test of the condition fails, as it did in this consutlation. Note that the ELSE segment had a CNF of 70. The CNF of the result was unchanged since the CNF of the Time variable defaulted to 100.

There are three additional comments that we wish to make about wp18.kbs. To help you understand these comments, let's look at a program listing for wp18.kbs. This listing is shown in Figure M6.3.

```
!The file wp18.kbs has one compound AND
!         IF-THEN-ELSE rule
!         with confidence factors.

!ACTIONS BLOCK

ACTIONS
          DISPLAY "This expert system WPHELP will advise you whether you need to buy
a word processor soon or wait.

Press the SPACEBAR to start the consultation.~"
            CLS
            FIND advice
            DISPLAY "Concerning the purchase of a word processor, WPHELP advises
            you to {#advice}.

Press the SPACEBAR to exit WPHELP.~ "
            CLS:

!RULES BLOCK
RULE 1
IF          Afford = Yes
            AND Help=Yes
            AND Time=Yes
            AND Need=Yes
THEN        Advice=proceed CNF 90
ELSE        Advice=wait CNF 70;

!STATEMENTS BLOCK
ASK Afford : "Can you afford the money to buy a word processor at this time?";

CHOICES Afford : Yes, No;

ASK Help: "Do you have some word processing help—people, tutorials, experience,
etc.—available to you ?";

CHOICES Help: Yes, No;

ASK Time: "Do you have the time to search, install, and learn a word processor?";

CHOICES Time : Yes, No;

ASK Need : "Do you need a word processor?";

CHOICES Need : Yes, No;
```

FIGURE M6.3 PROGRAM CODE FOR wp18.kbs

First, there are four CHOICES statements, one for each variable (C1). The range of the choice is the same for each variable (yes, no). Each CHOICES statement is preceded by an ASK statement, which prompts you about making your selection.

Second, the rule in the program has a CNF assigned to both the THEN and ELSE parts of the rule (C2). Notice that the sum of the two CNFs is not 100 but is greater than 100. We discussed the rationale for this occurrence when we described the MYCIN certainty factor scheme in Chapter 6. Both of these CNF's are entered by the expert system developer and/or the human expert.

The third comment (C3) relates to the use of the # symbol in the DISPLAY statement. The use of this symbol tells VP-Expert to display the final value of the CNF when displaying its recommendation on the screen.

Confidence Factors for Rules with OR Conditions

Multiple conditions in a rule may also be connected by OR. When this occurs, VP-Expert uses a different technique to calculate the CNF of the condition. From a procedural perspective, VP-Expert checks the conditions in order. If it finds a condition that is true, it does not stop but continues to check the other condition(s).

For example, suppose we have the following rule:

```
IF A CNF1
OR B CNF2
THEN K CNF5
```

If both conditions in the rule are found to be true, then the CNF of the condition is given by

CNF1 + CNF2 − (CNF 1 * CNF2)

In the rule, suppose that CNF1 = 80, CNF2 = 60, and CNF5 = 90. For the condition, we have

CNF = 80 + 60 − (80 * 60)/100
= 140 − 48
= 92
CNF (rule) = 92 * 90 = 83

This is a result that we would have expected from our discussion in the provisions section about the final CNF of the rule.

It is possible that there may be more than two true conditions in a rule. In this case, VP-Expert uses the results of applying the OR formula to the first two conditions as a CNF to be used with the CNF of the third condition. For example if our rule looked like the following:

IF A CNF1
OR B CNF2
OR C CNF3
THEN L CNF6;

then VP-Expert would proceed as follows:

1. Calculate the CNF for A OR B.
2. Use this result with the CNF for C in the OR formula.

The result of the second step would be the CNF for the condition. If more conditions existed in the rule and were connected by OR, VP-Expert would continue to apply the formula in a similar way.

Let's illustrate this calculation with a sample knowledge base. Your system may be ready to run a consultation. If so, choose wp19.kbs as the file you wish to consult. If this is not the case, boot your system, load VP-Expert, and proceed as before (Path = b:). Choose wp19.kbs for consultation.

You will be prompted to choose none, one, or more than one Activity. As before, assign a CNF to each selection (using the HOME and ENTER keys). For this consultation, select "Letters" with CNF of 80, select "Resumes" with CNF of 70, and "Notices" with CNF 85. Press the END key. Your screen should look like Figure M6.4.

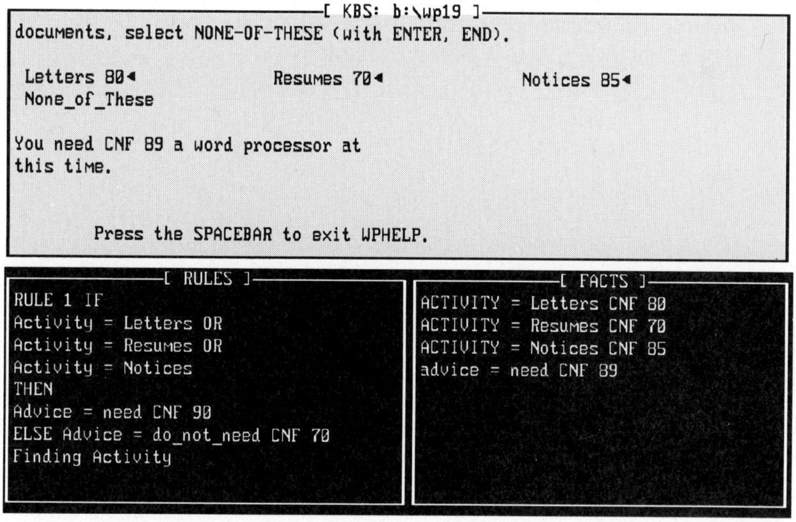

FIGURE M6.4 FINAL CONSULTATION SCREEN FOR wp19.kbs

You should note several things about this screen. As before, the CNFs which you entered for the different activities are shown in the Facts window. Second, the CNF has been calculated at 89 for the rule. How did VP-Expert arrive at this figure?

It first used the two conditions, Letter (CNF 80) and Resume (CNF 70) in the OR formula.

80 + 70 – (80 * 70)
= 150 – 56
= 94
where 56 = (80 * 70)/100.

Next, it used this result (94) with the third condition. Notice (CNF 85) in the OR formula.

94 + 85 – (94 * 85) = 99

Then

CNF (rule) = 99 * 90
= 89

Where 89 = (99 * 90)/100 with rounding.

You also may have recognized that Activity is a PLURAL variable (C1). Plural variables were discussed in Module 3 page 237. You should not assume, however, that all conditions using OR represent PLURAL variables. Indeed, it is valid to have conditions where different variables are connected with OR. In this case, VP-Expert calculates the CNF of the condition in exactly the same way, using the OR formula.

To complete our work with wp19.kbs, let's examine the program code in Figure M6.5. Some comments need to be made about the code. We have already looked at the fact that Activity is a Plural variable.

```
!The file wp19.kbs has a PLURAL variable,
!           Activity, in a compound OR IF-THEN-ELSE-BECAUSE
!           rule with confidence factors.

!ACTION BLOCK

ACTIONS
        DISPLAY "WPHELP will advise you whether you need a word processor or not.

Press the SPACEBAR to start the consultation.~"
          CLS
          FIND advice
          DISPLAY "You {#advice} a word processor at this time.
   C3
          Press the SPACEBAR to exit WPHELP.~";

!RULES BLOCK

RULE 1
IF Activity =Letters
OR Activity=Resumes                              C2
OR Activity=Notices
THEN      Advice=need CNF 90
ELSE      Advice=do_not_need CNF 70
BECAUSE"If you generate frequent letters, resumes, notices, or papers, then you need a
          word processor.";

!STATEMENTS BLOCK

ASK Activity : "Which of the following documents do you need to write for your business?

Select your answers by pressing the ENTER key. After you have made all your selections,
press the END key. If you don't need to write any of these documents, select NONE-OF-
THESE (with ENTER, END).";

CHOICES Activity : Letters, Resumes, Notices, None_of_These;

Plural : Activity;<----- C1
```

FIGURE M6.5 PROGRAM CODE FOR wp19.kbs

Our second comment concerns the THEN-ELSE part of the rule. The CNFs will come into the picture when the final CNF of the rule is calculated. In particualr, we have already seen the effect of the CNF of the THEN part of the rule in determining the final CNF for the rule. The only way that the CNF of the ELSE will be used is if the rule condition is found to be false (none of the conditions are satisfied).

Our final comment on this program pertains to the display of the final results. The use of the # symbol tells VP-Expert that the CNF of the final result is to be displayed.

Confidence Factors for Rules with AND/OR Conditions

The structure of the condition part of a rule could include the use of both the AND and OR connectives. For example, we might have a rule in the form RULE A

```
If Activity = Letter OR
  Activity = Resume AND
  Cost = low
  THEN Word_processor = D CNF 90;
```

This rule is different from the previous examples in that the condition has both AND and OR connectives. How does VP-Expert deal with the situation?

To calculate the CNF for the condition, VP-Expert takes the rule and splits it into two rules as follows:

```
Rule A1: IF Activity = Letter AND
Cost = Low
THEN Word_processor = D CNF 90;
or
Rule A2: IF Activity = Resume AND
Cost = Low
THEN word_processor = D CNF 90;
```

The AND and OR formulas are then used to calculate the CNF of the condition.

As an example, let's suppose that confidence factors have been input by the user so that the rules (after separation) appear as follows:

```
Rule A1: IF Activity = Letter CNF 90 AND
Cost = Low CNF 80
THEN Word_processor = D CNF 90;
or
Rule A2: IF Activity = resume CNF 70 AND
Cost = low CNF 80
THEN word_processor = D CNF 90;
```

VP-Expert applies the AND formula to the condition which yields a CNF of 80. The CNF for Rule A1 is then calculated as

80 * 90 = 7200/100 = 72

For Rule A2, the CNF of the condition is the minimum of 70 and 80, which is 70. The CNF for Rule 1A is then calculated as

70 * 90 = 6300/100 = 63

The CNFs for the two rules are then put into the OR formula to yield

72 + 63 − (72 * 63)
= 135 − 4536/100
= 135 − 45
= 90

Hence, the CNF of the original rule for our example is 90.

Threshold Values

VP-Expert allows the expert system developer to set a minimum, or *threshold value,* for the determination of whatever a rule condition is to be considered true. The assigned threshold value is compared to the rule condition CNF. If the condition CNF is less than the threshold value, the condition is considered false; that is, the rule condition fails.

The default value for the threshold in VP-Expert is 40 percent or CNF 40. The threshold value can be assigned **legibility** with the use of a threshold clause in the Actions block with the following format:

TRUTHTHRESH = <value>

where value is a number between 0 and 100. A threshhold value may be assigned to a particular rule by placing a TRUTHTHRESH clause after the THEN part of a value. A potential danger in assigning a threshold value to a particular rule is that all rules following that rule will also use the same threshold value which may not be desirable.

While a threshold value can cause a rule condition to fail, the threshold value does not cause a rule to fail. This is true even though the final CNF of the rule is less than the threshold value.

Let's illustrate the use of the threshold with an example. If you are at the 2Go option after running wp19.kbs, select 8Quit to return to the Main Menu, then select 6FileName and choose wp20.kbs. If you have exited form VP-Expert, return to it. At the Main Menu, select 7Path as b: and 6FileName as wp20.kbs. Now, run a consultation with wp20.kbs. When prompted, enter the following selections and associated CNF for each selection. For this example, select "Letters" with CNF 80, "Resumes" with CNF 70 and "Notices" with CNF 85, for the Activity variable. After making the selections, press END to end the consultation. Your screen should appear as in Figure M6.6.

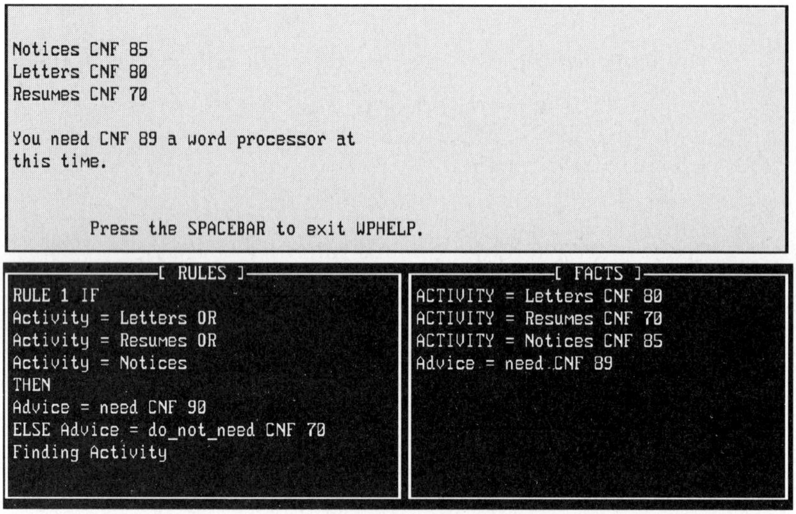

FIGURE M6.6 FINAL CONSULTATION SCREEN FOR wp20.kbs

The result of the consultation is that you need a word processor with CNF 89. (Applying the OR formaula to the rule condition yields a final CNF of 99, and the product of 99 and 90, the CNF of the conclusion, yields a final rule CNF OF 89.) Everything appears in order.

Was a threshold value used? Look at Figure M6.7, the program code for wp20.kbs. Note that there is a THRUTHTHRESH clause with a value of 85 (C1). Thus, if the condition CNF was less than 85, the rule condition would fail.

```
!The file wp20.kbs has a PLURAL variable,
!        Activity, in a compound OR IF-THEN-ELSE-BECAUSE
!        rule with confidence factor. TRUTHTHRESH and SORT
!        are also used

!ACTIONS BLOCK

ACTIONS
        DISPLAY "WPHELP will advise you whether you need a word processor or not.

Press the SPACEBAR to start the consultation.~"
          CLS
          TRUTHTHRESH = 85  <-- (C1)
                  FIND Advice
(C2) ---->      { SORT Activity
                { DISPLAY "The following documents are sorted in descending order by
                  their confidence factors.

                  {#activity}"
          DISPLAY " "
          DISPLAY "You {}advice} a word processor at this time.

          Press the SPACEBAR to exit WPHELP.~"
          CLS;

!RULES BLOCK

RULE 1
IF                Activity=Letters
                  OR Activity=Resumes
                  OR Activity=Notices
THEN              Advice=need CNF 90
ELSE              Advice=do_not_need CNF 70
BECAUSE           "If you generate frequent letters, resumes, or notices, then you need
                  a word processor.";

!STATEMENTS BLOCK

ASK Activity : "Which of the following documents do you need to produce? Select your
answer(s) by pressing the ENTER key. After you had made your selections, press the
ENTER key.
";

CHOICES Activity : Letters, Resumes, Notices, None_of_these;

Plural : Activity;
```

FIGURE M6.7 PROGRAM CODE FOR wp20.kbs

Results Sorted by Confidence Factors

When PLURAL variables are used in rules, it is often useful to be able to see a **ranking** of the variable values by their CNFs. It is then easy to see what relative weights were placed on the variable values by the user.

Our consultation with wp20.kbs illustrates this feature. Referring back to Figure M6.6, notice that the rules of the variable activity are shown in the Results window in the upper left corner. The values are ranked (sorted) by CNF from top to bottom.

This feature is invoked by the use of the SORT command. The format for the command is

SORT plural variable

It is placed in the Actions block after the FIND command (C2) as shown in Figure M6.7. The results of the sort are seen with the use of a DISPLAY statement which is shown in the declaration immediately below the SORT clause. See C2 on Figure M6.7.

Key Points

- VP-Expert makes use of the certainty factors concept through the use of confidence factors (CNF).
- Confidence factors are integers between 0 and 100 and represent a level (percentage) of confidence. CNF of 100 represents absolute confidence and a CNF if 0 represents absolutely no confidence. Most CNF values occur between the extreme values.
- Confidence factors can be assigned to rule conditions by the user by using the HOME key and entering a CNF value at the time when a value is selected for a variable during a consultation.
- If no CNF value is assigned by the user, a default value of 100 is assigned by VP-Expert.
- If there are multiple conditions connected by AND, VP-Expert assigns a final CNF for the condition by using the minimum value of the set of CNFs.
- If there are multiple conditions connected by OR, VP-Expert assigns the final CNF for the condition by using the formula CNF1 + CNF2 − (CNF1 * CNF2), where CNF1 and CNF2 are the confidence factors associated with conditional and condition2. If there are more than two conditions associated by OR, VP-Expert applies the formula to the first two conditions, uses that result with the third condition and so on.
- The confidence factor for the conclusion of a rule is entered by the expert system developer and/or the human expert.
- The final CNF for a rule is the product of the CNF for the condition and the CNF for the conclusion.

- For conditions that have both AND and OR connectives, VP-Expert splits the rule into two or more rules and applies the AND and OR formulas as appropriate.
- Threshold values for the minimum acceptable CNF for a rule condition to be true can be set by the expert system developer. The default threshold value is 20.
- The threshold value is entered with a TRUTHTHRESH clause in the Actions block or after the THEN part of an individual rule. In the latter case, all rules following the TRUTHTHRESH entry are affected.
- A rule condition can fail because of a threshold value, but the value cannot cause a rule to fail.
- The SORT clause is used to sort the values of a plural variable by the CNFs of the values in descending order.
- The SORT clause is entered in the Actions block after the FIND command.

Exercises

1. What are confidence factors?
2. What is the default value for a CNF?
3. How does VP-Expert calculate the CNF for multiple conditions connected by AND?
4. How does VP-Expert calculate the CNF for multiple conditions connected by OR?
5. What are threshold values? How are they used?
6. Why is the SORT command useful? Under what conditons is it used?
7. How is the final CNF for a rule calculated?
8. How are confidence factors entered for conditions?
9. How are confidence factors entered for conclusions?
10. Given the following rule, calculate the final CNF.
    IF A CNF 80 AND
    B CNF 70 OR
    C CNF 90
    THEN D CNF 85;
11. Calculate the condition CNF for the following rule.
    IF J CNF 60 OR
    K CNF 70 OR
    L CNF 90
    THEN M CNF 40;

Assignments

1. Copy wp18.kbs to your Data Disk as my18.kbs. Modify wp18.kbs so it has a threshold of 80. Run a consultation after the modification. What are the results?
2. Copy wp19.kbs to your Data Disk as my19.kbs. Modify my19.kbs so it can sort the plural variable values, and has a threshold value of 90. Run a consultation and enter the following CNFs.

   value CNF
   Letters 65
   Resumes 70
   Notices 75

   Describe the results of the consultation.

Module 7

IMPLEMENTING THE USER INTERFACE

An expert system is composed of three parts, the knowledge base, the inference engine, and the user interface. In this module we will concentrate on the features of VP-Expert that help us to implement and improve the user interface. Even if the knowledge base is accurate and the inference engine is flawless, an expert system without good communications between the intended user and the computer system minimizes the potential of the system.

In this module we will examine how VP-Expert formats the screen. We will see how text is displayed, how windows are created, how color can be utilized, and the potential for graphics output. Commands for effectively controlling the printer, the run-time environment, and a mouse are included. Finally in this module, we will run five new versions of old programs to describe many of the major points. We placed the program examples at the end of this module since certain commands were used before and many key points can be illustrated in one program.

Formatting the Screen Display

The *screen* is the major method of communications in most computer-based systems. How text is displayed on the screen, how the display is partitioned, and the use of color can add to the communications via the video display screen. Let's consider the display of text first.

Text Display

We have already had many examples of the use of the DISPLAY clause to send any text enclosed within quotes to the screen. Both uppercase and lowercase can be sent to the screen simply by inserting the desired text between the quotes. An appropriate mixture is necessary since the use of all uppercase text is cumbersome for the reader. More characters can be displayed than appear on the keyboard. These characters, including numerals, lowercase, uppercase, and special symbols, on IBM-compatible microcomputers use the *American Standard Code for Information Interchange (ASCII)*. This is a one to one correspondence between the numbers 0 to 255 and a set of corresponding symbols for IBM-compatible microcomputers. (Some ASCII codes are for control rather than display.)

To display a character or symbol not found on the keyboard, the CHR command is used. The CHR command is

```
CHR number, variable
```

After the command is executed, the symbol corresponding to the number is placed in the variable name. Then the DISPLAY statement can be used to print the symbol to the screen. For example,

```
CHR 65, Symbol
DISPLAY"Symbol"
```

would display A on the screen because the ASCII value of A=65. If the number in the example were 240, the equivalence symbol ≡ would appear. The complete list of symbols that can appear on the video screen is presented in the Appendices.

The DISPLAY statement has several interesting features. Values of variables can be sent to the screen by enclosing the variable within curly brackets. If a pound sign (#) is placed within the curly brackets, then the confidence factor associated with that variable is displayed to the screen. If an integer precedes the variable inside the curly brackets, then the screen will right-align that value of the variable in the designated number of spaces. The following examples illustrate these points:

```
Cost = 199.99
DISPLAY"Cost is {Cost}"        Cost is 199.99
DISPLAY"Cost is ${Cost}"       Cost is $199.99
DISPLAY"Cost is ${#Cost}"      Cost is $199.99 CNF 95
DISPLAY"Cost is ${8Cost}'      Cost is $   199.99
```

The FORMAT command can be used to change the formatting of the display of a numeric value of a variable. If

```
FORMAT Cost,7.3
```

were issued, then the DISPLAY command would yield

```
199.990
```

The first number after Cost identifies the number of places (including the decimal point) and the last number tells how many of the places are to the right of the decimal. In our example, of the 7 places, three are to the right of the decimal.

The DISPLAY clause has another interesting option. If there is a tilde (~) at the end of the string before the last quote, then the system will pause until the user presses a key. This is useful in scrolling long screens of text at the display terminal. We have used this option in the DISPLAY clause many times.

The placement of the text from a DISPLAY clause is important. In general, the display format of a screen is 25 rows by 80 columns. The choice of forty columns is also available on the IBM-PC. The video screen is laid out with 0,0 as the upper left corner and 24,79 as the lower right corner. If position x,y is on the screen, then x stands for the number of rows down, and y indicates the number of columns across. This is shown in Figure M7.1.

The other corners of the screen are 24,0 (lower left) and, 0,79 (upper right). The WOPEN and LOCATE commands will help us place text where we want it on the video screen.

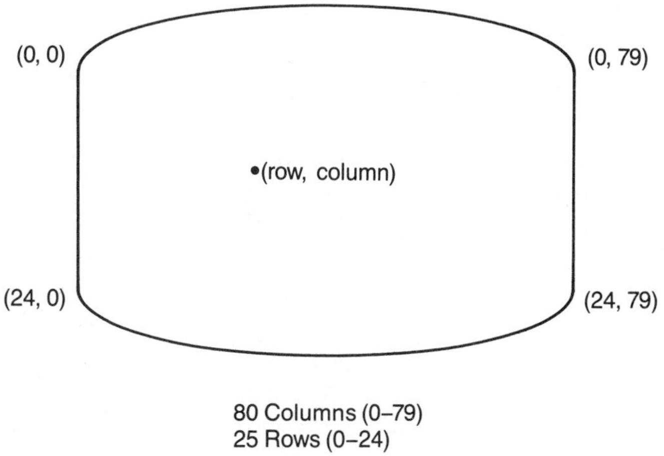

FIGURE M7.1 SCREEN LAYOUT FOR TEXT MODE

Windows

Windows, or rectangular boxes, are one effective way of organizing the layout of a screen. You have already seen the effective use of three windows one each for the Consultation, Rules, and Facts windows from the Main Menu. These boxes or windows help to organize the arrangement of information on the screen. VP-Expert has several commands, WOPEN, ACTIVE, and LOCATE, to facilitate the windowing effects for the user interface. Windows allow the screen to be partitioned in almost any arrangement. Consider the different window configurations in Figure M7.2.

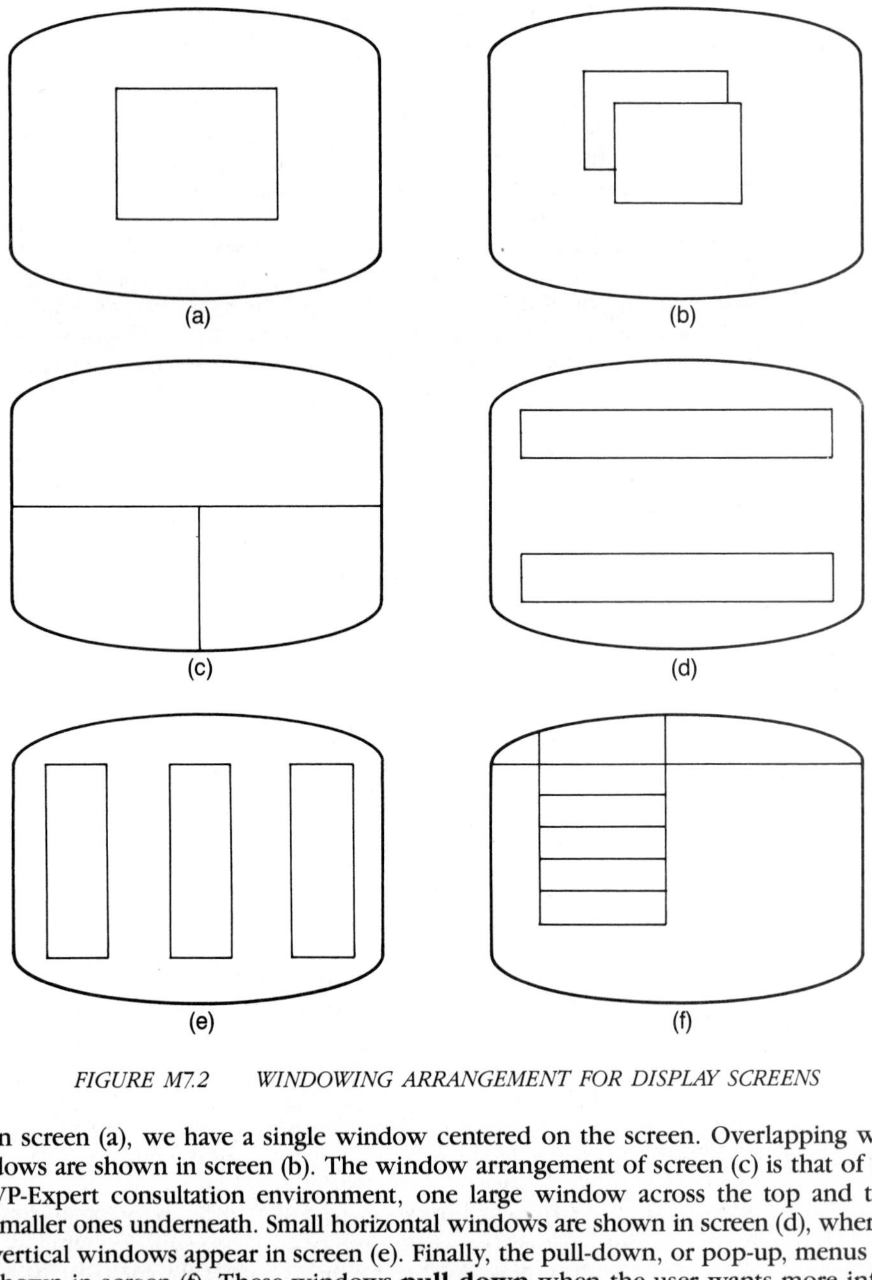

FIGURE M7.2 WINDOWING ARRANGEMENT FOR DISPLAY SCREENS

In screen (a), we have a single window centered on the screen. Overlapping windows are shown in screen (b). The window arrangement of screen (c) is that of the VP-Expert consultation environment, one large window across the top and two smaller ones underneath. Small horizontal windows are shown in screen (d), whereas vertical windows appear in screen (e). Finally, the pull-down, or pop-up, menus are shown in screen (f). These windows **pull down** when the user wants more information. There are many such arrangements of windows that could be designed for the interface to an expert system.

VP-Expert allows up to 9 windows on the screen at one time. To create a window, the WOPEN clause with the following parameters is used:

WOPEN window#,
row-start,
column-start,
number of rows,
number of columns,
background-color#

For example, WOPEN 1,4,6,8,30,background-color# would draw a window number 1 with its upper left-hand corner at 4,6. The window would be 8 rows deep and 30 columns wide. (Color will be discussed later.) The window is illustrated in Figure M7.3.

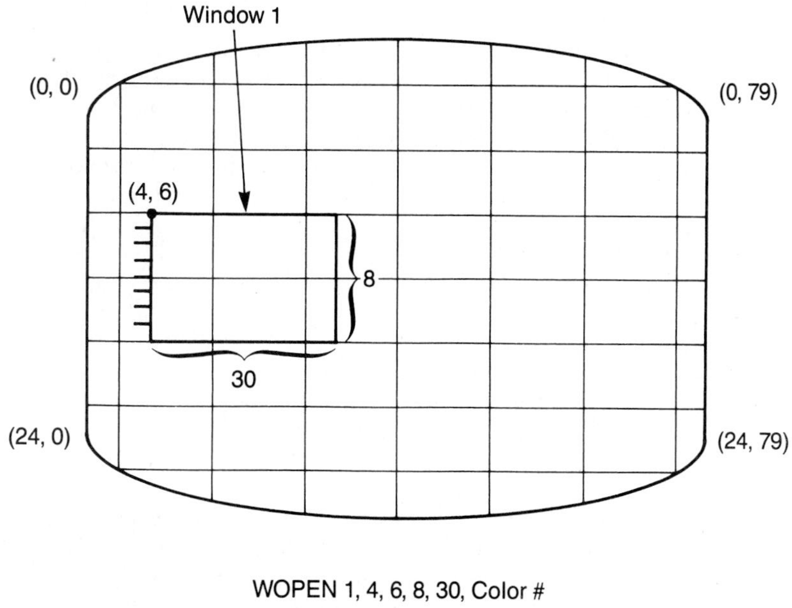

FIGURE M7.3 THE WINDOW CREATED BY WOPEN 1,4,6,8,30,Color#

The window numbers can range from 1 to 9. Nothing other than the background color can be displayed inside the window until the ACTIVE clause is executed. The format of the clause is

ACTIVE window#

Only one window can be active at a time even though several may be on the display screen at one time. A WOPEN clause for window 1 must precede a corresponding ACTIVE clause for window 1.

Once a WOPEN and ACTIVE clauses (with the same window number) have been executed, then the LOCATE command can be used to position the display of text within the active window. The format for this command is

LOCATE row-number, column-number

These two numbers are relative to the corner of the active window. For example LOCATE 2,3 from WOPEN in Figure M7.3 would locate any displayed text at two rows down and three columns across from 4,6. In other words, the text from a subsequent DISPLAY statement would start at 6,9 (counting from 0,0). This is helpful in placing text on the desired position on the screen. Unfortunately, when the inference engine uses the ASK statements, we have no control over this display except for blanks and similar markings inside the quotes.

Color

Whether *color* can be added to the user interface depends on the availability of a board (hardware) inside the microcomputer. This hardware is sometimes called a video adapter, graphics board, or graphics adapter. If your consultations have been in color, then there is a graphics adapter. If you do not have color display, then your screen display is white letters on a black background, or amber or green on a black background. Text that involves color will be displayed as black/white on a noncolor system.

There are several **de facto** standards that have evolved over the past five years in graphics adapters. They are listed below:

Color Graphics Adapter (CGA)
Enhanced Graphics Adapter (EGA)
Video Graphics Adapter (VGA)
Hercules Graphics Card

Even though there are many more types of hardware graphics borads, these are the most common. Unfortunately, each board works differently. The first three in the list are from International Business Machines (IBM) and are listed in ascending order of capability. Since the CGA has been around the longest, we shall make some comments on this adapter relative to VP-Expert.

The CGA allows color and text to be displayed in both 25 by 80 and 25 by 40 modes. You have a choice of 8 background colors and 16 foreground colors. A background color can be thought of as the color of the writing surface (display screen) and the foreground color is the color of the pen or ink used to write letters on the screen. If one selects the foreground and background color to be the same, then the text on the screen is invisible (useful for entering passwords). The color names and numbers are given in the following table.

Color Number	Foreground Color	Background Color
0	Black	Black
1	Blue	Blue
2	Green	Green
3	Cyan	Cyan
4	Red	Red
5	Magenta	Magenta
6	Brown	Brown
7	White	White
8	Gray	
9	Light Blue	
10	Light Green	
11	Light Cyan	
12	Light Red	
13	Light Magenta	
14	Yellow	
15	Light White	

Since the monitors, or video screens, vary in quality and contrast, red on one screen may not appear as the same red on another screen. There are two commands to set the background and foreground colors in Text mode. They are

```
BKCOLOR = background-color# (0-7)
  COLOR = foreground-color# (0-15)
```

The two clauses BKCOLOR = 0 and COLOR = 14 would write yellow letters on a black background. Be sure to check the physical appearance of the colors on the screen for the user. Certain combinations are difficult to read. Yellow or white on blue or black usually gives a good constrast. Of course, no colored text is seen on the foreground until a DISPLAY statement is executed. Windows on the screen can have different background colors, as you have seen in the consultation runs with VP-Expert.

Graphics

Graphics is another potential enhancement to the user interface. By *graphics* we mean the ability to draw circles, lines, polygons, and so on, at the screen. This is more than simply putting characters on the screen. Instead of controlling characters at the screen, we need to control finer portions of the screen called pixel elements or *pixels*. The more pixels, the better the quality of the displayed graphic. Text can also be displayed in Graphics mode. Text and Graphics modes are sometimes confused. Therefore, we shall call Text Graphics the mode where the computer can display symbols and letters, and Graphics modes those where the computer can draw lines, circles, polygons, and so on (pixel control), **in addition** to displaying text. Be careful how technical references refer to **graphics**.

How does the computer display graphics (pixels) at the screen? The answer depends on the graphics board. For example, on the CGA there are two commonly used graphics modes: 320 columns by 200 rows (Medium Resolution) and 640 columns by 200 rows (High Resolution). The Medium-Resolution mode allows only certain sets of four colors to be displayed at one time, whereas High-Resolution mode allows one color and black. The natures of Graphics modes and applications have to be carefully matched. There is a general trade off between resolution (number of pixels) and number of available colors for screen display (at one time).

The command for invoking a Graphics mode with the proper adapter is given by the clause

GMODE setting#

The GMODE setting numbers are illustrated in Figure M7.4 with setting descriptions and codes for adaptors.

		Adapter					
Setting	Description	MDA	CGA	MCGA	EGA	VGA	HGC
−1	restores screen to original mode	✓	✓	✓	✓	✓	✓
0	40 × 25 [text], 16 grey	✓	✓	✓	✓	✓	
1	40 × 25 [text], 16/8 color		✓	✓	✓	✓	
2	80 × 25 [text], 16 gray	✓	✓	✓	✓	✓	✓
3	80 × 25 [text], 16/8 color		✓	✓	✓	✓	
4	320 × 200 [graphics], 4 color		✓	✓	✓	✓	
5	320 × 200 [graphics], 4 gray		✓	✓	✓	✓	
6	640 × 200 [graphics], BW		✓	✓	✓	✓	
7	80 × 25 [text], BW	✓	✓	✓	✓	✓	✓
8	720 × 348 [graphics], BW for HGC						✓
13	320 × 200 [graphics], 16 color		✓	✓	✓	✓	
14	640 × 200 [graphics], 16 color			✓	✓	✓	
15	640 × 350 [graphics], BW				✓	✓	
16	640 × 350 [graphics], 4 or 16 color				✓	✓	
17	640 × 480 [graphics], BW				✓	✓	
18	640 × 480 [graphics], 16 color					✓	
19	320 × 200 [graphics], 256 color			✓		✓	

Adapter Code	Description
MDA	Monochrome Display Adapter
CGA	Color Graphics Adapter
MCGA	MultiColor Graphics Array
EGA	Enhanced Graphics Adapter
VGA	Video Graphics Array
HGC	Hercules Graphics Card

FIGURE M7.4 THE GMODE SETTING NUMBERS

Once a GMODE command is executed, there are a host of commands that can be used to draw rectangles, lines, polygons, and other drawing primitives. These graphics can enhance the visual display screen of the user interface. A special graphics library, VP-Graphics, can be added to the VP-Expert system for producing drawings and other presentation graphics.

Together, text, windows, color, and graphics can all be used to format the screen display for more effective communications in an expert system application.

Controlling the Printer

The *printer* should not be forgotten in implementing a user interface. The availability of printouts for needed information is a vital part of a useful business system. VP-Expert has four commands

PRINTON
PRINTOFF
PDISPLAY
EJECT

to help control the printing of needed information. We have already used the first two clauses: PRINTON and PRINTOFF. The clause PRINTON will cause all display statements to be sent to the printer until a PRINTOFF clause is encountered. The DISPLAY statements are also still sent to the screen. The text following an ASK statement is not sent to the printer. A message within the program code telling the user to check to be sure the printer is on is required.

The PDISPLAY will send any text found in quotes to the printer and not the screen. PDISPLAY does for the printer what DISPLAY does for the screen. The last command, EJECT, will cause the printer to eject a page or **roll up the paper** until the top of the next page is found. You need this feature when your printout ends in the middle of a page. You can see that attention to these small details in a business application will help the user interface.

Controlling the Run-time Environment

Another part of the user interface is the *run-time environment* for the expert system. Previously, we have been running our consultations by accessing the Consult Menu from the Main Menu. We can make this easier for the user by hiding some of these consultation features. There are three commands

EXECUTE
RUNTIME
ENDOFF

that help control the run-time environment. These three statements are placed before the Actions block, and each is followed by a semicolon. The EXECUTE statement will allow the user to run a selected file from the 4Consult option of the Main Menu. You do not have to enter 2Go of the Consult Menu to run a consultation. When the consultation is over, the EXECUTE command returns the user to the operating prompt A>, rather than the Main Menu. The RUNTIME statement, which we have already used, will turn off the Results and Facts windows for the consultation. Both of these commands are useful for the user of the program. We have used the windows from the inferences engine because we were interested in learning how an expert system works and how to create one. Many people, however, only want to run a consultation, not create one.

The third statement, ENDOFF, can be used to change the method of selecting an answer to a question through the keyboard. You can use ENDOFF for any question except one involving a PLURAL variable. If only one selection is to be made as the answer to a question, ENDOFF will turn off the need to press the END key. To make a selection, you may simply select your reply and press the ENTER key. The END key is no longer required. These three statements, EXECUTE, RUNTIME, and ENDOFF, can enhance our user interface to the expert system application.

Using a Mouse

A *mouse* is an alternative input, or control device, for the keyboard. Physically, it is a small device that is attached to your computer system. The mouse allows you to move the cursor around on the screen rather than using the arrow keys. To make a selection from a list or menu on the screen, you move the mouse on a table surface until the cursor is on the desired item, then you click, or select, the designated entry. A mouse is faster to use than keyboard arrow keys, but it adds an additional expense and is cumbersome for applications requiring extensive data entry. However, of all the possible input devices, the mouse has become the second most important input device (after the keyboard).

If you have a mouse connected to your computer system, you can use the VP-Expert commands that let you use the mouse for selecting; thus, replacing typing from the keyboard. The following commands help you to incorporate the use of a mouse in your user interface:

BUTTON
GETMOUSE
MOUSEON
MOUSEOFF
MOUSEX
MOUSEY

You can find detailed information on each of these commands in the Help facility of VP-Expert.

Exploring Examples

We will now run some sample programs to illustrate the points that we have made with VP-Expert commands. Get into VP-Expert at the A drive and place the Sample Files Disk in the B drive. Our first sample program will display some ASCII characters to the screen. Set the 7Path to b: and select wp21 for the 6FileName. After the consultation, obtain a printout of the program code for wp21.kbs. At the end of the consultation, your screen should appear as Figure M7.5.

```
The ASCII value for    50 is  2
The ASCII value for    51 is  3
The ASCII value for    52 is  4
The ASCII value for    53 is  5
The ASCII value for    54 is  6
The ASCII value for    55 is  7
The ASCII value for    56 is  8
The ASCII value for    57 is  9
The ASCII value for    58 is  :
The ASCII value for    59 is  ;
The ASCII value for    60 is  <
The ASCII value for    61 is  =
The ASCII value for    62 is  >
The ASCII value for    63 is  ?
The ASCII value for    64 is  @
The ASCII value for    65 is  A

         Press the SPACEBAR to exit WPHELP.

1Help     2Go      3WhatIf   4Variable 5Rule     6Set      7Edit     8Quit
1Help 2How? 3Why? 4Slow 5Fast 6Quit
```

FIGURE M7.5 ASCII CHARACTERS FROM 50 TO 65 FROM wp21.kbs

These symbols are the printable characters from 50 to 65. If you examine the program for wp21.kbs (Figure M7.6), you will see some interesting programming structures.

```
!The file wp21.kbs will print the ASCII characters
!                  from 50 to 65.
                   RUNTIME;
ACTIONS
                   DISPLAY "This expert system WPHELP will display
ASCII characters from 50 to 65.

Press the SPACEBAR to start the consultation.~"
                   CLS
                   FOR X = 50 to 65
                        CHR @X,Character
                        DISPLAY "The ASCII value for {5X} is {3Character}"
                   END
                   DISPLAY"
                        Press the SPACEBAR to end the consultation.~";
                   CLS;
```

FIGURE M7.6 PROGRAM CODE FOR DISPLAYING ASCII CHARACTERS (wp21.kbs)

Comment 1 is the CHR command. Notice that we placed the at symbol (@) in front of the variable X, which stands for a number. From C2 you can see the numbers (5 and 3) before the variables in the DISPLAY statement. These numbers tell how many spaces are provided for the display of the variables. Comment 3 identifies a new loop. The loop starts at the value 50 and continues until the value is past 65. One is added to the variable X by the system at the END of the loop. In other words, this addition is not coded inside the loop (as the WHILEKNOWN loop does). Comment 4 focuses our attention on the ending messge to the user. This message along with the tilde (~) keeps the displayed ASCII characters on the screen until the user presses the SPACEBAR. Without the last DISPLAY with a tilde, the screen would return to the Main Menu so fast that you could not read it. The tilde in the DISPLAY statement is an easy way to scroll through paragraphs of text or screen displays.

The RUNTIME statement above the Actions block (C5) removes the Rules and Facts window during a consultation. This statement is most useful after an expert system has been debugged and the system is ready for the user.

Let's run a consultation with a window. Exit the Consult Menu and select wp22.kbs from the 6FileName option. Run the consultation and obtain a printout of the code. We have eliminated the EXECUTE statement so the consultation ends at the Consult Menu. The last Consultation screen for wp22.kbs is shown in Figure M7.7.

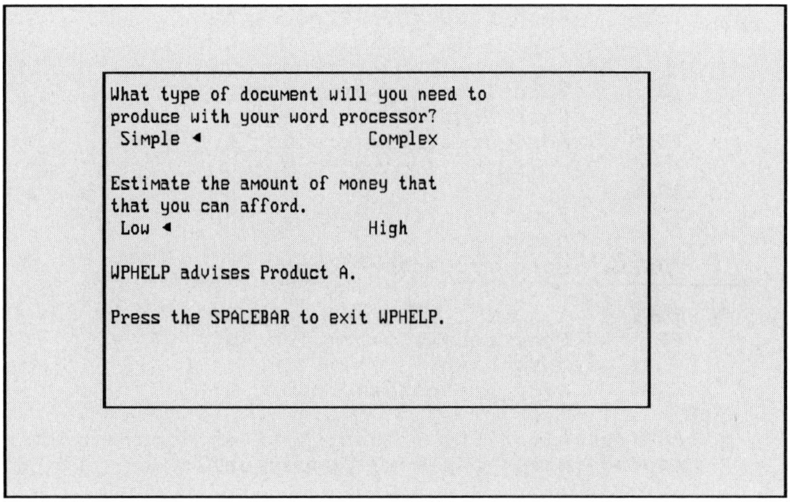

FIGURE M7.7 LAST CONSULTATION SCREEN FOR wp22.kbs

If you have color, the border is green, and the window is blue (background color) with light red (foreground color) letters. The program code for producing this window is detailed in Figure M7.8.

```
!The file wp22.kbs is wpl.kbs with a different
!      user interface using color and a
!      window for a run-time environment.

C1     RUNTIME;
       ENDOFF;
ACTIONS
C2     WOPEN 1, 3, 10, 15, 55, 1
       ACTIVE 1
       COLOR=12                C3
       LOCATE 3, 5
       DISPLAY "WPHELP will advise you on word processing."
       LOCATE  5, 5
       DISPLAY"Press the SPACEBAR to start the consultation.~"
       CLS
       FIND Word_processor                             C4
       DISPLAY "WPHELP advises {word_processor}."
       DISPLAY " "
       DISPLAY "Press the SPACEBAR to exit WPHELP.~"
       WCLOSE 1
       CLS;
```

(continued on page 366)

```
RULE 1
IF      Functionality=simple AND
        Cost=low
THEN    Word_processor=Product_A;

RULE 2
IF      Functionality=simple AND
        Cost=high
THEN    Word_processor=Product_A;

RULE 3
IF      Functionality=complex AND
        Cost=low
THEN    Word_processor=none;

RULE 4
IF      Functionality=complex AND
        Cost=high
THEN    Word_processor=Product_B;

ASK Functionality : "What type of document will you need to
produce with your word processor?";

CHOICES Functionality : Simple, Complex;

ASK Cost : "Estimate the amount of money that
that you can afford.";

CHOICES Cost : Low, High;
```

FIGURE M7.8 PROGRAM CODE FOR A WINDOW (wp22.kbs)

From Comment 1, note the use of the RUNTIME and ENDOFF statements for controlling the run-time environment. The RUNTIME turned off the Results and Facts windows, while the ENDOFF determined the ENTER key to be the only key needed to select answers to questions. In Comment 2, we point out that Window 1 was opened, made active, and then closed. In the WOPEN clause, the 1 indicates Window 1. The next two parameters (3 and 10) tell us that the upper left-hand corner of the window is 3,10. The next number (15) indicates that Window 1 is 15 rows deep and the next parameter (55) says that Window 1 is 55 columns wide. The last parameter (1) tells us that the background color of Window 1 is blue.

This window is where all our text is displayed in the COLOR=12 clause after the ACTIVE clause sets the text color to light red. In Comment 3 we show the use of the LOCATE command to position the light red text inside the active window. The tilde is necessary in the last DISPLAY statement, Comment 4, so that the screen stays visible for the user.

Our next example will show how we utilize two windows in the user interface. Select wp23 from 6FileName. Run this consultation and then obtain a printout of the program code. The last Consultation screen for wp23.kbs appears in Figure M7.9.

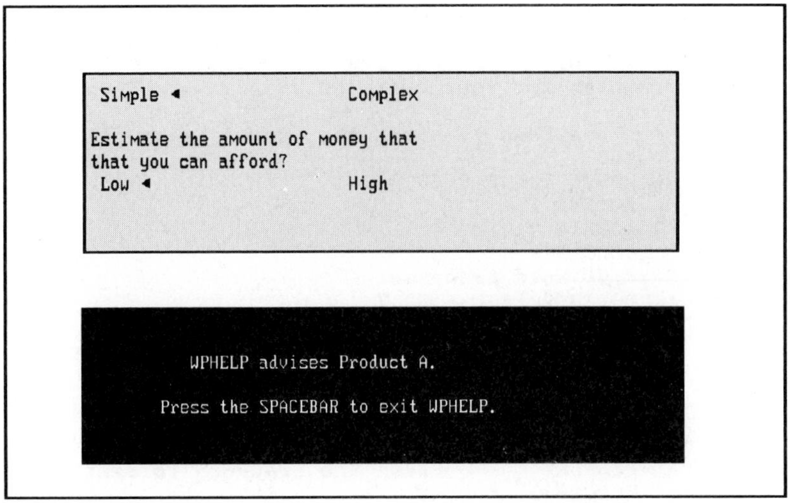

FIGURE M7.9 LAST CONSULTATION SCREEN FOR wp23.kbs

This program advises us on which word processors to select based on type of document and cost. The user interface has two windows, one for messages between the user and expert system, and the other for the advice from the consultation. The two windows partition the display screen horizontally. The program code is detailed in Figure M7.10.

```
! The file wp23.kb uses 2 windows.

        ENDOFF;
        RUNTIME;
ACTIONS
        DISPLAY "This expert system WPHELP will advise you on selecting
a word processor for your IBM compatible
microcomputer for your business.

Press the SPACEBAR to start the consultation.~"
         CLS
C1 ----> WOPEN 1,3,8,8,60,9
         ACTIVE 1
         LOCATE 2,0
         COLOR=7
         FIND Word_processor
C2 ----> WOPEN 2,14,8,6,60,7
         ACTIVE 2
         COLOR=9
         LOCATE 1,10
         DISPLAY "WPHELP advises {word_processor}.
         "
         LOCATE  3,7
         DISPLAY "      Press the SPACEBAR to exit WPHELP.~"
         WCLOSE 1
         WCLOSE 2
         CLS;

RULE 1
IF       Functionality=simple AND
         Cost=low
THEN     Word_processor=Product_A;

RULE 2
IF       Functionality=simple AND
         Cost=high
THEN     Word_processor=Product_A;

RULE 3
IF       Functionality=complex AND
         Cost=low
THEN     Word_processor=none;

RULE 4
IF       Functionality=complex AND
         Cost=high
THEN     Word_processor=Product_B;

ASK Functionality : "What type of document will you need to
produce with your word processor?";

CHOICES Functionality : Simple, Complex;

ASK Cost : "Estimate the amount of money that

that you can afford?";

CHOICES Cost : Low, High;
```

FIGURE M7.10 PROGRAM CODE FOR TWO WINDOWS (wp23.kbs)

From Comment 1 we see that Window 1 (for questions to the user) is opened, made active, and that text is located inside. The advice window, Window 2, is then made active (C2), and the results of the consultation are displayed. In the WOPEN clause of C1, Window 1 has its upper left-hand corner at 3,8 and is 8 rows deep and 60 columns wide. The background color (9) is light blue. Note that the clause COLOR=7 sets the text in Window 1 to white. From the WOPEN of C2, we conclude that Window 2 is located at 14,8 and is 6 rows deep and 60 columns wide. From the 7 in this WOPEN clause and the clause COLOR=9, we note the background and foreground colors in Window 2 are the reverse of Window 1. Even though two windows appear on the screen, note that you can only write to one at a time. The last ACTIVE clause identifies where the text from the DISPLAY statement is written.

Our next sample run will show us the use of **overlapping** windows in a consultation. Run wp24.kbs and then obtain a printout of the code. This consultation will retrieve word processing information from the database file wpdb.dbf.

The last Consultation screen is displayed in Figure M7.11. The questions and messages to the user are in the upper left and the results of the consultation on the right. We asked for word processors with good technical support, and displayed the entire record of each in the right window. The user was also told to turn the printer on for a hard copy of the results.

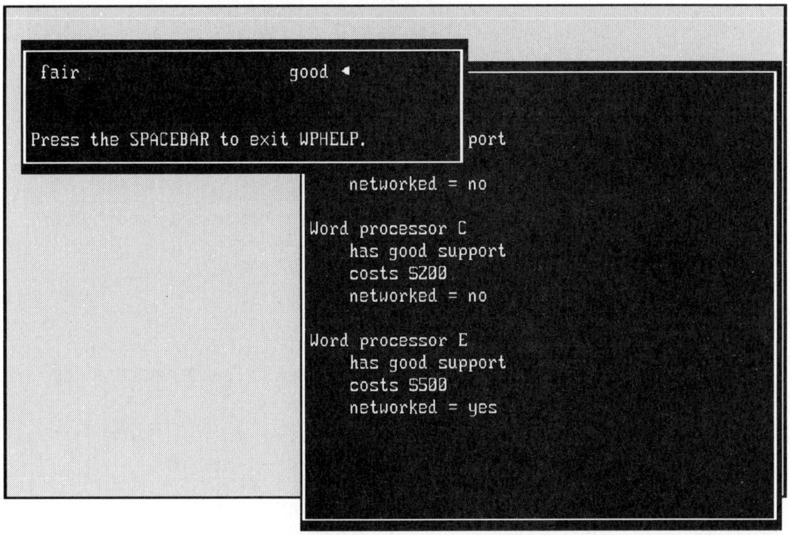

FIGURE M7.11 LAST CONSULTATION SCREEN FOR wp24.kbs

When we examine the program code (Figure M7.12), we again see the opening of two windows and the switching between the two windows. This is indicated in Comment 1 and 2. In C1, we open both windows. Window 1 has a background color of cyan (3) and Window 2 has a background color of white (7). In C2, Window 1 is made active with text in red (4), whereas Window 2 will have text in black (0). Note that there are 3 ACTIVE clauses so that text is written to Window 1, then Window 2, and then Window 1 again. This is why the last message appears in the first window. In C3 we find the EJECT clause which causes your printer paper to move to the top of the next page. This allows you to tear off your report without having to realign the printer.

```
!The file wp24.kbs will access information
!        from a database file called wpdb.dbf.
!        The field names in the database file are:
!        Word_proce, Networked, Support, Cost
!        Overlapping windows will be used.

          ENDOFF;
          RUNTIME;
ACTIONS
          DISPLAY "This expert system WPHELP will display
information from a database file. Be sure that
the printer is on.

Press the SPACEBAR to start the consultation.~"
          CLS
          PRINTON
         {WOPEN 1,2,2,5,44,3
  C1 --> {WOPEN 2,3,30,20,48,7

         {ACTIVE 1
         {COLOR=4
         {MENU List, ALL, wpdb, Support
  C2     {FIND List

         {ACTIVE 2
         {COLOR=0
          WHILEKNOWN Support
               GET List=Support,wpdb,ALL
               RESET Screen
 C3            FIND Screen
          END
          EJECT
          PRINTOFF       C1
          ACTIVE 1 <--
          DISPLAY "Press the SPACEBAR to exit WPHELP.~"
          CLS;

RULE 1
          IF Support <> UNKNOWN
          THEN Screen = Yes
                DISPLAY" "
                DISPLAY"Word processor {Word_proce} "
                DISPLAY"    has {Support} support"
                DISPLAY"    costs ${Cost}"
                DISPLAY"    networked = {Networked}"
          ELSE Screen = No;

ASK List :  "What kind of technical support do you
want for your word processor?";
```

FIGURE M7.12   PROGRAM CODE WITH WINDOWS AND PRINTER OUTPUT (wp24.kbs)

One more example is appropriate. If you have a color adapter, then program wp25 will let you select the background color that you want for your consultation run. If you do not have a graphics adapter, you will see only black and white. Run the consultation and obtain a copy of the program code.

Program wp25 advises you on selecting a word processor according to Functionality and Cost. After the opening screen, however, the color numbers appear on the display as shown in Figure M7.13.

```
What color do you want your background screen?
(The foreground color is set to white.)
Enter a number from the list:

          0 for Black

          1 for Blue

          2 for Green

          3 for Light Blue

          4 for Red

          5 for Magenta

          6 for Brown

          7 for White
█
```

FIGURE M7.13 CONSULTATION SCREEN FROM wp25.kbs

The user is to select the number of the desired color. The screen shows white text (7) on a blue background (1). If the user chooses white for the background, then almost nothing will appear at the screen, except certain words and colors controlled in the text of the ASK statement by the inference engine. After the selection is made, the screen changes color, and the consultation proceeds with a screen as selected. The program code for this consultation run (Figure M7.14) shows how we control color in text mode.

```
!The file wp25.kbs lets the user set the background color
!       for a WPHELP consultation.

        ENDOFF;
        RUNTIME;
ACTIONS
        WOPEN 1,0,0,24,79,1      C1
        ACTIVE 1
        COLOR=7
        DISPLAY "This expert system WPHELP will advise you on selecting
a word processor for your IBM compatible
microcomputer in your business.

Press the SPACEBAR to start the consultation.~"
         CLS
  C2     FIND Screen                  C3
         WCLOSE 1
         WOPEN 2,0,0,24,79,@Screen
         ACTIVE 2
         FIND Word_processor
         DISPLAY "WPHELP advises {word_processor}.
         "
         DISPLAY "      Press the SPACEBAR to exit WPHELP.~"
         WCLOSE 2
         CLS;

RULE 1
IF       Functionality=simple AND
         Cost=low
THEN     Word_processor=Product_A;

RULE 2
IF       Functionality=simple AND
         Cost=high
THEN     Word_processor=Product_A;

RULE 3
IF       Functionality=complex AND
         Cost=low
THEN     Word_processor=none;

RULE 4
IF       Functionality=complex AND
         Cost=high
THEN     Word_processor=Product_B;

ASK Functionality : "What type of document do you need to
prepare with your word processor?";

CHOICES Functionality : Simple, Complex;

ASK Cost:"Estimate the amount of money that
you can afford?";
           •
           •
           •
```

FIGURE M7.14 PARTIAL PROGRAM CODE FOR SELECTING BACKGROUND COLOR IN TEXT MODE (wp25.kbs)

From C1 we can see that the foreground color is white (7) and the background color (from WOPEN) is blue (1). The search for the desired new background color is identified with (C2) FIND Screen. The inference engine takes over and sends the text of the corresponding ASK statement to the screen. This value of the background color number is stored in the variable called Screen. In C3 we read that @Screen holds the user's choice and is the last parameter in the WOPEN clause. The consultation then proceeds with the new background color for the display screen. The foreground, or writing color, is still white. You may note from C3 that we opened a window as large as possible (80 columns by 25 rows) to override the settings by VP-Expert.

Thus, we have explored commands to control the screen, the printer, the run-time environment, color, graphics, and a mouse. We ran sample programs to illustrate the methods by which VP-Expert allows you to implement the user interface. If you have not read the guidelines in Chapter 7, we suggest that you do.

So far in the modules we have discussed in detail the implementation of the three major components of an expert system, the knowledge base, the inference engine, and the user interface. None of the three parts can be neglected if you are to design and implement a workable and usable expert system. In the next and last module, we will discuss additional commands that you can use to implement an entire system.

Key Points

- The user interface is one of the three major components of an expert system.
- The user interface is the total communications interface between the user and the expert system. The user interface is concerned with screen design, text, color, graphics, printer output, and alternative input or output devices.
- Text can be output to the screen with the DISPLAY clause. For displaying variable values, various parameters in this clause can format the size of the field or output the CNF associated with the value.
- For IBM microcomputers, there is a one-to-one association between symbols and numbers (0-255). This correspondence is called the American Standard Code for Information Interchange (ASCII) and can be displayed using the CHR command.
- Windows are rectangular regions of the display screen. Various arrangements of multiple windows on the video display can aid in the organization of information during a consultation.
- Windows can be created with the WOPEN clause. Text can be written within a given window after an ACTIVE clause is executed followed by LOCATE and DISPLAY commands.
- If a microcomputer system has a graphics board, then color can be utilized in the user interface. There are numbers associated with the background color and the foreground color. The BKCOLOR and COLOR commands are used to set these colors (for Text modes).

- Graphics can be utilized in the user interface. Graphics consist of circles, lines, polygons, and so on, in addition to text. To utilize graphics, use the GMODE command and the appropriate command to draw the graphic.
- IBM graphics boards include the Computer Graphics Adapter (CGA), the Enhanced Graphics Adapter (EGA), and the Video Graphics Adapter (VGA).
- Printing in VP-Expert can be controlled with the PRINTON, PRINTOFF, PDISPLAY, and EJECT commands.
- Three commands, EXECUTE, RUNTIME, and ENDOFF, can improve the run-time environment for the user of an expert system.
- There are a group of commands within VP-Expert to support a mouse for user input to an expert system.
- VP-Graphics is an add-on library to support presentation graphics in the user interface for VP-Expert applications.

Exercises

1. What is displayed to the screen from each of the following:

   Cost = 324

   a. DISPLAY "The Cost is {Cost}."
   b. DISPLAY "{Cost} is the cost."
   c. DISPLAY "The Cost is {10 Cost}."
   d. DISPLAY "The Cost is ${10 Cost.}"
   e. DISPLAY "The Cost is {# Cost}."

2. Using the ASCII table from the Appendices, enter the number that is associated with each of the following symbols.

   a. ? ________
   b. Q ________
   c. g ________
   d. 3 ________

3. Using the ASCII table in the Appendices, enter the symbol that is associated with each of these numbers.

   a. 27 ________
   b. 77 ________
   c. 127 ________
   d. 177 ________

4. In the following clause

   WOPEN 1,2,3,4,5,6

   a. which number identifies the background color?
   b. which two numbers give the row and column coordinates of the upper left-hand corner of the window?
   c. which number identifies the window number?
   d. which two numbers determine the width (rows) and length (columns) for the window?

5. Which of the following commands opens a window across the bottom half of your screen?
   a. WOPEN 3, 0, 40, 12, 7
   b. WOPEN 3, 10, 10, 40 12, 7
   c. WOPEN 3, 39, 12, 12, 40, 7
   d. WOPEN 3, 10, 0, 10, 40, 7
6. Given the clause
   WOPEN 9,3,4,12,20,8
   what are the coordinates of
   a. the upper left-hand corner?
   b. the lower left-hand corner?
   c. the upper right-hand corner?
   d. the lower right-hand corner?
7. Given WOPEN 3,7,6,4,9,7, enter the actual value for row and column for
   a. LOCATE 0,0 ________
   b. LOCATE 1,1 ________
   c. LOCATE 2,1 ________
   d. LOCATE 3,2 ________
8. Given the following code

   ```
   WOPEN 7,0,4,9,20,7
   WOPEN 9,4,7,9,20,9
   ACTIVE 7
   ACTIVE 9
   LOCATE (4,7)
   CHR 70,X
   DISPLAY "(X)"
   ```

   a. How many windows are created?
   b. Which window will be written to?
   c. Where will the output be written?
   d. What is the output?
9. In regular Text mode, the IBM-PC display screen has ________.
   a. 25 rows and 25 columns
   b. 80 rows and 25 columns
   c. 25 rows and 80 columns
   d. 24 rows and 79 columns
10. For each of the following, write two commands that will allow you to write
    a. red text on a blue screen.
    b. white text on a red screen.
    c. green text on a white screen.
    d. yellow text on a yellow screen.
11. To utilize graphics, what command must be executed?
    a. GRAPHICS
    b. GMODE number
    c. DRAW shape
    d. CGA

12. What is the printer output and screen output for the following sequence of code?

```
DISPLAY "X"
PRINTON
DISPLAY "Y"
DISPLAY "Z"
PDISPLAY "Q"
PRINTOFF
PDISPLAY "R"
```

Assignments

1. At the A prompt, place the Sample Files Disk in the A drive and your Data Disk in the B drive. Transfer wp21.kbs to your Data Disk with

   A> COPY wp21.kbs B:my21.kbs

   Use the editor to change the numbers in the FOR loop in wp21.kbs from

   FOR X = 55 to 65

   to

   FOR X = 40 to 54

   Run a consultation and obtain a printout of the results with SHIFT PRTSC.

2. Transfer wp22.kbs to your Data Disk with

   A>COPY wp22.kbs B:my22.kbs

   a. Use the editor and delete the tilde (~) from two DISPLAY statements. Run a consultation and record the results.
   b. Use the editor and delete the clause

      COLOR=12

      Replace this clause above the clause

      ACTIVE 1

      Run a consultation and record the results.

3. Transfer wp23.kbs to your Data Disk with

   A>COPY wp23.kbs B:my23.kbs

   a. Use the editor to change COLOR=7 to COLOR=5. Also insert EXECUTE; above the ENDOFF statement.
   b. Run a consultation and record the results.

4. Transfer wp25.kbs to your Data Disk with

   A>COPY wp25.kbs B:my25.kbs

   Rewrite the code so that

   a. the opening message appears in Window 1.
   b. the advice message appears in Window 2.
   c. the ending message appears in Window 3.

   Enter your revisions and test the results.

5. Transfer wp25.kbs to your Data Disk with
   A>COPY wp25.kbs B:my25.kbs
   a. Write the code to let the user select the foreground color in addition to the background color.
   b. Using the editor, add the new code to my25.kbs.
   c. Run consultations with your new version of my25.kbs
   d. Does your new program run correctly?
6. Transfer wp24.kbs to your Data Disk with
   A>COPY wp24.kbs B:my24.kbs
   a. The PDISPLAY command sends the output of the DISPLAY statements to the printer but not the display screen. Write the code to modify my24.kbs to let you send output to the printer or the screen, but not both.
   b. Using the editor, enter your changes and test the results.
   c. Change the program to let the user select output to the printer, screen, or both.
   d. Enter your changes and test the results.
7. If you have an EGA or VGA graphics adapter and mouse, run carpict.kbs from the Sample Files Disk.
   a. Record the results.
   b. Obtain a printout of the code.
   c. Circle the graphics commands.
8. Use the VP-Expert Help Facility to obtain a printout of the details of the following commands
   a. Window commands
      WOPEN
      LOCATE
   b. RUN-TIME commands
      EXECUTE
      RUNTIME
      ENDOFF
   c. Printer Commands
      PDISPLAY
      EJECT
9. Use the VP-Expert Help Facility to obtain a printout of the details of the following graphics commands:

Managing the Screen	Drawing the graphics
GBCOLOR	ELLIPSE
GCLS	RECTANGLE
GCOLOR	LINE
GLOCATE	

10. If your system has a mouse, use the VP-Expert Help Facility to print out the instructions for:
    a. BUTTON
    b. GETMOUSE
    c. MOUSEON
    d. MOUSEOFF
    e. MOUSEX
    f. MOUSEY

Module 8

SYSTEMS DEVELOPMENT WITH VP-EXPERT

This last module is designed to give you an overview of the power and flexibility available within VP-Expert. As you are designing and developing an expert system application, it is helpful if one of the team members is familiar with the features of the expert system shell. This will enhance the entire software engineering cycle.

This module is divided into two basic parts. This first section will take you through a short review and summary of the VP-Expert commands by category. We will summarize commands relating to the inference engine, confidence factors, loops, screen display and printer, database, and worksheets. New commands will be presented with more detail than commands previously covered. The categories are organized by commonalty rather than application.

The second section will give you an overview of some additional advanced features available for the software engineer.

Summary of Commands by Category

Inference Engine

The power of the **inference engine** is invoked when a FIND command has a variable with an UNKNOWN value. If the variable has a known value, then the FIND variable will be skipped and control will pass to the next command. When the FIND variable is activated, the inference engine will search the Rules, which are expressed in the IF-THEN or IF-THEN-ELSE format. If a value of the variable cannot be found there, then the search for the goal variable is extended to ASK variable commands. If the ASK statement is followed by a CHOICES statement, then the user will have a selection to make; otherwise, the user types in an appropriate response. This chaining of rules is altered somewhat if the Rule is preceded by a WHENEVER value. If the value changes, the Rule is automatically tested. The RESET command will change the value of a variable to UNKNOWN. Hence, a subsequent find variable command will initiate a search for the goal variable.

If the inference engine is attempting to FIND values for a PLURAL variable, there are several useful commands which only apply to PLURAL variables. The PLURAL clause allows the value of a variable to have multiple values. Hence, the inference engine continues its search even after it has found one value. These helpful commands involving a PLURAL variable are POP, COUNT, and SORT.

The POP command can be used to manipulate the individual values of the PLURAL variable. The syntax is

```
POP plural_variable, non_plural_variable
```

When this clause is executed, the most recently found value of the plural_variable is moved or stored in the non_plural_variable. The next POP clause will move the second value to the destination variable, and so on. Placing the POP clause inside a WHILEKNOWN loop can display the multiple values of a PLURAL variable. For example,

```
ACTIONS
        FIND Function
        WHILEKNOWN One_function
                RESET One_function
                POP FUNCTION, One_function
                DISPLAY "{one_function} is a desired feature."
        END;
                ....
        ASK Function : "Select five features you want in
                your word processing package.";
        CHOICES Function: ....;
        PLURAL : Function;
```

In this portion of code, the user selects five features that are desirable for word processing. The WHILEKNOWN loop displays these choices to the screen by the POP clause. The last value selected is the first function displayed. The fourth value selected by the user is the second value to be displayed. The stack of values, hence, is displayed from last selected to first selected.

Another clause used to implemented the PLURAL variable is COUNT. This instruction counts the number of values of a PLURAL variable. The syntax is

```
COUNT plural_variable_name, counter_variable
```

The COUNT clause will place the number of values for the plural_variable_name in the counter_variable. In our POP word processing example the clause

```
COUNT Function, Counter
```

would place the number 5 in the variable called Counter. Another useful command related to a PLURAL variable is SORT. The clause SORT plural_variable will sort the various values of the plural_variable by confidence factors (CNFs) in descending order. Hence, POP, COUNT, and SORT are clauses used to manipulate PLURAL variables.

Loops

Loops are clauses that cause a repetition of a given set of instructions. There are three repetitive structures in VP-Expert:

```
WHILEKNOWN variable_name
END

WHILETRUE condition
END

FOR variable = start_value to end_value
END
```

These three constructs, WHILEKNOWN-END, WHILETRUE-END, and FOR-END allow all the instructions between the stated key word and END to be repeated. In the WHILEKNOWN loop, the instructions are repeated until the END is reached and the value of the variable is UNKNOWN. As long as the variable has a KNOWN value, the instructions within the loop are repeated.

The WHILETRUE loop works in the same manner except that there is a condition after the key word instead of a variable name. The condition may be a simple statement, or a compound one using AND and OR connectives. As long as the condition has the value TRUE, the loop is executed. At the start of the loop, the system tests the condition. If the condition has a FALSE value, then control passes to the instruction after the END clause. If the first test of the condition is FALSE, then the loop is entirely skipped.

The FOR-END loop works on an automatic counter. The start_value and the end_value must represent numbers. At the END of the loop, the loop variable is automatically incremented by one. A test is made to determine if the variable is past the end_value. If it is, the loop is skipped; otherwise, the loop is repeated. It is possible, however, to use instructions within the loop to increase or decrease the control variable using assignment statements. These three loop constructs — WHILEKNOWN-END, WHILETRUE-END, and FOR-END — are very useful for system development work.

Confidence Factors

Expert systems development is concerned with the degree of certainty or confidence for conditions and conclusions. Hence, handling the *confidence factors* or CNFs is part of the systems development work. Three clauses — CNF, TRUTHTHRESH, and

SORT — assist with this task. The statement CNF = number can be inserted at the end of a conclusion in a Rule of the knowledge base. As the inference engine does its work, it uses these numbers to calculate the certainty of its final conclusion(s), the value(s) of the goal variable, or the FIND variable.

The TRUTHTHRESH is a clause that affects the firing of rules. If the condition of a Rule is true and the CNF of the condition is greater than or equal to the TRUTHTHRESH value, then the Rule fires. However, if the condition is true and the CNF value for the condition is below the TRUTHTHRESH value, the condition is re-evaluated to be false. This clause may occur in the Actions block and affects all Rules, or within the conclusion of a particular Rule, in which case it affects all actions by the inference engine after the Rule is fired. If there is no TRUTHTHRESH value in a program, VP-Expert assumes a TRUTHTHRESH of 40. Another command for certainty factors is the SORT clause. This command will sort the CNF numbers associated with the values of a PLURAL variable in descending order. In summary, CNF, TRUTHTHRESH, and SORT are instructions relating to certainty factors of conditions or conclusions. (Refer to Module 6 for further explanation of these commands.)

Screen Display and Printer

We will briefly overview the commands for controlling the *display screen* and *printer.* Text can be displayed with the DISPLAY statement. The FORMAT command can be used to format the display of numeric variables. The CLS instruction will clear the video display screen. The color of the background and foreground can be controlled with the BKCOLOR and COLOR clauses, respectively. Windows on the screen can be opened with the WOPEN clause and accessed via the ACTIVE and LOCATE instructions. The WCLOSE command will close a window.

One useful command relating to the screen and text is GETCH. This clause will cause the system to wait until the user enters a character at the keyboard. The syntax is

GETCH variable_name

VP-Expert waits until the user presses a key. When a key is pressed, it's corresponding ASCII value is placed in variable_name. The difference between the GETCH clause and the tilde within a DISPLAY statement is that the GETCH clause captures the ASCII code of the key pressed. This can be used as a control feature in VP-Expert programs.

The printer can be controlled with the PRINTON, PRINTOFF, PDISPLAY, and EJECT instructions.

Database

Database access to certain database packages is a powerful tool for expert systems development. VP-Expert has a variety of commands to support this feature. The MENU clause can be used to help generate choices from a database column. For large MENUs, the MRESET clause is used to release the memory used in the MENU clause. The GET clause is used to get a record from the database file. RECORD_NUM is a system variable that indicates the current number of the record from the database. The PUT clause will allow you to place new values back into the database file, whereas APPEND will allow you to add a new record to the database file. The CLOSE command will close a database file.

One useful command that we have not yet used is the INDEX clause. To speed access to a database file, the database management system may allow the creation of an index to a field or attribute of the database. These **indices**, or **pointers**, are stored in an INDEX file. If the database file to be accessed has an existing INDEX file, then VP-Expert can utilize this index. The clause is

INDEX index_file_name, database_filename_for_index

The first parameter is the name of the existing index file. The physical index file has a NDX extension. The second parameter is the database name of the field upon which the index is constructed. The advantage of using indexed database files is the increased speed of retrieval plus the fact that the index will list the values of the indexed field in order. The INDEX clause must be executed before a GET clause.

Worksheets

VP-Expert allows access to *worksheet information* or *spreadsheet information* during a consultation. Like database access, this is a powerful tool for the software engineer in expert systems. A worksheet can be read with the WKS instruction. The entire worksheet information is read into arrays in the microcomputer's memory. Hence, it may take a few seconds to load the information and more memory to hold the information. Worksheet information can be accessed by COLUMN, ROW, or NAMED ranges. Updated information can be written to the worksheet with the PWKS clause. The numeric format of the worksheet cell can be altered with the WFORMAT instruction.

Two instructions, WORKON and WORKSHEET, have not been used in our earlier modules. The WORKSHEET clause is used before a WORKON instruction. The format for WORKSHEET is WORKSHEET VP or WORKSHEET VPP. The "VP" is a setting for VP-Planner, while "VPP" is a program setting for VP-Planner Plus. The WORKSHEET clause indicates which spreadsheet program will be used and the subsequent WORKON clause identifies the worksheet file for the appropriate spreadsheet program.

The format of WORKON is

WORKON path, worksheet_file_name

The path is the name of the drive where the worksheet program is to be found. After this clause, the user is taken immediately to the opening screens of VP-Planner or VP-Planner Plus by the instruction. Control is passed from VP-Expert to either of the two spreadsheet programs where normal worksheet operations can be performed.

When you exit the spreadsheet software, you are returned to VP-Expert. If WORKSHEET is omitted, then VP-Expert assumes WORKON for VP-Planner. One WORKSHEET clause affects all subsequent WORKON commands until a new WORKSHEET instruction is encountered. (To utilize Lotus 1-2-3 or Symphony, use a CCALL, which we will discuss in the next section.)

An example is appropriate here. In a large scale expert system, we may want to update a special worksheet related to Chinese word processors. The following code accomplishes this:

```
RULE 12
IF Functionality = Chinese
THEN
          DISPLAY "Press any key to update information on
                    Chinese word processors.~"
          WORKSHEET VPP
          WORKON C:\vpp, ChineseWP;
```

If the Functionality is Chinese, then the Rule displays a message to the user and passes control to VP-Planner Plus to WORKON, the worksheet ChineseWP. VP-Planner Plus is found in the directory, vpp, on drive C. The advantage of this interface being used for two worksheet programs (not just work files) is apparent.

Hence, we have reviewed some VP-Expert commands by related category rather than by applications. A few new related instructions were added to our list. In the next section we will discuss some advanced features which the software engineer can utilize.

Advanced Features

VP-Expert has a variety of advanced features to aid the software engineer in implementing expert systems. We will overview these advanced topics under the following categories: chaining, text files, external programs, graphics, Dynamic Images, Smartforms, and HYPERTEXT. All of these features can add to the expert system implementation.

Chaining Knowledge-based Files

There are instructions within VP-Expert that allow the results of one consultation to be passed as input to another, but related, knowledge base. This is important because of the memory required for large expert systems on microcomputers. Three clauses, CHAIN, SAVEFACTS, and LOADFACTS, along with EXECUTE, make this *chaining*, or *linking*, possible. During a consultation with a given knowledge base, values of the variables assigned during that consultation can be saved into a text file with the clause SAVEFACTS file_name. The file name may have a drive specification in front of it. For example

```
SAVEFACTS c:WPdata
```

would save data on drive C under the name WPdata. This clause would then be followed by CHAIN new_kbs_file. This sequence command will deactivate the first .kbs file and the new .kbs file will take its place.

The new_kbs_file must have LOADFACTS: WPdata as one of the first clauses in the Actions block. The values from the old consultation are now available to the new .kbs file. The EXECUTE statement placed before the LOADFACTS clause will facilitate a smooth transition.

We could place the LOADFACTS and CHAIN clauses within the conclusion of appropriate rules, and then chain the user to the appropriate word processing information. For example

```
! The file Needs.kbs will analyze your word processing
!         needs and link to the appropriate information.

          Rule 24
          IF            Need = Technical_illustration
          THEN          LOADFACTS Temp
                        CHAIN Techill;
```

The user would be transferred to the new knowledge base program Techill.kbs, with the following partial code:

```
! Techill.kbs contains information on
! technical illustration packages.

EXECUTE;
ACTIONS
        LOADFACTS : Temp
```

The most important advantage of using the CHAIN clause is the reduction of the memory size needed to run the linked knowledge-based programs rather than one large one. The educational version of VP-Expert allows the chaining of three knowledge based files. The regular version is not limited in the number of files that can be chained.

Text Files

VP-Expert has several instructions to enhance the transfer of *external text file information* to and from consultations. The clauses, RECEIVE, SHIP, FDISPLAY, and SHOWTEXT, provide for the transition of text material to and from a consultation.

The RECEIVE clause transports a line of text from an external file into a VP-Expert variable. The format of the instruction is

```
RECEIVE text_file_name, variable
```

The current line of text found in the external text_file_name is placed in the VP-Expert variable. The external file is an ASCII text file which may or may not have a drive specification. When the first RECEIVE clause is executed, the first line from the file is read into the receiving variable. The receiving variable after the RECEIVE command can hold lines up to 1,000 characters in length. This is an advantage over the usual 20-character limit on values assigned to VP-Expert variables. Subsequent RECEIVE clauses extract the second line, the third line, and so on. When RECEIVE and DISPLAY commands are placed inside a WHILEKNOWN-END loop, the entire contents of the external file will be displayed to the screen. For example,

```
WHILEKNOWN Description
        RECEIVE WPdata, Description
        DISPLAY "{Description}"
END;
```

The contents of the file WPdata will be transferred to the variable Description and then displayed on the screen.

The opposite action is implemented with the SHIP clause. The command

```
SHIP text_file_name, variable
```

will transfer the value of the variable to the external text file. If the text_file_name does not exist, the system will create it and place the contents of the variable as the first information on the file. If the file already exists, the information will be written at the end of the file. Placing SHIP inside a WHILEKNOWN-END loop will write many lines of text to the external file.

A more powerful version of SHIP is the FDISPLAY clause. This clause has the format

```
FDISPLAY text_file_name, "text"
```

Instead of a variable to hold the information, the information inside the double quotes is written to the external file indicated. The value of variables can be embedded within this text. For example,

```
WHENEVER Change
IF          Cost < (New_ cost)
THEN        FDISPLAY WPdata, "{Word_proc} has a new cost of
            {Newcost}.";
```

Both the text and the values of the two variables, Word_proc and New_cost, will be written to the text file WPdata. One interesting use of the FDISPLAY clause is to record the results of a consultation. If an FDISPLAY is placed after each DISPLAY statement, then the results of the consultation will be saved to disk.

Another clause that handles text is SHOWTEXT. This clause will display a page of text from a special indexed text file. The syntax is

```
SHOWTEXT text_file_name, variable
```

The text_file_name must have a .TXT extension and must be created with the BASIC program INDEXER.BAS. The file is created with a special index. When the clause SHOWTEXT is executed, a page of text from the external file with the heading listed in the variable is displayed to the screen. For example, the code

```
DISPLAY "Information on Package A"
        PRINTON
        Package = (Package_A)
        SHOWTEXT WPdata, Package
        PRINTOFF
```

would find, display, and print the page of text in the file WPdata whose heading is Package_A. This is a useful technique for handling large amounts of textual information.

External Programs

Another advanced feature of VP-Expert is it's ability to call *external DOS programs*. In addition to calling external worksheet programs, VP-Expert allows a consultation to call other programs with the CCALL, CALL, and BCALL clauses.

The CCALL instruction allows the consultation to call an external DOS file that has a .COM extension. COM files are limited to 64K. The syntax of the clause is

```
CCALL file_name, "parameters"
```

The file name must have a .COM extension, but it is not used in the CCALL clause. The command line parameters are optional. After the new program is executed, control returns to the consultation.

The CALL command is almost identical to CCALL, except that it calls .EXE files. EXE files can be of any size and are relocatable object files. Hence, for this reason, we can say that CALL is more powerful then CCALL. The syntax of the clause is the same as CCALL. Because of the additional memory, you have to be careful not to conflict with the memory requirements of VP-Expert. These clauses allow you to integrate additional programs, such as telecommunications, graphics, and programs to do mathematical calculations into a consultation. For example, if Rule 25 were fired,

```
Rule 25
IF word_processor=technical
THEN CALL C:\Symbols," "
```

the system would call, load, and execute the file named Symbols.EXE which would display the technical symbols available in the designated word processor. When Symbols.EXE finished execution, you would be back in the calling consultation. Symbols.EXE could be a program written in another language. The ability to incorporate these external DOS programs enhance both the expert system and the development time and costs.

A third clause, BCALL, turns control over to a DOS batch file. The file must have a .BAT extension. Batch files are text files that contain commands for the operating system. They are useful in starting other programs without the user having to type in several lines of commands. The BCALL command functions the same as CCALL and CALL and has the same syntax.

Two additional commands, CLROFF and CLRON, affect the screen for CCALL and CALL. Following a CCALL or CALL clause, the CLROFF instruction cancels the normal clearing of the Consultation screen. The effect is that the user still sees the same Consultation screen. This allows the external program to execute transparently to the user. In other words, background processing is allowed. The CLRON clause is used to turn off the effect of the CLROFF clause. Consider the example.

```
CLROFF
DISPLAY " Wait please."
CCALL C:\Forecast, " "
CLRON
CALL C:\Graphics, " "
```

When CLROFF is executed, the Consultation screen remains, a wait message is displayed, and the program Forecast.COM is run in the background. When the forecasting program to project the savings of our word processor has finished, the CLRON command allows the screen to be cleared when the CCALL clause activates the Graphics.EXE file, which displays a bar chart of the five-year forecast of savings. Indeed, these five clauses, CCALL, CALL, CLRON, CLROFF, and BCALL, are power tools for the software engineer in expert systems.

Graphics

VP-Expert contains a set of tools for creating drawings on the Consultation screen. These *graphics primitives* cannot be used unless the microcomputer system has a graphics adapter. To utilize graphics drawings, you must first set the proper setting code with the GMODE clause. Then a background color, GBCOLOR and a drawing color, GCOLOR, must be selected.

Once these clauses have been executed, lines, polygons, circles, and ellipses can be drawn. The MOVETO command moves the **drawing pen** to a new X,Y position on the screen. The PSET clause sets a particular pixel to the given drawing color. The LINETO clause draws a line (in the GCOLOR color) from the current cursor location to the indicated new point. A series of LINETO commands can generate a polygon. The RECTANGLE clause draws a rectangle on the screen, and the ELLIPSE instruction draws an ellipse or circle on the display. The FILL command can be used to fill the interior of a polygon, rectangle, ellipse, or circle with the preselected drawing color.

Text can also be incorporated into these drawings. The GLOCATE clause will locate the X,Y position where the GDISPLAY clause will display text. When a graphics program is finished, you can return VP-Expert to its default screen setting (text and color only) with TMODE.

Dynamic Images

VP-Expert offers an additional feature for implementing user interfaces called *Dynamic Images.* A Dynamic Image is a predefined graphic object (drawing) that is dynamically linked to a value of a specific variable. When the value of the variable changes, the linked Dynamic Image is changed. These Dynamic Images include gauges, buttons, form fields, meters, and time-series graphs. For example, a **gauge** could be used to indicate the rating of the performance of a word processing package. A **meter** could indicate the expected productivity gains from using the specialized word processor. Combinations of Dynamic Images could be used to create a control panel where the user selects symbols instead of word items from menus.

All Dynamic Images work in Graphics mode. Two of the images, FORMFIELD and LBUTTON, are text images, whereas other images, such as METER and BUTTON, are graphics images. Both types of images require X,Y coordinates to determine the upper left corner of the enclosing rectangle; however, the values of the coordinates vary in different Graphics modes. The text images range from 0 to 79 for X (column) and 0 to 24 for Y (row).

A Dynamic Image is not displayed on the screen until the value of the variable to which it is linked (associated) has a known value. As long as the associated variable has an UNKNOWN value, the image is not displayed. Once the image is shown on the screen, however, it can be erased by issuing the RESET command with the linked variable.

The Dynamic Image instructions are statements. The BUTTON statement displays a button image which is linked to a YES or NO variable. The LBUTTON statement is the same except the displayed button contains a Text label. FORMFIELD displays a rectangular box, or form field, containing the value of the linked variable, whereas DBFORM displays a vertical array of rectangles or form fields corresponding to the fields of a .dbf file. The METER statement displays a meter image, while the HGAUGE and VGAUGE commands display horizontal and vertical slide gauges, respectively. The TRACK instruction displays a time-series graph linked to the last 50 values of a given variable.

It is also possible to create your own Dynamic Images for use within a consultation. This can be effected by combining a series of graphics primitives with the HOTREGION statement. The HOTREGION statement creates an invisible **hot**, or **active**, region. When this region is clicked on by a mouse, the associated variable toggles between YES and NO. You now have your own custom-made image linked to a variable value to control its display on the screen. All of the Dynamic Image statements can add creativity and functionality to the user interface of the expert system application.

SmartForms

Another advanced feature of VP-Expert is the ability to create *SmartForms* of screen displays that resemble regular paper forms. Unlike the traditional paper forms used in business, the VP-Expert SmartForm can adapt to the user's responses. As the user fills out a form, the value of the response determines which form field will pop up next. For example, in a SmartForm application where the user is filling out an upgrade agreement with the vendor of a word processing package, the reply to the question, Are you networked?, would determine what part of the form would come up next. Comparing the SmartForms approach to the traditional questioning (interview style), the SmartForms approach presents the user with a group of questions, allows him or her to change answers on the screen, and simulates the actual paper form used in the business application.

Creating a SmartForm involves several steps. First of all, the Actions block must have a GMODE setting, a WHILETRUE-END loop to keep VP-Expert in a loop until the user has completed the form, and a TMODE clause to resume Text mode. WHENEVER rules are used to activate actions depending on the replies from the user in the SmartForm. These WHENEVER rules can offer advice if certain information is entered into a field, can remove irrelevant fields, add new fields to the form, and maintain consistency between the fields in the forms. The FORMFIELD statement with the LBUTTON command can be used to create the form fields and link the reply to the click of a mouse when finished. Obviously, this SmartForm feature can enhance those expert systems involving extensive data entry with forms.

HYPERTEXT Feature

Another useful feature available for VP-Expert applications is *HYPERTEXT.* HYPERTEXT is similar to SHOWTEXT and RECEIVE text in that it reads externally stored textual information into a consultation. HYPERTEXT, however, works only in Graphics modes, is activated whenever a variable is initialized, and appears inside a window. The interesting feature of HYPERTEXT is that the textual information is linked to other HYPERTEXT information. When the displayed information contains uppercase HYPERTEXT words, the user can click on these words with a mouse and the system will replace them with additional text related to the HYPERTEXT word. This allows the user to browse through information and to find additional information on key words.

HYPERTEXT is a special Dynamic Image. When it is not being used in a consultation, it must be removed from the screen. The HYPERTEXT window disappears when the linked variable is UNKNOWN. The use of the HYPERTEXT feature can add flexibility to the expert system application.

Conclusion

The many features of VP-Expert can enhance the applications development of an expert system. Combining the graphics, Dynamic Images, and HYPERTEXT features is limited only by the design and imagination of the software engineer. The total development of an expert system application rests on the accuracy of the knowledge base and the consistent, creative, and meaningful implementation of the user interface. VP-Expert has all the power tools for the creation and implementation of useful expert systems in the business world.

Key Points

- Instructions related to the inference engine are
  FIND
  ASK, CHOICES
  RESET
  RULES
- Commands involving a PLURAL variable of a FIND clause are
  POP
  COUNT
  SORT
- Three loop structures for VP-Expert programs are
  WHILEKNOWN variable
  WHILETRUE condition
  FOR variable = start_number to end_number
- Confidence factors can be implemented and utilized by
  CNF
  TRUTHTHRESH
  SORT (PLURAL variables only)
- Useful commands for controlling the screen are
  CLS
  DISPLAY, FORMAT
  COLOR
  BKCOLOR
- Commands to process text characters are
  CHR
  GETCH
- Commands to utilize windows are
  WOPEN
  ACTIVE
  LOCATE
- Printer commands include
  PRINTON
  PRINTOFF
  PDISPLAY
  EJECT

- Database files can be utilized with
  - MENU
  - GET
  - INDEX
  - MRESET
  - PUT
  - APPEND
  - CLOSE
  - RECORD__NUM
- Worksheet (spreadsheet) related instructions include
  - WKS
  - PWKS, WFORMAT
  - WORKSHEET
  - WORKON
- Commands to accommodate the linking of knowledge-based files are
  - CHAIN
  - SAVEFACTS
  - LOADFACTS
- Commands to incorporate text files into a consultation are
  - RECEIVE
  - SHIP
  - SHOWTEXT
  - FDISPLAY
- Commands that will call specific external DOS files are
  - CCALL calls .COM files
  - CALL calls .EXE files
  - BCALL calls .BAT files
- The CLROFF and CLRON commands toggle the clearing of the screen before the execution of CCALL or CALL.
- The following instructions implement chaining
  - CHAIN
  - LOADFACTS
  - SAVEFACTS
  - EXECUTE
- Commands to set the graphics screen are
  - GMODE
  - GBCOLOR
  - GCOLOR
- Instructions to draw graphics include
  - PSET
  - MOVETO
  - LINETO
  - RECTANGLE
  - ELLIPSE
  - FILL
- Commands to control text on a graphics screen are
  - GLOCATE
  - GDISPLAY
  - TMODE

- Mouse input can be implemented with
  - GETMOUSE
  - MOUSEX
  - MOUSEY
- Dynamic Images can be implemented in graphics modes with
  - BUTTON
  - LBUTTON
  - HGAUGE
  - VGAUGE
  - METER
  - TRACK
- Dynamic Images involving text are
  - DBFORM
  - FORMFIELD
- Custom Dynamic Images can be created with graphics primitives and HOTREGION.
- SMARTFORM allows the creation of dynamic data entry forms.
- HYPERTEXT is textual information which allows the user to obtain related information on keywords.

Exercises

1. Draw an arrow from one parameter to the other to indicate the direction of movement.
   a. POP X,Y
   b. SHIP X,Y
   c. RECEIVE X,Y
   d. COUNT X,Y
   e. SHOWTEXT X,Y
2. In the following commands, draw a box around file names and circle variable names.
   a. CALL X
   b. FDISPLAY X, " "
   c. RECEIVE X,Y
   d. POP X,Y
   e. INDEX X,Y
3. Which of the following instructions do not require any parameters?
   a. GETCH
   b. POP
   c. CLROFF
   d. EXECUTE
   e. CHAIN

4. Which of the following commands could execute Lotus 1-2-3 during a consultation?
   a. CHAIN
   b. CCALL
   c. WORKON
   d. WKS
   e. LOADFACTS

5. Given the code below, what can you assume about file X, in each instruction?
   a. CCALL X ," "
   b. BCALL X, " "
   c. SHOWTEXT X, "Jones"
   d. INDEX X,Y
   e. WORKSHEET X

6. Circle the commands that apply only to a PLURAL variable.

POP	TRUTHTHRESH
CALL	COUNT
SORT	FIND
CNF	WHENEVER
GETCH	CLROFF

7. Circle the commands that work only in a Graphics mode.

ELLIPSE	PUT
MOUSEX	PSET
LINETO	LOCATE
GETCH	WINDOW
RECTANGLE	GCOLOR

8. Answer the following questions about the code

```
        FOR X=2 to 5
                DISPLAY "{X} "
        END
```

   a. What is the start value?
   b. What is the end value?
   c. How many times is DISPLAY executed?
   d. What is the value of X when control passes to a command after the END?
   e. What is displayed on the screen?

Assignments

1. Readme.kbs is a file which demonstrates how to start a graphics screen and use the LBUTTON and BUTTON commands. It is on your Sample Files Disk. You must first change the GMODE setting to match your adapter.
   a. Copy Readme.kbs to your Data Disk.
   b. Run a consultation.
   c. What does the expert system do?
   d. Obtain a printout of the code.
   e. Circle the graphics primitives and new commands.

2. Formdemo.kbs is another file on your Sample Files Disk. It demonstrates the use of the FORMFIELD command. Repeat the instructions for Assignment 1.

3. Fromage.kbs is a file that demonstrates the use of the FORMFIELD statement and WHENEVER rules. It is a cheese advisor system on your Sample Files Disk. Check the GMODE setting before running. Repeat the instructions for Assignment 1.

4. Tempsim.kbs is a demonstration file of graphics primitives on your Sample Files Disk. It is combined with Dynamic Images to simulate data acquisition of the current temperature. Repeat the instructions from Assignment 1.

5. Transfer wp25.kbs to your Data Disk as my25.kbs.
   a. Redesign the program to use the GETCH instruction.
   b. Using the editor, enter your changes.
   c. Run a consultation.
   d. Record the results.

6. Transfer wp9.kbs to your Data Disk as my9.kbs
   a. Rewrite the program using a WHILETRUE-END loop.
   b. Using the editor, enter your revisions to the code.
   c. Run a consultation with your revised code.
   d. Record the results.

7. Try the use of the CHAIN command. Rewrite wp4.kbs and wp1.kbs so that if wp4.kbs advises that you need a word processor, you are automatically taken to a consultation with wp1.kbs. Copy both files to your Data Disk using different file names.

8. Use the VP-Expert Help Facility to obtain details on Dynamic Images:
   BUTTON
   LBUTTON
   HGAUGE
   VGAUGE
   METER
   TRACK

9. Use the VP-Expert Help Facility to obtain details of two Dynamic Images with text:
   DBFORM
   FORMFIELD

10. Use the VP-Expert Help Facility to obtain details about HYPERTEXT.

11. The README.TXT file on the Sample Files Disk contains useful information about the commands and latest improvements to VP-Expert. Obtain a printout by entering
    A> COPY B:README.TXT LPT1
    The Sample Files Disk is in the B drive.

12. File Readme.kbs on your Sample Files Disk demonstrates the use of HYPERTEXT. The expert system file reads the HYPERTEXT Readme.txt file. Run a consultation in VP-Expert with Readme.kbs.

A

VP-EXPERT COMMAND HIERARCHY CHART

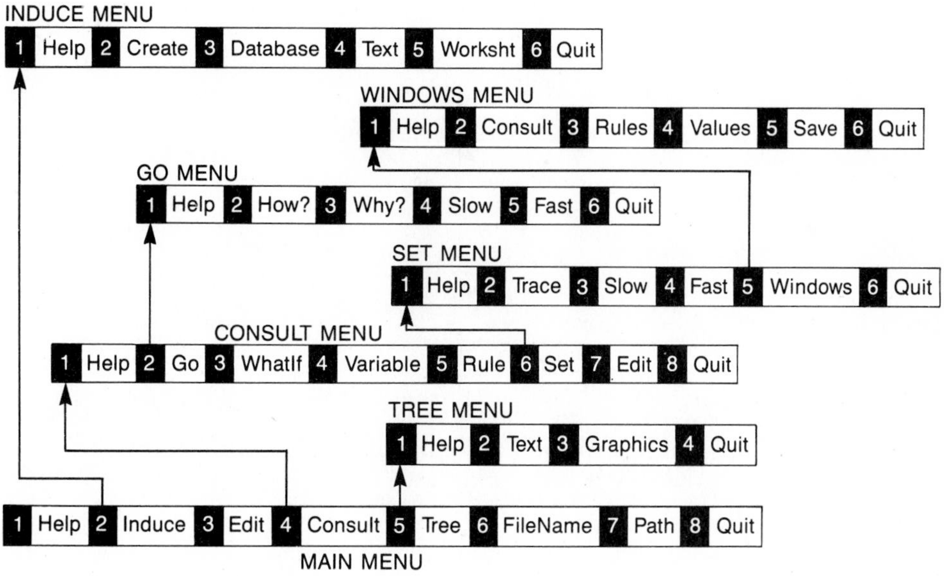

B

TABLE OF ASCII CHARACTERS

ASCII CODE	DISPLAY	CONTROL SEQUENCE	CONTROL CHARACTER	ASCII CODE	DISPLAY	CONTROL SEQUENCE	CONTROL CHARACTER	ASCII CODE	DISPLAY	ASCII CODE	DISPLAY	ASCII CODE	DISPLAY	ASCII CODE	DISPLAY
0		Ctrl 2	NUL	16		Ctrl P	DLE	32		48	0	64	@	80	P
1		Ctrl A	SOH	17		Ctrl Q	DC1	33	!	49	1	65	A	81	Q
2		Ctrl B	STX	18		Ctrl R	DC2	34	"	50	2	66	B	82	R
3		Ctrl C	ETX	19		Ctrl S	DC3	35	#	51	3	67	C	83	S
4		Ctrl D	EOT	20		Ctrl T	DC4	36	$	52	4	68	D	84	T
5		Ctrl E	ENQ	21		Ctrl U	NAK	37	%	53	5	69	E	85	U
6		Ctrl F	ACK	22		Ctrl V	SYN	38	&	54	6	70	F	86	V
7		Ctrl G	BEL	23		Ctrl W	ETB	39	'	55	7	71	G	87	W
* 8		Ctrl H	BS	24		Ctrl X	CAN	40	(	56	8	72	H	88	X
* 9		Ctrl I	HT	25		Ctrl Y	EM	41	)	57	9	73	I	89	Y
10		Ctrl J	LF	26		Ctrl Z	SUB	42	*	58	:	74	J	90	Z
11		Ctrl K	VT	*27		Ctrl [	ESC	43	+	59	;	75	K	91	[
12		Ctrl L	FF	28		Ctrl \	FS	44	,	60	<	76	L	92	\
*13		Ctrl M	CR	29		Ctrl]	GS	45	-	61	=	77	M	93	]
14		Ctrl N	SO	30		Ctrl ^	RS	46	.	62	>	78	N	94	^
15		Ctrl O	SI	31		Ctrl _	US	47	/	63	?	79	O	95	_

*These characters cannot be entered in LABEL mode. Characters 0 through 31 (ASCII) cannot be entered in EDIT mode.

ASCII CODE	DISPLAY	ASCII CODE	DISPLAY	ASCII CODE	DISPLAY	ASCII CODE	DISPLAY	ASCII CODE	DISPLAY	ASCII CODE	DISPLAY	ASCII CODE	DISPLAY	ASCII CODE	DISPLAY
96	‘	116	t	136	ê	156	£	176	░	196	─	216	╪	236	∞
97	a	117	u	137	ë	156	¥	177	▒	196	┼	217	┘	237	φ
98	b	118	v	138	è	158	₧	178	▓	198	╞	218	┌	238	ε
99	c	119	w	139	ï	159	ƒ	179	│	199	╟	219	█	239	∩
100	d	120	x	140	î	160	á	180	┤	200	╚	220	▄	240	≡
101	e	121	y	141	ì	161	í	181	╡	201	╔	221	▌	241	±
102	f	122	z	142	Ä	162	ó	182	╢	202	╩	222	▐	242	≥
103	g	123	{	143	Å	163	ú	183	╖	203	╦	223	▀	243	≤
104	h	124	¦	144	É	164	ñ	184	╕	204	╠	224	α	244	⌠
105	i	125	}	145	æ	165	Ñ	185	╣	205	═	225	β	245	⌡
106	j	126	~	146	Æ	166	ª	186	║	206	╬	226	Γ	246	÷
107	k	127	Δ	147	ô	167	º	187	╗	207	╧	227	π	247	≈
108	l	128	Ç	148	ö	168	¿	188	╝	208	╨	228	Σ	248	°
109	m	129	ü	149	ò	169	⌐	189	╜	209	╤	229	σ	249	∙
110	n	130	é	150	û	170	¬	190	╛	210	╥	230	µ	250	·
111	o	131	â	151	ù	171	½	191	┐	211	╙	231	τ	251	√
112	p	132	ä	152	ÿ	172	¼	192	└	212	╘	232	Φ	252	ⁿ
113	1	133	à	153	Ö	173	¡	193	┴	213	╒	233	Θ	253	²
114	r	134	å	154	Ü	174	«	194	┬	214	╓	234	Ω	254	■
115	s	135	ç	155	¢	175	»	195	├	215	╫	235	δ	255	

C

ANSWERS TO ODD-NUMBERED EXERCISES

Chapter 1

1. According to WEBSTER'S SECOND EDITION NEW WORLD DICTIONARY, intelligence is "the ability to learn or understand from experience; the ability to acquire and retain knowledge; the ability to respond quickly and successfully to new situations; or the use of the faculty of reason in solving problems, directing conduct, etc., effectively."

3. Answers will depend on your particular situation.

5. Advantages
   1) Solution of complex problems
   2) Increase in productivity
   3) Prevention of the loss of human expertise
   4) Removal of people from working in selected dangerous environments.

   Limitations (disadvantages)
   1) Large overhead in time, money, and resources.
   2) Time required to learn new computer languages.
   3) Lack of inexpensive, usable, and reliable AI development tools to implement needed systems.
   4) Lack of qualified professionals to work on teams to implement AI systems.

7. Data processing systems (DPS) use predetermined procedures to manipulate huge volumes of data. Management information systems (MIS) summarize and select data from the massive DP files so as to give meaning to the computer output. Decision support systems (DSS) are designed to help managers make more effective and efficient decisions. They can be used when problems become too large or complex for an MIS to be adequate, especially when the individual does not have any relevant past experience in solving the problem. Expert Systems (ES) are systems that are designed to simulate the behavior of a human expert as he or she attempts to solve some complex problem in a particular domain. Both DSS and ES evolved from similar disciplines, but the general goal of an ES is to replace human knowledge while the general goal of a DSS is to assist rather than replace the expert.

Chapter 2

1. An expert system is a computer program that emulates the behavior of human experts who are solving real-world problems associated with a particular domain of knowledge. The most basic difference between an expert system and a conventional computer program is that expert systems manipulate knowledge while conventional computer programs manipulate only data. Conventional programs are algorithmic in nature and therefore guarantee a solution to a problem, while expert systems use heuristic (rules of thumb) and inferential (reasoning) processes and therefore do not guarantee a solution to a problem. Expert systems and conventional computer programs are similar in that they are both computer software designed to accomplish a specific task.

3. The early efforts at expert system development began in the 1950's with the work of Newell, Shaw, and Simon, who created a system called the General Problem Solver (GPS). Other groups, such as Minsky and McCarthy, and Ledburg, Buchanan, and Feigenbaum also did significant work. In the 1970's researchers realized that expert systems should be built with narrow-scoped problem domains and also realized that the quality of the knowledge possessed by the expert system was at least as important as the inference techniques used by the system. These two realizations, along with advancements in microcomputer technology, were the real catalysts to advancements in the 1970's and 1980's. Expert systems had begun to move from the research to the commercial environment.

5. The two types are—1) Knowledge engineering languages/systems (shells) and 2) High-level programming languages. Shells are easier to use by inexperienced expert system builders but are not as flexible relative to the range of potential problems to be solved because the inference engine is pre-constructed. High-level programming languages offer greater flexibility to the range of problems to be solved but are more difficult because the inference engine must also be constructed and decisions about how knowledge is to be represented must be made.

7. Advantages:
   1) The knowledge base is (usually) permanent and easy to maintain.
   2) The system is relatively inexpensive to maintain and can be used in several locations at the same time.
   3) The system is easy to document and produces consistent results.

   Limitations:
   1) The system cannot learn from experience.
   2) The knowledge acquisition process is not well understood.
   3) Not all problems are candidates for expert systems.
   4) All knowledge put into the expert system must be represented in the same form.

9. A word processor is a software program that manipulates text.

Chapter 3

1. There are four models for knowledge representation

3. Antecedent = If today is Tuesday and the temperature is above 60 degrees
   Consequent = I will go fishing
   A = today is Tuesday
   B = the temperature is above 60 degrees
   C = I will go fishing
   Example
   A = T
   B = F
   A and B = F
   C = F
   IF (A and B), THEN C = T
   Answers will vary to the last part of the question, depending upon your situation.

5. Example
   1. Monte Carlo
   2. 789321
   3. 1985
   4. Black
   5. 305
   6. Chevrolet

   Answers will vary.

7.

Frame name	Monte Carlo
License plate number	789321
Year of model	1985
Color	Black
Type of Engine	305

9.

A	B	NOT A	NOT A AND B	A OR NOT B	B → A
T	T	F	F	T	T
T	F	F	F	T	T
F	T	T	T	F	F
F	F	T	F	T	T

11. IF functionality is simple and cost is low,
    THEN select a word processor equal to A.
    IF functionality is simple and cost is high,
    THEN select a word processor equal to A.

Chapter 4

1. Backward Control. We know what the goal state is in advance (the light bulb is on). We know that to turn the light bulb on we need to flip the light switch.

3. C
   B, E
   H, I
   D, F, A, H, I
   D
   G
   None
   C,B,D,E,F,A,G,H,I
   C,B,E,D,F,A,G,H,I
   Both methods would be the same.

5. If A and B then F
   If C and D then G
   If F and G then H
   If E and H then I

7. For example.
   Node 5 = 100(0) + 10(1) + 0 − (100(0) + 10(1) + 1) = 1
   Node 8 = 100(0) + 10(2) + 0 − (100(0) + 10(2) + 0) = 0
   Formula: 100A + 10B + C − (100D + 10E + F)
   Where
   A = number of rows, columns, diag. with 3 X's
   B = number of rows, columns, diag. with 2 X's and 0 O's
   C = number of rows, columns, diag. with 1 X and 0 O's
   D = number of rows, columns, diag. with 3 O's
   E = number of rows, columns, diag. with 2 O's and 0 X's
   F = number of rows, columns, diag. with 1 O and 0 X's

9. (a) Blue
   (b) 14
   (c) 55

Chapter 5

1. Waterman [1986] suggests that three questions need to be answered.
   1. Is expert systems development possible for the problem solution?
   2. Is expert systems development justified for the problem solution?
   3. Is expert systems development appropriate for the problem solution?

3. It is often difficult for an expert to express thoughts pertinent to subject domain. Because an expert has a deep knowledge about the subject, as he or she talks assumptions are made about the qualifications of the listener (knowledge engineer). If the listener is unprepared for the subject, what the expert says is likely to be meaningless; causing frustration during the communication process and possibly resulting in a waste of time as each tries to understand the other.

5. Introspective modeling involves examining portions of the expert's previous experience. It aids in the interview process because the interviewer is better able to understand the point of view and past experience of the expert.

7. The art of listening is the ability to fully understand what we hear. This is important to a knowledge engineer because during an interview, the knowledge engineer must be continually aware of the potential impreciseness of language in the verbal communications with the expert and must gain an understanding of the experts thinking process.

9. If a high-level programming language is going to be used, any of the four models of knowledge representation discussed in Chapter 3 could be used. Most expert system shells use the rule as the form of knowledge representation.

11. The knowledge engineer queries the expert to try to capture his or her knowledge and to determine what strategies he or she uses to solve a given problem. The query/response process, the key to the knowledge-acquisition process should be, ideally, a flow of the expert's knowledge and strategies with minimal or nonexistent gaps.

Chapter 6

1. Uncertainty can be considered as the lack of adequate information needed to make a decision.

3. 1) Reasoning errors can occur in the rule as a whole.
   2) There is uncertainty involved in determining how the knowledge should be combined in the antecedent. Giarratano and Riley [1989] note that there are 3 basic areas of uncertainty pertaining to rules, — individual rules, conflict resolution rules, rule compatibility.

5. Because most expert systems are rule based, and even if each individual rule can be verified, there is no guarantee that the inference chain will give valid results. Uncertainties exist as inference chains are formulated. Conflict resolution is used to determine the order in which rules are fired (executed).

7. Because rule incompatibility occurs when two rules have the same antecedent but have conflicting consequences, which causes a lack of adequate information to make a decision.

9. The original definition of the certainty factor for a given hypothesis H and the given evidence used the difference of the measure of belief (mB) and the measure of disbelief (mD). mB and mD were probably numbers assigned by the physicians (experts).

11. VP-Expert uses the term "confidence factor" instead of "certainty factor." Its calculations are similar to those of MYCIN.

13. (a) 70
    (b) 40
    (c) 74
    (d) 68
    (e) 84
    (f) not possible using the VP-Expert method.

Chapter 7

1. The user interface is the total communications medium between the participant and the expert system.

3. Keyboard — cursor keys

5. Checking
   1. Cost of Checks
   2. Monthly service charge
   3. Rate of Interest

   Savings
   1. Money Market
   2. Certificates of Deposit
   3. Closing Costs
   4. Rate of Interest

   Mortgage
   1. Escrow
   2. Principal
   3. Points
   4. Fixed
   5. Adjustable Rates
   6. Closing Costs
   7. Insurance
   8. Rate of Interest

7. ■ Main Menu
   1Disk 2Create 3Edit
   ■ Disk Submenus
   1Save 2Getfile 3Quit
   ■ Create Submenu
   1Document 2Spreadsheet 3Database 4Outline
   ■ Edit Submenu
   1Typeover 2Insert 3Delete

9. (a) Uses all capitals.
   (b) User could be confused by the instruction. It should read: "Select one of the above."
   (c) Does not limit the number of menu selections from five to seven per screen.
   (d) Each item selection should be numbered.
   (e) Error message should be self-explanatory.
   (f) Should not use blank screens.

Chapter 8

1. An expert system is a piece of software; therefore, its development process can use principles of software engineering.

3. The expert system life cycle includes the following phases: development, use/integration and updating/maintenance. The development phase is where the expert system is actually created. In the use phase, the expert system is put into the role of solving problems related to the domain area. The updating/maintenance phase is where the knowledge base is updated or modified and where errors are corrected.

5. The development phase of the expert system life cycle is analogous to the development phase of the conventional software system life cycle in that the same basic steps are used. However, there are some differences. For example, a conventional software system is designed to deal with a single application or problem, and its specifications are developed in conjunction with the user who has a task to be accomplished. On the other hand, an expert system is intended to solve a range of applications or problems in a narrow domain of knowledge. Knowledge must be put into a form that can be understood by the expert system. While formal specifications are not developed with a conventional software system, the domain of the knowledge in an expert system must be clearly defined. The knowledge engineer works generally with the human expert to acquire true knowledge, but does not work with the user.

7. 1) Validate the choice and definition of the problem to be solved.
   2) Make initial determination of the appropriateness of the chosen development tool.
   3) Assess the initial completeness of the knowledge acquisition process.
   4) Initially evaluate the design of the expert system.
   5) Provide an initial test of the reactions of potential users.
   6) Allow management to see initial results of the expert system development process.

9. The 4 major areas are:
   1) Scarce Resources — It is very difficult to free resources for expert systems development within a company or organization because expert systems is a new technology, relatively unfamiliar to many computer specialists.
   2) Development Time — The knowledge acquisition process cannot be rushed. Also, many organizations increase the size of the team working on the development. This takes extra time and can be counterproductive if the number in the group exceeds the optimum team size.
   3) Sources of Errors — The sources of errors in an expert system include: the human expert, the knowledge engineer, the knowledge base, the inference engine, and the user interface. Most of these errors should be corrected during final system evaluation, although the total elimination of errors is very difficult.
   4) Inherent Limitations — The current state of the expert systems technology has some inherent limitations. They are not capable of acquiring knowledge directly without the knowledge engineer. They are not capable of dealing with knowledge that has a mixed representation. They cannot refine their own knowledge bases and cannot learn from experience.

Chapter 9

1. Expert systems of the future will likely be able to deal with more than one knowledge representation scheme at the same time. New knowledge representation schemes will be developed that will be more powerful and easier to use, and allow the use of single time dimension.

3. 1) Decrease the amount of time required to acquire the knowledge.
   2) Decrease the skill level required of the person acquiring the knowledge.
   3) Automate some aspects of the knowledge acquisition process.
   4) Enable users and human experts to add the knowledge.

5. They are used to locate duplicate or contradictory rules in the knowledge base.

7. System development tools will be more powerful and easier to use with the appearance of new shells. They will include graphics and more natural-language interfaces. Intelligent design tools will aid the knowledge engineer by determining problem domain characteristics, ensuring that all important problem attributes are considered, determining which knowledge representation scheme(s) and inferencing mechanism(s) are used, assessing system user capabilities and selecting appropriate user interface design schemes, and helping detect appropriate shells for given applications.

9. The use of natural language is an attempt to make the human/machine interface as human-like as possible. The current status of natural language technology is that there is much progress to be made. The problem of natural language processing is very complex and solutions will not be easily found.

11. User interfaces in expert systems of the future will be verbal and "user-friendly" with increased attention by the expert system developer to the quality of the interface.

13. Cost will always be a problem, while hardware costs tend to decrease, software development costs tend to increase. The development of automated tools will hopefully help decrease costs in the future.

Module 1

1. a. 1) The knowledge base
      2) The inference engine
      3) The user interface
   b. 1) They can give advice of investments
      2) They can determine the acceptability of a credit application
      3) They can predict backorders
      4) They can control inventory
      5) They can design investment portfolios

3. We need to protect ourselves against the accidental loss of data and damage to programs.

5. a. 1. DISKCOPY
   d. 2. VER
   c. 3. FORMAT
   b. 4. COPY

7. d

Module 2

1. Quit, Edit, Path, Help
3. Go, Variable, Rule, Edit, Help
5. b
7. Help, How?, Why?, Slow, Fast, Quit
9. e

Module 3

1. All variables are valid except for COST-7 and COST/.
3. RULE
   BECAUSE "Product X has tutorial and telephone help."
   RULE 1
   BECAUSE "Product X has tutorial but does not have telephone help."
   RULE 2
   BECAUSE "Product X does not have tutorial but does have telephone help."
   RULE 3
   BECAUSE "Product X does not have tutorial or telephone help."
5. See Figure C.1

```
!The file wp3.kbs with one compound AND
!         IF-THEN-ELSE rule.

!ACTIONS BLOCK

ACTIONS
         Display "This expert system WPHELP will advise you on whether you need
to buy a word processor soon or wait.

Pass the SPACEBAR to start the consultation."
          CLS
          FIND advice
          DISPLAY "concerning the purchase of a word processor, WPHELP advises
          you to {advice}.

          Press the SPACEBAR to exit WPHELP."
          CLS

!RULES BLOCK

Rule 1
IF        Afford=Yes
          AND Help = Yes
          AND Time = Yes        Relational Operators (4)
          AND Need = Yes
THEN      Advice = proceed CNF 90
ELSE      Advice = wait CNF 70;

!STATEMENTS BLOCK

ASK Afford : "Can you afford the money to buy a word processor at this time?";
```

CHOICES Afford : Yes, No;

ASK Help : "Do you have some word processing help—people, tutorials, experience, etc.—available to you?";

CHOICES Help : Yes, No;

ASK Time : "Do you have the time to search, install, and learn a word processor?";

CHOICES Time : Yes, No;

ASK Need : "Do you need a word processor?";

CHOICES Need : Yes, No;

FIGURE C.1

7. a. 3
   b. Advice
   c. 3
   d. 3
   e. IF Name = I
         AND Type = J
         AND Model = K
      THEN Advice = L

9.

Cost	Warranty	Advice
400	Yes	OK
400	No	No
800	Yes	Maybe
800	No	No

Module 4

1. a. Trace, d. Fast
3. Path, Filename, Consult, Set, Trace, Go, Tree, Text
5. Document=Type4
   Functionality=Complex
   Cost=High
   Word_processor=Product_B
7. RUNTIME-Statement
   ASK-Statement
   CHOICES-Statement
   FIND-Clause
   DISPLAY-Clause
9. c. 0 and 100

Module 5

1. b. GET

3. a. MENU Reply, ALL, wpdb, Word_Proce
   b. MENU Reply, ALL, wpdb, Networked
   c. MENU Reply, ALL, wpdb, Support
   d. MENU Reply, ALL, wpdb, Cost

5. a) Answer is: The entire table

b)	A	B	C	D	E
c)	fair	good			
d)	200	500			
e)	no	yes			

7.

a)	A	B	C	D
b)	D	E		
c)	A	D		
d)	E			

Module 6

1. Confidence factors are the same as certainty factors. They are a measure of belief/disbelief in an assertion.

3. It uses the minimum value of the set of condition CNFs.

5. Threshold values represent a minimum acceptable CNF for a rule condition to be considered true.

7. The final CNF for a rule is the product of the CNF for the rule condition and the CNF for the rule conclusion.

9. Confidence factors for rule conclusions are entered by the knowledge base developer at the time the rule is entered into the knowledge base.

11. First, calculate CNF for J or K.
    60 + 70 − (60 * 70)/100
    = 88
    Using this value (88) with "or L",
    88 + 90 − (88 * 90)/100
    = 99
    which is the CNF of the rule condition. The final rule CNF is
    99 * 40 = 40

Module 7

1. a. The cost is 324.
   b. 324 is the cost.
   c. The cost is   324.
   d. The cost is $ 324.
   e. The cost is 324. CNF 95.
   (NOTE: e. assumes that the confidence factor of Cost is 95. The command will print whatever confidence factor is associated with COST at that time.)

3. a. ESC
   b. M
   c. DEL
   d. ?

5. d.

7. a. Row = 7 Column = 6
   b. Row = 8 Column = 7
   c. Row = 9 Column = 7
   d. Row = 10 Column = 8

9. c.

11. b.

Module 8

1. a. The most recently found value of the plural-variable X is moved or stored in the non-plural-variable Y.
   b. The value of the variable Y is transferred to the external textfile X. X is created if it does not already exist.
   c. The current line of text found in the external text file X is placed in the VP-Expert variable Y.
   d. The number of values for the plural-variable X are placed in the counter-variable Y.
   e. A page of text from the external file X with the heading listed Y is displayed to the screen.

3. c. CLROFF
   d. EXECUTE

5. a. X is an external DOS file that has a .COM extension that is not used in the CCALL clause. This file X is limited to 64k in size.
   b. X is a DOS batch file with a .BAT extension. Batch files are text files that contain commands for the operating systems.
   c. X is a text file with a .TXT extension that was created with the BASIC program INDEXER.BAS. X was created with a special index.
   d. X is an existing index file with an NDX extension that contains indices or pointers to a field or attribute of the database named in Y.
   e. X is VP or VPP, which indicates which spreadsheet program, VP-Planner or VP-Planner PLUS, will be used. X is not a file.

7. ELLIPSE
   LINETO
   RECTANGLE
   PSET
   GCOLOR

D

USING VP-EXPERT WITH A HARD DISK

VP-Expert can be run from a hard disk system. To create a directory of VP-Expert files, obtain the root directory of the C drive, the hard disk, and check the amount of available memory. Type

C:\> DIR

All of the files and the directories on your disk will be listed along with the amount of memory available. VP-Expert requires 600K of storage. Create a subdirectory for VP-Expert files by issuing the following command:

C:\> MD VPX

Move to this new subdirectory by typing

C:\> CD\VPX

The system should respond with C:\VPX to indicate that you have changed from the root directory to the VPX subdirectory.

Assuming that you have already made backups of the VP-Expert disk and the Sample Files Disk, copy all of the files from the VP-Expert disk to the VPX subdirectory. Place the VP-Expert disk in the A drive and type the following:

COPY A:*.* \VPX

The screen will display the name of each file as it is copied to the subdirectory. You may transfer all of the files from the Sample Disk to the same subdirectory. Place the Sample Files Disk in the A drive and type in the same COPY instruction.

To start VP-Expert, type vpx at the C:\VPX subdirectory prompt. If you wish to access or create files on another drive or directory, select the 7Path option from the Main Menu of VP-Expert. The spreadsheet, database, and VP-Expert help files are expected to be on the B drive. If your system does not have a B drive, then use the SUBST command at the DOS level. If you are using the A drive for data files, then the following command

```
C:\ SUBST B: A:\
```

will allow the A drive to be used when the B drive is expected.

REFERENCES

Apple, 1987. *Human Interface Guidelines.* Reading, Massachusetts: Addison-Wesley.

Bonnet, A. and C. Dahen. 1988. "Oilwell Data Interpretation Using an Expert System and Pattern Recognition." *Proceedings of IJCAI — 88.*

Brown, G.M. 1988. *Human – Computer Interface Design.* Norwood, New Jersey: Ablex.

Buchanan, B. and E. Feigenbaum. 1978. "DENDRAL and METADENDRAL: Their Applications and Dimension." *Artifical Intelligence,* vol. 11.

Buchanan, B. and B. Shortliffe, eds. 1984. *Rule-Based Expert Systems,* 205-301, 571, 596. Menlo Park, California: Addison-Wesley.

Buchanan, B. and E. Shortliffe. February 1977. "Production Rules as a Representation in a Knowledge-Based Consultation System," *Artifical Intelligence.*

"DELTA/CATS-1". The Artifical Intelligence Report, vol. 1, no. 1, January 1984.

Frenzel Jr., L. 1987. *A Crash Course in Artifical Intelligence and Expert Systems.* Indianapollis, Indiana: Howard Sams.

Giarratano, J. and G. Riley. 1989. *Expert Systems: Principles and Programming.* Boston, Massachusetts: PSW-Kent.

Goyal, S. et al. 1985. *COMPASS: An Expert System for Telephone Cable Maintenance.* Waltham, Massachusetts: GTE Laboratories, Inc.

Gresnerietal, R. 1984. "YESMVS: A Continuous Real-Time Expert System." *Proceedings of the American Association for Artificial Intelligence.*

Hendler, J. Ed. 1988. *Expert Systems: The User Interface.* Norwood, New Jersey: Ablex.

"INVEST: An Expert System for Financial Investments." Summer 1988. *IEEE Expert.*

Martin, J. and S. Oxman. 1988. *Building Expert Systems.* Englewood Cliffs, New Jersey: Prentice-Hall.

McDermott, J. January 1982. "Domain Knowledge and the Design Process." *Design Studies,* vol. 3, no. 1.

Pressman, O. 1982. *Software Engineering: A Practical Approach.* New York: McGraw-Hill.

Rubin, T. 1988. *User Interface Design for Computer Systems.* New York: Helsted Press.

Shortliffe, E. and B. Buchanan. 1985. "A Model of Inexact Reasoning" in *Rule-Based Expert Systems.* Reading Massachusetts: Addison-Wesley.

"Similarity Networks: A Knowledge Representation for Information Analysis and Retrieval." July/August, 1988. *Artifical Intelligence.*

Waterman, D. 1986. *A Guide to Expert Systems.* Reading, Massachusetts: Addison-Wesley.

Wetherbe, J. 1988. *Systems Analysis and Design.* St. Paul, Minnesota: West.

Wright, J. et al. October 1984. "ACE: Going From Prototype to Product with an Expert System." *Conference Proceedings of the Association for Computing Machinery.*

INDEX